Governance Structures in African Securities Exchanges

Demutualization Theory, Conflict of Interest, and Challenges

Samuel O. Onyuma

School of Business & Economics
Laikipia University - Kenya

INDIA · SINGAPORE · MALAYSIA

A book is written when there is something specific that has to be discovered. The writer doesn't know what it is, nor where it is, but knows it has to be found. The hunt then begins with the writing.

– Roberto Calasso, The Celestial Hunter

TABLE OF CONTENTS

PREFACE

Securities exchanges are critical to an efficient financial system. Their rules and regulations influence price discovery and least-cost allocation of capital. The exchange's governance structure is a key determinant of these rules and regulations. Corporate governance is concerned with the resolution of collective action problems among dispersed investors and the reconciliation of conflicts of interest between various corporate claimholders. In the last decades, the governance structure of securities exchanges has undergone a momentous change – they have moved from being member-controlled and owned cooperative entities to demutualized shareholder corporate exchanges.

Over the past years we have witnessed substantial changes in the ownership and governance structures of securities exchanges worldwide. Recent surveys indicate that a substantial majority of the world's exchanges would like to demutualize in the coming years. Government regulators around the world have expressed concern about the effect of exchange ownership and governance reforms. This book delves into the main mechanisms of corporate control, discusses the main legal and regulatory issues in securities markets, and examines the comparative corporate governance structures in securities exchanges. A fundamental dilemma of corporate governance in securities exchanges emerges from this analysis.

Demutualization of a securities exchange is an entire journey by which a non-profit member-owned mutual organization is transformed into a for-profit share-owned corporation. It is therefore the process of transforming from a member owned, not-for-profit, entity to a for-profit, investor-owned corporation which involves changing the legal status, structure and governance of an entity. In the case of a securities exchange, the proprietary rights of the members are converted into shares and the exchange can subsequently be listed on its own trading platform. Securities exchanges have been demutualizing because of international competition and technological challenges to traditional modes of trading securities. The change from a member-owned organization to a for-profit shareholder corporation triggers a number of questions about ownership, management and regulatory oversight. For instance, when a demutualized exchange is listed on its own board, some regulatory oversight needs to be transferred to a government capital market's regulator.

The book therefore discusses the evolution of exchange investor protection and corporate ownership of securities exchanges. Challenges in regulation have emerged in the wake of demutualization. The main effect of regulation is to make demutualized securities exchanges to be accountable to the owners, the intermediaries and the listed companies. It should promote the geographical proximity of shareholders to the boards of directors of securities exchanges. And this can only be achieved through demutualization. For these reasons, demutualization has been widely viewed as a means for securities exchanges to streamline their governance structures, improve and expedite decision-making, and raise the much needed capital for their development.

The concept of demutualization still remains a hazy one, however, along multiple dimensions the factors that distinguish a demutualized from a mutualized exchange, the factors that motivate demutualization, c onflict of interest that may arise, and the implications of demutualization for the way in which exchanges are regulated. In seeking to clarify the meaning of demutualization, this book seeks to clarify the sources of conflict between the role of a securities exchange as a commercial enterprise acting in the interests of its owners and its role as a quasi-regulatory body.

This book therefore examines individual securities exchange governance mechanisms, particularly their ownership and management mechanisms in various countries. The book analyses the effect of corporate governance institutions and ownership structures on securities exchanges. The managerial entrenchment may worsen securities exchange investment performance. The book is an outgrowth of the current paradigm shift in the ownership and management of securities exchanges that calls for the need to update literature in the field. It focuses on developing a greater understanding of corporate governance issues in securities exchanges, including demutualization by discussing the challenges it creates and how these might be resolved. It also develops common themes and lessons from demutualization case studies and how different countries have evolved different approaches to exchange demutualization.

Traditionally, securities exchanges have been self-regulatory organizations. But because demutualization is at least perceived to create a conflict of interest between the profit motive of an exchange and its regulatory function, there have been a number of major changes, some proposed and some actually implemented, in the regulatory requirements and oversight of securities exchanges. The book therefore examines how the forces of automation, competition, and demutualization are rapidly changing the industrial organization, ownership, and capital structure of the financial exchange industry. It proposes the conditions under which demutualization becomes optimal from the perspective of mutually owned exchange owners.

Using demutualized exchange around the world as the touchstone and bringing in examples of other mutual exchanges, the book shows what needs to be done to upscale the operational and management efficiency of securities exchanges – particularly in Africa – and improve what has become history's greatest system of wealth creation so that it benefits not just a few greedy insiders but all stakeholders. Some evidence and arguments may help us better understand the potential of a securities exchange as a for-profit enterprise.

The book is therefore unprecedented in its purpose as it presents a contextualized material on corporate governance and its application to securities exchanges. Having examined every shade of opinion on the subject, it offers the most judicious assessment to date of the ownership, management and regulatory issues in securities markets. The book answers the following questions relating to demutualization: how will demutualization of a securities exchange enable greater and swifter capital market development; what is the role of capital markets regulator and of the government in relation to a demutualized exchange in a nation; what is the right self-regulatory model for a nation's securities market; how should conflicts of interest be effectively managed; what investment is needed to enhance the effectiveness of a nation's securities market; and how can the demutualization of a securities exchange facilitate a country's destiny to be a leading capital market both globally and in its continent?

Governance Structures in African Securities Exchanges: Demutualization Theory, Conflict of Interest & Regulatory Challenges is therefore a magisterial offering with many virtues. It is comprehensive, thoroughly researched, richly informative, and seriously erudite – both respectful of the foundation of which securities exchanges have grown – innovative, forward-looking, and inspiring. The book should inform and stimulate debate on key development issues of securities exchanges and is therefore expected to remain a foundational work of securities market governance history.

Finance scholars and university students interested in studying the important link between corporate governance and securities markets development will find the book a valuable learning and research reference material, as it can be used as supplementary text for lectures on financial markets and institutions, management of financial institutions and securities exchanges, contemporary issues in financial market. Moreover, industry practitioners such as fund managers, investment bankers, stockbrokers, securities markets regulators and securities exchange managers interested in developing their markets will also find the book important in designing reforms targeted at promoting securities markets' development.

– Samuel O. Onyuma
Nakuru, Kenya.

ACKNOWLEDGEMENTS

The prospect of writing this text has been both exciting and intriguing. One name is on the front of it, but a great many others are powerful contributors to its development as many of my colleagues in the academia and financial industry read the entire manuscript. I am grateful to several people for their response to surveys and review of manuscript drafts. I cannot overstate the importance of their contributions in helping me to make this most market-driven text possible.

I received my first encouragement as a postgraduate student at the University of Maryland Eastern Shore, long before I knew anything about securities exchanges, their governance structures and commercial focus. While Prof. Jogmohan Joshi (may his soul rest in peace) first commented publicly during my master's thesis defence that I would make a good College Professor, Prof. George Shorter, later advised me to publish a book based on lectures I would give when I become a Professor. Although it seemed unimaginable to me at that time, I have never forgotten the confidence they had in me. I look forward to the time I will also read a book written by one of my students.

I am immensely grateful to my former Professors, Emmanuel T. Acquah and Ayodele Julius Alade at University of Maryland at Eastern Shore, who gave me the confidence to think for myself thus developing interest in financial industry leading to the development of this book. I also thank my students who first suggested that I write a book on securities exchanges from the institutional viewpoint. Particular thanks go to the students in the Masters and Doctoral classes in Finance Theory, Finance Seminar, Financial Institutions & Markets, Investment Finance, and Management of Financial Institutions at Egerton University, Laikipia

University, Kabarak University, Chuka University as well as University of Nairobi. I appreciate their challenge and encouragement as well as the nuggets some of the suggested which enhanced the book's quality. They are the greatest traction in turning an abstract idea into a usable learning tool.

I am very grateful for the invaluable experts' comments received from participants during the 24th Annual African Securities Exchanges Association (ASEA) Conference of 2022 hosted by Bourse Regionale des Valeurs Mobilieres (BRVM), the regional securities exchange of the West African Economic and Monetary Union, held in Abidjan Côte d'Ivoire; the 2021 virtual Annual ASEA Conference hosted by Bourse de Casablanca; the 2014 ASEA Conference on Capital Markets Development in Africa in Diani, Kenya and the 2019 Conference held in Kasane, Botswana; the 2023 World Federation of Exchanges Annual Clearing and Derivatives Conference hosted by Johannesburg Stock Exchange in Johannesburg, South Africa; as well as the seminar participants at the 2018 Conference on the Theories and Practices of Securities and Financial Markets in Kaohsiung, Taiwan. The participants' views and suggestions helped to improve the quality, gist and focus of this book. I am also grateful for the invaluable assistance received from staff at World Federation of Exchanges, African Association of Stock Exchanges and securities exchanges as well as capital markets regulators from Africa, Europe, America, Middle East and Asia Pacific for allowing me to utilize their print and website materials and information used to bring clarity to certain issues.

Much gratitude also goes to the editors and technical staff at Notion Publishers and anonymous reviewers for their insightful comments and suggestions. I am most indebted to my able grammarian, Anne Juma of Egerton University and Prof Eliud Kirigia of Laikipia University, who gave freely and generously of their time and editing skills, and provided endless piercing insights that have shaped the text. Together, they read the entire manuscript and in several places suggested extensive revisions. They severely criticized the chapters, which gained greatly in clarity of exposition as a result of my efforts to meet their objections. The reviewers went patiently through the manuscript, served as a sounding board for testing ideas, and again and again forced me to a more rigorous thinking and clearer of expression. They coped with the reviewing and editing of this text as not only was it written at breakneck speed but it has also been subject of fine-tuning by myself as the months tickled down to publication. Without their contribution and constant encouragement, perception of logical weakness, and willingness to discuss difficulties, I doubt whether this book would have appeared in its present form. I acknowledge, in a special way, the support I obtained from Joseph Omwanda, who printed all the reviewed documents and the many drafts of the manuscripts. He was patient with my persistent demand of reading through only printed documents.

Furthermore, I acknowledge the encouragement I received from my lovely wife Agatha, son Gift, and beautiful daughters Wendy and Natalie for their inspiration, patience and support during the writing of this book. Agatha's uncomplaining acceptance of the hardship a wife must bear when her husband is involved in the painstaking process of finishing a book was astonishing. Lastly, and most importantly, is the gratitude to Dolrose, my dear mama, who has been a source of support and learning, and who taught me the value of love, hard work, integrity and responsibility. She also encouraged me to cross rivers ahead, including River Yala. I am of course responsible for all defects that remain, some of which are undoubtedly due to my stubbornness and resistance to relent to some other viewpoints, since, and as Cardinal Newman says, "…a man would do nothing, if he waited until he could do it so well that no other man would find fault with what he has done…"

Chapter One

THE NATURE OF SECURITIES EXCHANGES

A securities exchange is a formal organization, licensed and regulated by the securities exchange authority of a country. It is physically located and is made up of members that use the exchange and its systems to trade on the listed stocks. It is therefore an elaborate and organized market that enables investors to acquire and dispose of securities at prices that are fair and equitable. Such a system is convenient to both buyers and sellers of securities since it performs the important function of financial intermediation in an economy. The securities traded at a securities exchange include shares, bonds, exchange traded funds, options and futures. Members of a securities exchange must *buy a seat* on the exchange to obtain the rights to trade securities on the exchange floor or through its trading system.

Securities exchanges are therefore institutions that offer market transaction services to facilitate trading, allowing them to profit from the listing and other transaction fees they impose on listing firms and other customers. Exchanges sell a bundle of services for listed firms; specifically, the provision of liquidity to compensate for temporary imbalances in order flow; monitoring of trading patterns, dispute resolution and corporate governance in exchange-listed securities, the development of standardized contracts to reduce transaction costs for investors in listed stocks, and the provision of reputational capital to listing firms.

There are three models of a securities exchange, which may be considered by those aspiring to construct one. There is the self-regulated model, which involves players in the market determining how it is run and operated, as in the case of the London Stock Exchange. The second model involves regulation by a government, as is the case in Kenya, where the Capital Markets Authority is in charge of setting the laws, rules and regulation governing the securities market. The third model is where there can be a mixture of both the self-regulation as well as the government input in the running of the exchange. This form is common in North American exchanges like the National Association of Security Dealers and Automated Quotation – Nasdaq stock market, and New York Stock Exchange (NYSE).

Members of the exchange must buy a seat on the securities exchange to obtain the rights to trade securities on the exchange floor or dedicated electronic trading terminals. Financial intermediaries wishing to organize themselves into a securities exchange must be licensed by the relevant securities market regulator. Similarly, to be listed, a firm must apply and satisfy the listing requirements stipulated by the exchange and securities market regulator, with respect to minimum capitalization, shareholders' equity, average closing share price, etc. After being listed, the exchange may delist a firm's stock if it no longer meets the exchange continuous listing requirements.

The Origin of Securities Exchanges

Whereas it is not possible to state exactly when the first securities exchange was started, there is some evidence that the Dutch were the first people to trade in stocks. As early as 12th century in France, there was unofficial trading in debt and government securities by some brokers. In existence is a list of stocks, which were being traded in Amsterdam as far back as 1585. The key features of the early financial innovations – safe and rapid international movement of funds in the bill of exchange, and safe and liquid long-term investment in the perpetual annuity – were successfully blended by 1609 in the shares of the Dutch East India Company (*Vereenigte Oost-Indisch Compagnie*).[1] At that time, the directors of the company called Heeren XVII converted the initial investment that had been made in the first three voyages into a permanent capital fund. Investors could not recover their capital from the company, but were entitled only to whatever dividends that might be declared each year, as well as the right to transfer their shares to another investor.

---

1   Neal, L. (1999) The Rise of Financial Capitalism: International Capital Markets in the Age of Reason. Cambridge: Cambridge University Press.

The operating control of the Heeren XVII was independent of shareholders because it derived from the political compromise among the six cities written into the original charter. This allowed for foreign investors because their participation would increase the working capital available to the Dutch without infringing on their power to control the far-flung enterprise. The combination of a permanent capital and 'separation of operating control from ordinary stockholders made these shares ideal for active trading in the secondary market that arose on the Amsterdam Beurs.

Britain was the second country to engage in the trade of stocks and this was towards the end of the 17th Century. In the United States of America, before the America war of independence, most capital financing and securities arising there from were handled in the London Stock Exchange. The outbreak of the war of independence cut off access to the British capital market leading to the establishment of separate securities exchanges in America. This then marked the beginning of modern securities markets as they are known today. From these humble beginnings, securities exchanges continued to spread to other countries in the World until they reached the level and state with which we are now familiar.

Despite the earlier origins of both securities exchange and newspapers in Amsterdam, it was in London that the first regularly printed stock price list occurred. The earliest printed evidence of price quotation came from a weekly newspaper price list printed by Whiston, *The Merchants Rememberancer*, for 4th July 1681.[2] However, it did not give actual prices for the shares, as it just reported on the shares of the East India Company which were at their highest level and the Royal African Company which were at its lowest. The first actual listing of actual prices came in the 3rd January 1682 issue of Woodlley's Price Current.[3] The early-days securities exchanges experienced many scandals and crashes, as there was little or no regulation and almost anyone was allowed to participate in the securities

---

2   Cope, S. R. (1978) The Stock Exchange Revisited: A new Look at the Market in Securities in London in the Eighteenth Century. *Economica*, 45(177):1-21.
3   Jacob M. (1954) Notes on Some London Price-Current, 1667-1715. Economic History Review, 2nd Series, 7:244.

exchange. In fact, there was informal hawking of shares in the street of London by 1668.

However, as the volume of trade increased with more companies floating their shares, the need for organized market place escalated. Consequently, the traders decided to begin meeting outside a coffee house, which they used as a market place. Eventually, they moved inside the coffee house, later took it over and changed its name in 1773 to London Stock Exchange. Over the years, the concept of securities exchanges and their importance as platforms where firms could raise further capital spread throughout the world as colonial masters conquered other countries in different continents. The same colonial masters started securities exchange in Africa early in the nineteenth century.

Securities exchanges deal in securities including equities, debt instruments and mixtures of both. The supply of suitable securities was therefore provided first by the formation of joint stock companies and towards the end of the seventeenth century, by the appearance of permanent national debts, which were receiving increased attention as means of financing government expenditures. The common feature of joint stock companies was that common owners would provide the required capital and participate in profits, or absorb losses while leaving the management of the enterprise to professional managers.

Evolution of Securities Exchanges

Typically, securities exchanges evolved through three distinct stages. The initial stage was characterized by an informal network of stockbrokers who would meet at a physical place and match orders from the public – the buyers and sellers. This meeting of the stockbrokers to match the order constituted a securities market. The second stage of the evolution came when these networks of stockbrokers gradually formalized into not-for-profit mutual or member-owned organizations that employed governance structures akin to those of associations or cooperatives. This stage brought about the earliest version of the modern-day securities exchange. Then, the securities exchanges were established using the capital of the members – stockbrokers – and in some instances with assistance of Government.

During this stage the stockbrokers owned the exclusive rights to trade on and manage the securities exchange as well as the ownership rights. They even had the right to admit or reject any new entrants to the market.

As the securities exchanges grew in relative importance to their host economies, capital markets regulation evolved and strengthened, primarily to protect the interests of the investing public. Consequently, it was recognized that the stockbrokers' exclusive rights to trade on the market ought to be separated from their ownership and management rights. This ushered in the third and the current stage of the evolution of securities exchanges: the age of demutualized for-profit securities exchanges. Most securities exchanges have therefore transformed from mutual or member-owned organisation to companies limited by shares.

Importance of Securities Exchanges

Several studies have reached the conclusion that deep securities markets improve the capital allocation, as reflected by higher returns and lower cost of capital from higher valuations. The cumulative effect of deeper capital markets has a positive impact on innovation and growth.[4] This is important for countries that have to compete by increasing productivity and must foster technological upgrades of their production. Over the past few decades, the world securities markets have surged, and emerging markets have accounted for a large amount of this boom. Even in regions where securities exchanges are a new phenomenon, for instance in Africa, new securities markets have recently been established in Angola, Somalia, Lesotho and Rwanda. Prior to 1989 there were just only 5 securities markets in sub-Saharan Africa and 3 in Northern Africa. Currently, there are 29 securities exchanges.[5] Securities market development has been central to the domestic financial liberalization programs of most African countries. It seems any program of financial liberalization in Africa is incomplete without the establishment and development of securities markets.

4   Andritzky, J. R. (2007). Capital Market Development in a Small Country: The Case of Slovenia. IMF Working Paper No. 07/229, Washington, DC: International Monetary Fund.

5   Onyuma, S. O. (2020). Securities Market Development in Africa: Mobile Financial Services, Efficient Remittance Flows & Diaspora Investment Securities. Notion Press.

The drive towards the establishment of securities markets in developing countries during the last few decades may be linked to other important developments in the global economy. The financial markets of many advanced countries have undergone tremendous changes and become increasingly integrated. These changes have resulted from the operation of a number of interrelated factors such as the progressive deregulation of capital markets both internally and externally; the internationalization of securities markets; the introduction of new financial products allowing riskier and bigger financial investments; and the emergence and the increasing role of new actors, such as institutional investors, in the capital markets.[6] These developments in the securities markets of advanced countries have led them to seek liberalization in the international trade and exchange of services in world trade negotiations.

Therefore, the establishment of securities markets in developing countries and the liberalization of capital accounts can be seen as parts of this global trend. Securities markets in these countries are expected to boost domestic savings and increase the quantity and quality of investment. Securities markets are seen as enhancing the operations of the domestic financial system in general and the capital market in particular. However, critics argue that securities markets might not perform efficiently in developing countries and that it may not be feasible for all countries to promote securities markets given the huge costs and the poor financial structures.

The financial intermediation in many African countries relies mostly on the banking system with established lending relationships, while the development of the non-bank financial sector is far behind their peers in other continents. The dominance of bank lending has resulted in a lack of equity financing, as bank lending is biased towards existing corporations and securities markets are shallow. Therefore, developing more complete and deeper securities markets would enhance the growth potential and innovation in many developing countries.

---

6   Onyuma, S. O. (2017) Financial Deepening Determinants Influencing Securities Markets Development in Kenya. Doctoral Thesis (Laikipia University).

The critical role of long-term finance in economic development of a country cannot be gainsaid. A well-organized securities market is crucial for mobilizing both domestic and offshore capital. In fact, countries with well-developed securities markets seem to be more developed than those with thin securities markets. In many developing countries, however, capital has been a major constraint in economic development.

The provision of funds to finance domestic capital formation is a key factor in the prospects for long-term economic growth in developing countries. The reality of a much reduced supply of foreign funds and other sources like commercial banks compel governments in many developing countries to pay increased attention to securities market development as a way of improving domestic resource mobilization, enhancing the supply of long-term capital and encouraging the efficient use of existing assets.[7] In fact, the ongoing debt crisis in these countries serves to focus attention on the importance of equity rather than debt, particularly in the financing of projects with long gestation periods.

Securities market development can also contribute to financial stability of a country. More diversified and liquid markets could attract investments from African institutional investors that currently prefer to invest abroad. Deeper local markets that are well integrated with the global financial markets enable all types of investors to maintain a diversified global portfolio and better manage their risks, while becoming capable of absorbing the large pension savings that the aging population is expected to accumulate. A broader investor base also enables companies to raise capital at lower costs, while banks can develop alternative sources of revenue from investment services. With more firms active on capital markets, market oversight would increase transparency and accountability in the corporate sector. Therefore, markets serve as the "spare wheel" for financial systems and support the overall financial stability.

Additionally, securities markets have an important role to play in financial liberalization and deepening. Apart from providing a means of

---

7   Yartey, C. A. (2006). The Stock Market and the Financing of Corporate Growth in Africa: The Case of Ghana. IMF Working Paper No. 06/201. Washington, DC: World Bank Group.

diversifying risk for capital raisers and investors, securities markets play other roles. For example, they are a mechanism for capital allocation and corporate monitoring, and a means for government to exercise market-based rather than direct fiscal and monetary policies.

In poorest developing countries, firms rely mostly on internal resources and informal credit markets for financing with commercial banks being the main financial institutions but informal credit markets also play a vital role.[8] However, the loan contracts of such banks are generally short term, and formal markets for long-term debt or equity do not exist, thereby constraining both corporate and economic growth.

There also exists a need for securities markets even for less-developed economies because the securities markets can significantly enable them raise the level of domestic savings and contribute to a more efficient allocation of such savings among competing investments. Through the securities markets, a variety of financial instruments with varied term-to-maturity, risks, yields and liquidity, are added to the traditional types of financial assets such as demand and savings deposits. Thus the availability of this wider range of financial assets can induce individuals to increase their rate of current savings. This is because securities markets enable savers to achieve a better wealth composition and also permit adjustments in the wealth composition with speed and at low cost whenever circumstances change. Moreover, competition among the users of securities market funds, including firms, government and individuals will tend to increase the efficiency with which capital is used, thereby directly influencing the economic growth rate of a country.

Efforts to integrate markets and plans for single currency are both an opportunity and a challenge for securities market development in developing countries. Up to now, financial integration mainly took place through bank finance from abroad and portfolio investments in foreign securities. With the possible removal of currency risk, the scale and scope

---

8   Yartey, C. A. (2008). Macroeconomic and Institutional Determinants of Stock Market Development in Africa: Is South Africa any Different? IMF Working Paper No. 08/35. Washington, DC: World Bank Group.

of financial integration is set to deepen in many countries. This process can bring sizeable benefits for many countries as international integration helps to overcome the domestic markets' small size and limited scope for risk diversification. Also, financial integration could complicate the development of securities markets domestically due to greater competition and pressure to find niche markets with a local comparative advantage.

The size of domestic markets in developing countries is not sufficient to soon become a thriving market place on its own. However, developing nations' experience of running small local market places with relatively sophisticated market infrastructures may prove valuable in the process of integration. Preserving the local market does help to maintain and expand securities market access for smaller issuers and improve the investment opportunities of locally oriented investors.

Furthermore, most developing economies have continued to face greater development challenges such as low levels of economic growth, increasing population, and adverse effects of globalization, which have affected their rate of economic development. These economies have continually been unable to fully mobilize sufficient resources because they lack sufficient instruments for long-term capital mobilization and the securities markets remain largely underdeveloped. Moreover, the supply of capital is required to maintain the momentum of the growth in their GDP. An organized and developed securities market in developing countries therefore serves as a medium for transferring part of the firm ownership of foreign corporations to the local citizens. The securities market, for instance could, be used to transfer the ownership of the many state parastatals through the government privatisation program to improve their efficiency, management and public ownership.

Such realization elsewhere has made developing countries to increasingly focus on building an environment that fosters sustainable local capital mobilization. Thus, developing the securities market becomes an important area of policy focus. In jumpstarting the development of securities markets, policy has been geared on trading technology, market size and depth, and reforming the laws regulating trade practices and restructuring the ownership and management of the securities exchange.

Critics of the securities markets, however, argue that the actual operation of the pricing and takeover mechanism even in well-functioning securities markets lead to short termism and lower rates of long term investment particularly in firm specific human capital. It also generates perverse incentives, rewarding managers for their success in financial engineering rather than creating new wealth through organic growth.[9] In addition, the takeover mechanism does not perform a disciplinary function and that competitive selection in the market for corporate control takes place much more on the basis of size rather than performance. Therefore, a large inefficient firm has a higher chance of survival than a small relatively more efficient firm.

These critics further argue that securities market liquidity may negatively influence corporate governance because very liquid securities market may encourage investor myopia. Since investors can easily sell their shares, more liquid securities markets may weaken investors' commitment and incentive to exert corporate control.[10] These problems are further magnified in emerging market countries with their weaker regulatory institutions and greater macroeconomic volatility. These limitations of securities markets have led many analysts to question the importance of such markets in promoting economic growth in emerging markets.

Moreover, such critics of the securities market also argue that market prices do not always accurately reflect the underlying fundamentals when speculative bubbles emerge in the market.[11] In such situations, prices in the securities market are not simply determined by discounting the expected future cash flows, which according to the efficient market theory, should reflect all currently available information about fundamentals. Under this condition, the securities market develops its own speculative growth dynamics, which may be guided by irrational behaviour. This irrationality is

---

9   Singh, A. (1997). Financial Liberalization, Stock Markets, and Economic Development. *The Economic Journal*, 107: 771–782.

10 Bhide, A. (1994). The Hidden Cost of Stock Market Liquidity. *Journal of Financial Economics*, Vol. 34, pp. 31–51.

11 Binswanger, M. (1999). Stock Markets, Speculative Bubbles and Economic Growth. Cheltenham: Edward Elgar Publishing.

expected to adversely affect the real sector of the economy as it is in danger of becoming the by-product of a casino, due to gambling tendencies.

Global Trends in Securities Markets

Securities exchanges around the world have been undergoing institutional and microstructure reforms because of the rapid evolution of the global securities and futures industry, the fierce competition faced by exchanges among themselves and also from alternative trading systems (ATS) which bypass traditional exchanges.[12] National boundaries are no longer hurdles to the flow of capital and investments. As technology advances, investments and firms migrate to those markets with high transparency and liquidity, low transaction costs, well diversified product base, sound regulation, high quality of service and robust trading infrastructure. The following is a discussion of some of the global trends being witnessed in securities markets.

Globalization of Markets. Increasingly, securities issuers and investors are migrating to markets that provide the greatest liquidity and best execution. Exchanges find themselves having to compete among themselves and against new market players. The traditional value of an exchange is being eroded by the proliferation of electronic communications networks (ECNs), which are positioning themselves as virtual exchanges and providing a single electronic access point to multiple markets. A combined securities exchange is capable of offering larger size and product range to compete in the industry and emerge a winner.

Market Integration. Securities exchanges worldwide are rethinking their strategies and operations to improve their services, reinforce their competitive positions and optimise their performance. Overseas, markets are rapidly integrating vertically (linking together trading, clearing and settlement functions into a single transaction chain) and horizontally

---

12 ATS are government-regulated electronic trading systems that match orders for buyers and sellers of securities. They are not a national securities exchange, however, they may apply to the capital markets regulator to become a national securities exchange. All current ATSs are dark pools - trading systems that allow their users to place orders without publicly displaying the size and price of their orders to other participants in the dark pool.

(combining securities and futures products into a single organization) and developing alliances with other securities exchanges.

Sophisticated and Demanding Securities Issuers. There still exists stickiness to shares as financial investments, making trading in the domestic market more likely than in a foreign market. Nevertheless, it has become much easier for capital raisers to access other markets, and some firms, especially blue chip firms, no longer look to raise capital in their domestic markets alone. The main driver of the decision on where to list is the cost of finance. There are two aspects of access for capital seekers: practical (delivering a prospectus and receiving the applications) and regulatory (registering the prospectus). Therefore, firms may prefer to list in regional or other securities exchanges that can provide them with a large investor base and high liquidity.

Securities Exchange Competition. As securities markets become more globalized and investors become more sophisticated, competition from other fields has also become an increasing challenge. Stocks of major listed firms on the New York Stock Exchange could be traded easily in Beijing and, increasingly, also in South Africa or London. Financial and equity based derivatives, for example, are even less geographically bound and fierce international competition in this area has already been seen. International competition has also meant that international stockbrokers are now trading in a variety of markets, which make them sensitive to cost differences and the relative inefficiencies of competing exchanges.

Advances in Technology. New financial technology allows new players to compete effectively. Building trading platforms is also expensive for exchanges. If such platforms can be shared across financial products being traded can influence and result in customer advantages. Technological advances have led to significant changes in the landscape of both on-exchange and off-exchange transactions. The technology improvements have lowered the entry barriers to establishing new securities exchanges, thus enabling emergence of a widespread alternative and proprietary trading systems whereby trades are executed off-traditional exchanges. In fact, the new breed of ECNs in securities markets that have emerged are already siphoning an unknown amount of securities trading from traditional securities markets and intermediaries.

Blurring of Product Distinctions. As the differences between securities and derivatives products have become more blurred, the ability of different markets to compete has increased. A combined entity would be able to align securities and derivatives business strategies more closely, minimize operating costs by sharing overheads, and increase its value-positioning against other exchanges, locally and internationally.

Opening Up of Financial Markets. More governments and securities regulatory authorities are gradually opening up their national capital markets in order to attract international participation. They are beginning to understand that opening their borders is capable of improving the standards of financial markets by making them more competitive and efficient, attracting a larger and more diverse investor base and allowing for knowledge and skills to be transferred to the domestic markets. This is likely to result in increased development of the domestic markets.

Institutionalisation of Securities Markets. Institutional investors and large, proprietary trading operations of investment banks, stockbrokers, dealers and other securities firms such as fund managers have become extremely powerful and more globalized. They are diversifying their trading and portfolios through various markets and trading facilities as a means of minimizing transaction costs and increase liquidity. Also, demands from investors to have direct access to securities exchanges and representation in their governance prosper the growth of the alternative and proprietary systems.

More Sophisticated Investors. With better market knowledge and access to both information and markets through the Internet, investors are looking for more innovative financial products to invest in. They try to minimize their transaction time and cost by attempting to bypass certain intermediaries. Their goal is to search for higher returns by lowering their risk.

Corporate Governance. Traditionally, securities exchanges have been operated and managed as cooperatives envisaging member-owned, controlled, and managed institutional structures. Currently, the issue of corporate governance is a world agenda, and relates to how management of firms can be improved in a way that the management is accountable to the owners. Securities exchanges have not been left behind, as they are also competing in the governance race. Through governance, securities exchanges are changing their organizational structures through demutualization – an entire process by which a non-profit member-owned mutual organization is transformed into a for-profit share-owned corporation.

Securities exchanges around the world have been demutualizing because of international competition and technological challenges to traditional modes of trading securities. The Stockholm Stock Exchange, also known as Stockholmsborsen, became the first securities exchange to become a for-profit share-owned exchange with brokers and listed firms becoming shareholders. Today, demutualization is becoming the norm and the in-thing in securities markets and many securities and futures exchanges have demutualized, and several more have set the machinery in motion. It would be surprising if there are any exchanges for which the question of whether to demutualize is not at least on the radar screen.

The change of a securities exchange from a member-owned organization to a for-profit shareholder corporation triggers a number of questions about ownership, management and regulatory oversight. For instance, when a demutualized exchange is listed on its own board, some regulatory oversight needs to be transferred to a government regulator. In many countries, demutualization of the major national securities exchange has been accompanied by general securities regulatory reform. In Africa, not much has taken place in this governance structure transformation, as we are going to see, just a few of them being led by Johannesburg Stock Exchange (JSE) and Nairobi Securities Exchange (NSE), have undergone this process.

Recently, a large number of mutual securities exchanges have converted to publicly listed companies. Global securities market competition and advances in technology costs are causing securities exchanges around the world to examine their business models and become more innovative. Many of the securities exchanges are responding by demutualizing. Increased competition and divergence in the interests of the trading members has led to a decline in the prosperity of securities exchanges. Some of the securities exchanges arrived at a point where their viability was at stake and had to restructure their governance system. Traditionally, securities exchanges have been run as mutual companies to ration access to trading floors by charging substantial membership fees. Electronic trading systems however lead to a decline in marginal cost of adding a new member to almost zero which also constitutes a reason for the process of demutualization.

Especially in Europe, the deregulation of the financial markets by initiatives such as the Single European Market but also by the Big Bang reforms in UK, opened the path for increased competition from foreign institutions. Given the circumstances that have prompted the change in the governance of exchanges, it is reasonable to surmise that the conversion from mutual structure to publicly traded self-listed exchange structure will be value-enhancing for the exchange itself and also has the potential to improve the quality of the securities market. The improvement in performance could occur because self-listing provides managers of the exchange the free hand to pursue profitable business opportunities that they otherwise would not have been able to undertake under the mutual not for-profit structure. Also, self-listing leads to greater scrutiny of management by investors, thus management in turn could respond to the monitoring with greater efforts.

Securities exchange demutualization can offer the greater flexibility to respond to demands of rapidly changing business environment and creates a framework, which is intended to maximize value of the exchange to its members. Additionally, exchanges can benefit from access to capital markets in ways not available to a non-stock membership corporation. It can also provide the ability to pursue opportunities to engage in business combinations and joint ventures. It is also reasonable to surmise that because of the for-profit motive, the listed exchanges will embark on strategies that will increase order flow to their markets. The increase in trading volume could lead to a fall in bid-ask spread and improve the quality of the market.

The for-profit business model can also enable a securities exchange to put in place programs and incentives that will increase order flow to the exchange. Some exchanges are providing subsidies to market makers in order to attract them to their trading platforms. This initiative could help attract more international intermediaries and institutional investors to the market and the increase in trading volume can lead to reduction in bid-ask spread. These improvements can arise from greater production of information and the trading activity of these investors. Institutions that hold stocks of the firm may increase research efforts and the number of analysts may increase accordingly. The process toward exchange demutualization may seem inevitable, but it is not one not to be taken lightly. It raises a number of issues for the markets, its stakeholders and its regulators. Securities exchanges have evolved from informal trading sessions in coffeehouses to organizations competing globally for market share. The governance structures that worked well in the early days have therefore increasingly became a hindrance, as exchanges need to react quickly to domestic and international developments. These are the intricate issues that form the gist of the book.

The Thrust of This Book

Securities exchanges are critical to an efficient financial system. Their rules and regulations influence price discovery and least-cost allocation of capital to corporations. Their governance structure is a key determinant of these rules and regulations. Recently, the governance structure of several securities exchanges has undergone a momentous change – they have moved from being member-controlled (owned) cooperative entities to demutualized exchanges.

This contributes to the current debate on securities exchange governance structures. It achieves this through a deep literature dive by documenting the wave of demutualization and providing a critical analysis of the demutualization phenomena. The book is therefore an outgrowth of the current paradigm shift in the ownership and management of securities exchanges that calls for the need to update literature in the field. It provides perspectives and dimensions of demutualization based on a review of literature and experience. It focuses on the meaning and significance of demutualization; factors driving the demutualization of securities exchanges; ownership, legal and strategic approaches being adopted in the process of demutualization; key benefits of demutualization; regulatory challenges and securities exchange responses to these challenges; and financial viability of demutualized exchanges.

In a more specific way, the book analyses the reasons for the exchange governance change and assesses its impact on various aspects of a securities exchange. It examines a few demutualization cases, which occurred for different reasons. It also undertakes to explore, in a more detailed manner, analysis of the change in exchange governance structures by discussing the role of competition as a motivation for demutualizing. In addition, it examines how demutualization affects both the securities exchange and the investors who trade on such exchanges. An analysis of the impact of demutualization in two separate instances, in which competition plays very different roles, is also provided. It therefore zeroes in on developing a greater understanding of demutualization as a concept.

Based on the literature on the economics of conversions, this book generates a set of general observations that might inform private and public policy perspectives on the future role of user-owned and controlled organizations in market economies. In doing so, the book may serve as a platform for further discussion among scholars, policymakers, practitioners, securities exchange leaders and regulators in their quest to understand and affect the ongoing process of demutualization.

Indeed, the securities exchange corporate governance topic is therefore important from both practical and academic perspectives. From a practical viewpoint, due to its implications for investors, regulators and policymakers, practitioners are obviously interested in why securities exchanges demutualize. From an academic viewpoint, there is extensive literature on the functions that securities exchanges perform, but limited literature on their corporate governance structures and the impact of such structures on exchange trading costs, growth and development.

In terms of the pedagogy adopted, this book maps the global landscape of securities exchanges – with a focus on demutualization of exchanges. Data to inform this landscape were collected through a variety of methods, including surveys, desk research, engagement with a community of practice, networking with stakeholders, participation in conferences, case study presentations, and workshops attended. The project has therefore been achieved through the literature synthesis from books; securities exchange management, ownership and membership manuals. Information about the institutional evolution and ownership and management of securities exchanges were gathered from multiple primary and secondary sources. The majority of demutualization information was obtained by visiting the websites of individual securities exchanges and emailing their CEOs with a short survey.

The author was, therefore, able to verify the information on securities exchange competition, demutualization and self-listing of exchanges with that provided in other studies extensively acknowledged in the book. The author further derived other data and information on securities exchanges like market performance from financial reports, exchanges' Internet websites, World Federation of Exchanges Internet database, and published academic papers. Several e-mail interviews regarding restructuring the governance structures of securities exchanges were conducted with key CEOs in both developed and emerging exchanges in Europe, America and Asia Pacific in 2015. Personal interviews were conducted in the year 2016 during the 18th African Securities Exchange Association conference in Diani, Kenya with securities exchange CEOs from Nairobi, Uganda, Dar es Salaam, Nigeria, South Africa, and Botswana, whose exchanges had completed or were undergoing demutualization.

The author, therefore leveraged on a number of proprietary methodologies and tools, reviewed extensive documentations, undertook analysis and conducted many email and face-to-face discussions with officials of securities exchanges and market regulators, and other industry groups like association of stockbrokers and investment banks.

In terms of structure, this book is divided into 10 chapters with an introduction in Chapter 1 explaining the meaning, origin and importance of securities exchanges. In discussing the various dimensions and issues involved in the process of securities exchange demutualization, Chapter two (2) presents an overview of corporate governance, its importance and its application to securities exchanges. This is followed by Chapter three (3) which provides a broad discussion of the nature, theoretical underpinnings, reasons for and process of demutualization, the decision-making and pointing the important issues to be considered. In setting forth the critical issues in a demutualized securities exchange and what market regulators must confront in connection with the demutualization process, Chapter four (4) discusses the ownership and management issues as well as potential problems during and after demutualization.

While Chapter five (5) details the possible conflict of interest raised by exchange demutualization and how such conflicts can be dealt with. In addition, Chapter six (6) discusses the resultant regulatory and oversight issues and attempts by demutualized exchanges to deal with the problem of conflict of interest in regulation. Chapter seven (7) presents the post-demutualization lessons being learnt reflecting mergers and acquisitions, market values as well as financial performance. Chapter eight (8) looks at the prospects and challenges of exchange demutualization in Africa and presents four successful demutualization cases for JSE, NSE, Zimbabwe Stock Exchange (ZSE) and Botswana Stock Exchange (BSE) to depict how demutualization is taking shape in African securities exchange landscape. Chapter nine (9) re-assesses whether a non-profit mutual securities exchange structure might have been efficient in attracting firms' listing by linking demutualization to the lemon problem and hostage taking. Finally, Chapter ten (10) provides a synopsised wrap-up of demutualization, while presenting important strategic directions for a successful demutualization of securities exchanges in Africa. The book then ends with a general conclusion.

Chapter Two

CORPORATE GOVERNANCE IN SECURITIES EXCHANGES

Introduction

In this chapter, a discussion is presented on corporate governance issues inherent in organizations and how it can be applied to securities exchanges. It begins by exploring its meaning, importance and securities exchanges governance structures and how such structures may be changed. World over, organizations are facing major financial problems that lead to their eventual collapse with disastrous social and economic consequences that raise concerns on how they are managed. Thus, the issue of the quality of corporate governance at all levels of management comes to the fore. Good corporate governance practices are necessary owing to the great expectation on organizations from shareholders, creditors, regulatory authorities and the public. The survival of corporations depends on them embracing global corporate governance standards. Corporate governance establishes effective, competitive and sustainable organizations that contribute to the welfare of the society by creating wealth, employment and solutions to emerging corporate challenges such as corruption and mismanagement. The need for legitimate, accountable and responsive organisations that are managed with integrity and transparency and that recognizes and protects shareholders' rights and interest calls for the promotion of good corporate governance practices even in securities exchanges. The concept of corporate governance is just gaining its importance in many developing financial markets.

Meaning of Corporate Governance

Corporate governance has become high in the global arena. However as a definitive concept, there is no globally applicable definition of corporate governance.[13]

The 1992 Cadbury Report simply described corporate governance as the system by which companies are directed and controlled. It can be confined to the Corporate Governance Tripod, that is, the relationship between shareholders, directors and management. An increasing number of definitions refer to the fact that many other groups have an interest in a company. Corporate governance is an umbrella term that includes specific issues arising from interactions among senior management, shareholders, boards of directors, and other corporate stakeholders. It is also the system by which business entities are monitored, managed and controlled. The OECD in an attempt to standardize the governance principles across the countries has chalked out five areas which cover the rights of shareholders; the equitable treatment of shareholders; the role of stakeholders; disclosure and transparency; and the responsibilities of the board. Despite the wide discussion on corporate governance in most of the forums, still it is difficult to suggest a single definition because there are so many varying views on the meaning of corporate governance. Available analysis has also cast doubt on the universality of rule-based corporate governance practices.[14]

Consequently, several academics view corporate governance differently, depending on their orientation.[15] However, corporate governance is basically the manner in which power is exercised in the

---

13 This section draws in part on the summary of the literature on corporate governance in Onyuma, S. O., Cheruiyot, T. K. & A. N. Okumu (2007) Debt as a Tool for Monitoring and Controlling Firms in Emerging Economies: The Kenyan Experience. African Journal of Business & Economic, 2(1):24-45; and Onyuma, S. O. (2005) The Emerging Role of Creditors in the Corporate Governance of Debtors: Evidence from Kenya. *Egerton Journal of Humanities & Social Sciences*, 5 (2):151-171.

14 Liang, H. & Homanen, M. (2019). Universal Corporate Governance. European Corporate Governance Institute (ECGI) - Finance Working Paper No. 585/2018. ECGI.

15 See Dimsdale, N & Prevezer, M., (1998). Capital Markets and Corporate Governance. In H. J. Blommestein (ed) The New Financial Landscape, pp 257-261, Clarendon Press, Oxford.

stewardship of a firm's total portfolio of resources, with the objective of maintaining and increasing shareholder value. It is concerned with creating a balance between economic and social goals, and between individual and societal goals while encouraging efficient resource use and accountability in the exercise of power and stewardship. It can thus be viewed as the establishment of an appropriate legal, economic and institutional framework that allows organisations to thrive as institutions for advancing long-term shareholder value and maximizing human-centred development while remaining conscious of other responsibilities to stakeholders, the environment, and the community. Simply stated, corporate governance depicts a set of relationships between an organisation and all its stakeholders and a means of achieving optimum organisational performance. Thus, in terms of the financial system, it represents the sets of relationships between organisations and their suppliers of finance which have long-term consequences for future procurement of finance, and general organisational performance.

Corporate governance includes the set of rules and incentives by which the management of a firm is directed and controlled in order to maximize the profitability and long-term value of the firm for the shareholders. It regulates the contractual relationships between stakeholder groups, in particular, the principal-agent relationship between shareholders and management. The separation of ownership and control allows shareholders and managers to focus on their respective competitive advantage: the provision of risk capital on the one hand and the management of investment portfolios on the other hand. The contractual governance of management behaviour is necessarily incomplete and direct monitoring may be under-provided. Therefore, the management is in the position to seize residual control rights and may squander the shareholders' investment returns. If left unregulated, shareholders will under-provide finance and firms will not be able to take advantage of all value-enhancing investment opportunities. Thus the codification of corporate governance into national law or codes of best practice becomes a necessary and effective means of alleviating the under investment and limiting the implied agency costs.

Corporate governance is therefore a broad term that encompasses:[16]

- Rules and market practices which determine how widely-held firms make decisions.
- The transparency of the corporate decision-making process and the accountability of its directors, managers and employees.
- The information, which firms disclose to investors and the protection of minority shareholders.
- Issues of company law, security laws and the listing rules of a country's securities exchanges.
- The accounting standards applicable to listed firms, competition or antitrust laws and bankruptcy or insolvency laws.
- The government regulatory agencies with which firms and their shareholders deal and the regulators' actions to ensure compliance with applicable laws and regulations.
- The courts that are called upon by shareholders, directors and managers to resolve corporate governance disputes and enforce government regulations.

There are four major players affected by corporate governance:

- Shareholders who provide capital in exchange for the rights to profits and increase in corporate value.
- The board of directors who represent the basic interests of shareholders and sometimes those of other interested parties. The board selects management, provides general direction to the managers and oversees management performance.
- The management who has the responsibility of overseeing the day-to-day operations of the firm and reports to the board. Management is responsible for maximizing corporate profits and shareholder value.
- Other stakeholders mainly financial creditors – whose interest is on maximizing the probability of debt repayment, employees, suppliers and the public at large.

---

16 Oli, J. (2001) Corporate Governance in Korea at the Millennium: Enhancing International Competitiveness. Law and Economics Working Paper No. 196, Stanford Law School.

There are interrelated factors contributing to the proper functioning of the corporate governance system. Internal factors include the board of directors, providers of capital, management and stakeholders. External factors include the environment that ensures effective governance, including the law, regulation, competitive markets, the media, transparency and high standards of reporting.

Importance of Corporate Governance

Corporate governance is now the subject of much discussion in boardrooms, lecture halls and the media. Corporate governance systems have evolved over the centuries, often in response to corporate failure or systemic crises. Every major corporate failure is often as a result of incompetence, fraud and abuse and is usually met by assessing the inherent system of corporate governance.[17] Corporate governance has received more attention than it ordinarily would have, due to a series of corporate collapse that affect not only those directly connected with the firms concerned such as directors, shareholders and auditors but also those affected by its existence like employees, customers, suppliers and the environment.

The financial systems in developed and developing countries have had many problems. The financial systems worldwide, for example, have experienced severe problems with many organisations being liquidated or placed under statutory management. Lapses in corporate governance have caused the collapse of, and financial crisis in, large world corporations stretching from America, Europe, Asia and of, recently, Africa. Such corporations include Adelphia, Barings, Daiwa Bank, Enron, Global Crossing, Maxwell Affair, Rites Aid Corp, Tyco, Sunbeam, Vivendi, Waste Management, MCI-WorldCom and Xerox. Even before these corporations filled the world news, a Belgium-based corporation Lernout & Hauspie Speech Products was already involved in banking and securities fraud in Belgium and across Europe, USA and Asia. These corporations were involved in, among others, financial engineering, accounting fraud, debt

---

17 Iskander, M. & Chamlou, N. (1999). Corporate Governance: A Framework for Implementation. World Bank Group.

hiding, fraudulent sales and revenue reporting based on bank loan, pyramid schemes and destruction of documents containing material evidence. Africa has not been left behind since many large corporations such as Steinhoff, New Frontier, Sasol and Tongaat Hulett, among others have gone under in South Africa due to lack of good corporate governance practices. Also, in Kenya such lapses have caused the collapse ARM Cement, Mumias Sugar, Tuskys Supermarkets, Nakumat Supermarkets, Spencon and Kenya Finance Bank. Central Banks from many developing countries have liquidated many commercial banks and non-bank financial institutions, while some under operation have accumulated large amount of bad debts due to poor corporate management.

Some stockbrokers like Shah Munge, Francis Thuo & Partners, Nyaga Stock Brockers, Discount Securities (Kenya) and investment advisors like Armstrong, and Bayou Group – a Connecticut hedge business (USA) have even been suspended from securities exchange trading by securities market regulators for getting involved in financial maleficence and corruption-related deals. In addition, China had to punish 16 executives of state-owned corporations for accounting frauds and also issued a $61 million fine on Zhejiang Securities for manipulating the securities market and conducting illegal trades. All these cases point to the lapse in owners' monitoring and control aspects in organisations' activities. In addition to poor regulation, the occurrences of major corporate failures such as the collapse of world corporate giants, have pointed to the lack of a proper corporate governance systems as one of the main reasons for their collapse. The present economic turmoil faced by many countries, for example, the Asian economic crisis, the continuing economic turmoil in Russia and the global financial turmoil originating from US mortgage linked securitization have combined to push the issue of corporate governance to the centre stage. These financial crises show that even strong economies lacking transparent control, responsible corporate boards and shareholder rights collapse quite quickly as investors' confidence erodes.

Globalisation processes such as the liberalization and internationalisation of economies, development in telecommunications, the integration of securities markets, as well as transformations in the ownership structure of firms with the growth of institutional investors, privatisation and rising shareholder activism, have increased the need for efficient firms and financial markets. Globalisation is forcing many firms to tap international financial markets and thus face greater competition. This has led to restructuring and a greater role for mergers and acquisitions and to expanded markets for corporate control. In an increasingly globalized economy, firms need to tap domestic and international capital markets for capital and investment and the quality of corporate governance is increasingly becoming the criterion for investment and lending. Corporate governance is a significant factor considered by institutional investors when making investment decisions and ownership stakes. Many shareholders now compare ownership rights and governance structures as part of their due diligence reviews of companies. International investors are also convinced that the appropriate governance structures reduce risk and promote performance, and that shareholder participation can motivate companies' boards to produce higher long-term returns. Companies that enjoy good corporate governance have a competitive advantage in attracting capital over those whose practices discourage shareholder participation.

For the whole economy, good corporate governance practices mean a more efficient corporate sector and a higher level of economic growth. An active, dynamic and imaginative management pushes firms into new markets, provide new or/and cheaper services to customers and reacts rapidly to outside pressure. For instance, privatisation around the world has forced governments and firms to accommodate the needs of private investors who require good governance practices. Corporate governance encourages more transparent management practices, in order to attract more investment flows. Cross-border analysis is a noteworthy feature of corporate governance's rise to prominence.[18]Improving corporate governance standards helps improve the management of firms in areas such as setting company strategy, ensuring that mergers and acquisitions

---

18 Teemu, R. (2000). Conceptualizing Corporations and Kinship: Comparative Law and Development Theory in a Chinese Perspective. *Stanford Law Review*, 52:1599-1603.

are undertaken for sound business reasons and that compensation systems reflect performance.[19]

Upholding standards for transparency in dealing with investors and creditors helps in preventing systemic crises. Increasingly for developing economies, a healthy and competitive corporate sector is fundamental for sustained growth that withstands economic shocks and renders benefits to the society as a whole. Therefore, corporate governance has become, and is likely to remain a powerful tool for attracting foreign investments, as capital and investments will go where there is protection of investors. Companies in both developed and emerging markets have learned that corporate governance becomes a vital issue as they begin to go public, to merge with local and foreign companies, to tap international financial markets and to operate in a truly competitive domestic and international business environment. Even securities exchanges have not been left behind as they also consider corporate governance as vital.

Setting Codes for Good Corporate Governance

Who sets corporate governance codes? Codes of good corporate governance present a comprehensive set of norms on the role and composition of the board of directors, relationships with shareholders and top management, auditing and information disclosure, as well as the selection, remuneration and dismissal of directors and top managers. The codes serve to improve the overall corporate governance of corporations, especially when legal environments fail to ensure adequate protection of shareholders' rights. Countries are usually classified into four legal families according to the origin of their legal systems: English, French, German and Scandinavian. Countries with an English origin or common-law legal system provide better protection to shareholders than countries with a civil law legal system such as French, German and Scandinavian origin. The code serves to compensate for the lack of protection in the legal system and would be more likely to be adopted in civil law countries. In common-law countries,

---

19 Aguilera, R. & Cuervo-Cazurra, A. (2000). Codes of Good Governance Worldwide. CIBER Working Paper No. 00-105.

codes of good governance developed much earlier with the securities exchange and managers' associations being the main actors in developing codes whereas civil-law countries, created codes later, with managers and directors' associations taking the lead. Thus the legal system can be considered as a conditioning factor in the development of the codes of good governance.

Another important factor affecting the issuance of the codes is the issuer. Issuers can be securities exchanges, governments, director's associations, managers' association, professional associations or investors. The securities exchange is more likely to set the first code in common law countries, while the government is more likely to issue the first code in civil-law countries. Differences in who issues the code denote differences in the enforcement of the codes. For instance, government and securities market issuers might exert coercive pressure for the adoption of the codes of good governance, whereas associations and investors might apply normative pressures for adoption. In many developing countries, the government, through the capital markets regulators and securities exchanges, play a crucial role in the development of a corporate governance code. In most countries, corporate governance rules are the subject of binding law or regulations. In other countries, rules involve market institutions or merely common practices, sometimes written down in corporate governance codes and enforced through listing or disclosure rules, and sometimes simply embodied in investor expectations.

Corporate governance rules are neither entirely mandatory nor entirely voluntary in nature, but a mixture of both. Any reform proposal must include judgments on which issues should be addressed by a mandatory rule, which issues require mandatory disclosure but not binding rules, and when the adoption of a practice should be purely voluntary. It is worth mentioning that Hong Kong, Korea, Malaysia, Singapore and Thailand have all adopted codes of best practice of corporate governance and have linked them to the listing rules of their securities exchanges. The most recent country is China whereby China Securities Regulatory Commission issued a code of corporate governance for listed companies.

Since the nature of governance is defined in terms of the power wielded at a securities exchange, the analysis of governance draws heavily from the theory of the organisation, including the nexus-of-contracts, property rights, principal-agent problem, and the transaction cost approaches. The thrust of the transaction cost approach is that the governance structure adopted by an organization will be the one which minimizes the combined costs to all participants – institution's owners, members, controllers, management, staff, customers, suppliers, and financiers – dealing with the organization. The two key elements of governance are the assignment of ownership, monitoring and control. The cost incurred by those participants who are not its owners or controllers, are altogether minimized. It is therefore important to increase the understanding of a range of conceptual issues focussing on those aspects of governance which are not subject to legal or regulatory intervention specific to the securities markets since such intervention may affect a securities exchange's governance by constraining the organizational structure of the exchange or by limiting the choices that an exchange and its board may take concerning the exchange's operations and activities.

A number of securities exchanges mostly in developed countries like the UK and the US, and some in developing nations including those in Africa like Nairobi, Nigerian, Ghanaian, Egyptian and Johannesburg securities exchanges, among others, have set codes for corporate governance. Market institutions such as the Kuala Lumpur Stock Exchange, the Malaysian Exchange for Automated Dealing and Securities (Mesdaq), the Securities Clearing and Automated Network (Scans), the Malaysian Central Depository (MCD), the Futures Exchange and Clearing House, and many others in developing and emerging markets have recently voluntarily developed a Code of conduct for their market institutions. Such codes are to serve as a guide to their directors, managers, and employees to clarify their obligations and to provide general governance guidelines that apply to the institutions and persons within the institutions. The setting of the codes for market institutions like securities exchanges is deemed important; to explain and clarify the manner in which issues of inherent conflicts of interests and duties within these market structures should be addressed. Moreover, securities exchanges that impose corporate governance requirements on their listed companies and members should also adhere to the highest standards of conduct and thus lead by example.

One of the essential issues in corporate governance is its credibility. Market regulators and rules play an essential role for enforcement. To promote effective enforcement, rules must be effectively enforced and transgressions must be penalised. While the effectiveness of regulators in enforcing good governance is crucial, shareholder activism is key to ensuring good governance. Shareholders could take steps to enforce governance such as setting up a minority shareholder watchdog group. Furthermore, compulsory education programs for the directors of a firm seeking listing should be mandated as a pre-requisite to listing, along with mandatory accreditation for all the existing directors of listed firms. In many countries appropriate programs have been developed for this purpose. The training arms of most exchanges are expected to launch some of the director accreditation programs in their countries. This is intended to help with the problem that directors tend to be subjected to law and statutory responsibilities without having a full understanding of the significance of their responsibilities. Furthermore, market participants consider that education in relation to corporate governance should not be only confined to director accreditation. Training and education must be pursued at all levels for all those who can contribute to promoting and enhancing good corporate governance practices.

Corporate Governance in Securities Exchanges

Literature on corporate governance as an important indicator for organization performance in developing countries is still scanty. It is against this background that the text devotes itself to issues of corporate governance within the context of capital markets, specifically the application of the concept in securities exchanges. Most academic evaluations of governance have concentrated on the state, firms and other organizations while ignoring institutions like securities markets and regulators of such markets. Whereas securities exchanges are the best known and talked about capital markets, they are also organizations with owners and other interested stakeholders.

In analysing the nature and conduct of securities exchanges, there has also been a tendency of ignoring their inner structures by viewing them merely as a trading system or impersonal instrument guided by their managers and not as corporates. These approaches are not rich enough in detail to explain the nature and conduct of securities exchanges. Rather, a thorough understanding of the behaviour of a securities exchange can be attained by viewing it as a system made up of sub-systems, people and behaviours.

It is worth exploring who has what power at a securities exchange, how and why they obtain it, and how they exercise it. These issues are collectively referred to as governance and are closely intertwined and one cannot address one without addressing the others. For example, the choice of what governance structure a securities exchange adopts depends on the effects that different structures have on securities exchange behaviour. Second, the governance of a securities exchange will be affected both by the formal and legal constructs within which a securities exchange operates, such as its constitution and any contractual and non-contractual issues.

Securities Exchange Organizational Structures
There are three governance structures that have most commonly been adopted by securities exchanges within the African continent and elsewhere. These include, non-profit, the consumer cooperative, and the for-profit structures.[20] Although historically most securities exchanges have been non-profit organisations, there have been some consumer cooperative securities exchanges, and recently, there is a trend for securities exchanges to incorporate themselves as for-profit corporates. The following is a simple review of the essential elements of these forms and the relative costs to financial intermediaries if a securities exchange adopts any of these structures. The discussion covers only basic governance elements of each structure, and it is assumed that associated with each of the three organizational structures is a simple and well-defined objective function

---

20 For details, see Onyuma, S. O. Paradigm Shift in Stock Exchanges: Automation, Management, Competition, Integration and Regulation of Securities Markets(forthcoming); Lee, R. (2000) What is an Exchange: The Automation, Management and Regulation of Financial Markets. Oxford: Oxford University Press.

that is maximized by the securities exchange adopting it. Attention is focused only on the costs that would be incurred by the market participants in a securities exchange, like the financial intermediaries who trade on, and are consumers of the services offered by the exchange, while ignoring the incentives facing other types of securities exchange parties. It assumes that all the financial intermediaries trading on a securities exchange can be modelled by a single representative organisation structure. The implications of a securities exchange adopting each of the three governance structures depend on the applicable jurisdiction. However, a number of essential elements associated with each legal form may be identified, and these are discussed in the next sub-sections.

Non-profit Exchange Structure

The central characteristic of the governance structure here is that the non-profit securities exchange is restricted from distributing any profit or surplus that it earns, outside the exchange. Given that such surplus is not distributed to the exchange's management, a non-profit exchange is also typically only allowed to pay a reasonable compensation to its management. Following the simplest characterization of a securities exchange as a non-profit organisation is as complex as a commercial-mutual non-profit.[21] It is commercial in the sense that a non-profit's income accrues primarily from providing services for a fee to its clients like offering financial intermediaries a marketplace on which to deal. It is mutual since the agents who are the main source of a non-profit's income also control the exchange. For instance, the financial intermediaries who trade on a securities exchange also own and control it. A commercial mutual non-profit organisation is controlled by, and managed for, the consumers of the organisation. It cannot distribute any profits and operate if its cumulative losses exceed its cumulative gains. The idealized objective function of such an organisation is that it maximizes consumer surplus subject to break-evening.

---

21   Chambers, S. & Carter, C. (1990). US Futures Exchange as Non-profit Entities. *Journal of Futures Markets*, 10:79-88.

Consumer Cooperative Exchange Structure

The second governance structure, which a securities exchange may adopt, is consumer cooperative form. This governance structure revolves around the notion of membership. The key attribute of a cooperative exchange is that the services it provides are mainly for the use by its members, and that membership is limited only to those members who consume its services.[22] The formal control of such a securities exchange, like the assignment of voting rights, is allocated solely to its members on an equal basis, so that each member has only one vote regardless of the number of shares he owns or the amount of equity he has in the cooperative. Transfer of ownership interests is normally prohibited or limited. The initial investment is normally paid by the initial members either on an equal basis or in an amount proportionate to the amount of patronage a member is expected to bring to the exchange.

The economic benefits associated with membership may also be allocated on an equal basis or on the basis of a member's patronage of the exchange, and not necessarily according to the amount of equity a member has in the exchange. Although outside equity may be issued, it may have no voting rights attached to it, and sometimes may be restricted to earn a maximum rate of return. Net earnings are often to retire the investments of a member, with the oldest outstanding shares normally retired first through a revolving sinking fund. The key difference between these non-profit and consumer cooperative exchange is that the consumer cooperatives exchange may make distributions in cash through dividends to its owners – members – while the non-profits one is only allowed to do so in kind. Nevertheless, these two structures are not always judiciously distinguished in eye of the law. The idealized vision of the objective function of a consumer cooperative exchange is to maximize consumer and producer surplus, with profits being distributed to the members of the exchange.

---

22   Sendo, K. J. (1987). Cooperative Mergers and Consolidation: A Consideration of the Legal and Tax Issues. *North Dakota Law Review*, 63: 377-404.

For-profit Exchange Structure

The governance structures of for-profit organisations are extremely complex and to capture their structures, it is worth deciphering their characteristics by contrasting them with the above two exchange governance structures. First, unlike non-profits, for-profit exchanges are not required to retain all profits within the exchange and such profits may be distributed to shareholders. Second, unlike consumer cooperative exchange, for-profit exchanges may allow market participants other than its clients and non-market participants to have voting rights, and may also allow non-members to be their clients, thus, the notion of membership is not easily applicable.

In a securities exchange context, the differences between the non-profit and for-profit governance structures is that although non-profit exchanges are not allowed to distribute any profits earned, they can effect a similar result by lowering the fees they charge their members for the various services that they offer, or by offering rebates to their members. While the payment of a dividend by a for-profit exchange will primarily benefit its large owners, however, the reduction of fees and/or the payment of rebates at non-profit securities exchange will primarily benefit the large users of the exchange's services. This is ideally the type of governance structure, which securities exchanges aspiring to grow in the future, should strive to envisage.

It is notable that factors such as technological development, introduction of new trading platforms, deregulatory incentives and network externalities, economies of scale and cost reduction encourage securities exchanges to modify their strategies as well as organization structures. In a competitive financial environment, securities exchanges must maximize their profits to survive. Therefore, they opt to modernize their trading platforms to be more competitive and eventually transform their governance structures and commercial focus. Such evolution allows them to reduce costs, increase their market share, diversify their products and respond better to new challenges. However, there are likely to arise some profound change affecting the internal structure of securities exchanges and their transition to a new market model – the for-profit.

Until recently, securities exchanges have been considered part of the national identity and, therefore, untouchable monopolies with a mutualized structure. This situation is untenable given the increasing international competition arising from new technology and regulatory reforms. Securities exchanges are being pushed to react more and more like other firms seeking to maximize their profits. This transition to a for-profit or firm model, unimaginable a few years earlier, is at the heart of the changes affecting securities exchanges globally. A natural question that arises relates to the effects of this phenomenon on the ownership, management and functioning of securities exchanges and on their recently adopted transformations and strategic realignments.

Mutually Owned Securities Exchanges

Traditionally, a securities exchange was primarily a physical location for trading shares. Trade was conducted in person, and multiple securities were traded at the same location to maximize liquidity. Given the need to conduct exchange in person, space constraints restricted access to securities exchange members who were intermediaries for investor transactions. The limited access gave securities exchange members market power as they collected brokerage commissions and had a privileged view of trading flows that enabled them to make monopoly rents. These rents were protected by the high barriers to entry caused by limited space and network externalities – the more people traded on the securities exchange, the better was the price discovery. As a consequence of this, even more traders wanted to trade on such exchanges.

The floor-based trading system was not distinct from its members and was member-owned and operated on a non-profit basis. Securities exchanges were naturally non-profit – as cash profits were returned to the members in the form of lower access fees or rebates – in an effort to curb monopoly power and regulate pricing. Member ownership was efficient since customer ownership enabled users of a securities exchange to protect themselves against monopoly expropriation.[23] Each member owned one

---

23   Hansmann, H. (1996). The Ownership of Enterprise, The Belknap Press of Harvard University Press. Cambridge, Massachusetts. London, England.

share with attached voting rights and the exchange adopted a majority voting system.

The 1980s saw advances in electronic communications which meant trading could be done from anywhere via computerized systems meaning that a centralized physical location became less important. As barriers to entry fell, off-floor trading systems began to compete with the traditional securities exchanges, and, for the first time, the traditional securities exchanges felt the pressure on revenues. Notable examples include Reuter's Instinet system which trades Nasdaq unlisted securities, or the London's SEAQ-I – a screen-based system trading international securities – which competed with European exchanges such as Stockholm, Amsterdam and Milan.

Regulatory barriers to entry also fell, for example, in 1993 the Swedish Government enacted legislation to end the monopoly of the Stockholm Stock Exchange. In USA, the SEC implemented the Order Handling Rules to promote greater competition between the Electronic Communication Networks and Nasdaq. Also, the fixed costs needed to start an exchange decreased; consequently, the market became increasingly contestable. According to the theory of contestable markets, an incumbent monopoly is unable to exploit its market power, even in an increasing returns industry due to the threat of potential competition. It assumes zero sunk costs, and free entry and exit.[24] That is, traditional securities exchanges faced the threat of potential competition as a few large dealers could circumvent the exchange, start trading with each other, and siphon off significant trading volume.

Most traditional securities exchanges found it difficult to respond to competition because of their mutual governance structure. They had heterogeneous members – local market makers, broker-dealers, international banks etc. – who made private cost-benefit evaluations and could not be compelled to vote in favour of any policy change. For example, there was resistance to the introduction of automated trading platforms in

---

24   Baumol, W. J., Panzar, P. C. & Willig, R. D. (1982). Contestable Markets and the Theory of Industry Structure, New York, Harcourt Brace Jovanovich.

all traditional securities exchanges, and once introduced, to exploiting its full potential. In automated trading the computers match the buy and sell orders and thus reduce the role of the intermediary.

The international banks proposed electronic auction trading, but as it affected the profits of local members such as the German Kursmakler and the Amsterdam Hoekman, they resisted it. In USA, Nasdaq market-makers blocked the incorporation of mandatory price-time priority in the SuperMontage trading system so that they could continue matching trades internally.

In the member-owned mutual exchanges, the policy decisions were focused primarily on maximizing the member's utility. To respond to competition, the traditional securities exchanges required a residual claimant who would provide the right incentives to maximize securities exchange value as opposed to the members' individual profits. To achieve this, many securities exchanges in Europe and Asia moved towards demutualization – the separation of membership from ownership.

Mutuality and Floor Trading

The traditional model of an exchange as an organized mutual association is a remnant of the era before automation of exchange trading system. As trading required visual and verbal interaction, securities exchanges were necessarily designated physical locations where traders would meet at agreed times. Access to the securities exchange had to be rationed to prevent overcrowding and, when single-price periodic call-auctions were prevalent, to ensure that simultaneous full participation was physically feasible.

Given that trading systems were simply rules governing the conduct of transactions, securities exchanges were naturally run by the traders themselves as cooperatives. Organizing trading floors as companies selling transaction services would have been infeasible, as there was no system distinct from the traders themselves – only an empty room. Rationing access to the securities exchange was generally done through a combination of substantial initial and annual membership fees, in order to ensure self-selection by high-volume users. Non-members naturally wished to benefit from the network externalities of concentrated trading activity, commonly referred to as liquidity, and therefore paid members to represent their buy and sell orders on the securities exchange floor. This is how exchange members came to be intermediaries – the brokers, for investor transactions. In fact, securities exchanges organized stockbrokers into a classic cartel with respect to brokerage commissions – which were determined by the same stockbrokers.

Mutuality and Automated Trading

The economics of automated auction trading are radically different. The placement and matching of buy and sell orders can now be done on computer systems, access to which is inherently constrained neither by the location nor the numbers of desired access points. In a fully competitive market for electronic markets, the traditional concept of membership becomes economically untenable. As the marginal cost of adding a new member to a trading network declines towards zero, it becomes infeasible for a securities exchange to impose a fixed access cost, or membership fee. Rather, only transaction-based, the variable cost, charging is sustainable.

Indeed, this trend is evident among automated securities exchanges faced with significant competition: Deutsche Börse and OM Stockholm, for example, have eliminated membership fees. The transactors on electronic networks, therefore, come to look much more like what are normally considered clients or customers of a firm than members of an association. And since an electronic auction system is a valuable proprietary product, not costlessly replicable by traders, it is feasible for the owner to operate it, and sell access to it, as a normal for-profit commercial enterprise. This contrasts with a traditional securities exchange floor, whose value derives wholly from the physical presence of traders.

The fact that an automated securities exchange can be operated as a commercial enterprise, unlike a traditional floor-based exchange, does not in itself make an economic case for a corporate rather than mutual governance structure. However, such a case emerges naturally from an analysis of the incentive structures under which a mutualized and corporate securities exchange operates. Exchange members are the conduits to the trading system, and they thereby derive profits from intermediating non-member transactions. They can, therefore, be expected to resist both technological and institutional innovations which serve to reduce demand for their intermediation services, even where such innovations would increase the economic value of the securities exchange itself. If the members are actually owners of the exchange, they will logically exercise their powers to block disintermediation where the resulting decline in brokerage profits would not at least be offset by their share in the increase in exchange value.

As a major economic benefit of automated auction trading is the elimination of the need for trade intermediation, mutualized securities exchange can be expected both to have difficulties introducing automated systems and, once introduced, allowing their full potential to be exploited by non-member investors. Both of these effects exist, for instance, the largest UK-based market-makers on the LSE fought to block the adoption of electronic auction trading in the mid-1990s. Similarly, NYSE specialist firms have long fought against automated matching of investor orders and display of their limit order books to the trading floor and the wider public. Also, Nasdaq market-makers blocked the incorporation of mandatory price-time priority in Nasdaq's trading system upgrade, known as SuperMontage, successfully arguing that customers should be allowed to trade with them even if they were not posting the best price, or the earliest best price. They could simply agree to match the best posted price. Non-member-based commercial trading system operators, on the other hand, have always chosen both to operate automated auction structures and to do so without any intermediation requirement – except for retail orders, for which such operators have traditionally not wished to manage the credit risk function.

What are the efficiency costs inherent in securities exchange continuing to operate as broker-dealer cooperatives? Recent empirical evidence suggests two primary ones: higher trading costs (and therefore lower returns) to investors, and higher capital costs to listed companies. Domowitz & Steil (2002) estimate total trading costs to be 28-33 percent higher through NYSE and Nasdaq traditional broker members than through non-intermediated for-profit trading system operators, now commonly referred to as ECNs. The implication was that European securities exchanges trading fees alone would fall a massive 70 percent if these exchanges were to move to a reformed governance model: eliminating membership and allowing direct investor access. Historically, mutualized exchanges have sought to fix commissions and prevent price competition.

For-profit non-member-based trading system operators, on the other hand, have the opposite incentive: to mitigate access costs to their system imposed by intermediaries. The emergence of commercial rather than mutualized trading operations should also result in lower capital costs to listed companies. Domowitz & Steil further demonstrate not only that disintermediating trading reduces trading costs, but that trading cost reductions in turn reduce the cost of raising equity capital. The halving of total trading costs which they document in the USA between 1996 and 1998 resulted in an 8 percent decline in equity capital costs to S&P 500 companies. The authors further estimate that the elimination of mandatory broker intermediation at the European exchanges would result in at least a 7.8 percent savings to European blue-chip companies.

The New Exchange Governance Structures
Competitive pressures not only forced the traditional exchanges to demutualize, it made them relinquish at least some ownership in the securities exchange as well. That is, in most governance restructured securities exchanges, the members did not retain 100 percent ownership. A firm usually allocates ownership through power or authority; exchange governance structure reform is an example of this as customers of the exchange were given ownership shares to acknowledge their new-found power to switch trading venues.

Traditional securities exchanges had monopoly power; all public firms had to list on the exchange and all traders had to trade on it. With electronic competition, the exchanges' customers – the listed companies and the retail firms providing order flow – have choices. Now, the trading system becomes a stand-alone entity that needs customers to survive. The power structure shifts, with the larger customers having monopsony power; consequently, the traditional exchange has to provide them with incentives, such as ownership, to continue to do business with it.

Existing evidence explains how deregulation and technological change through the 1990s has changed the nature of the firm, and introduced new corporate governance mechanisms. In this new firm it may be more efficient to allocate formal control rights to parties such as workers and customers who have a lot of de facto power within the enterprise. For example, the Stockholm Stock Exchange (SSE) was the first to demutualize in 1993, with 50 percent ownership remaining with the members and 50 percent going to the listed companies. The Helsinki and Copenhagen stock exchanges had a 60-40 split between members and listed companies, while Amsterdam Stock Exchange allocated 50 percent ownership to members and auctioned 50 percent to listed companies and institutional investors.

Therefore, electronic networks have brought competition to the traditional securities exchanges, which adversely affect members' revenues. It was difficult for the traditional exchanges to bring in policies to counter competition due to their heterogeneous membership and mutual governance structure. Thus, they demutualized to introduce a residual claimant who would maximize the exchange's value by increasing trading volumes and revenues. Furthermore, the erstwhile members gave substantial ownership to the exchanges' customers in the demutualized exchange, to encourage them to continue to trade on the dominant exchange.

Sources of Transaction Costs in Exchange Governance Structures

Each of the governance structures, when adopted by a securities exchange, will impose different transaction costs on the financial intermediaries trading on a securities exchange. The following are the major sources for such transaction costs.

Incomplete Contracts. The first source of transaction costs that result due to adoption of a particular governance structure is the existence of incomplete contracts. Contracts are incomplete because it is costly to specify how a contract should operate under all circumstances, and since not all outcomes can be anticipated in advance. The presence of incomplete contracts may affect the most efficient allocation of ownership and this may be important when the parties in a business relationship make sunk investments.[25] The standard paradigm is one in which partners are locked in a relationship ex-post because of investments that have substantially higher value within the relationship than outside. So long as one party cannot specify ex-ante how the surplus should be divided between the two by being unable to write a comprehensive contract, the division will depend on ex-post bargaining positions which will depend on the organizational context. Where relationship-specific investments are large, it is not worth the use of a securities exchange, because parties will fear that they will be unable to appropriate the returns from their investments in an ex-post non-competitive bargaining environment. Bringing the transaction within the organisation will offer safeguards against opportunistic behaviour the – the moral hazards.

In order to avoid the possibility that the organisation may seek to exploit these clients who have made investments that are firm specific, it may be cost-efficient for the organisation to be governed by its clients, through a non-profit or cooperative structure. Certainly, there are sunk costs to a financial intermediary of being associated with a particular securities exchange like having to implement the necessary electronic links because a securities exchange employs an automated trading system. For example, all the stockbrokers in Kenya must now invest in a computerised system in order to participate in the NSE's automated trading system, as well as the clearance, settlement, and registry system.

However, the cost to an intermediary of switching its order-flow from one securities exchange to another do not generally appear to be so high that once it has become a member of the first securities exchange, it is effectively locked into only dealing on that securities exchange. Relatively cheap alternatives are typically available, either by leasing space on the second securities exchange if it operates a trading floor, by hiring electronic capacity to deliver orders to the second securities exchange if it operates an

---

25   Hart, O. (1991). Incomplete Contracts and the Theory of the Firm. In O. Williamson & S. Winter (eds.) The nature of the Firm: Origins, Evolution and Development. New York: Oxford University Press; Williamson (1996). The Mechanics of Governance. Oxford: Oxford University Press.

automated trading system, or by routing orders through a member of the second securities exchange and paying the required brokerage fees.

Ownership in the context of incomplete contracts is the set of residual rights of control associated with an asset, where residual means the set of rights that have been pre-specified contractually. The possibility that bargaining about the returns to an asset may occur after an initial contracting period, may make it optimal for ownership to be allocated to those participants who have made investment decisions specific to the asset. Agents' importance as trading partners and agents' investment decisions are significant determinant of the optimal allocation of ownership rights. When an agent is identified as being indispensable to an asset, it may be optimal to grant ownership to him, otherwise, the possibility of bargaining outcomes, which are inefficient, is again increased. To the extent that the financial intermediaries in a market have been the only agents who could usefully employ the services offered by securities exchanges, their indispensability may have been one of the factors making their ownership of exchanges relatively cost-efficient. Although other market participants can now use an exchange's services, but the importance of this determinant of securities exchange governance will shrivel.

Long or Short-Termism Problems. The other source of costs resulting from having particular governance structure is the termism problem, which may arise when an owner's claim on the net cash flow generated by his asset is shorter than the productive life of the asset. Should this happen, and when the market for the asset is not competitive, the return to the owner will be less than the return generated by the asset. There will therefore be under-investment in such assets compared to the situation where such problems were not present – a problem that may arise in non-profit and cooperative exchanges. In non-profits, claims to incremental net earnings cannot be bought and sold. In cooperatives, the capitalization and transfer of future net earnings is likely to be only partially effective at best even though an outside equity can only be transferred by relinquishing trading rights. Both in non-profit and cooperative securities exchanges, termism problems may occur, as members reducing their use of an exchange's services will undervalue investment assets compared to the discounted cash flows the investments are expected to yield. They will not want to pay more fees now for benefits they may not see in the future.

However, those members for whom patronage is expected to grow over the life of an investment will place a higher value on the asset. This may create control problems at securities exchanges where all members are required to make the same investments, given that investment incentives may differ between exchange members. A different type of termism problem for a securities exchange may be brought about by the structure of for-profit organisations since claims to net earnings can be capitalised and transferred in for-profit securities exchanges, and therefore the financial potential of the long-term investments necessary for exchange marketing and product development, can be appropriately evaluated by such securities exchange owners. The shareholders of for-profit securities exchanges may be more short-termist than those of non-profit and cooperative securities exchanges. The pressure on for-profit organisations to pay dividends rather than retain their earnings for reinvestment, may allow non-profit and cooperative securities exchanges to make longer term, but more profitable investments, than for-profit securities exchanges.

Inability to Diversify Investment Risks. Typically, in the non-profit or cooperative structured securities exchanges, the members' ability to diversify their investments in their securities exchange, while still retaining the right to trade on the exchange, is usually low. This is because the shares of such securities exchanges cannot easily be bought and sold while retaining trading rights. A securities exchange seat ownership is therefore an illiquid form of wealth. The volatility of seat prices will make bankers cautious to take a seat as collateral for a loan of an amount close to the seat's market value. Members of non-profit and cooperative structures securities exchanges will therefore be unlikely to arrange their investment portfolios so as to reflect their personal preferences for risk. This may make them demand greater return on their investments, or make less of an investment, than their counterparts in for-profit securities exchanges.

Monopoly Derived Costs. Usually, a for-profit organisation which is monopolistic in nature strives to maximize producer surplus by raising prices and reducing output compared to the competitive outcome. This will not be optimal for clients of the organisation who would prefer that the lower price and higher output competitive outcome are derived. Evidence[26] indicates that both the non-profit and cooperative forms may, however, be able to deliver the lower price and higher output. Just like the for-profit organisation, a non-profit producer has the capacity to raise prices without much fear of customer complaints, but lacks the incentive to do so because those in charge are barred from taking home any resulting profits. Available evidence[27] further shows that cooperative structure tends to arise in situations in which the organization's clients feel a need to maintain control of prices set by the enterprise particularly when the enterprise is a monopoly. In order for the non-profit or the cooperative structure to be adopted by a monopolistic producer, the costs to clients of exercising control over the organisation by switching to one of these governance structures must be lower than costs they would incur by contracting through the market with the monopolistic for-profit organisation.

Provision of Trading Systems. If one considers where there is only one governance system, operated on a for-profit basis, and not owned and controlled by the financial intermediaries for their use, and restrict the amount of services available, compared to what would happen if there were many such systems competing with each other. If the cost of exercising control over a trading system is not too high, in such a case, the financial intermediaries owning the securities exchange may wish to operate the trading system as a non-profit or cooperative form.

Provision of Brokerage and Dealing Services. The provision of brokerage and dealing services is another source of transaction costs resulting due to the adoption of a given governance structure. Thus, the other source of monopoly which is of interests to financial intermediaries, therefore, relates to the provision of broking and dealing services to investor-clients. By restricting competition between themselves through limiting the number of stockbrokers and charging minimum commissions, financial

---

26   Hansmann, H. B. (1980). The Role of Non-profit Enterprise. *Yale Law Review*, 89: 835-898.
27   Hansmann, H. B. (1981). Reforming Non-profit Corporation Law. *University of Pennsylvania Law Review*, 129: 497-623.

intermediaries have been able to exploit some monopoly power over their clients. This can be viewed as a monopolist operating in an upstream market who provides an indispensable factor of production to a downstream market. The securities exchange is the monopolist, the indispensable factor of production is the trading system, and the downstream market is the one for whom securities broking and dealing services are provided by financial intermediaries. The securities exchange owners can refuse to sell the use of the trading system to those brokers who are not members of the cooperative, thereby reducing unwanted competition. This is what has happened in Kenya where for the seventy years since securities exchange inception, the number of stockbrokers was six, thirteen, eighteen for decades, and then twenty-one.

The governance structure of a securities exchange may thus help the stockbrokers to sustain such a cartel-like tendency by limiting access to the exchange trading system. The cooperative governance structure on the one hand may be employed by financial intermediaries to reduce the effects of a monopoly which they face for the provision of the trading system. On the other hand, the same governance structure may be used to strengthen the cartel which they operate for the provision of brokerage services in a securities market.

This notion that securities exchanges are organized as cooperatives because a cooperative is an effective mechanism for sustaining a cartel amongst stockbrokers has been refuted by scholars who argue that an outside owner could implement the same outcome by similarly restricting the numbers of stockbrokers and raising commissions.[28] This argument, however, ignores the issue of how any monopoly profits that arise are to be distributed. The outcomes at a monopolistic for-profit securities exchange and at a monopolistic consumer cooperative exchange may be indistinguishable from an investor's point of view,

---

28 Hart, O. D. & Moor, J (1997). Cooperatives vs. Outside ownership. Working Paper, Harvard University, London School of Economics, and University of St. Andrew, 16th October; Hart, O. D. and Moor, J (1994). The Governance of Exchanges: Members' Cooperatives versus Outside Ownership. Working Paper, Harvard University and London School of Economics, April.

in that the same relatively limited number of stockbrokers would be operating and they would be charging the same (relatively high) fees to investors. The two different governance structures are likely to have different effects on the distribution of profits. At the for-profit securities exchange, the owners of the exchange may seek to appropriate the monopoly profits by charging the intermediaries a high transaction fee, which the intermediaries would in turn pass on to investors. At the consumer cooperative, however, the intermediaries may look to obtain this money through relatively high commissions, and setting themselves a relatively low transaction fee.

Further evidence of the importance of governance points to whether a monopolistic securities exchange would be willing to grant access to its trading system directly to investors. A non-profit or cooperative monopolistic securities exchange whose members are financial intermediaries would be reluctant to do so as this might lead to the financial intermediaries being disintermediated, and thereby endanger the livelihood of the members whose very welfare the securities exchange existed to serve. This is the common situation in Africa and many developing countries in South America. On the other hand, a monopolistic for-profit non-member-owned system would have no such doubts, as it would not have to satisfy the preferences of the financial intermediaries trading on its system.

Financing Options. The other factor associated with the various organizational forms that may bring about cost differences across the governance structures, is financing.[29] This is because a for-profit securities may issue dividend-paying and voting equity to anybody, whereas a cooperative exchange may only issue dividend-paying but non-voting equity to non-members. But a commercial mutual non-profit exchange may only issue non-voting and non-dividend-paying equity to non-clients. A for-profit exchange may therefore be able to raise finance more cheaply than the other two governance structures. Major securities exchanges globally have transformed their governance structures from non-profit

---

29   Berglof, E. (1990). Capital Structure as a Mechanism for Control. In M. Aoki et al. (Eds) The Organisation as a Nexus of Treaties. New York: Sage Publication: 237-362.

mutual cooperative ones into for-profit structures. This has enabled them to raise equity finance through self-listing of their shares.

Legal Benefits. Some legislation may favour particular organisational forms and bring about cost differences across governance structures. Such legal benefits may give non-profit securities exchanges advantages over their for-profit counterparts in many areas of legislation in different countries. The advantages may, for example, occur in the treatment of securities regulation, bankruptcy, antitrust, unfair competition, copyright, social security, and minimum wage. Some non-profits organizations, though not securities exchanges, receive an exemption from paying income tax.

Legal Constraints. Lastly, the legal constraints facing a securities exchange may also result in costs because the functions which non-profits are allowed by law to undertake may be restricted, as opposed to for-profit organisations. They are allowed to establish trade associations, a category in which securities exchanges may often be classified. Some jurisdictions similarly limit the activities of cooperatives, in some instances only allowing agricultural associations to incorporate as cooperatives. But even some informal and semiformal financial institutions like savings and credit societies have been allowed to operate as cooperatives although not fully owned by members. The developments, for example, in the informal and semiformal financial subsector in many developing countries are attributable to the supportive environment created by government ministries in charge of cooperative affairs.

Securities Exchange Governance Issues

Governance is one of the pertinent issues considered with regard to the implementation of demutualization of securities exchanges. While the primary motive behind good governance practice is to deliver the best to all the stakeholders, still investors, as the backbone of a securities exchange, and their interest remain as the focus area of any reform in the securities market. Investor confidence is the most important capital on which a securities exchange can pursue its economic and social objectives.

Over the years, the inadequacy of proper governance practices and standards of transparency in many traditional securities exchanges have eroded investors' confidence in many of the economies and as a result a demutualized structure has found favour. Securities exchange governance has, therefore, become high in capital development agenda. During the last few years among many issues, governance has become the pertinent issue considered with regard to the implementation of demutualization of securities exchange. The structure of an exchange exists because of the trusts imposed on it by the investors. This simply demands that the structure has to deliver the best to them. This ultimately emphasizes on the operational transparency and viability of securities exchanges.

The actual governance structures of existing securities exchanges seem to be so diverse and complicated that the assumptions of the three organisational structures discussed above are far from representing how securities exchanges operate in practice. The following are the implications of such variety and complexity and the ramifications of relaxing the assumptions made earlier.

Formal Exchange Structures

To be able to distinctively state the formal governance structure of a securities exchange, it is important to understand the constitutional rights and duties that are allocated to the key participants at the exchange, such as its owners, members, traders, board, committees, and management.[30] This calls for the evaluation of issues relating to the type of shares available in a securities exchange, rights and duties like voting, trading and representation associated with the different types of shares, how such rights and duties can be varied, and who may own which shares, transferring shares, appointments to the board and directors' powers, appointment and firing of managers, and when to put to a ballot decisions at a securities exchange.

Different securities exchanges have different ownership structures. The owners of a securities exchange may typically be classified as intermediaries, issuers, investors, management, and the government.

---

30 Capital Markets Authority (2016) Code of Corporate Governance for issuers of securities to the public, Gazette Notice No. 1420 - March 4, Government Press.

At futures and commodities exchanges, classification may include floor brokers, floor traders, futures commission merchants and producers. The voting rights associated with being an owner vary at some exchanges like JSE, as each member is granted one share and one vote in general meetings of the exchange; at others, members who do more business have been granted more shares, and correspondingly more votes, than their smaller counterparts. Futures exchanges with more than one trading pit may issue several classes of shares with different rights or duties attached to them.

The different types of membership are frequently designed to attract new participants to an exchange in order to trade new products. The exchange board representation also differs across securities exchanges since in some exchanges investors are granted access to the board, in others they are not. The method of selecting the chairman of a securities exchange also varies. Sometimes the chairperson is elected by the board of directors like in Chicago Mercantile Exchange (CME), sometimes by the full electorate of all the members of the exchange like in NSE. In other countries, the chairperson is sometimes appointed by the state. For example, the Shenzhen Stock Exchange and Shanghai Stock Exchange can be characterized as quasi-state institutions insofar as they were created by government of China and their leading personnel are directly appointed by the China Securities Regulatory Commission. The Tashkent (Republican) Stock Exchange established in 1994 is mainly state-owned but has a form of joint-stock company since the Republic of Uzbekistan has a state share ownership in the authorized capital of the exchange of 26 percent.[31]

The mission of most securities exchanges is to develop and operate an efficient and transparent securities market to the best international standards for the benefit of all stakeholders. Exchanges hope to achieve their mission through trading system automation, legal and markets reform and customer focus.[32] The internal organization of many exchanges

---

31   See https://www.uzse.uz/abouts/history

32   Kibby, K. (2001) The Role of the Nairobi Stock Exchange in Kenya, Presentation by NSE Chief Executive to Students of the Columbia Business School. Thursday, 4th January.

exemplifies the complexity of the formal governance structure typical of many exchanges. Their objectives are contained in Memorandum of Association, which lays down the objects, and those which are the most relevant for its activity as a securities exchange – showing multiplicity of objectives. Such exchanges may state their purpose as being to:

- Carry on the business of an investment exchange and clearing house; to provide, manage and regulate markets in, and clearing and settlement services with respect to transactions in investments of all kinds, including financial instruments, and to provide facilities for the transaction of the business of broking, dealing, market-making, investment management and financial advice, as well as other businesses in the field of financial services.

- Act as an authority for the admission of investments to be traded or dealt in on the exchange or securities market and to maintain any official list for the time being required or recognised by the law.

- Provide the listed firms' information and depository services individually or through an agent; and provide, maintain and operate systems for and in connection with the evidencing and transfer of investments and to regulate the use of such systems.

- Act in any statutory, supervisory, regulatory or public capacity pursuant to statute or otherwise in relation to investments or financial matters of any kind or any market relating thereto.

- Enter into arrangements of any kind and to co-operate and share information with other exchanges, governmental and non -governmental authorities, bodies and persons in any part of the world, and in particular with those having responsibility for the supervision or regulation of financial services.

- Promote high standards in the investment service industry and in particular to make, administer, monitor, and enforce rules governing access to and use of any services and facilities provided by the exchange and the qualification and conduct of persons engaging in the securities, and to make arrangements for the investigation of complaints in respect of business transacted by means of the exchange's services and facilities.

- Establish and maintain, by levying of contributions, by insurance or otherwise, compensation schemes for the benefit or protection of the public or of any class of person.

Most securities exchanges in Africa and other developing markets in South America have designated themselves a non-profit structure such that their net revenues can only be applied towards the promotion of the objects of the exchange, and no portion of these revenues can be paid directly or indirectly to their members. The memorandum also states how the exchange is to be controlled. Only members of the exchange may be owners of the exchange, and all members of the exchange must become owners. There are restrictions on the number of memberships that may be obtained. The rights attached to membership may be changed either with the consent in writing, or with the sanction of an extraordinary resolution passed at a general meeting of the exchange members. Every member has the right to attend and vote on a resolution which is put to a poll at a general meeting, if present either in person or by proxy. Resolutions may be passed on a show of hands or on a poll by a majority of the votes, subject to there being a quorum.

For instance, the NSE as of March 4th 2010 had twelve directors including a chairman and two vice chairmen.[33] The board of directors was made up of a chief executive, chairman who was a registered member of the exchange, five member-brokers, four outsiders representing interests of fund managers, bankers, insurers, etcetera, and a company secretary. Directors were appointed either on the recommendation of other directors, or by a member representing a substantial voting rights of all members. The directors had powers to recommend a person for appointment only if he was already a director retiring by rotation, if he was approved by the chairman, or if he represented a key economic sector. The directors were

---

33 www.nse.or.ke

empowered to manage the exchange being headed by a chairman and the chief executive officer.

Since 1991 representatives of investing institutions and listed companies had been invited to the board of directors of some securities exchanges in UK and USA where exchange reforms have been undertaken, thus giving them some influence over the securities exchange control, but not the ownership of the exchange,[34] though such efforts are yet to be introduced in many developing securities markets. The chairman usually calls a directors' meeting. Each director has one vote on any issues put to the vote in such a meeting, and in case of a tie, the chairman has a casting vote. In general, the quorum necessary to hold a vote in a directors' meeting is two-thirds of members, of whom not less than five must be non-executive directors. The directors may elect or remove the chairman of the exchange.

An application for membership could be made by an incorporated stockbroker or investment banker. In order to be a member, an institution had to be conducting business at the exchange, be suitable to do so by being technically competent, had sufficient knowledge and experience, and had adequate systems and controls, and be appropriately authorized by the capital or securities markets regulator. The securities exchange's rules outline the types of business that might be conducted on the exchange. The main categories of institutions allowed to become members in many markets, for example are stockbrokers, investment bankers, and securities dealers. There were therefore restrictions on investors being members and having direct access to the securities exchange's trading systems. In fact, all trading transactions at the securities exchanges can only be undertaken by an investor through a stockbroker who is a member of the securities exchange.[35]

Powers of the Board

Explaining the behaviour of a securities exchange by trying to identify one main objective that the exchange seeks to maximize is a fruitless effort.

---

34 See Lee (2000) *What is an Exchange: The Automation, Management and Regulation of Financial Markets.* Oxford: Oxford University Press.

35 See the NSE Management and Membership Rules. Nairobi: NSE.

The personalization of the organisation implied by asking questions such as what should be the objective function of the corporation is seriously misleading as the corporation is not an individual, but a fictitious legal entity which serves as a focus for a complex process in which the conflicting objectives of individuals are brought into equilibrium within a framework of contractual relations. Thus the behaviour of an organization is similar to that of a market as it is the outcome of a complex equilibrium process. Whether securities exchanges are seen as corporations or as markets, their behaviour is also best viewed as the outcome of a complex equilibrium process. It is not only the contractual relationships at a securities exchange that determine its governance structure. Rather, the constitutional arrangements, and some relationships determined by either contractual or constitutional factors, can be critical in influencing its nature and behaviour. The multiplicity of these relationships implies that conflict is endemic to securities exchanges.

Some of the many ways in which such multiplicity of objectives and conflict can emerge are varied. For example, different ownership groups may attempt to promote their own competing interests and seek to minimize the particular fees that they are required to pay. Some securities exchange members may also be exchange competitors, and these participants are likely to pursue different goals from those followed by non-competitors. Elsewhere in Europe and America, many financial intermediaries, for example, operate their own internal order-matching systems in competition with the exchange of which they are members. Some members may themselves have internally conflicting interests and these conflicts may affect the securities exchange as well as the intermediaries themselves. The larger securities exchange members, who pay most of the revenues to the exchange, may wish to wield greater power than the exercise of their voting rights that the exchange would grant them, given the relatively small number of votes that they typically own. Particular types of conflicts may also arise if securities exchanges have different types of members with divergent goals where they want to keep their contract expenses down, but also want as much trading and information infrastructure as possible placed on the trading floor.

The board, the management, and some committees at different securities exchanges, each plays a vital role in exchange governance. The nature of their roles and their relative importance are difficult to measure since it is hard to obtain relevant information, given that board and committee minutes and management memoranda are almost kept confidential, and the power of the three institutional structures appears to differ across securities exchanges. The fact that an exchange's board of directors is granted the constitutional authority to decide on a wide range of issues is often taken as evidence that the board plays a critical role in the securities exchange's governance. The growing complexity and value of the services provided by securities exchanges has meant that only the most political of issues are now being referred to directors of large securities exchanges, and the management of exchanges are, therefore, gaining more power at the expense of their boards. This may be particularly relevant for non-profit securities exchanges. Thus, the notion that the boards of non-profit organisations in which non-profit securities exchanges fit are policy-making, goal-evaluating organisational units may not be borne out in practice.

Securities exchanges' boards do not seem to be formulating policy but rather ratifying policy that is presented to them by the staff. The executive committee in cohort with top management may be the only organ within the board structure where policy is designed.[36] Certain situations like organizational transformations may increase the probability that boards enact policy, but as a rule they do not. Instead, they are used more or less effectively for external linking functions. The extent to which the committees established at a securities exchange have either any formal power delegated to them by the exchange's board, or any informal power vested in them, varies considerably. One exchange at which committees have been very powerful is the Chicago Board of Trade (CBT).[37] Here, the exchange's committee structure shows the complex manner in which

---

36 See Cadbury, A (2002) Corporate Governance and chairmanship: a personal view, Oxford University Press, Oxford.

37 See Crawford (1994) Report Calls for CBOT Reform. Futures and Options World, March, No. 274:19.

committees can influence exchange governance. Through restructuring the exchange's organization, three main benefits of the committee system were identified:[38] it provided a mechanism through which the owners of the exchange could influence its activities and business direction, allowed the knowledge and expertise of the membership to be captured for the benefit of the exchange, and served as a vehicle for building consensus and communicating with the broader exchange members. The costs of the CBT system indicated an unbalanced representation of different membership groups on the various committees, with agricultural traders generally over-represented. The committees' decision-making processes were slow and often ad hoc. There was over-involvement by the committees in detailed operations creating diffused responsibility and accountability. Participation in committee work was time-consuming for management and members; and priorities for the exchange were generated from the bottom up, and not within a strategic framework. The implication is that attempting to characterize the role that committees play in exchange governance is also complex.

An indication of the multiplicity of goals which a non-profit securities exchange may be mirrored in the capacities that are believed appropriate for its executives. The ideal model for the chief executive officer of a non-profit organization has been identified as a mix of the political wheel-dealer, the capitalist venturer and marketer, the disciplined technical manager, and the master of interpersonal relations. In addition, the perfect candidate for the position of the chief executive of the securities exchange has been identified in Kenya as an intelligent, businessman, with knowledge and experience in accounting and finance, and more so a stockbroker. The chairman, for example at the NSE, comes from its registered stockbrokers. However, the qualification of such chairmen given the above descriptions is not clear.[39] If chief executives of securities exchanges meet these standards, they evidently need to reconcile competing interests. An important quality necessary in

---

38 See Allen, B. & Hamilton Inc. (1994) Final Report of the Implementation Committee. CBT, 8th, March.

39 See Nairobi Securities Exchange management and Membership Rules. www.nse.co.ke

establishing a securities exchange or a new trading environment is dynamism often associated with an autocratic tendency in an individual. Securities exchange boards have frequently sought to find a new management that is better able to operate through consensus by interested stakeholders.

Securities exchange leaders, partners, and suppliers are amongst the types of market participants who may be able to affect an exchange's governance structure. The role Reuters played at GLOBEX trading system is an example.[40] Initially, Reuters was viewed merely as the provider of the hardware and software for this system, whereas the participating exchanges were viewed as the creators and sponsors of the markets trading on the system. The convoluted history of the system's development meant, however, that Reuters became more involved with its governance in addition to being responsible for the efficacy of its operations. In addition, the partnerships in the ownership of CDSC have been influential in its governance structure, as have the stockbrokers who over the years have shaped the governance structure of NSE. The end-investors or the clients of the financial intermediaries on a securities exchange may also have a strong influence on exchange governance even if they have no direct constitutional rights at, or contractual agreements with the securities exchange. Their power lies in the possibility of their diverting order-flow away from a securities exchange if they believe its governance principles are against their interests.

Even if it is hoped to ascribe a single objective function to a non-profit securities exchange, and it is assumed that this should be the maximization of consumer surplus, the manner in which this objective should be interpreted has been conceived in several ways. There exist models in which a non-profit securities exchange may seek to maximize the profits of its members by granting just that number of memberships which leads to a profit-maximizing bid-ask spread.[41] Other thinkers argue that exchanges seek to maximize their members' utility by maximizing total trading volume. In addition, non-profit securities exchanges, may pursue

---

40   See Stewart and Ivory (M-Books) (1996) New Electronic Trading Services: Consultation Feedback- Response, LSE no. 052, 14th February.

41   Saloner, G. (1984) Self-Regulating Commodity Futures Exchange. In R. Anderson (ed) The Institutional Organisation of Futures Markets. Lexington, MA: Lexington Books.

other goals, like maximising the quality and quantity of services that they offer, or their annual budget, all subject to the constraint that revenues equal costs; the quality maximization might be imputed to managers who are empire builders or who seek to serve as the board; and maximization of an exchange's budget may be followed because it enhances the importance of, or justifies a higher salary for, the exchange managers.

An effort to measure what objectives securities exchanges seek to maximize calls for the evaluation of how they have been valued when issuing new shares or seats. In addition to a securities exchange's balance sheet and income statement, other relevant valuation criteria have included seat prices, trading volume, open interest, average daily volume, assets of the exchange such as proprietary technology or contracts it has developed that have a use outside the exchange, and the extent to which trading on the exchange is vulnerable to competition by ECNs, over-the-counter (OTC) trading or other futures exchanges. Conflict between the objectives that a securities exchange seeks to realize is often evident and may be caused by the goals that the exchange publicly states that it seeks to pursue. The objectives that non-profit securities exchanges officially follow are normally not the financial returns they achieve, but those reflected in their mission statements. Such objectives are often ambiguous in nature and difficult to measure. The ambiguity in, and conflict between, the objectives pursued by a non-profit securities exchange can create opportunities for internal politics, goal displacement, and conflict between its official mission and the goals it actually follows. Non-profit exchanges are thus frequently seen as temporary alliances of separate groups, each interpreting the exchange's purpose a little differently. Most non-profit securities exchanges, for example, identify the efficiency and integrity of their markets, both of which are extremely vague concepts, as being key objectives. In fact, non-profits are often thought to have many goals which can be inconsistent, contradictory, or incoherent, and it is often unclear even at what level or with respect to what units the attainment of such goals should be measured.

Possible tension between the official goals of a securities exchange and those it actually pursues is not limited to non-profit exchanges alone since for-profit securities exchanges are progressively also defining the goals they pursue in much wider terms than simply the returns that they achieve and often have mission statements similar in nature to those pursued by non-profit securities exchanges. The assumption that the maximization of profits is the main goal of such exchanges is also doubtful. The CBT vision statement of 1993[42] provides an example of the ambiguity typical in the purpose of a securities exchange. It stated that the exchange would be the premier, innovative, aggressive, global venue for the risk transfer and clearing of commodities, securities, financial instruments and other products, and that trading opportunity would be maximized by focusing on satisfying customer needs. Ownership returns were to be maximized by professionally managing the exchange as an efficient and profitable business.

From the statement, trading opportunity was defined to mean not just volume of contracts but a breadth and depth of potential possibilities and courses of action. Moreover, ownership return was defined to mean not just seat value but also a variety of ways in which to derive earnings based upon operational performance. Also, the intent to provide flexibility to the exchange in its choice of action and the goals that this vision statement promotes is clearly ambiguous. Initially, Stockbrokers Botswana was the only brokerage firm responsible for all buy and sell activities, reporting, and other operations of the Botswana Stock Exchange.[43] However, conflicts arose when reorganization was made to promote foreign investment and bring in more market players. This brokerage firm saw a deliberate effort to snatch from it all the activities it performed before. Therefore, the internal politics and the personalities at an exchange are therefore critical factors in affecting its governance and may highlight the specific identity of important exchange participants and the manner in which conflicts are presented and resolved at a securities exchange.

---

42 See CBT (1993) A Strategic Framework for the Chicago Board of Trade. Report to Board of Directors, July.

43 Irving J. (2005) Regional Integration of Stock Exchanges in Eastern & Southern Africa: Progress and Prospects. IMF Working Paper No. 05/122.

Efficiency of a Particular Securities Exchange Structure

The factors complicating securities exchange governance structures discussed above may also affect the efficiency of the different governance structures for an exchange in a number of ways, as discussed below.

Democratic Decision-Making

One of the ways in which the complexity and ambiguity of the objectives of a securities exchange can affect the efficiency of its governance structure is by democratic management. There is a wrong assumption that the decisions taken by an exchange reflect the preferences of a single market participant. A securities exchange should adopt a more complicated democratic management as opposed to a dictatorial approach, thus creating different costs. By avoiding making such assumptions and accepting the fact that a complete contract can be written that covers all the decisions to be taken by a securities exchange, then the manner in which the exchange decisions are made should be specified in order to analyse its governance structure. The best way of typifying such a decision-making process is to consider it as a democratic approach, and that, given the preferences of all the securities exchange owners, would determine how decisions are made at a securities exchange. For example, it can be specified that each exchange owner is granted one vote on relevant issues and the alternative with the highest number of votes wins or a two-thirds majority win is required. The democratic approach adopted will influence the quality of the decisions made and lead to the imposition of different costs on various securities exchange stakeholders. Globally, most securities exchanges have a two-thirds majority rule in its decision-making system.

The costs of collective decision-making may be high, especially if the ownership of a securities exchange is heterogeneous and one group of stakeholders seeks to use this mechanism to maximize its own welfare by exploiting other groups or clients to the extent permitted by competition. There may exist strong incentives for coalition-forming to capture the available benefits, resulting in some costs. However, if there is a simple way for balancing securities exchange stakeholders' interests and even in cases where stakeholders' interests diverge considerably, such costs associated with collective decision-making may not be enormous so long as there is an agreed method of sharing the benefits accruing from the securities exchange by each individual party, there will be less complaints.

A securities exchange management may apply different voting structures which are cost-efficient for different types of decisions. Democratic management has been successful in cooperative organisation structures. The system used to choose the tenets of democratic principles should minimize bargaining costs between securities exchange members, and maximize the possibility of effecting an outcome in which there is minimum gap between benefits obtained by different members of the cooperative.[44] A wide benefit gap amongst members is undesirable as members do not know in advance of choosing the type of decision-making method, how successful they are going to be, and therefore would wish to ensure that should they fail, the method adopted will not too adversely affect their interests. By lowering the number of agents participating in the decision-making, bargaining costs are likely to go down.

The more centralized the decision-making process, the more strongly the divergent preferences securities exchange members have over the decision-making alternative selected. It may even be beneficial to one person with decision-making responsibility, especially on issues that, to a lesser, extent affect securities exchange members. In fact, more important securities exchange policy decisions should be made by a two-third majority. A demerit of the cooperative exchange governance structure is that such democratic decision-making may not be efficient since the views of the decisive-median voters in the securities exchange do not represent those of all the membership, or its average voter. Thus the attractiveness of the decisions of such an exchange may be reduced by a skewed distribution of members caused by an increasing gap between the preferences of the median voter and the average voter.

However, there being no competition, other outside securities exchange owners (like when exchange shares have been distributed to listed companies,

---

44 Zusman (1992) Constitution Selection of Collective Choice Rules in Cooperative Enterprise. Jornal of Economic Behaviour and Organizations, Vol. 17:353-362.

banks, firms providing trading platform) may behave monopolistically by raising prices and restricting supply and thus excluding many members from the exchange than would happen in a competitive structure. The increase in the skewness of the distribution across membership does not in any way affect the incentives facing outside ownership.

Since cooperative securities exchange owners' shares cannot be traded, and because a separation of voting from trading rights may not be allowed, other costs may arise in non-profit or cooperative exchanges because no single member can easily influence the decisions taken by the exchange itself by buying the votes of other members to exert control. This effort is expensive and is likely to reduce the liquidity of such a securities exchange and the value of controlling it. But through the democratic process, which suffers from a free-rider-effect, each voter will only obtain a small part of the gains realized by his actions, even though he will have to incur all the costs necessary to undertake such activities.

Costly actions designed to increase the value of a securities exchange are, therefore, unlikely to be taken in some non-profit or cooperative exchanges than in for-profit exchanges unless an owner of a membership is allowed to lease his membership to somebody else allowing the owner to retain the voting rights, while the lessee keeps the trading rights. For investment purposes, a securities exchange member can thus acquire a number of seats and retain the voting rights associated with those memberships. Therefore, if votes are allocated on the basis of one vote per membership owned, rather than one per member, the concentration of voting claims would arise in a securities exchange.

Principal- Agent Problem

The second way in which the complexity and ambiguity of the objectives of a securities exchange can affect the efficiency of its governance structure emanates from the tension between its owners and managers. The agency problem which occurs because the management of a securities exchange cannot be assumed simply to follow the desires of its owners or clients, and this, together with the presence of asymmetrical information, may result in a principal-agent problem. Organisation owners (principals) do not usually manage the organisation themselves, but employ a management team (agents) to act on their behalf in running the entity. The principal-agent problem arises if the management has different preferences from those of the owners and are able to advance their own interests at the expense of those of the owners. It also occurs due to the presence of asymmetrical information between management and owners. This may happen when the owners are unable to control and monitor directly the performance of the management, and thus cannot evaluate whether self-interested actions by their agent are occurring. In assessing the effects of principal-agent problems on the relative efficiency of the non-profit, cooperative and for-profit structures for a securities exchange, the important issue is whether such concerns give rise to different costs for the different governance structures.

Methods of reducing principal-agent problems include establishing an incentive scheme for management so as to align its interests with those of the shareholders through paying the management a salary based on the returns earned by the exchange. Although appropriate in for-profit exchanges, there are two problems with applying this approach in non-profit securities exchanges. First, management is not legally allowed to share in the residual earnings of non-profit entities. They may, therefore, face a smaller incentive to seek cost-efficiency than would be present in for-profit exchanges. A securities exchange can go about this problem by employing a bonus plan for staff, which is based on volume increases. Although compensation packages are also subject to the discretion of the securities exchange's membership, they may be linked to the residual earnings of an exchange. Second, the objectives of a non-profit securities exchange may be more ambiguous than that of a for-profit exchange, making it harder to develop an appropriate incentive scheme for management even if permitted by law. This can provide the management of a non-profit securities exchange the opportunity to advance its own interests thus imposing greater transaction costs than for-profit securities exchanges.

The market for corporate control can be used to reduce principal-agent problems. If the management of a for-profit securities exchange becomes inefficient, a predator can take-over an exchange, and install a new manager who maximizes the value, thereby realising an arbitrage profit. However, the market for control of both non-profit and cooperative exchanges is likely to be limited since those buying such an exchange cannot reap the benefits of any enhanced efficiency achievable as a result of a hostile-takeover through an increase in earnings. This may reduce the incentive for management to act efficiently since it is not subject to outside scrutiny. The fact that the rewards of improved efficiency cannot be reaped through enhanced earnings does not mean that there is no market for control of non-profit or co-operative securities exchanges. If the clients of such exchanges were able to gain the benefits of any efficiency that could be effected by a takeover, through lower fees, for example, they would have an incentive to encourage such takeovers. In fact, there have been some mergers between non-profit exchanges for this reason.[45]

The principle-agency problem can also be reduced by the organizational structure adopted.[46] The organisational structure of a securities exchange influences the relative costs imposed by principal-agent problems if information to the securities exchange's owners about its performance is made available. The non-profit or cooperative exchange owner will have less external information available to them to evaluate the performance of their management than would the owners of for-profit securities exchanges because the shares of non-profit and cooperative exchanges are not readily tradable. Financial intermediaries trading on a securities exchange may have better information about management performance than any outside owners because they take direct receipt of the services provided by the exchange and can better and more cheaply monitor the quality of services provided by the securities exchange. The need for the owners of a securities exchange to monitor and control management will be low if the exchange faces competition thus reducing the possibility of management inefficiency.

---

45 See Onyuma, S.O. Paradigm Shift in Securities Exchanges: Automation, Management, Competition, Integration and Regulation of Securities Markets (forthcoming).

46 Ricketts, M. (1994) The Economics of Business Enterprise: An Introduction to Economic Organisations and the Theory of the Organisation, 2nd Edition. Harvester, Hertfordshire.

Changing the Governance Structure of a Securities Exchange

Various governance structures may be applied in a securities exchange at different stages of its development. The Botswana Stock Exchange is an example where the formal governance structure of a trading system allowed for the possibility that the owners of the system could exploit market participants since there was effectively only a single individual, the Stockbrokers Botswana, who controlled all aspects of trading. Investors might have felt vulnerable both to overpricing and to the possibility that any information they released to this individual might be used against them. The good reputation of the individual in question, and the relatively high costs of establishing any alternative governance structure, however, probably meant that stakeholders were willing to forgo any potential benefits that might be obtained under a different governance structure in favour of the existing one. There are two important ways in which the governance structure of an exchange may come under pressure to change.

The first is the desirability and consequences of transforming a securities exchange from a non-profit into a for-profit entity, generally referred to as demutualizing. Worldwide, securities markets have seen a trend amongst exchanges to consider alternative governance structures to the traditional non-profit or cooperative ones. This has resulted in a growing number of new for-profit trading systems being developed in the securities markets and transformation of many non-profit or cooperative organized securities exchanges into for-profit entities in Europe, Asia, Africa and the USA.[47] The greater pressure of competition in the securities markets implies that a balance of the costs and benefits of for-profit governance structures is necessary. The cost of collective decision-making in a non-profit or cooperative securities exchange is likely to be relatively burdensome compared to those that would be incurred in a for-profit securities exchange. Also, the benefits to financial intermediaries of having a non-profit or cooperative organized exchange in a securities market are

---

47 Onyuma, S.O (2006) Regional Integration of Stock Exchanges in Africa. African Review of Money, Banking & Finance (Supplement Issue) December, pp. 99-124.

likely to be relatively low given the difficulty of obtaining any monopoly profits.

Given the possibility of gaining membership from more than one securities exchange, members may have a proportionally greater voting power at an exchange than the amount of business they bring to the exchange that they have sought to transform to a for-profit securities exchange structure. In the USA, having a majority of the votes at several exchanges, have been strong campaigns to switch to for-profit status. This has not occurred outside the USA, where the fastest-growing exchanges are controlled mostly by the institutional owners like stockbrokers, investment bankers and securities dealers. If a securities exchange is able to exploit clients other than just its membership while retaining its monopoly, its entire membership may seek to transform the exchange into a for-profit company structure. Some are even brooding the idea of listing, while others have listed their own shares on their own trading boards.

Given the extent to which securities exchanges are trying to obtain revenue from the users of their price and quote data, who are not necessarily securities exchange members, pressures to transform to for-profit structures are likely to be more in the future. The benefits to financial intermediaries of operating a non-profit securities exchange are therefore diminishing. Even if an intermediary-owned non-profit securities exchange were believed to maximize consumer surplus, the identities of the securities exchange's consumers are changing. Both the magnitude in number and the diversity of the end-investors on a securities exchange, also mean that any benefits that might accrue to these participants of owning and operating an exchange are likely to be affected by cost of collective decision making.

There are many ways in which a non-profit securities exchange can be transformed to for-profit status. For instance, members could share in the profits a securities exchange obtains from its core business, through dividends or distributions. It can also create for-profit subsidiaries or affiliated business entities for the provision of certain specific services.[48]

---

48   See Gorham, M. (1997) Exchange Subsidiaries Proliferate. Futures Industry, 8th September: 15-18.

Dividend-paying shares may be issued free or sold to members, or indeed to other market participants, although demanding dividend payments at a membership-exchange is likely to lead to the redistribution of either profits or power in an exchange. Those securities exchange members who pay the most to their exchange are those who most use the services provided by the exchange, and should the securities exchange transformation result in each member receiving the same number of dividend-paying shares, then there will be a redistribution of revenue that they pay to the exchange.

However, if voting rights are kept according to the dividend rights, the smaller members will find their powers diluted. Although this is not possible under many securities exchange applicable laws, it may lead to conflict between the members and the owners of the securities exchange, with regard to how the securities exchange should be run, and may also make management more independent. One solution to this is to separate membership from ownership of a securities exchange. Permitting the free transferability of a securities exchange shares has the capacity of influencing the intensity of competition in the securities market for the services provided by such securities exchanges. An intermediary or member who perceives that a securities exchange with tradable shares may be a potential competitor may buy up the exchange's shares in order to pre-empt such competition.

The second important way in which the governance of an exchange may come under pressure to change is when the exchange becomes extremely large and complex, thus unmanageable. This means that the interests represented on it are too diverse for a single forum to be able to reconcile them. However, the presence of conflicting objectives is endemic to the nature of non-profit and cooperative exchanges, and sufficient for an exchange to become unmanageable. Securities exchanges the world-over have never been able to realize the objectives of all the various stakeholders of their markets. The range of preferences that market participants may reveal concerning an exchange's decisions becomes so diverse, and the strength with which they express their views about these decisions becomes so powerful, that the securities exchange becomes unmanageable. The reason why securities market participants have become more vocal than before about revealing their views on decisions made at a securities exchange is because they feel by doing so they can affect the exchange's decisions. Recent advancement of cheap technology now allows small groups of market participants, and even single traders, to develop their own dealing or trading systems to satisfy their own trading preferences. Should participants feel that a securities exchange no longer meets their needs they can divert their order flow away from their securities exchange more easily than before, and this, therefore, gives them some leverage in trying to affect the decisions taken by a securities exchange. A securities exchange should be viewed as unmanageable if it cannot meet the needs of all its stakeholders because their differences of opinion may be vocal and the securities exchange may lose business because various interests are not adequately represented on its governance policies. But the critical issue to consider also is the extent to which its governance structure is still cost-efficient for some of the rational securities exchange stakeholders. Given the importance attached to demutualization, the next section is dedicated wholly to this concept.

Historically, most exchanges were not-for-profit organizations owned by their members. Over the past few years, there has been a trend among securities exchanges to consider alternative governance structures to these traditional mutual or cooperative models. In most cases, the exchange is transformed into a for-profit shareholder-owned company. A demutualized exchange may take many forms, each raising its own issues. Some exchanges have demutualized and become public companies listed on their own exchanges. Other exchanges have demutualized but have remained private corporations.[49] Still others are subsidiaries of publicly traded holding companies. There are a variety of issues which securities exchanges and capital market regulators have addressed in recent years

---

49   The Australian Stock Exchange is a public company listed on its own exchange. As we shall see, Amsterdam Exchange and The Toronto Stock Exchange organized as private corporations. The London Stock Exchange arranged for an off-market trading facility for its shares. The Pacific Exchange in the United States converted its equity business into a wholly owned subsidiary of the exchange and the OM Stockholmsbörsen AB is a wholly owned subsidiary of a listed company.

when considering the regulatory consequences of changes to the ownership structure of exchanges in their jurisdiction. Generally, these changes have involved conversion from a not-for-profit member-owned mutual exchange to a shareholder-owned demutualised exchanged, which is likely to be a for-profit corporation through a process known as demutualization. The specific circumstances of demutualization with respect to each jurisdiction and securities exchange[50] will differ, but there are some generic issues or regulatory responses that have arisen or may conceivably arise in the future. These issues and many more are discussed in depth in the next chapters.

Automated Trading System and Exchange Governance

Is it possible that the conversion from a floor-based trading system technology to computerized technology may affect the governance structures of a securities exchange? There exist some existing discussions relating to this issue.[51] It had been earlier mentioned that securities exchanges have traditionally been organized as mutual associations, operated by member-brokers and dealers, under varying degrees of state control. The member firms are often the legal owners of the securities exchange and, in some cases, actually own shares in the exchange as a corporate entity, although elsewhere, securities exchanges are legally state institutions. This mutual structure is a remnant of the era before automation, when securities exchanges were of necessity floor-based. The inherent limitations of floor space required access limitations. Access was rationed through the sale of a fixed number of memberships (or ownership seats). Since a non-automated trading floor itself has little more than commercial real estate value, it is logical that the members themselves should operate the floor as a cooperative structure. These members necessarily become intermediaries for all others wishing to trade the securities exchange's contracts, and a portion of their profits derives from entry barriers. In an automated auction market, there is no inherent technological barrier to providing unlimited direct access.

---

50 For example, it may make a difference whether or not concentrations or types of ownership interests in the exchange are limited.

51 See Domowitz, I. and Steil, B. (2000) Automation, Trading Costs, and the Structure of the Securities Trading Industry. LSE conference paper.

There is, therefore, no longer an economic logic for securities exchanges being organized as intermediary cooperatives.

An automated system operator can sell access direct to all those who wish to trade and charge for this service on a transaction basis. The marginal cost of adding an additional user to a network is virtually zero, thus negating any economic value to membership as such. The operator should be able to select its governance structure on the same basis as a normal commercial firm. Whereas an automated exchange can be organized along traditional mutual lines, it is questionable whether such a structure is optimal in the type of competitive environment. Automation of the trading system permits demutualization, the separation of the ownership of the exchange from membership. The incentive problems inhibiting demutualization are similar to some of those inhibiting the adoption of technology, the vested financial interests.

Demutualization is now rapidly being adopted in practice, and all such examples begin with a conversion from traditional floor trading technology to automated trade execution. For trading service enterprises with no prior history of mutual governance structure, the mutual structure is routinely avoided in favour of a for-profit joint-stock corporate structure. As automation initiatives continue to proliferate, a revealed preference argument may indeed suggest the optimality of a demutualised securities exchange structure, relative to its mutual counterpart. The incentive structure under which a mutualized securities exchange operates is different from that under which a demutualised one does. As securities exchange members are the conduits to the trading system, they derive profits from intermediating non-member transactions. This, in turn, means that members may resist innovations that reduce demand for their intermediation services, even if such innovations would increase the value of the securities exchange. If the members are actually owners of the securities exchange, they will logically exercise their powers to block disintermediation where the resulting decline in brokerage profits would not be offset by their share in the increase in the value of securities exchange.

Several securities exchanges, especially in Asia, America, Africa and Europe have in the past several years chosen to demutualize thus detaching ownership from membership. This transformation of governance structure has had the effect of diluting the influence of former members over the commercial activities of the securities exchange. If the financial interests of non-member owners differ significantly from those of members, such a transformation is likely to impact significantly on the securities exchange's behaviour. The first exchange in the world to demutualize in 1993 was Stockholm Stock Exchange followed by Helsinki (1995), Copenhagen (1996), Amsterdam (1997), the Australian Exchange (1998) and Toronto, Hong Kong and London stock exchange in 2000.

The SSE initiative came on the back of major competitive inroads into Swedish equity trading made by London's SEAQ-I between 1987 and 1990, a period in which Stockholm's turnover declined by a third and its market share of global reported Swedish equity turnover dropped as low as forty percent. The members retained half of the shares in the new Stockholm corporate structure, and half were allocated to listed companies. The shares later became freely tradable in 1994, and in 1998 they were listed on the exchange itself. Following the demutualization, SSE became the first securities exchange in Europe to offer remote cross-border membership in 1995 and direct electronic access for institutional investors in 1996, although trades must still be notionally executed via a sponsoring member. Local Swedish members resisted both of these initiatives but could not block them given their minority interest. Non-member owners, in contrast, had an unambiguous incentive to support these measures. The securities exchange as a commercial enterprise appeared to have performed well following the demutualization. Turnover quadrupled in the first two years of demutualised operation, and the exchange's share price rose nearly sevenfold. This shows how securities exchange governance structures may bring about important benefits to the exchange and its other constituents.

The SSE model has since been widely emulated by other automated exchanges, the biggest difference among them being in the initial allocation of shares. Helsinki and Copenhagen exchanges, for example, applied a sixty-forty share split between members and listed companies. Amsterdam Stock Exchange allocated fifty percent to members and auctioned off fifty percent to both listed companies and institutional investors. Australia

Stock Exchange allocated all shares to the members but listed them on the exchange itself the day following the demutualization. Member-based exchanges are demutualizing in order to approximate better the incentive structure of a public company with a diversified shareholder base. In contrast, trading system operators in USA and UK, which have entered the market with automated auction products, have avoided the mutual structure entirely. Such companies were in the past called proprietary trading system operators and more recently, ECNs. Instinet (owned by Reuters), POSIT (owned by ITG), and Lattice Trading (owned by State Street) are formally regulated as brokers but sell order-matching services on a transaction fee basis direct to institutional investor-clients.

Some like Arizona Stock Exchange and LSE-based Tradepoint are classified by their respective national regulatory authorities as exchanges but operate in an identical manner. OptiMark and BondConnect (owned by State Street) have chosen a third route since legally they are neither brokers nor a securities exchange and as such have licensed their trading products to existing bodies that are classified by their regulators as exchanges. Securities exchanges operating in a competitive environment can usefully be analysed as organisations offering trading products in a market defined by the salience of network externalities. The degree to which this formulation approximates reality depends on the level of contestability in the market for trading services and the incentive structure under which securities exchanges operate. Trading automation has, in fact, significantly increased both market contestability and the incentives of exchanges to exploit network externalities. These incentives are manifested, among others in the transformation of exchange governance structures toward conventional corporate models. A majority of securities exchanges in Africa are still envisaging the non-profit mutualized governance structures and are yet to adopt full automation and competitive structures. However, many of these exchanges have indicated their desire to demutualize by 2030 into publicly owned company that will be self-listed on the same securities markets.

Therefore, corporate governance systems usually improve with demutualization for a number of reasons. The board of directors becomes more diversified. As a mutual, the board will often largely reflect that of cooperatives. The idea of shareholder value introduces new disciplines to management. Hopefully, the culture shifts to a service culture. This is partly dependent on the ability of management to act as agents of change and of staff to embrace change. The social culture probably plays a role as well as the single group of owners. Their perspective is that of a broker, although their interests are not always uniform. A more diversified board represents a greater diversity of business views.

The priority of the board shifts from the brokers' interests to shareholder value. This changes the organization in many ways and, significantly, introduces customer focus. There is a widening of the groups recognized as customers. Staff can be rewarded in line with improved efficiencies. It is usual for a mutual not to distribute profits and use any reserves to even out good and bad years. The levelling effect also applies to staff salaries, so staff may expect regular pay increases and promotions regardless of the exchange's financial performance. Profit distribution changes that occur allow better rewards in good times and for productivity gains. Market disciplines will apply, particularly if the exchange self-lists. Because the exchange company is paying a return on its capital, it can be measured against other exchanges doing the same.

For these same reasons, a number of securities exchanges worldwide have either demutualized or are planning to do so in the near future. Also, a few securities exchanges from Africa have also expressed the desire to adopt a for-profit structure when they finally convert into public limited companies. The only ones, which have demutualised are JSE (2006), NSE (2014), Dar es Salaam Stock Exchange (2016), Uganda Securities Exchange (2017), Botswana Stock Exchange (2017) and NGX (2021). In fact, the shift by the NGX made it the 57th exchange worldwide to embrace such a transformation since Sweden's SSE piloted the move.

Chapter Summary

In this chapter, issues relating to corporate governance including the monitoring and control of exchange managers by shareholders are discussed in depth. Second, the nature of the three governance structures that have been adopted by securities exchanges like non-profit, the consumer cooperative, and the for-profit forms and how they influence the governance structure an exchange have been presented. Third, the relative costs to financial intermediaries of an exchange adopting each of these governance structures for the establishment of a securities exchange were also covered. The diversity and complexity of the governance structures of securities exchanges were explored, and the assumptions made in each structure analysed. Whereas the detail of securities exchanges' constitutional structures is recognized, the simplicity of the exchange's objective functions pursued by securities exchanges adopting each of the three organizational forms, are however in doubted.

Moreover, the transaction costs incurred by market participants other than financial intermediaries are espoused and the implications for exchange governance of the behaviour of these other types of stakeholders are discussed. The manner in which these factors affect the transaction cost comparison, and thus relative efficiency of the different organizational exchange structures was adequately discussed. Fifth, the chapter pointed out the need to transform a securities exchange from a non-profit into for-profit form, exchanges becoming unmanageable and the adoption of automated trading as some of the ways in which the governance of an exchange may come under pressure to change to for-profit structures. Lastly, the chapter explained how automation of the trading system may influence the governance structure of a securities exchange. The focus of the next chapter is on the hard-core rubrics of the nature and scope of demutualization.

Chapter Three

NATURE OF DEMUTUALIZATION OF SECURITIES EXCHANGES

Introduction

Demutualization involves the conversion of a securities exchange from a not-for-profit member-owned institution to a for-profit shareholder-owned corporation. The main motivation for demutualization and the structure of demutualized exchanges vary among countries. However, a number of themes emerge that are common to different demutualization cases that have been undertaken. In this chapter, the nature, meaning of demutualization, as well reasons why securities exchanges demutualize is presented. The chapter also provides the common models of demutualized exchanges including some examples of securities exchanges, which have demutualized. It therefore provides background information for the build-up of the other chapters on the process of converting to a demutualized exchange, the structure, potential conflicts of interest and regulation of a demutualized securities exchange.

Governance Structures of Securities Exchanges

Historically, securities exchanges in developing and developed markets operated as mutual organizations. Mutual funds were once the most important vehicles of investment. For instance, in the United States, ownership of stocks, bonds and money market mutual funds rose from six (6) percent of the USA households in 1980 to 37 percent in 1996 while the total assets held by mutual funds soared by 2,100 percent from $135 billion to \$3.5 trillion at the end of 1996.[52] The basic characteristics of a mutual organization are that the institution neither have shareholders nor share capital. Ideally, the mutual organization is one owned and managed by its members.

Generally, securities exchanges offer a variety of services to listing firms, such as trading liquidity, execution of services, signalling function for listed firms, monitoring of trading to prevent manipulation and insider trading, provision of standard rules to reduce transaction costs as well as clearing of buy and sell order transactions. Traditionally, securities exchanges operate as a club of brokers, offering services as monopoly operators serving, largely, under a mutual governance structure. In fact, when a securities exchange is owned by its members, the ownership is similar to that for a country club. The members of the club enjoyed rights of ownership, decision-making through one member, one vote, and trading. And value enhancement of a securities exchange is achieved by restricting access to the services offered by the club.

Several ways exist in which external bodies and public interest representatives can influence the policies of a securities exchange. Legal and regulatory frameworks vary considerably, as does the degree of oversight of the securities exchanges by government regulatory authorities. Exchange membership may be open to any persons who satisfy stipulated requirements or it may be closed. Should membership of an exchange be acquired through seats on the securities exchange, the seats are usually not freely transferable. The most distinguishing feature of the traditional securities exchange structure is its cooperative governance model that depicts a close identity between ownership of the exchange and the direct use of its trading services. The owners of the mutual exchange are also its customers. The owners-customers may share in the net gains of the exchange in proportion to their ownership interest. Decisions are usually made democratically, on a one-member, one-vote basis and often are made by committees of representatives of member firms. The ability to influence

---

52   Alexander G, Jones, J. & Nigro, P. (1998). Mutual Fund Shareholders: Characteristics, Investor Knowledge and Sources of information, *Financial Services Review*, 7(4): 301-316.

the decisions of a securities exchange is thereby separated from the level of economic interest a member has in the securities exchange.

Ownership rights may not be freely tradable or exchangeable and on cessation of membership, those rights are forfeited. Because the organization's constituting documents may expressly or implicitly adopt a non-profit objective and prohibit the distribution of surpluses, mutually owned exchanges are seldom able to raise capital from anyone other than their members. On the other hand, most for-profit securities exchanges are organized as corporations with share capital in which the owners, principal decision-makers and customers are three separate groups. The shareholders vest decision-making power in a board of directors who are subject to election and removal by shareholders and this power is exercised on a day-to-day basis by the management of the exchange company. The voting rights of shareholders usually are proportionate to their economic interest in the securities – one-share, one-vote. Ownership rights are distinct from trading privileges, and for-profit securities exchanges may raise new capital from a variety of sources.

Mutually owned exchanges have provided served to their stakeholders, and markets are increasingly recognising that a trading infrastructure, as well as modern corporate and governance structure, is essential to reducing transaction costs, attracting funds from investors, and attracting new firms to raise their capital requirements.[53] Accordingly, securities exchanges globally have been involved in massive demutualization exercises. Since 1993, the word has witnessed substantial changes in the governance structures of securities exchanges and majority of securities exchanges are likely to restructure their governance systems.

Across the globe, consequently, securities exchanges are now rethinking their business strategy and model in order to find ways of how best to survive. In the process, securities exchanges have evolved towards new corporate, legal and business models to strengthen governance and face the competition. Securities exchanges are now increasingly changing their

---

53 Akpesey, P. (2008). Publicly Owned Stock Exchanges - Prospects and Challenges: http://www. modernghana.com

business model and restructuring themselves due to the simultaneous convergence of a number of many factors. The most notable of these has been the rapid advancement and innovation in technology that has facilitated ATS, including ECNs, and growing market competition and integration as well as globalization induced partly by cross-border listing and portfolio flows, need for good corporate governance in exchanges, the urge to open up ownership of exchanges to public investors, and the need for increased capital. Together these developments have eroded the significance of physical national securities exchanges and their trading floors. This process of transformation from a member's associations into for-profit corporation is referred to as demutualization.

Evolution of Securities Exchanges

Typically, securities exchanges evolved through three distinct stages. The initial stage was characterized by an informal network of stockbrokers who would meet at a physical place and match orders from the public – the buyers and sellers. This meeting of the stockbrokers to match the order constituted a securities market.

The second stage of the evolution came when these networks of stockbrokers gradually formalized into not-for-profit mutual or member-owned organizations that employed governance structures akin to those of associations or cooperatives. This stage brought about the earliest version of the modern-day securities exchange. Then, the securities exchanges were established using the capital of the members – stockbrokers – and in some instances with assistance of Government. During this stage the stockbrokers owned the exclusive rights to trade on and manage the securities exchange as well as the ownership rights. They even had the right to admit or reject any new entrants to the market.

As the securities exchanges grew in relative importance to their host economies, capital markets regulation evolved and strengthened, primarily to protect the interests of the investing public. Consequently, it was recognized that the stockbrokers' exclusive rights to trade on the market ought to be separated from their ownership and management rights. This ushered in the third and the current stage of the evolution of securities exchanges: the age of demutualized for-profit securities exchanges. Most securities exchanges have therefore transformed from mutual or member-owned organisation to companies limited by shares.

Meaning of Demutualization

Securities exchanges have traditionally been mutual associations owned by their members and operated on a not-for-profit basis. Any profits are therefore returned to members in the form of lower trading costs or access fees, but this has not always been the case. There are differences in the manner in which securities exchanges are owned, operated and regulated. They differ in terms of the role of the board and the staff of the securities exchange, the powers of the chief executive and the chairman, and the composition and powers of exchange board committees. Securities exchanges have a variety of voting structures and the balance of power between different users also varies among them. Since 1993, many securities exchanges worldwide, through the process of demutualization, have converted to for-profit companies.

As a concept, demutualization is neither a very new concept nor very sophisticated. The essence lies with the separation of ownership and management as well as trading rights. It seems to be well driven by the good intentions of proper governance, which has taken a new turn after the collapse of many large corporations during the 21st Century. Whereas there is no exclusive definition of a mutual organization, it is an enterprise owned by its members and provides a variety of service to the members for their benefit. They are, therefore, not for-profit organizations, and are restricted in their capacity to raise equity, and are characterized by diffused decision-making power.

The term mutualization means that the organization's funding is strictly undertaken by members of a mutual organization, whose membership is restricted by certain criteria and most non-profit oriented. Demutualization requires that the knots and bolts of mutualization are loosened in such ways as to fit the needs of not only members but for other stakeholders. The inhibitive features differ across different securities exchanges, and hinges on corporate governance and regulatory quality with it. Before their demutualization, securities exchanges seemed to have been infested with lack of professionalization, broker-banker nexus, conflict of interest, corruption and cartel-like operations, which led to financial scams and erosion of confidence of investors from lack of trust.

Demutualization is, therefore, the transition from a mutual organization limited by guarantee in which there are no shares, and every member has one vote, to a company limited by shares in which there is one vote per share. The concept is also used to describe the process by which a company limited by shares in which every member is required to have the same number of shares, converts to a more usual economic model, or simply one where the link between membership in the securities exchange company or ownership of a share in it, is broken.

Demutualization is, therefore the separation of ownership from management and trading membership in the exchanges. It is a mechanism to reduce the overbearing influence of the stockbrokers on the management of the securities exchanges and thereby put a better governance practice in place. Demutualization implies the transition from a mutual company, in which there are no shares, and every member has one vote, to a company limited by shares and one vote per share. It also describes the process by which a company limited by shares in which every member is required to have the same number of shares, converts to a more usual economic model; or simply one where the link between membership in the exchange-company or ownership of a share in it, is broken. The process, therefore, leads to a change in the legal status, structure and governance of a securities exchange from a non-profit, protected interest, to a profit oriented one.

The process of demutualization involves a change in ownership structure and a change in legal and organization form. With regards to the ownership structure, members' seats are monetized and values assigned per seat. Members of the exchange then either keep or sell their shares. The process therefore, separates the trading rights from ownership rights. This, however, is only a technical definition because if shares of a demutualized exchange are only held by stockbrokers, then the securities exchange would remain a mutual entity. Demutualization is better thought of as a process that brings about balance among interest of different stakeholders in the corporate and governance structure of a securities exchange. It provides the exchanges with a for-profit motive and access to economic and human capital to develop its business. In most cases, ownership restrictions are placed, for example 5-10 percent non-controlling stakes, on individuals and groups to prevent potential takeovers by other securities exchanges. The legal and organizational change normally entails the exchange becoming a typical profit making company with limited liabilities and abiding by the relevant company laws as well as capital markets regulations.

The recent structural changes witnessed in many securities exchanges have brought the commercial objectives into the forefront and simultaneously the relationship among the board of directors, management and other stakeholders has come under severe scrutiny. The central idea with demutualization does not only rest on the basic status of the organization, that is, whether it is for-profit or not-for-profit. There are several for-profit organizations even securities exchanges, which are not demutualized. The crux of the problem therefore lies with the ownership of the securities exchange. Separation of ownership and membership is the fundamental ingredient of demutualization as well as the essence of effective governance. The critical issues are essentially those arising from permitting non-brokers to own a stake in the securities exchange, and brokers not to have an ownership interest of any kind or to have ownership to a limited extent.

In the new competitive environment, the promise of demutualization is that, along with the capital necessary for investments in technology, the shareholders of the newly demutualized securities exchange provide a new corporate governance structure that is far more effective in managing conflicts among market participants. Thus, rather than being set up mainly to preserve the current revenue stream of the securities exchange members, the new governance structure is designed to maximize the *residual* value of the exchange that accrues to the shareholders. Although the members may continue to be the dominant owners for some time, demutualization is likely to end up transferring considerable ownership and decision-making power to outside investors. And this means that the old consensus decision-making of the exchange members is eventually going to be supplanted by a professional management team presumably motivated by significant share ownership to increase efficiency and profits.

Being the change in legal status of a securities exchange from a mutual association with one vote per member – and possibly consensus –based decision making, into a company limited by shares, with one vote per share – with majority – based decision making, demutualization process entails first converting memberships (seats) into shares. This step may or may not be followed by a public issue of those shares. In this manner, a quasi-governmental institution transforms itself into a profit-oriented, publicly traded company in which ownership and trading privileges are effectively separated. Stockbrokers are no longer owners but customers of the securities exchange. Directors of the exchange company are elected by shareholders and answerable to them. Demutualization makes sense if it induces a change in the exchange's objective from managing the interests of a closed member-based organization with a central focus on providing services for the benefit primarily of the members-brokers and keeping costs and investments limited to financing agreed by member-brokers, into a company created with the objective of maximizing the value of the shares by focusing on generating profits from servicing the demands of their customers such as stockbrokers and investors in a competitive manner.

Governance is one of the pertinent issues considered with regard to the implementation of demutualization of securities exchanges. So what are the motives behind demutualization of securities exchanges? While the primary motive behind good governance practice is to deliver the best to all the stakeholders, still investors, as the backbone of the securities exchange, and their interest remain as the focus area of any institutional reform in the securities market. Investor's confidence is the most important capital on which a securities exchange can pursue its economic and social objectives.

There are several motives behind demutualization securities exchange. Over the years, the inadequacy of proper governance practices and standards of transparency in many traditional exchanges have eroded the investor's confidence in many of the economies and as a result a demutualized structure has found favour. The growing competition among the securities exchanges, the presence of global companies in most of the important international securities exchanges and the advent of new information technology has warranted the worldwide move to demutualization. Since the present management structure of most of securities exchanges are dominated by the stockbrokers, the governance has been a constant casualty. It is thus imperative for better governance that the securities exchanges are to be demutualized with corporate structure.

Before securities exchanges are demutualized in some countries, there have been cases of consolidation of some domestic and regional securities exchanges. Mergers and acquisitions have been witnessed in Europe and the USA. Demutualization, although alone does not provide solutions to the entire existing problem, the new management structure with proper representation from the professionals with minimum control of the stockbrokers on management can pave the way for better governance practices. Earning sufficient return for the shareholders in a securities exchange and at the same time rendering quality and unbiased service to the listed companies and to the investors are the two crucial indicators of the efficient governance and to address these twin issues the demutualized management mechanism shall definitely prove handy and also provide the necessary cushion to absorb the risk of the changing new business environment.

What, therefore, are the major changes entitled in demutualization of securities exchanges? The conversion of exchanges from mutual to demutualized structure involves two key features; first, a change in the ownership structure, and second, a change in legal as well as organizational form. Both need to be accompanied by adequate safeguards to ensure appropriate governance. Depending on the nature of ownership and legal forms adopted, the demutualized exchanges, given their corporate model and facing growing competitive pressures, focus on evolving strategic positioning which, depending on a number of conditions, could involve greater market consolidation, vertical integration and financial product diversification.

In terms of the ownership structure, the transformation from the mutual member-based to demutualized securities exchange involves the transfer of ownership from members to non-members. There are various ways that dilution of membership can be achieved. Sequentially, it involves the conversion of existing member seats by monetizing these and assigning a certain value per seat. Once the valuation is done, the members can opt to convert their membership to share ownership or to sell off their interest to non-members. In most cases of demutualization of securities exchanges, members have opted to retain their share ownership. A self-listing of shares on the exchange facilitates the unlocking of the members' equity and buy-out of the interest of the traders, thus leading to the monetization of the value of the members' seats. A securities exchange with freely transferable shares, rather than membership rights, can form equity-swap-based strategic alliances or mergers with other exchanges, domestically or in different countries or time zones. Such alliances are stronger and offer greater credibility than pure cooperation agreements between securities exchanges.

To avoid securities exchanges operating in special or limited interests, securities market regulators often place restrictions on ownership by one equity holder or a group of holders to non-controlling stakes of 5-10 percent. Limits on ownership stakes could affect potential takeovers by other exchanges. Such take-overs could have merit in terms of the efficiency and economies of scale of the market especially where more efficient participants acquire inefficient ones. Recognizing the synergies of take-overs, most demutualized securities exchanges have provisions in place to allow other exchanges, or technology partners, the possibility of acquiring or swapping strategic stakes. The reluctance to relinquish control to strategic partners or owners remains, however, one reason why non-equity, swap-based cooperative alliances have been more prolific in the securities exchange industry. Indeed, several hostile take-over attempts (including Hong Kong Exchange takeover move on LSE in 2019, Nasdaq attempt to acquire LSE in 2007, the OM Gruppen's move to acquire the LSE in 2000, as well as the takeover bid for Sydney Futures Exchange by the Australian Stock Exchange in 1999) failed due to the voting strength still exerted by the brokers.

With regard to the legal structure, many securities exchanges worldwide are registered as private limited companies with a paid-up capital base, while others operate as member associations or cooperative arrangements. As at December 2000, FIBV statistics indicated that ninety percent of its member exchanges, accounting for sixty percent of market capitalization, were private limited companies. Almost forty-six percent of these were legal company exchanges with inside ownership. Around twenty-five percent of the exchanges – accounting for twenty-one percent of market capitalization – had been privatised, thirteen percent of these exchanges - accounting for eight percent of market capitalization – were registered as listed companies and the remaining seventeen percent had other types of status with some being state-owned or semi-public entities. However, most of the exchanges are legal entities registered as private limited companies. By then, five securities exchanges in Asia have been fully demutualized, with three of these listed on their own exchange, and another two had announced plans to demutualize by 2005. In Europe, 15 exchanges had demutualized; while in Africa, only one exchange had demutualized by 2007. In USA, seven securities exchanges had demutualised. Securities exchanges that have demutualized are presented in Table 4 in the next section, while those which have listed their shares on their own listing boards are presented in Table 5 in Chapter 4.[54]

The legal structure for demutualized securities exchanges is based on considerations similar to those for any profit-making company including decisions on the number of shareholders, voting procedures, limitation of liability, accounting and reporting requirements – based on taxation laws and partners/shareholders' access to information of the company – and distribution of dividends – re-investment needs or distribution to partners, taxation. In most jurisdictions, a limited liability company has been observed to be the traditional and preferred option for profit-making ventures involving more than a close group of partners. The methods for transforming an association into a limited liability company varies between jurisdictions, but in principle, the existing members agree to transfer the

---

54 This list may not be exhaustive since exchanges are currently in the race to demutualize and even self-list. Cooperation agreements are being signed even in a daily basis and so is the decision to demutualize.

assets and operations of their association to a newly formed company, in exchange for shares in that new company.

Technical Meaning of Demutualization

Remarkably, there seems to be no standard definition of a demutualized securities exchange. In informal discussion, the emphasis is often placed on whether or not a securities exchange is run on a for-profit basis. However, the central question is not whether a securities exchange is legally able to distribute its surplus income back to its owners to maintain the definition of for-profit status, but rather who owns the exchange in the first place. For-profit securities exchanges are, therefore, not necessarily demutualized – in fact, most are not.

Separation of ownership and membership is fundamental to the concept of demutualization. Why do securities exchanges choose to bring in non-members as owners? Exchange officials often maintain publicly that they must sell ownership stakes to outsiders as a means of raising capital for expansion and technology investment. However, raising capital seems to be generally a secondary aim, or absent as an aim altogether. Most securities exchanges that have demutualized have had no immediate need for fresh capital. Amsterdam Stock Exchange actually used its demutualization as an opportunity to return excess capital to the members. Furthermore, if capital is, in fact, necessary, it can normally be raised from the member firms without having to turn to outsiders.

The primary function of demutualization is to reduce the control of local intermediary firms over the strategic positioning of a securities exchange. This is in recognition of the fact that securities exchanges operating in a competitive financial market must ultimately be able to reduce capital costs for a significant subset of companies, and raise investment returns for a significant subset of savers, relative to the next-best financing alternative – whether that be another securities exchange, the bond market, or the banking sector. Financial market intermediaries, in seeking to maximize their own profits from trade intermediation, can act to impair the ability of a securities exchange to serve firms and investors with maximum efficiency. It is not surprising that officials of mutualized securities exchanges rarely argue this publicly, and instead claim that demutualization is needed to expand their capital bases. But it is in reality typically a response to members frustrating their efforts to implement less intermediated trading structures, to expand direct trading access to foreigners or institutional investors, or to merge with other securities exchanges. All of these efforts can serve to reduce demand for the services of existing members.

Nevertheless, under what conditions will securities exchange members actually accept new outside ownership? The key issues tend to be the degree of competition or potential competition, which the exchange faces, and the degree to which the largest member firms operate internationally. Competition makes it difficult for securities exchange members to protect their intermediation franchise and, therefore, makes them more open to governance reform and outside ownership. It is not surprising that the pioneer demutualizers were three Nordic and Amsterdam exchange. These exchanges operate in small and highly open national economies. Each faced significant competitive threats from abroad, particularly London, to trading in their key blue chip stocks. The NYSE, on the other hand, has yet to see effective competition materialize, and the members, therefore, successfully resisted the high profile demutualization initiative launched by its board chairman in 1999, until eight years later in 2006 when demutualization was becoming the in-thing in securities markets.

The internationalization of membership also facilitates demutualization. Large international banks which are members of numerous securities exchanges have much less motivation to defend mutualization than local players. Locals have a strong incentive to maintain institutional barriers to disintermediation of their services, whereas larger international players tend to see governance reform as an effective weapon for increasing their strategic control of a securities exchange vis-à-vis the locals – typically by replacing one member, one vote and committee-based decision making with decision-making tied more directly to the size of the ownership stake. The same argument holds for trading automation. Locals tend to dominate market-making and specialist functions. It is no surprise that it was the large international banks which championed the cessation of floor trading in Amsterdam

Stock Exchange and market making in LSE in the mid-1990s, whereas the locals fought bitterly to stave off automated trading.

The mere fact that a securities exchange can be partially owned by specific non-members does not itself suggest that the incentive structure guiding its behaviour will be materially different from that of a wholly mutualized exchange, or that its interests will be better aligned with those of investors and issuers. In many cases, outside ownership is limited to not-for-profit or mutualized entities such as the national central bank or the broker-owned central securities depository – securities clearance and settlement entities which have little or no incentive to challenge broker interests. Deutsche Börse and the Paris Bourse prior to their initial public offering (IPO) in 2001 were already organized as for-profit companies, although ownership stakes, which were controlled almost exclusively by members, could not be sold without approval of the supervisory board, which effectively meant that they could not be sold. These securities exchanges, therefore, had an incentive structure almost precisely identical to that of a mutualized exchange.

In essence, therefore, what is essential to a successful demutualization, then, is that non-members are free to buy equity stakes in the securities exchange from current member-owners. This is what makes it possible to change the incentive structure in a firm. If we classify as demutualized all exchanges which permit members freely to sell their equity stakes in the exchange to non-members – albeit perhaps with limitations related to maximum shareholdings – it is still clear that there are huge differences in governance structure among demutualized securities exchanges. At one extreme is the Borsa Italiana, which is demutualized according to this definition, but is nonetheless 90 percent owned by Italian financial intermediaries. It therefore functions more or less as it did prior to its demutualization or, more accurately, prior to its privatization, as it was effectively sold by the Italian Treasury. At the other extreme is OM Stockholm, which is self-listed and which has a highly diversified shareholder base, approximately a quarter of which is foreign. London-based Virt-x, a Pan-European blue chip securities exchange dominant only in Swiss SMI index stocks, has a complex ownership structure: 40 percent of its shares is owned by the Swiss Exchange, itself a mutual association; 38 percent is owned by a consortium of major USA and European financial institutions; and 22 percent free-floats on the AIM small cap market of the London Stock Exchange, a competitor.

Theoretical Underpinning of Demutualization

Since the start of the demutualization wave in early 1990s, debate ensued about the impact of this transformation and while many researchers and policy makers have praised the demutualization of securities exchanges, some securities exchanges have been more sceptical and tend to be reluctant in undertaking the demutualization decision. Existing literature focuses on assessing the impact on the performance of the demutualization agenda. While assessing the performance of demutualized securities exchanges provides useful insights for policy makers on the usefulness and value of this process, it remains important for policy makers to link the implementation of demutualization to the nature of the securities exchange, including its existence, behaviour and its relationship with the market and the external factors. Such description is explained thoroughly by the theory of the firm. This section provides a description of how the demutualization process is linked to the theory of the firm, the reasons behind it as well as its consequences.

Agency theory provides the theoretical underpinning for many empirical studies of demutualization. According to this theory,[55] the choice of an organizational form and the concomitant property rights structure affects the ability of the firm to transform inputs into outputs – that is, it affects efficiency. Evidence[56] exists arguing that the property rights structure in alternative forms of organization may give rise to organizational flaws and, consequently, inefficiency. Such literature[57] has described the property

---

55   Chaddad, F. R. & Cook, M. L. (2004). The Economics of Organization Structure Changes: A US Perspective on Demutualization. *Annals of Public and Cooperative Economics*, 75(4): 575-594.

56   Jensen, M. C. & Meckling, W. H. (1979). Rights and production functions: an application to labour-managed firms and codetermination, *Journal of Business*, 52(4), 460-506.

57   Fama, E.F. & Jensen, M.C. (1985) Organizational forms and investment decisions. *Journal of Financial Economics*, 14, 101-119.

rights structure of alternative forms of organization – including investor-owned corporations and mutuals – and deriving a set of hypotheses regarding their expected behaviour and relative performance. More specifically, restrictions on mutual residual claims give rise to capital acquisition and governance constraints, whereas the separation of ownership from control leads to agency costs between managers and shareholders in companies.

Agency theory posits that the choice of organizational form is endogenous and depends on the exogenous *rules of the game* found in the institutional environment. Moreover, this choice is driven by efficiency considerations, since it is expected that in free markets competition will weed out inefficient forms of organization. If a firm adopts a less than optimal organizational structure, it will not be able to compete against more efficient forms of organization. The main agency theoretical hypothesis is that organizational change occurs when economic efficiencies are to be gained. This hypothesis, however, does not predict the direction of ownership structure change. In other words, a firm will choose among organization forms to minimize production and agency costs.

Contrasting to this point of view, alternative hypotheses regarding the decision to convert are found in the demutualization literature. Some authors[58] suggest the wealth expropriation hypothesis; according to which demutualization is initiated by management and board of directors' desire for windfall gains and stock compensation plans. Another hypothesis is that the nature of patron's equity in securities exchanges may predispose high performance securities markets to restructure as investor oriented firms. If the market value of a cooperative exceeds its book value, members with limited patronage horizons can realize the value of their cooperative shares only by selling or converting the business. A more balanced view[59] however, argues that the choice of organizational form is driven by transaction

---

58   Mayers, D. & Smith, C.W. (2000). Ownership structure and control: Property-casualty insurer conversion to stock charter. Working Paper No.FR00–15: The Bradley Policy Research Center, University of Rochester.

59   Hansmann, N. H. (1996). The Ownership of Enterprise, The Belknap Press of Harvard University Press, Cambridge.

costs minimization and predicts that the mutual form will prevail when contracting costs are higher than risk bearing costs.

There are different strands of theoretical and empirical literature on possible effect of demutualization of securities exchanges. Empirical analyses of the governance of securities exchanges are relatively few. The theoretical literature on mutuals and cooperatives is relevant. However, the large volume of contributions is closely related to organizational forms of securities exchanges. A few focuses on the user welfare of different governance setups for securities exchanges, analyzing the relative merits of a mutual structure and outside ownership in dependence of the level of competition and the diversity of member interests.

Hart and Moore (1996) made two main findings; first, outside ownership becomes more efficient than a mutual structure as the members of the mutual become more diverse in terms of preferences. Second, outside ownership becomes more efficient than a mutual structure as a securities exchange faces more competition. However, they do not explicitly analyze competitive interaction between securities exchanges with different organizational forms, nor do they investigate dynamic considerations that concern the viability of securities exchanges under competitive pressure. Pirrong (2000) takes a different approach to analyze governance issues. In contrast to Hart & Moore (1996), Pirrong does not compare different owners of securities exchanges, but focuses on different types of users that may organize their securities exchange either as a for-profit or as a not for-profit entity. He then describes governance mechanisms to mitigate conflicts of interests between the members. He further presents an analysis of competition between securities exchanges based on switching costs and liquidity effects, respectively.

Krishnamurti, Sequeira & Fangjian (2003) have analyzed the market quality of securities exchanges with different organizational form and found evidence that the demutualized National Exchange of India provides a higher market quality than the mutual Bombay Stock Exchange. Mendiola & O'Hara (2003) focus on the post-IPO performance of publicly listed securities exchanges and found that they outperform both the general market and other IPOs. Furthermore, they found a positive link between the fraction of equity sold to outside investors and securities exchange performance.

Other empirical attempts to compare different governance regimes in the securities exchange industry mainly rely on frontier efficiency methods. While Schmiedel (2001) employs a parametric stochastic frontier model to evaluate the cost efficiency of European securities exchanges, controls for demutualized exchanges within the regression and reports a positive impact of demutualization on cost efficiency. Schmiedel (2002) applied a non-parametric method and found the mean of factor productivity gains to be higher among mutual securities exchanges.

Using univariate probit regressions to evaluate the propensity of exchanges to demutualize, Ramos (2005) found evidence that competitive pressure has a positive effect on the likelihood of exchanges to demutualize. In addition, using a five-year sample of 26 securities exchanges, Serifoy (2006) employed a more involved estimation technique to provide evidence for the impact of organizational forms on investment decisions at securities exchanges, in addition to using a bivariate probit approach to account for potential endogeneity issues stemming from the study's governance variable. Serifoy presented a model that explains why securities exchanges have increasingly demutualized in recent years. This is due to the fact that mutual securities exchanges cannot effectively compete against other exchanges, especially against outsider-owned, for-profit trading platforms. It was demonstrated that they can survive against competing exchanges when they demutualize. Furthermore, Serifoy explained the ongoing trend of diversification among securities exchanges by showing that outsider-owned exchanges will have a higher propensity to do so vis-a-vis mutual exchanges. In particular, Serifoy found evidence that competitive pressure induces securities exchanges to demutualize and that publicly listed exchanges are more likely to invest into related business activities.

Recent research[60] has empirically found that technology driven growth opportunities, product driven growth opportunities and increases

---

60   Jain, C., Jain, P. K. & Taylor, D. (2022). Causes and Effects of Worldwide Demutualization of Financial Exchanges. Available at SSRN: http://dx.doi.org/10.2139/ssrn.3886562.

in market concentration are the main stimulants for demutualization. These factors remain strongly significant in explaining demutualization after controlling for market capitalization, trading volume and economic freedom environment within the country where the exchange is domiciled. They also analyzed the impact of demutualization from the perspectives of other stakeholders in financial markets and found that turnover and liquidity for investors improved after demutualization, helping reduce the cost of capital for corporations. Demutualization, therefore, seems to generate more benefits to securities exchanges than does the mutual governance structures.

Global Forces Towards Demutualization of Securities Exchanges

There are a number of forces pushing securities exchanges to demutualize and change their organizational and management structures. Currently, it seems to be the in-thing in the securities exchange industry. In fact, about 70 securities exchanges had demutualized by end of 2020. Forces of *globalization* and *consolidation*-integration dictates that securities exchanges have to reorganize themselves to become viable entities of international standards. Stiff *competition* amongst securities exchanges and between exchanges and alternative trading systems calls for mechanisms to minimize costs and generate more revenues in order to shield themselves from such competition.

Globally, the migration of order flow seems to be putting pressure on securities exchanges to rethink their ownership, management and commercial focus. For some exchanges, already more than fifty percent of trading and listing have migrated offshore. Trading migration makes it difficult for countries to sustain full-fledged local securities exchanges. The increased migration will thus make it more difficult for small securities exchanges to survive. If they do not act quickly, there is a great risk that blue chip firms listed on these exchanges will migrate to other regional securities exchanges. As trading volumes further decrease, financing the fixed overhead of maintaining market oversight, clearing and settlement systems, generating enough business for local investment banks, accounting firms and other support services will become even harder, especially for smaller emerging securities markets. Migration of order flow puts pressure on securities exchanges worldwide. Such trading order flow migration makes it difficult for countries to sustain fully-fledged stand-alone local securities exchanges. The following is a detailed discussion of these forces.

Globalization of Securities Markets. Historically, stockbrokers and securities exchanges were locally focused. Securities exchanges did not face meaningful competition from other exchanges in distant places. Domestic securities exchanges developed when the telegraph and telephone made it easier to deal on a distant exchange. Advances in telecommunications have, however, enabled securities issuers and investors to access foreign securities markets. As nationality has become less of a defining characteristic of securities markets, global centres have grown in importance, and the relevance of national securities exchanges has been challenged. This challenge is more acutely felt in relatively small home markets. Today, either the NYSE or the National Association of Security Dealers and Automated Quotation – Nasdaq stock market – in USA is the major market for several European and Canadian listings. Globalization will lead to further consolidation and integration of securities exchanges. The move is already on in Europe, America, Asian Pacific and even integration talks are on in African among the African securities exchanges.[61]

Integration and Consolidations. Acquisitions, mergers, consolidations and other forms of strategic alliances are also affecting securities markets and securities exchanges globally. Mergers among securities exchanges and derivative exchanges in the USA are redefining the competitive landscape and creating super-exchanges. The merger of Nasdaq and American Stock Exchange (AMEX) for instance, created a securities exchange with a market capitalisation of US$1.9Tn offering an unprecedented variety of financial products. Strategic alliances and consolidation are also occurring in Europe, for example the Euronext, as well as in other parts of the world. These alliances are motivated by a variety of factors. Scale is increasingly

---

61   See Onyuma, S. O. (2006) Regional Integration of African Stock Exchanges. *African Review of Money, Finance & Banking* (Supplementary Issue): 99-124.

important, particularly in leveraging technology costs and other investment opportunities. Through these alliances, securities exchanges seek to attract more investors by harmonizing distinct trading environments and by offering greater product variety. Strategic alliances are a means of pursuing the conventional wisdom that liquidity attracts liquidity, thus liquid markets will continue gaining more liquidity from other markets.[62] Integration of securities exchanges calls for harmonizing regulatory rules and laws for uniformity, and has been a force during demutualization as demutualized securities exchanges have been seen pursuing mergers, acquisitions as well as different forms of strategic alliances aimed at integrating their markets with other exchanges, locally as well as globally.

Global Competition. Currently, securities exchanges are no longer the sole primary and secondary market makers or the sole service providers of trade execution, signalling or other activities. This is largely because of the widespread proliferation of ATS and ECNs that have been supported by the technological revolution and the introduction of high capacity hardware, software packages and Internet facilities. The ATS and ECNs have allowed efficient and effective matching of the buy and sell orders of customers at lower transaction costs, while offering price transparency, trader anonymity and extended trading hours. Large global stockbrokers are able to price-match within their own order-stock and only report the net position as a trade to the securities exchange thereby avoiding transaction costs. Given the competitive edge, the market share of the ECNs has grown significantly. In 2022, ECNs accounted for 65 percent of Nasdaq shares traded (compared to 25.5 percent in 1999) – although they only accounted for about 12 percent of the listed shares traded. Of the several ECNs, Island alone accounts for 38 percent of the ECN's market share. Instinet makes up another 31 percent, ArcaEx 29.3 percent (formed through the merger of Archipelago and REDIBook), Bloomberg Tradebook 7.5 percent and Brut ECN 6.9 percent, the rest is accounted for

---

62   Onyuma, S. O. (2006) Regional Integration of Stock Markets in Africa. *African Review of Money, Banking & Finance,* (Supplementary Issue): 99-124.

by other networks.[63] Having attracted substantial trading, ECNs are also entering into strategic alliances or tie-ups with other securities exchanges, or are offering services such as quotations and listing of shares to further raise revenues.

The competition among the securities exchanges and with ECNs has increased both domestically, regional and globally. Consequently, securities exchanges are no longer monopolies but must now be run as efficient corporate enterprises. For these reasons, stiff competition has been a major factor in decisions to demutualize many securities exchanges. Earlier, floor-based securities exchanges had limited space and so permitted only a limited number of exchange memberships or seats. Therefore, securities exchanges, even those that were not floor-based were organized as mutuals – owned and controlled by their broker-members. Thus, the mutual structures predominated when securities exchanges had monopoly power and the interests of members were capable of being protected.[64] Therefore, the fight to provide listing for firms, securities trade clearing, trading and data services will increase drastically due to the competition between securities exchanges searching for growth beyond national borders, as well as competition from non-exchanges such as ATS and ECNs.

Technological Advancements. Major changes in the structure and operations of securities exchanges have generally coincided with breakthroughs in communication and data processing technologies. Prime examples are the emergence of telegraph technology, which helped some securities markets to establish their dominance in the late 19th century, and the advances in network technology that led the way to the development of over the counter markets in the 1980s.[65] The recent technological improvements have enabled the development of the continuous electronic auction market in Europe. Continuous auction systems are trading systems that allow automatic execution of matching buy and sell orders. Currently,

---

63 GFSR (2022) National Association of Securities Dealers (NASD). JP Morgan, H&Q, Global Finance Staff Research.

64 Aggarwal, R, (2002) Demutualization & Corporate Governance of Stock Exchanges. *Journal of Applied Corporate Finance*, 105-113.

65 Aggarwal, R. (2002).

all European securities exchanges operate some version of this continuous electronic trading system. In Africa, Asia and USA, however, many securities exchanges continue to operate as traditional, floor-based systems, in which only broker-members are allowed to be on the floor and trade. For such exchanges, electronic trading systems present a major competitive challenge. Both advances in technology and innovation will enable new business models and drive further change, including more tailored financial products and services enabled by more standardized processes and systems within the market.

Internationalization of Exchange Membership. The internationalization of exchange membership also facilitated demutualization. Local players (mostly brokers) have a strong incentive to maintain institutional barriers to disintermediation of their services, whereas international players tend to see governance reform as an effective weapon for increasing their strategic control of the exchange *vis-à-vis* the locals – typically by replacing-one member, one-vote and committee-based decision making with decision-making tied more directly to the size of the ownership stake.

Therefore, the recent transformations in the global environment have added new dimensions to the trading, clearing, settlement and listing functions of the securities exchanges. Many of these functions have come under actual or potential competitive threat. The need to meet the demand from its customers for lower transaction costs; more efficient services and new products are now becoming more crucial for the survival of the many securities exchanges. The driving forces behind demutualization are, therefore, found to be growing competition among securities markets, increasing listing of global companies and securities exchanges around the world and the overall changes in market place due to the advent of new technology. The Boston Consultative Group[66] has summarized the effect of these factors and others on securities exchanges as illustrated in Figure 1.

---

66   Boston Consultative Group (2003). Key Learning Related to the Demutualization of Stock Exchanges. Conference Paper, Instanbul, April 10th, Boston Consulting Group.

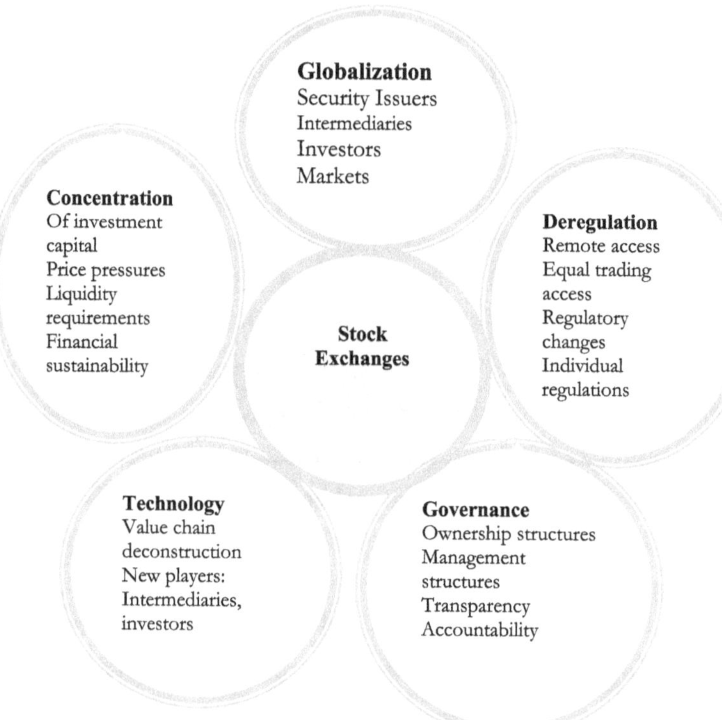

Figure 1: *Global Trends Shaping Securities Exchange Landscape & Demutualization*
Source: Boston Consulting Group, 2003

Competition and Mutual Securities Exchanges

Competition has been noted as one of the global trends taking place in securities exchanges. Competition has even been blamed on the demutualization of securities markets. For instance, Mendiola & O'Hara (2003) have analysed the empirical effects of the change in exchange governance. In particular, they look at the effect of exchange conversions to publicly traded companies on the exchanges' performance and valuation. Examining accounting and return data for ten securities exchanges, they found that exchange performance, measured by exchange returns, tends to improve after the change in corporate governance.

By considering how increasing competition and the traditional exchanges subsequent demutualization affect their order flow and trading costs, one could consider the demutualization of the London Stock Exchange. Introduction of the residual claimant helped LSE regain order-flow. LSE demutualized in response to increasing competition from exchanges such as Tradepoint. Therefore, the post-demutualization changes in trading volumes and costs may reflect the actions of the competing securities exchanges. That is, the impact of demutualization may be confounded by the effect of competition. To address this problem, it is worth examining securities exchange, which demutualized for reasons other than significant competition.

Specifically, the privatization of Borsa Italiana can be used as a benchmark to evaluate the impact of demutualization. The Borsa Italiana was not demutualized by its broker-members as a response to competition, but was privatized by the government, in spite of members' resistance. The government through securities market regulator in the country could decide to make the securities exchange a public firm (as opposed to a public utility) to bring in efficient and rational decision-making. For example, in the USA, the SEC in 2006 drove the agenda of taking the NYSE public. The LSE and Borsa Italiana, therefore, demutualized under different competitive environments. In the next section, a brief history of the two exchanges is presented and an explanation provided why and how they demutualized.

The Borsa Italiana Exchange. Like the other continental European exchanges, Borsa Italiana (Milan Stock Exchange) faced severe competition from SEAQI. Steil (1996) provides empirical evidence of the increase in London's share of trading compared to Borsa Italiana from 1989 to 1991. In addition, there was considerable off-exchange trading in the Italian equity market due to the existence of statutorily fixed commissions on the exchange. To avoid paying the 0.7 percent commission to an *agente di cambio*, a bank receiving a client's order would trade with another bank off the securities exchange (so that it could retain a 0.35 percent commission) or, even better, cross the trade in-house (in which case it would appropriate the entire 0.7 percent commission from the two clients). In some years the off-exchange trading volume was estimated to be over three times the trading volume on the securities exchange.

To cope with both these issues, Borsa Italiana Exchange in Milan adopted an automated continuous trading system in 1991, replaced the *agenti di cambio* (local members) with the *Società di Intermediazione Mobiliare* (SIMs), who could trade on their own account and could be owned by domestic banks, insurance companies and securities firms. The Borsa Italiana also liberalized commissions and made a rule to concentrate all trade on the official exchange. The local members agreed to open membership to other outsiders because of the concentration rule which implied that all trades had to go through the securities exchange and hence order flow (and thus commissions) increased, while the Italian banks accepted the concentration rule because it was introduced together with the liberalization of commissions and the elimination of the local broker-members' monopoly.

Thus, in 1991 the members of the Milan Stock Exchange took steps as a group (without demutualizing), to stem competition. This increased trading volume on the Milan exchange, and it regained substantial order-flow from SEAQ-I.[67] Then in 1997, demutualization of this exchange was initiated by the government as a part of its privatization initiatives. The demutualization of the Milan Exchange was not forced due to competition and member heterogeneity; it was privatized by the government. At the time of demutualization, Milan had 70 percent market share and a better trading system compared to SEAQ-I – its main competitor, (the order-driven trading system on Borsa Italiana was preferred by investors compared to the quote-driven SEAQ-I system). Also, the Italian equities market was not big enough to attract significant attention from the Pan-European exchanges such as Tradepoint, which were actively trading Swiss and Dutch stocks.

The London Stock Exchange. The LSE was demutualized by its members to respond to competition. To understand why, let us first look at the history of LSE. The abolition of exchange controls led to the *big bang* reforms of LSE in 1986, in spite of resistance by its broker-members. The

---

67 Steil, B, (1996). *The European Equity Markets: The State of the Union and the Agenda for the Millennium*, The Royal Institute of International Affairs.

reforms involved scrapping the single capacity system of *jobbers* and *brokers*, opening dealership to banks and other financial institutions, liberalizing commissions, and introducing SEAQ (for UK stocks) and SEAQ-I (for international stocks) - the screen-based quote-driven trading system, where dual-capacity dealers could post their quotes. The LSE became a private limited company, and each member firm obtained one share. These reforms were very successful and helped LSE maintain its dominant position in Europe's equity markets. Several continental European exchanges reacted to the competition from SEAQ-I, by scrapping floor trading and adopting order-driven auction trading systems. Thus, LSE lost substantial international order-flow back to the European exchanges. Also, competition for UK equities continued to intensify.

From September 1995, LSE's dealer market faced competition from Tradepoint, a new automated order-driven market for UK stocks. Tradepoint was set up by former executives of LSE who had tried unsuccessfully to introduce continuous auction market at the LSE. Tradepoint later merged with the Swiss Exchange (SWX) to form Virt-X – a pan-European blue-chip exchange in June 2001. As electronic trading networks such as Tradepoint established themselves in the UK, the UK regulatory authorities removed the earlier restrictions on market makers that had prevented them from quoting, on other electronic markets. *Jobbers* ran around the trading floor buying and selling shares for stockbrokers, and made the difference between what stockbrokers were willing to pay for shares and the price they actually paid. The stockbrokers made commissions by buying and selling for investors.

The ECNs quoted on their networks, prices better than those they were quoting on LSE. Thus, these electronic networks had the potential of bringing buyers and sellers together well within the LSE spread. Tradepoint allows institutional traders to trade directly without broker-dealer intermediation. It initially offered continuous trading for the largest 400 UK stocks, and in March 1996 it expanded its market to more than 900 shares. As Tradepoint began to gain market share, LSE had to slash its fees to undercut Tradepoint. In addition, Tradepoint introduced remote access to US-based institutions in March 1999. SEC allowed Tradepoint in until it had less than 10 percent of the global market for London-listed securities.

Also, in January 1996 the Paris Bourse launched Eurocac – a continuous auction system – to trade non-French equities. Eurocac also featured a market-making element: for each stock, at least one market maker ensures permanent bid and ask price display for a minimum value of Franc one million. Eurocac trades are not subject to stamp duty, and its fee structure provides incentives for limit orders and penalties for market orders, to maximize the liquidity of the market. Finally, under Article 15.4 of EU Investing Services Directive, automated order matching systems located anywhere within Europe became potential competitors of LSE.

The increasing potential competition worried LSE officials. They wanted to replace SEAQ with an updated system with order-matching capabilities. In October 1997, LSE introduced the Stock Exchange Electronic Service (SETS) – an order-driven trading mechanism, to complement SEAQ the existing quote-driven dealership market. This was a hotly debated issue between the board of LSE and the main market-makers, and led to the abrupt dismissal of the chief executive, Mr. Michael Lawrence, in January 1996. This debate brought to the fore the heterogeneity in LSE's membership and the need for change. Lee (1998) presents a case study of this debate which highlights how and why LSE was forced to demutualize. Finally, on July 30th 1999 LSE announced its intention to demutualize. The shareholders voted in favour of this on March 15th 2000 and its shares began trading on a matched-bargain facility exchange on July 24, 2000. Each of the 297 members of LSE swapped their existing single share for 100,000 shares in the new exchange-company, representing 0.34 percent of its capital.

Comparing demutualization due to competition by the LSE, to demutualization without competition by Borsa Italiana, Hazarika (2005) found that on LSE, trading volumes and dealer spreads decline before demutualization. This suggests that LSE members were facing declining revenues due to competitive pressures; presumably, it is these competitive pressures that led the LSE to demutualize. In contrast, in Milan where the government (and not the exchange) forced the demutualization – in fact, the exchange saw increasing volumes, and relatively constant spreads before demutualization. This is consistent with the fact that Borsa Italiana was not facing serious competition and that its members resisted demutualization.

Post-demutualization, trading volumes increased significantly on LSE. Thus, the introduction of the *residual claimant* helped the dominant exchange regain order-flow from the competition. Moreover, in an examination of trading costs, monthly average spread measures on LSE decreased further in the year after demutualization. This indicates that demutualization continues the effect of competition; the incentive structure of a demutualized exchange brings in policy change, which continues to lower trading costs.

In the case of Borsa Italiana too, which faced limited competition, trading volumes increased post-demutualization. Interestingly, the post-demutualization increase in trading volumes was substantial compared to LSE. Specifically, Borsa Italiana's market share increased to 98 percent (from 71 percent) within ten months of demutualization. Strikingly, however, in the post-demutualization period, trading costs increased on Borsa Italiana.

There is therefore an important role for competition in securities exchange landscape. In the case where a securities exchange demutualizes in a non-competitive environment, the policies brought in by the residual claimant have an immediate impact. The securities exchange captures the entire order-flow and eliminates the little competition, which is out there. Further, the owners of the demutualized securities exchange have no incentives to lower trading costs. This indicates that early demutualization, prior to the advent of significant competition, actually leads to further/ complete dominance by the primary securities exchange, making the introduction of potential competition even more difficult in the future. This suggest that introducing a residual claimant in the governance structure of securities exchanges is definitely beneficial for the exchange, as demutualization helps the securities exchange increase order-flow. The impact of this governance change for investors is not that unequivocal; demutualization is beneficial to investors only if a securities exchange faces competition. If the exchange demutualizes in a competitive environment, investors are better off, as trading costs continue to decline post-demutualization. In contrast, a demutualized securities exchange in a non-competitive environment could make investors worse off.

Why Would a Securities Exchange Demutualize?

From the above discussion on competition as a driving force towards exchange demutualization, the cardinal question, which is often asked, relates to whether competition is the dominant force. In essence then, why would a securities exchange be demutualized? There are several forces behind the demutualization of securities exchanges. The recent transformations in the global environment have added new dimensions to the trading, clearing, settlement and listing functions of securities exchanges. Many of these functions have come under actual or potential competitive threat. The need to meet the demand from its customers for lower transaction costs; more efficient services and new financial products are now becoming more crucial for the survival of securities exchanges. The driving forces behind demutualization are found to be growing competition among securities exchanges, increasing listing of global companies in many securities exchanges around the world, and the overall changes in market place due to the advent of new technology.

A look at the traditional role and governance structure of securities exchanges reveals that the typical floor-based securities exchange is a quasi-governmental organization that is protected from competition due to regulatory and currency barriers. These exchanges provide a range of services and earn fees from listing, membership, transactions, clearing and settlement services and data dissemination. Often, they have monopoly access to clearing, settlement and depository facilities. Access to the securities exchange is rationed by a combination of high initial and annual membership fees.[68] Most traditional exchanges are non-profit; broker-members invest a small portion of their profits in technology and facilities for the exchange and any profits beyond this are returned to the members through rebates, such as reduced transaction fees or in-kind provision of services.

---

68 Steil, Benn, (2002) Changes in the ownership and governance of stock exchanges: causes and consequences, Brookings-Wharton papers on financial services, 61-91.

It is safe to argue that the floor-based securities exchanges are member-owned to protect the traders' specialized human and reputational capital from expropriation by an outside owner; and to protect the outside owner from holdup by traders. Hart & Moore (1996) emphasize the decision-making aspect of the governance structure. The central idea of their argument is that authority to make decisions lies with the owner(s) of the securities exchange. The owner(s) have the residual rights of control and make decisions such as which parties will have access to the exchange, what should be traded, and what will be the rules of trading and fee structure. Hart and Moore further argue that both outside ownership and a members' cooperative are inefficient, but in different ways and for different reasons. The outside owners are interested in maximizing securities exchange profits, and hence decision-making is focused on the marginal user – the analogy they draw upon is that of the monopolist who inefficiently restricts supply to raise prices. The cooperative is inefficient because the views of the decisive voter are not necessarily those of the membership as a whole. The traditional securities exchanges are, therefore, seen to have a homogeneous membership and thus a member-owned cooperative is the more efficient governance structure. The residual rights of control are with the broker-members, each of whom has one vote and decisions are made by majority voting.

The reason why most floor-based exchanges are non-profit is because higher member heterogeneity – in terms of costs of providing brokerage services – allows low-cost members to enforce a non-profit mutual structure. The low-cost broker-members can credibly threaten to collude and leave the securities exchange if the high-cost members demand a for-profit structure that would lead to a redistribution of profits away from the low-cost providers. Therefore, when trading is floor-based, all members have the same incentive structure and member-ownership is the more efficient governance structure. Further, the 'one-member one-vote' governance system helps small local broker-members maintain a strong influence on securities exchange policies.

It has been argued earlier that electronic networks introduced competition to the traditional securities exchanges. For instance, the introduction of SEAQ-I[69] in London in 1986 is a classic example of the introduction of competition to monopolistic floor-based exchanges in continental Europe. Through SEAQ-I, a quote-driven system, dealers in London provided an immediate and deep market for large block trades in European blue-chip firms. Pagano (1998) explains that the dealers were available on the phone throughout the trading day compared to the European call auction markets, where trading outside the call auction, if allowed, was in very small amounts. The introduction of SEAQ abolished the trading floor in London; dealers chose to post quotes on computer screens rather than trade through open-outcry on the floor.

Furthermore, the monetary union and the implementation of the Euro eliminated currency barriers; the listing firms did not have to list on their national securities exchanges anymore. In addition, the European Union's Investment Service Directive (ISD) allowed exchanges in regulated markets to offer remote membership to intermediaries in other countries. This led large European banks to start concentrating their trading in London. Thus, the dominant position of virtually all the continental European exchanges was challenged by a single electronic network in London. In responding to this challenge, however, the continental exchanges were stymied by their mutual structure; any change in policy had to be voted in by the membership. The broker-members were interested in maximizing their individual profits, and resisted policy changes, such as reductions in commissions or remote cross-border memberships, that would decrease their profits even if the change would increase securities exchange revenues.

In addition, the value of any proposed change differed sharply across the broker-members of the securities exchange, and since each member's valuations were private, cost-sharing rules could not be implemented to ensure a net benefit for every broker-member. Moreover, the mutualized structure implied that no one could coerce the broker-members to compel participation. Thus, the cost of collective decision-making increases with member heterogeneity. Hence, there was a need to bring in a principal – a residual claimant who would take decisions with the aim of maximizing

---

69 SEAQ-I is an acronym for Stock Exchange Automated Quotation.

securities exchange value. This called for the need to separate ownership from trading access, to demutualize. Theoretically, Hart & Moore (1996) show that as securities exchange faces competition, outside ownership of the exchange becomes relatively more efficient than a members' cooperative.

Although competitive pressures could and did force the exchanges to implement individual changes (for example, in Amsterdam, the international banks championed successfully for the cessation of floor trading and introduction of electronic auction trading in the mid-1990s), some members of the securities exchanges realized that continued competition would erode securities exchange revenues unless they brought in a permanent governance change. They put pressure on the local securities exchange broker-members and forced them to accept demutualization. For example, in LSE, several international banks threatened to move their trading elsewhere in the 1990s if the governance structure did not change. Some two large marker makers argued that the commitment level of broker-members differs widely, thus one member one vote did not reflect the reality of the market structure, and that the LSE's best customers' had to expect the service to be tailored to their needs.

The decisions by securities exchanges to demutualize are, therefore, based on the recognition that the old member-owned association structure fails to provide the flexibility and the financing needed to compete in today's competitive environment. In the long run, for-profit securities exchanges run by management and disciplined by profit-seeking investors should produce better-financed securities exchanges with greater ability to respond quickly to preserve the value of their franchises. Besides helping securities exchanges adapt to a fast-changing marketplace, demutualization is also likely to promote the exchanges' efforts to leverage their brand values by expanding into new business areas. Therefore, equipped with better financing, more flexible decision mechanisms, and heightened accountability to shareholders, demutualized securities exchanges are likely to emerge as leaner, more competitive, and more transparent institutions capable of creating real value to a wider owners and the society.

The reasons for demutualization may vary from securities exchange to securities exchange. However, most of the reasons and benefits discussed below appear to be common to many demutualized exchanges. Some of these benefits have also been highlighted by some thinkers.[70]

Address a Global Corporate Trend. Since demutualization is concerned with the separation of ownership and management, it is well driven by the good intentions of proper governance, which has taken a new turn after the collapse of many large corporations, locally and internationally. In developed countries, demutualization has been motivated primarily by the need to compete with other securities exchanges, both conventional exchanges and alternative trading systems like ECNs. Failure to compete means losing both liquidity and listings to others. Competitive pressures are caused and intensified to a large extent by technological developments that are bringing geographical neutrality to the business of securities exchanges. In order to compete, securities exchanges require efficient decision making structures and large amounts of funds for investment in technological infrastructure. A mutual structure is an obstacle in both decision-making and access to capital, thus causing a wave of demutualization the world over.

A look at how increasing competition and the traditional exchanges' subsequent demutualization affect their order-flow and trading costs, one could consider the demutualization of the LSE. Introduction of the 'residual claimant' helped LSE regain order-flow. LSE therefore demutualized in response to increasing competition from exchanges such as Tradepoint. Therefore, the post-demutualization changes in trading volumes and costs may reflect the actions of the competing exchanges. Thus, the impact of demutualization may be confounded by the effect of competition.

In some countries, such as Australia, USA, and Britain, demutualization has largely been voluntary and the regulator and the government merely facilitated the process. In other countries, the desire to address governance problems of securities exchanges has been the driving factor behind demutualization. Therefore, there are other exchanges, which have demutualized for reasons other than significant competition. The initiative to demutualize was often that of the government or the apex regulator of the securities market. For instance, in Kenya, Nigeria, Singapore,

---

70   See Karmel (2000); Akhatar (2002).

Hong Kong, and Malaysia, securities exchanges have demutualized due to pressure from the government and regulators to do so. Specifically, the privatization of Borsa Italiana can be used as a benchmark to evaluate the impact of demutualization since the exchange demutualized as a result of the government requirement.

Improve Ownership and Managerial Structure. Currently, the traditional distinctions between securities exchanges' activities and the activities of their members and clearing members have become increasingly blurred. Members and clearing members decided their affairs, but some of them competed directly with their exchanges by developing off-exchange products and businesses and by joining alternative market initiatives. Demutualized securities exchanges' boards therefore believe that demutualization can enable the management to reduce the impact of these conflicts, by creating a governance and management structure that is more agile and swift in its ability to respond to competition and other conflicting members' behaviour.

Admittedly, the traditional ownership and management structure of securities exchanges is not readily adaptable to an emerging competitive environment. It is difficult to implement new policies and new strategic directions because members, acting through committees or voting on constitutional amendments, must bless each significant change. Also, a securities exchange's enterprise value can be increased for the benefit of its equity owners. The management of the demutualized exchange can be free to make decisions regarding listing contracts electronically, changing clearing and transaction fees when appropriate, or expanding existing product and service offerings. Therefore, most demutualization case[71] are intended to modernize the corporate governance structure, improve the efficiency of a securities exchange corporate decision-making process and position the exchange to compete more effectively in the evolving marketplace. As a for-profit entity, an exchange has the ability to issue

---

71 See CBOT Registration Statement, <http://www.sec.gov/Archives/edgar/edgar/data/ 111746310000950131015010062/ds4a.txt>.

capital stock, the flexibility to continue to evaluate the ownership structure and to consider value-enhancing transactions in the future.

Demutualization, therefore, restructures governance at the securities exchanges on a sustainable basis. The ownership rights and trading rights are de-linked. It thus increases the role of non-member stakeholders in the affairs of the exchange. Management is in the hands of professional managers. The board of directors and broker committees do not run the day-to-day management of the exchanges. The role of the board is policy making, supervision of management and laying down strategic direction. The new structure of governance leads to independent, efficient, and transparent decision making in the interest of all stakeholders, particularly investors.

Improve Financial Decision-making Model. In addition, the cost of capital to securities exchange members has been high. As a result, members, through fees, dues, and transaction charges, or through special assessments, become the primary source of working capital. Therefore, demutualization is a necessary step in modernizing governance and management for achieving growth in the future of an exchange. It can allow a securities exchange to unlock its equity value, enhance its business and partnership opportunities, and position itself to become more responsive to customer needs. The commercial decision-making thus diminishes broker-member political influences. Commercial pricing of services and a profit-making objective ensures that resources are allocated to those business initiatives and ventures that enhance, or have the potential to enhance, stockholder value. The securities exchange's ability to obtain financing at favourable rates depends on whether lenders believe it is investing it prudently. In fact, future growth capital can also be raise by the exchange company via an IPO at cheaper cost.

Create a Catalyst for Pursuing New Business Strategies. Continuing financial innovation and demand for new risk management and derivative products are fuelling global growth in exchange-traded and over-the-counter products. To capitalize on this potential, a demutualized securities exchange is able to attract outside investment, further expand its current technology platforms, and broaden its financial products and service offerings. Thus, a demutualized securities exchange can raise capital for strategic affiliations, technological improvements or new systems and pursue new profitable business strategies and opportunities. This can therefore aid cross-border investments.

IPO Makes Shares Publicly Traded and Widely Held. Some securities exchange boards[72] believe that it is in the interest of both its shareholders and the investing public for shares to be publicly traded and widely held through an IPO. As a for-profit, stock-based company governed by the market's leading participants, demutualized exchanges are more agile, flexible, and effective in responding to industry and market conditions. Public ownership through an IPO and the capital it provides can allow an exchange to continue to improve its market by allowing a securities exchange to compete effectively with domestic and international competitors, facilitating the sale of remaining equity ownership, and creating a liquid acquisition currency for an exchange. Such an IPO can also provide a valuation benchmark and liquidity for current investors and allow an exchange to control the development of the trading market for its shares. An exchange's interest is therefore aligned with the interests of key participants, thus have both an initial infusion of capital and easier ongoing access to capital. Future exchange share value appreciation can later be used for future negotiation of mergers and acquisition of other target securities exchanges.

Remove Tension and Conflict amongst Members. The diversity of interest among securities exchange members can be a continuous source of tension and conflict. Members are only able to realize economic value from their right to trade on the floor, but member firms compete with one another in a variety of businesses, including OTC market-making in listed securities.[73] Demutualization offers greater commonality among equity owners and avoids concentration of ownership power in a particular group of securities exchange participants.

---

72   Nasdaq to Become a Public Company, available at <http://www.Nasdaqnews.com/news/ pr2001/ne_section01_140.html>.

73   See Testimony of Richard A. Grasso before the Senate Banking Commission, 28 September 1999, available at <http://www.nyse.com/speech/NT0002458E.html>.

Keep Pace with Technological Advancement. A major driver of demutualization of securities exchanges is computer-based screen trading, which has replaced floor-based manual trading on most securities exchanges. As customers have direct access to computer screens, securities exchange memberships no longer have as much economic value, and clearing and settlement firms rather than traders have become a dominant force in securities exchange activities. Additionally, the move from floors to screen–based trading requires considerable capital investment. Demutualization thus offers an opportunity to buy out trader interests since they are no longer necessary and shift power to other firms, while raising capital for continued modernization of trading systems. Continued investment in technology serves as an effective way to meet competition from ATSs and upstairs trading as well as justifying the scale of the traditional integrated securities exchange model.

Trading technology has, therefore, become the main force behind any structural changes of securities exchange. The surge of new technology, which warrants a shifting from floor-based trading to a screen-based trading, has helped in the expansion of the population, both broking and investing, thus created a new demand for securities exchange governance. Also, the trading market automation permits demutualization, meaning that the corporate structure of organization of a securities exchange is feasible when computerized securities trading replaces floor-based trading. For example, in the mid -1990s, the floor-based trading was converted to automated trading in many of the Europe and American securities exchanges due to the pressure of large international banks and subsequently most of them have transformed them into demutualized structure.

Adopt Profit Motive for Growth and Development. Globally, there is a sustained pressure on the securities exchange to grow, develop its business and increase its profitability. It serves as a strong incentive for increasing liquidity in the market and introducing new financial products. A demutualized securities exchange does not remain a traditional securities exchange but graduates into a securities exchange offering a broad range of financial products and services. It also seeks new and diversified ways of increasing its revenues streams, such as share registration, selling back office software and data.

Improve Market Liquidity. The most important reason for demutualization is the shift from floor based to electronic trading. Liquidity no longer exists in a physical location and it is no longer in the best interests of a securities exchange to be dominated by floor-trading members. Rather, a securities exchange wishes to put securities trading screens in as many locations as possible.

Providing a Signal and a Currency for Working with Strategic Partners. Technology firms, as well as other firms interested in acquiring an equity stake in a securities exchange, are likely to prefer to work with a demutualized exchange, rather than a member-owned mutual institution. Demutualization and conversion of memberships or seats into shares create a valuable currency for strategic alliances and other a platform for an exchange aligning itself to important strategic investors and other partners.

Unlocking Members' Equity Values. Demutualization separates the trading rights from ownership rights. Members are able to retain their trading rights and are free to sell shares of their demutualized securities exchange. In a mutual securities exchange, a broker-member cannot sell his membership card or seat without foregoing his trading rights. Becoming publicly quoted would also give securities exchanges and their management a clearer idea of what exactly they were worth. As the business model for securities exchanges changes, demutualization can unlock the equity values of exchange memberships or seats and provide shareholder returns to former broker-members. Over the years, many retired securities exchange owners experienced substantial declines in their seat values and turned to income from leasing. These owners have become generally less interested in member opportunity on the trading floor and more interested in maintaining their asset values and deriving income from their assets. They have become more like traditional shareholders than securities exchange members. Demutualization therefore unlocks the equity value in securities exchange memberships or seats, and provides shareholder returns to them. Many securities exchange members are interested in selling only a portion of their equity interest in a securities exchange, but these broker-members have been unable to do so because they cannot sell less than an entire exchange membership or seat. By unlocking the value of membership cards or seats for all members without loss of trading rights, securities exchanges may invest these proceeds to upgrade their trading systems and other strategic business units.

Remove Barrier to Entry for New Brokers. Mutual securities exchanges restrict market entry by other brokerage firms. In a demutualized securities exchange, trading rights are given on the basis of qualifications and merit. There is no ceiling on the maximum number of trading rights thus removing scarcity value of a membership card or seat. Trading rights are non-transferable and are granted by the securities exchange itself. A number of new market entrants, particularly, financial institutions thus acquire trading rights. Capital adequacy, professionalism and large networks of financial institutions raises the standards and reach of securities market intermediation, thus acquiring global status.

Internationalize Exchange Membership. Experience has shown that the internationalization of securities exchange membership, in itself, also facilitates demutualization of securities exchanges. Local market players, mostly stockbrokers, have a strong incentive to maintain institutional barriers to disintermediation of their services, whereas international market players tend to see governance reform as an effective weapon for increasing their strategic control of a securities exchange compared to the locals. This is typically achieved by replacing one-member, one-vote and consensus-based decision making, with such decision-making based on the size of the share ownership stake. Stockbrokers in a demutualized exchange can then become brokers for other exchanges which could have acquired their exchange, or been acquired by their securities exchange, thus improving their international image.

Greater Ability to Attract Listings. With an improved perception and availability of wider range of financial products and other services, a demutualized securities exchange is well placed to attract listings and facilitate capital formation. With more transparency created following demutualization, more firms are likely to seek listing on securities and derivative exchange which such a demutualized exchange may ultimately takeover or merge with.

Become More Commercial & Responsive. Securities exchange do have the desire to be more commercially nimble and respond to market needs more quickly, unimpeded by broker-member committees and their diverse interests. Demutualization exactly provides exchanges with all these opportunities. It also enables exchanges an access to the local and global capital markets for fund raising. Such funds become instrumental in an exchange's pursuit to modernise its operations and systems.

Access to Economic Capital. Many securities exchanges need money for modernization of their systems and businesses. While they could tax their members through extra dues, the securities exchanges may need more money than the members are willing to provide, so it has to look to outside investors who are not members for money, and thus it sells shares to them. A demutualized exchange is therefore able to raise capital from multiple sources as a normal for-profit listed company. Thus, it can obtain capital from issuing its shares to the public. Thus, an important source of economic capital is the new shareholders, institutions and individuals who then bring in huge funds. Access to economic capital allows large investments required in the technological infrastructure to broaden access to the market. A demutualized exchange is also able to borrow from conventional lenders, such as banks. Through diversification of revenue sources, a demutualized exchange has a pool of capital to resort to for development.

Therefore, a competitive securities exchange must be able to respond quickly to global competitive forces and technological advances through financing. With the capital raised from an IPO or private investment and a heightened awareness of accountability to stakeholders, a securities exchange should have both the incentive and the resources to invest in the competitiveness of its information and trading systems. To be competitive, financial products and services must not only be timely and cost-effective, but also reliable.

Counter Competition from ATSs. Demutualization has the capacity to increase competition between securities exchanges for market share, as investors demand a return on their investment. An ATS is a privately operated computerized system that performs many of the functions performed by securities exchanges by centralizing and matching buy - and sell-orders and providing post-trade information. The stiff competition from ATSs has forced traditional securities exchanges to examine their role as trading arenas and to take measures that facilitate more competitive future commercial strategies. Usually, ATSs are often operated by securities exchange members or member-affiliates and are similar to such exchanges because they allow two participants to meet directly on their systems and are maintained by a third party who also serves a limited regulatory function by imposing requirements on each subscriber.[74] Although some ATSs have been in operation for many years, technological advances, trading value increases and pressures on trading profits have enabled some of them to become serious competitors to securities exchanges.

The US Securities and Exchange Commission (SEC) became concerned that ATSs would impair the fair and orderly functioning of securities markets. In December 1998, SEC implemented the Regulation that permitted ATSs to continue to be regulated as broker-dealers, but required them to comply with rules designed to improve transparency and surveillance, as well as systems capacity, integrity and security of ATSs. Most securities market regulators in EU and the US have also proposed a rule governing ATSs.[75] Many broker-dealers have internal systems to automate the firm's execution of customer orders, particularly firms that internalize or purchase order flow. These systems are not generally considered ATSs because all trades effected on internal systems, generally referred to as upstairs trading, involve only the operator of the system and not external parties. Upstairs trading occurs when a securities exchange member matches customer orders against other customer orders or against its own inventory position within the firm, rather than exposing the order to auction on their securities exchange. The market only learns of the trading activity after

---

74 See Jeffrey W. Smith et al. (1998) The Nasdaq Stock Market: Historical Background and Current Operation, Nasdaq Working Paper, http://www.academic.Nasdaq.com/docs/wp98_01.pdf.

75 These ATSs have also emerged in some African markets, yet market regulators have not found it proper to come up with the requisite regulations for them. In my upcoming book "Paradigm Shift in Securities Exchanges: *Automation, Competition, Governance, Integration & Regulation of Securities Markets in Africa*" I have provided a discussion on the emerging ATSs presence in African securities markets.

it has taken place. The upstairs trading has been on the rise as a result of several factors, among them regulatory changes that permitted investment dealers to trade as principals and to internalise orders.

Consolidation of investment dealers and their willingness to commit capital to facilitate trade have improved the services offered. As trading moves away from the central order book of a traditional securities exchange, the exchange's ability to maintain sufficient liquidity is impaired. Block trades in the upstairs market account for the majority of the volume and value of the transactions on many securities markets. Although traditional exchanges offering bundled services may offer scale and liquidity advantages, there is a growing role for specialty, and niche player exchanges. It is unclear how demutualization will improve the competitive position of traditional exchanges against ATSs. However, it is unlikely that traditional securities exchange business models, offering more integrated services than ATSs, will become obsolete, so long as they remain competitive in terms of price, variety and quality of their services, and are financially sustainable.

While the securities exchange industry may evolve to a point where low cost or niche players realize even greater opportunities than today, full service securities exchanges believe integrated services will continue to play an important role in the industry. Consequently, securities exchanges will be using a more streamlined business model resulting from demutualization to invest in core and new trading modalities and technology, integrate market information and perhaps integrate the ATSs themselves into the traditional securities exchange model. They would also be able to restructure market support mechanisms for retail investors, and improve value propositions for listed firms by offering more services and maintaining liquidity. Lastly, securities exchanges would be able to enhance their global specialization strategy through strong brand management and by becoming more entrepreneurial organizations.

Access Talented Human Capital. With better governance structures and access to economic capital, securities exchanges are able to attract highly qualified and competent management professionals. With the induction of these professionals, the management practices and culture changes and the exchanges will be able to introduce new products and services in their markets.

Attracting Participation of Securities Investors. A demutualized securities exchange is more profit-oriented due to its stakeholders' accountability. However, in today's competitive environment, a securities exchange must be responsive to the needs of its many stakeholders, including participating organizations, listed firms, and institutional and retail investors. Securities exchanges may perceive a need to shift power within the exchange from one group of members to another and to afford institutional customers direct access to the different exchange facilities. Separating exchange membership from ownership may be a politically and economically feasible way to effect such a shift and resolve conflicts of interest between exchange members and between securities exchanges and their members.

Furthermore, a demutualized exchange can afford both institutional investors and retail investors the opportunity to become shareholders unlike a mutual structure where only broker-dealers may be members. The assets managed by institutional investors have grown significantly in recent years and the trading needs of institutional investors differ dramatically from those of retail investors. Particularly, institutional investors have a strong preference for anonymity when they are effecting large block trades. They also require much greater liquidity to accommodate block trading and place far more emphasis on negotiating the lowest price. A demutualized exchange will have greater flexibility to accommodate these needs of institutional investors as customers, and potentially, as owners.[76]

Reduce Control of Local Financial Intermediaries on the Exchange. The primary function of securities exchange demutualization is to reduce the control of (particularly local) intermediaries over the strategic positioning of the exchange. This is in recognition of the fact that securities exchanges operating in a competitive financial market must ultimately be able to reduce capital costs for a significant subset of firms, and raise investment returns for a significant subset of investors. For example, the growing competition among some of the American, Asian and European exchanges

---

76   See Toronto Stock Exchange: A Blueprint for Success, (8 October 1998).

makes it difficult for members to protect their intermediation franchise, and therefore makes them more open to governance reform and outside ownership.

Pass Good Market Regulation and Laws. It is difficult to pass rules that are good for the securities market overall if they will hurt certain subgroups of members, because the members have a vote and can block them. This is the same reason why, in general, a firm should not be owned entirely by its employees – after a while, the employees just pass rules to help themselves and not the larger firm or society. With demutualization, such practice becomes a thing of the past.

Investors' Need for Low-cost Faster Trading & Better Flexibility to Adapt New Situations. There is also the growing concern among the investor community, which has brought the need for demutualization to the fore front. The focus is obviously on the investor's side. The need for low-cost faster trading and better flexibility to adapt new situations has been cause of concerns for investors. Demutualization is expected to bring the international technology, good governance and as well as the global competition. In all the fronts investors are going to get a better bargain. The automation of the securities market and intermediaries shall enable investors to trade faster, more cheaply, and with an impressive and ever-expanding universe of mostly free financial information at their command. This will help expose foreign investors to listed firms at home and local investors to firms abroad.

The efficiencies created by these economies of scale can then be passed on to investors and securities issuers alike. Simultaneously, the enhanced governance structure shall protect their rights and privileges through the rule enforcement and other investor protection mechanisms. Since investors will remain as the primary customers, as in case of other corporate houses, the new structure will definitely envision to put in place all the mechanism to attract more of them and also to build a strong customer relationship base.

Therefore, keeping in place the present mutual structure of securities exchange, which is mutual in nature, the demand of the new economy would not be properly met. The broker-owned structure should be diffused by the infusion of professionals from the wider industry. In fact, it is increasingly believed that a demutualized securities exchange can adapt more quickly; raise more capital; attract better administrators; centralize control in a small, better-equipped groups; and as a result, deliver higher profits to its owners – the shareholders. With the objective of maximizing the value to the investors as well as to the members of the securities exchange through the investment in new technology and to meet the competitive pressures from the environment, it has become imperative that the demutualization process should be hastened in the developing markets with a strong footing. This is because demutualization can improve the efficiency and transparence in a securities exchange and improve the investors' confidence in the securities exchanges, which is paramount for their development. All in all, demutualization seems to be the cure for the challenges bedeviling the mutual exchanges, including, the fast eroding investors' perception worldwide, particularly in developing markets of Africa, Asia and South America.

Along with these reasons for demutualization, there are other benefits that demutualized securities exchanges stand to derive, which would be impossible if they remained mutual organizations. These other benefits, as further discussed, are so overwhelming that they are now considered part of the reasons why securities exchanges undergo demutualization.

Increase Access to Exchange Services. Demutualization also increases access to services of a securities exchange and removes excessive investment costs for fund holders. For instance, stockbrokers usually package non-trade related fees (research, computer systems and IPO access) into institutional traditional commissions often known as soft commissions or bundled commissions and pass them on to clients. With demutualization, fund holders can directly access such information without the use of the brokers. Such governance restructuring can also instill efficiency and better structures in securities exchanges and results in commercial gains for such exchanges.

Opening Up Exchange Trading Rights. Based on the for-profit motive, most demutualized securities exchanges have included provisions to admit new trading partners and permitted eligible applicants – new customers – unrestricted commercial access to the services of the exchange. Some securities exchanges, however, have adopted a moratorium period on the issuance of new trading rights. If share ownership were a requirement for trading membership, it would be relatively easy for existing exchange members to protect their market share by refusing to sell existing or issue any new shares, thus barring new entrants from joining the exchange. If new shares can only be issued to the active trading members, then the public, financial institutions, institutional investors and others would generally not be able to invest. The question of a broader ownership base of a securities exchange, as a public listed firm, is critical in situations where securities exchanges need to raise funds for future investments. Broader ownership would help avoid potentially large swings in the value based on the trading of a limited number of shares only. When share ownership is separated from the trading right, the question of the compensation of existing trading members arises especially since trading rights are granted freely to new members, while the existing exchange members had to acquire their trading memberships.

If existing shareholders continue to retain their shares, then they would enjoy the trading rights granted to the shareholders and there would be no need to compensate them for trading rights since for both the old and new shareholders, the economic value that the shares now represent would always be inclusive of the right to trade provided such rights have been granted by a securities exchange. For shares to have economic value there must be an expectation of dividends, at some point in the future. The introduction of a dividend policy, which does not exist in mutual exchanges, coupled with a listing of the shares, thus transfers the value of a securities exchange share ownership from the right to trade, to the right to receive dividends and trade the shares. These issues should, in theory, minimize the resistance to demutualization of a securities exchange by its stockbrokers. However, a moratorium on the granting of new trading rights has often been introduced to lessen the competitive impact on smaller stockbrokers and investment bankers.

Solve Inherent Exchange Mutual Structure Problems. Demutualization is expected to solve some of the inherent mutual structure problems bedeviling securities exchange by opening up trading rights, admitting new trading partners, and broadening ownership such that the public can invest in securities exchanges. The absence of these in mutual securities exchanges tends to breed poor governance structures. In a mutualized securities exchange, traders and brokers enjoy monopoly power through exclusive rights and access to trading systems, resulting in a protection of vested interests for traders. In a demutualized securities exchange, there is a vote per share and once incentives for equity stakes to nonmembers exist there is separation of powers. Decision making in such exchanges is on ownership structure not trades intermediation. Thus, demutualization induces better corporate governance systems. In addition, undue governmental influence in mutual securities exchanges in Africa is likely to be absent in demutualized exchanges since appointment of government officials become unnecessary due to the fact that a demutualized securities exchange is a private company.

The mutual securities exchange structures only function well if a securities exchange is a provider of trading services with limited competition and the interests of its broker-members are homogeneous. If greater competition exists and the interests of members diverge from one another and from those of the securities exchange, the mutual governance model ceases to function well. Consensus decision-making becomes slow and cumbersome as evident in various forms of cooperative societies, like in developing countries in Africa, where their activities are dominant. Such securities exchanges are unable to respond quickly and decisively to changes as well as other emerging issues in the market. The financial products and services offered by demutualized securities exchanges – a corporation that operates in a more customer-focused manner – is able to respond more easily and quickly to changes in the business environment and meet competitive challenges.

The demutualized corporate model enables exchange management to take actions that are in the best interests of customers and the securities exchange itself. Separation of ownership and trading privileges enables a securities exchange to achieve greater independence from its members with respect to its regulatory functions. The securities exchange owners' interests are aligned with those of the securities exchange itself, and seek to maximize the profits of their exchange. In a governance structure in which consensus need not necessarily be reached, owners are able to influence decision-making, and strategic decisions are made by management in a much more efficient manner. A major advantage of a demutualized structure versus a mutual or co-operative one is the requisite degree of transparency. Demutualized securities exchanges must account to their shareholders not only regarding the financial bottom line, but also regarding issues arising in corporate governance. In one of the later chapters, a section on implications for disclosure requirement is provided detailing an extract from the financial reports of some exchanges to depict how demutualized securities exchanges have to account to its stakeholders, and the extent to which they are upholding tenets of good corporate governance practices.

Improvements in Corporate Governance Practices. Traditionally, when securities exchanges are managed as mutual organizations, clubs and cooperatives of traders and brokers, they allow members exclusive rights of access to trading systems and platforms. Operating under this mutual structure, securities exchanges enjoyed quasi or full monopoly on trading and they derived profits from the intermediation of non-member transactions. Since members under the mutual structure were owners of the exchange, they imposed rights to trading and disallowed direct access to the trading floor to any outsiders. Stockbrokers could inadvertently resist changes if these entailed additional costs, loss of revenue or competitive threats. This resistance eventually impedes the ability of the firm to react quickly to a rapidly changing market environment. Also, in some developing countries if securities exchanges enjoy a legal or decreed national monopoly, government-appointed officials and stakeholder representatives are often represented on the board. While in the short-run such appointments may prove conducive to mitigating entrenched vested interests, in the long-run these can prove counter-productive leading to unhealthy government interference.

With the changing economics of automated auction trading and its easy access electronically, the economics of member-cum-trading floor based securities exchanges has lost its merit. As a result, it has generated pressures to replace the age-old reliance on one-member, one-vote and the committee-based decision structure where control is vested with the interest groups that have exclusive rights of intermediation at a securities exchange. Under demutualization, there is increased acceptance to the separation of ownership from membership that automatically provides trading rights. This segregation helps introduce effective corporate governance if there are accompanying improvements in the incentive structure[77], which allow securities exchanges to sell their equity stakes to non-members and outsiders. The decision making is then based on this new ownership structure, not on rights of intermediation, and there is an effective oversight of a governing board and a company structure to support it.

Upon demutualization, the economic ownership of a securities exchange is separated from trading membership. It is not appropriate that interest groups like trading members have exclusive authority over the decisions of a securities exchange. Some securities exchanges have granted less than fifty percent of the voting rights to the broker-members on the board of demutualized exchanges. To gradually decrease stockbroker influence on the board, securities exchanges have appointed independent directors – directors that are non-trading owners. The appointment of government appointed officials, a common feature of securities exchanges in developing economies, has been viewed as controversial given that a demutualized securities exchange is a private sector firm operating in a competitive environment. Where stockbroker influences are often daunting, the continued role of the representative(s) of the securities market regulator can support the transition of securities exchange till such time as the market regulation is changed to allow securities exchanges to operate in a fully competitive manner.

77　Steil, B. (2002) Changes in the Ownership and Governance of Securities Exchanges: Causes and Consequence. In Brookings-Wharton Papers on Financial Services. Washington D.C.: Brooking Institution Press.

Moreover, with an appropriate board representation, it is important that the management of a securities exchange is fully qualified and motivated to act not only in the best interests of the shareholders, but also to conduct the business in a prudent manner so as not to disrupt the orderly and fair trading in the securities markets. To ensure that this public interest is satisfied, *fit-and-proper* screening of the board and management, similar to tests put in place in the banking regulations of many jurisdictions, could be undertaken. Securities exchange management should be accountable to its board, which would determine management's appointment and remuneration, supervise the strategic direction and audit the financial and operational results, including risk management, and if needed, effect the removal of management. To ensure effective supervision and auditing of management, it would seem prudent to ensure that a majority of board members are truly independent directors. To remain competitive, a securities exchange must follow best international ethical practices and procedures in order to ensure that institutional investors do not shift their investments to other alternatives perceived to be fairer and more secure. Therefore, it is in the profit-motivated exchange's best interest to ensure fair and transparent practices; and good corporate governance needs to be an integral part of a securities exchange once it is driven by the profit motive.

Effecting Alliances, Mergers and Consolidations. When securities exchanges demutualize, it is usually a historic moment for them. They gain the financial and strategic strength to undertake acquisitions, mergers, and other strategic alliances. After being demutualized, most securities exchanges have revisited their commercial strategy to improve viability, enhance business prospects and increase their market share. Majority of the exchanges have opted to consolidate, merge and/or integrate their domestic markets, build alliances by establishing cross-border linkages with other securities exchanges within or outside the region, and merge with other securities exchanges globally. Greater emphasis has been largely to re-group businesses to broaden the markets, and to offer issuers and investors better distribution networks and improved liquidity.

A demutualized securities exchange is able to enter into both domestic, regional and continental alliances with other securities exchanges through equity swaps. Such alliances provide an opportunity for investments and cross-listings from other countries like the Gulf and the Middle East. There are also possibilities of future listing of international Islamic debt instruments on demutualized securities exchanges.

Improve Domestic and International Recognition. Demutualization leads to domestic and international recognition. A demutualized securities exchange is an open and transparent company. This helps improve the perception of securities exchanges and enhance confidence of domestic and international investors.

Improve Market Quality and Exchange Performance. A look at the potential sources of the reductions in spreads on demutualized securities exchanges shows that, consistent with the predictions of the laws of demand and supply, the increased order flow, market share, and increased listings following demutualization, contribute to the falling spreads. Interestingly, they have also found that demutualized securities exchanges that subsequently self-list by going public after demutualization experience incremental improvements in market quality.[78] In addition, the conversion of exchanges from member-owned not-for-profit to for-profit companies or demutualization improves stock liquidity, with positive relation achieved through the market development level and the exchange strategy channels. In fact, this positive relation is stronger for securities exchanges with higher operating performance and revenue diversification. Moreover, the competitive effects of demutualization exhibit asymmetric patterns on exchange market share. Furthermore, domestic order flow and the level of market development enhance the positive impact of exchange demutualization on the securities exchange market share.[79]

---

78 Abukari, K. & Otchere, I. (2020). Has stock exchange demutualization improved market quality? International evidence, Review of Quantitative Finance and Accounting, 55(9): DOI: 10.1007/s11156-019-00863-y.

79 OECD (2014). Privatisation and Demutualisation of MENA Stock Exchanges: To Be Or Not To Be? OECD Directorate for Financial and Enterprise Affairs.

In sum, demutualized securities exchanges become primed to move aggressively to capitalize on their strengths, especially for those with highly regarded proprietary technology that supports their equity, option and regulatory systems and their multiple licenses to trade stocks, options and futures – all are assets that they may later leverage with potential strategic partners. With the capital raised, they can also continue to invest in their technology and to manage their finances prudently, positioning themselves to face the future with confidence. With future financial strength, their internal growth and key assets, they can be looking to ally with strong, innovative third parties. The developed demutualized exchanges are capable of building on their reputation as the marketplace that delivers leading edge technology, multiple trading opportunities and product innovation at the lowest cost in the industry. Cases of mergers and acquisitions brought about by demutualization are presented in chapter on post demutualization of securities exchanges.

The demutualization plans provide the best opportunity for both members and seat owners to maximize their value. The goal of the demutualized structure is to streamline decision-making, provide a more flexible capital structure, and separate the regulatory functions from other businesses. This new structure provides securities exchanges with the ability to enter into strategic transactions by using their capital stock as a new form of currency, and enhances their ability to raise outside capital for technological innovation, and product development and other critical initiatives. Demutualization therefore is the first line of response in tackling critical issues faced by modern day securities exchanges in their pursuit of growth and development, financial sustainability good corporate governance and attainment of international standards.

The following issues presented in Table 1 are brought about by demutualization of securities exchange.

Table 1: Issues Addressed by Responding to Demutualization

Exchanges Growth & Development Issues	Key Benefits of Demutualization
Deficiencies and Inefficiency caused by mutualized ownership and management structures.	• More efficient and flexible funding obtained from local and foreign securities markets. • Exchanges are now profit-oriented thus focused to revenue maximization and costs reduction strategies. • Public duty culture is replaced by service provision culture. • Incentives to strive for operational efficiency. • Incentives to work towards competitive advantage.
Conflict of Interests in Decision Making Process.	• Separation of owners from managers. • Separation of owners from direct users or traders. • Specific clearly defined roles for both market regulators and market players.
Stiff competition Between Exchanges and ATS and ECNs.	• Ability to play a part and benefit from service deconstruction like through increase in trade volumes. • Flexibility in responding to competitive pressures particularly from new entrants like ATS, ECNs. • Structurally ready for fitting for global integration of capital markets especially equity markets
Stunted Growth and Limited Cooperation Market Opportunities.	• New structure enables effecting domestic and international mergers, joint ventures or other strategic alliances. • Broader access to growth and development finance. • Increasing liquidity and product diversification through cross-border cooperation or integration.

Lastly, securities exchanges are also aspiring to take advantage of growth opportunities. Securities exchange demutualization has the capability of completely changing their business framework of exchanges. A look at some demutualized exchanges reveals that it has opened the securities exchanges up for new global opportunities. It has also presented cross-sector opportunities, which may lead to a substantial growth of securities exchanges. Table 2 presents how demutualized exchanges can open themselves to such opportunities.

Table 2: Growth Opportunities for Demutualized Securities Exchanges

Areas	*Growth Opportunities*
Organic Growth	• The rise in new firm listings on securities exchange. • Striking alliance with technology firms to build a global order-routing interface to provide international investors with better access to the market. • Increased levels of trade in both equities and derivative instruments. • New financial product development like exchanges traded funds (ETF).
International Alliances	• Involvement in the Global Equity Market initiative with other exchanges. For instance, ASX has developed such initiatives with NYSE, Euronext, Hong Kong, Mexico, Sao Paulo, Tokyo and Toronto exchanges • Alliance with other exchanges to design, develop and establish an active electronic link between exchanges. For example, ASX has an alliance with Singapore Exchange for developing its active electronic system • Signing MOUs with other exchanges. For example, ASX has signed MOUs with Indonesia, Korea, Malaysia, Philippines, Singapore, Taiwan, Thailand, Tokyo & Hong Kong exchanges

Areas	*Growth Opportunities*
New Business Portfolio	• Entering into beneficial joint ventures. ASX, for example, has entered into a joint venture with Perpetual forming ASX Perpetual Regis tars- a share registry business • Acquiring stakes in investor relations group. ASX now owns 50 percent in such a firm going by the name, Orient Capital. • ASX has also acquired 15 percent of Bridge DFS that operates the IRESS Order System- an order routing network between Australian & New Zealand institutions and their brokers.

Challenges of Demutualization of Securities Exchanges

Many questions arise with demutualization of securities exchanges. For instance, where should the listed exchange stock be traded? On the exchange itself? How will the exchange police the trading of its own stock? Also, major companies can buy a lot of shares and then control the exchange and then decide to not police so closely the trading of its own shares on the exchange. Most of the problems relate to governance issues. I do not think all securities exchanges are likely to demutualize and self-list because most mutual exchanges – in spite of what you read in the media – work pretty well and not so many wants to take a chance on messing it up. Again, some demutualization exchanges such as Nasdaq have not done so well after demutualization.

The changes in the governance structure through demutualization are, therefore, not without challenges. While exchange demutualization may unlock capital and bring attendant benefits in terms of responsiveness to customers,[80] rewarding participants for usage and improved decision making, it does pose challenges in terms of governance, reconciliation and management of a wider range of interests and stakeholders. Thus

---

80 McDowall, B. (2004). IBC's 8th World Stock Exchange conference: Unity in diversity? http://www.it-director.com/business/content.php?cid=7486

demutualization is not in itself a long-term panacea. In some instances, the historical mutual structure was considered to be a better business model.[81]

Remember, most securities exchanges were originally founded by stockbrokers themselves in order to have premises and infrastructure where they could meet to do business in an organized manner, with secure and pre-determined rules for trading. Initially, this structure was quite basic as the first securities exchange was just four walls and could hardly be described as a business, much less a profitable one. Nobody except the interested parties – the brokers, and in some cases governments – was willing to invest the funds needed to organize infrastructure and pay running costs. Collusion amongst stockbrokers was rampant and price fixing was a common practice. Because brokers had different level of power and influence, such were exercised and determined certain decisions at the securities exchange. It was not uncommon, for instance for chairman of the exchange to issue different opinion from that of the influential stockbroker(s). Mutual securities exchange structure also gave the owners leeway for engaging in unethical practices. Cases of unauthorised trading on clients' securities were common as a result of self-regulation. This resulted in erosion of the integrity of the brokerage fraternity but also that of the securities exchange itself. So long as stockbrokers were earning their commissions, the need to modernize the trading system and develop the securities exchange was lacking.

Demutualized securities exchanges are very sensitive to the issues of transferability of shares, particularly in situations where the shares of a listed exchange are freely transferable. Secondly, demutualization neither ascertains better regulation nor does it reassure investors about the value of the risk. In addition, demutualized financial market infrastructure may encounter difficulties stemming from regulatory oversight when attempting to respond to new opportunities and threats. This is because regulatory oversight takes up an extensive period before the approval of new policies. Thus demutualization separates the regulatory and corporate authority of

---

81 This issue is addressed later in another section, where it is asserted that there were instances where non-profit mutual exchange structure was good in many respect.

a securities exchange, which creates a conflict of interest. Moreover, a new problem of conflict presents itself when a securities exchange attempts to self-list its own shares on itself. This type of conflict is clear in satisfying its own listing obligations. It can also create the problem of conflict between management and the exchange owners – the shareholders. Furthermore, demutualization poses difficulties in area pertaining to regulation and supervision, particularly in the non-liberalized market in Africa, such as in Ghana, among others. Also, other legal issues may also threaten the demutualization process given that certain jurisdictions, where the securities exchange relates to guaranteed limited company status requires reorganizing the demutualization procedure to alter members or seats into shares.

There are, therefore, potential problems which demutualization may bring about. One of such problems is the *divergence of interest between exchange shareholders and members*. What a shareholder wants and what a member wants is not the same thing. The loyalty of the new shareholders in a national securities exchange is questionable. Empirical research evidence on the effects of the loyalty of shareholders on the stock return volatility is limited. However, the pressure to maximize return for demutualised funds investors may have contributed to the current global financial turmoil by encouraging business decisions with higher risks.

Most of the problems are due to the *difficulty of changing rules that benefit society but hurt the members*. Recently, due to the increasing use of computers, the way trading is done has changed very rapidly. Now securities all over the world can be traded anywhere, so securities exchanges no longer have a monopoly on trading domestic securities. As a result, a local securities exchange has to compete with securities exchanges around the world. This new competition and the new and ever-changing methods of trading create a need for ever-changing rules and the modernization of trading infrastructure. Mutually owned securities exchanges have a relatively difficult time keeping up with these changes in a competitive environment. In the past, most securities exchanges were stand-alone entities and there was not much innovation in how trading was done – so there was little need to change the rules. Some securities exchanges demutualized, but were then taken over by securities exchanges from other jurisdictions.

As whether demutualization achieve anything that stringent regulatory control cannot in an exchange which already has a small board with near-50 percent non-stockbroker representation and independent management, it can be argued it do not. On the face value, a securities exchange can raise money, but cannot do all other things. Stringent regulatory control, outside representation, and independent management do about the same thing, besides raising money, and may in fact be less messy governance-wise. The real point is that a securities exchange holds a special place in society and is not just like any other corporation. As a result, it is probably true that its governance and ownership structure should not look like the average corporation. After all, corporations should be allowed to go bankrupt and fail – yet *having a securities exchange go bankrupt, fail, or be taken over in a hostile takeover would be pretty disruptive for a society.* Corporate governance in a demutualized ownership structure basically requires that the firm can go bankrupt, fail, or be taken over. This may not be the best structure for any important part of society. If the securities exchange can be demutualized, why not the military?

There is also the problem of devolving regulatory responsibilities to securities exchanges. Securities market regulators have been seduced by the familiar. The belief appears widespread among regulators that the traditional mutual structure of securities exchanges they regulate – exchanges which often pre-date by centuries any formal self-regulatory obligations imposed on them – is somehow more consistent with devolved self-regulatory obligations than a demutualized structure. There are no grounds for believing this. As has been discussed, mutualized exchanges appear no less prone to malpractice or commercial risk-taking, nor is there any logical reason why they should be.

This does not mean that market regulators do not need to revisit the self-regulatory obligations they impose on securities exchanges. On the contrary, the inevitability of increased inter-exchange competition, particularly from other markets, will only serve to intensify the conflicts which have always existed between the commercial interests of both exchange members and owners, on the one hand, and self-regulatory obligations on the other. The more such conflicts exist, the worse one can expect a securities exchange to be able both to compete and to regulate effectively.

There are certain regulations common to most developed markets which require at least the active cooperation of securities exchanges in order to enforce. The clearest one is perhaps restrictions on insider trading. At the very least, regulators will require an accurate and comprehensive audit trail of transactions in order to identify suspect trading activity. But insider trading regulation simply cannot be wholly privatized, since it is highly unlikely that any securities exchange would find that its regulator's definition of insider trading is consistent with that which it would apply if its goal were merely to maximize transaction revenues. In the US insider trading regulation, as practiced by the SEC, the regulation of insider trading cannot be justified on the grounds that it promotes the goals of efficiency, fairness, or market integrity. As the Supreme Court recognized in Chiarella and Dirks, the only conceivable justification for banning insider trading is that such trading involves the theft of valuable corporate property from its rightful owner. The attempts to justify insider trading regulation on other grounds simply reflect efforts by a farrago of special interest groups to obtain private advantage through the regulatory and legislative process.

This view may obviously not be universally shared, but the sheer diversity of views on the appropriate definition and effects of insider trading only goes to highlight the reason why it cannot be privatized: there is no compelling evidence that what market regulators, for example, chooses to define as insider trading has a negative effect on market efficiency or turnover. Indeed, it is more than plausible that market efficiency and turnover would be higher without such regulatory restrictions. A securities exchange is exceedingly unlikely, therefore, to adopt a regulator's highly idiosyncratic insider trading policy on its own volition. The best that the regulators can hope to accomplish is that a securities exchange will cooperate effectively in maintaining audit trails and reporting activity which most regulators, for good reasons or bad, do not like. The broad implication is that self-regulation is only effective as a substitute for statutory regulation where its objective happens to be consistent with a securities exchange's commercial interests, in which case, of course, it is unnecessary to impose it.

A further cost of devolving regulation down to officially designated domestic securities exchanges is implicit in the risk of stifling competition. The ECN operating in the US Nasdaq market have often complained that the regulatory fees they pay to the National Association of Securities Dealers (Nasd) are effectively used to subsidize the Nasdaq trading system, of which the Nasd is the dominant owner and which competes with ECN services. Self-regulatory obligations must not be devolved such that an incumbent market operator is effectively given regulatory control over its competitors, or potential competitors. The UK government acknowledged this when it removed from the London Stock Exchange its designation as the primary UK listing authority, transferring that power up to the Financial Services Authority.

In fact, *corporate governance seems to be crux of demutualization*. Despite of wide discussion on corporate governance in most of the forums still it is difficult to suggest a single definition. Because there are so many varying views on what corporate governance is as a definitive product, there is no globally applicable definition of corporate governance. The 1992 Cadbury Report simply described corporate governance as the system by which companies are directed and controlled. It can be confined to the Corporate Governance Tripod, that is, the relationship between shareholders, directors and management. An increasing number of definitions refer to the fact that many other groups have an interest in the company. It is an umbrella term that includes specific issues arising from interactions among senior management, shareholders, boards of directors, and other corporate stakeholders. It is the system by which business entities are monitored, managed and controlled. Additionally, some demutualized exchanges have preferred to remain as private companies. A question can be asked whether it is preferable for securities exchanges themselves to be listed. Now, if the stock of a securities exchange is not tradable, then why bother to demutualizing? Such exchanges would not derive benefits of demutualization.

Common Governance Models Adopted by Securities Exchanges

There are two journal-published formal mathematical models of securities exchange governance choice – the first by Hart and Moore (1996) and the second by Pirrong (2000). Although presented as general models, they each focus on highly idiosyncratic and simplified options for governance and characteristics of securities exchange members. This limits their applicability in terms of understanding the drivers of the current demutualization movement.

Hart and Moore (1996) analyzed the efficiency of a securities exchange run as a members' cooperative relative to that of a for-profit exchange with a single outside owner. Efficiency was defined in terms of the proximity of the price that would be set for a unit of securities exchange services under each structure to the cost of supplying it. Trader-members are presumed to differ only along the dimension of size, defined in terms of their demand for exchange services (for example, trading volumes). It is assumed that under the members' cooperative structure, profits will be distributed equally among all exchange members, and that members therefore face a trade-off between the desire for cheap trading and the desire for exchange profits. Given this model of the governance choice, the members' cooperative structure will be perfectly efficient (that is, price equals cost) where member – size is identical, and that the outside owner structure becomes relatively more efficient as the skewness of the member size distribution is increased - an illustration of the so-called median voter theorem.

In fact, the introduction of a competing securities exchange disciplines the pricing policy of the for-profit exchange, increasing its relative efficiency, while having no effect on the pricing policy of the members' cooperative. Thus, growing inter-exchange competition should have the effect of increasing the prevalence of for-profit securities exchanges. A different rendition of the governance choice problem yields very different results. Pirrong (2000) also examines the impact of member heterogeneity on governance structure, and concludes that it has the opposite effect:

more heterogeneity favours a not-for-profit structure, which Pirrong likens to the traditional members' cooperative exchange.

There are several reasons for the different outcomes of the two models. First, Hart and Moore (1996) and Pirrong (2000) define the governance choices very differently. Hart and Moore's version of the traditional members' cooperative exchange is one in which all profits are distributed equally among members, whereas Pirrong's version allows no distribution. Furthermore, Hart and Moore's version of the for-profit exchange separates ownership from membership entirely, whereas Pirrongs' version does not separate them at all: it merely allows distribution of profits to the member-owners. Confusingly, then, Pirrong's version of a for-profit securities exchange is consistent with Hart and Moore's version of a members' cooperative. Second, the source of member heterogeneity is different in the two models. Hart and Moore assume that members differ only in the quantity of securities exchange services – trading – they demand, whereas Pirrong assumes that they differ only along an efficiency dimension – that there are higher and lower cost brokerage services providers. Third, Pirrong's model, unlike Hart and Moore's, allows for securities exchange members to collude and defect from the exchange. He uses this feature to show that low-cost members can prevent high-cost members from extracting too much surplus from them by credibly threatening to form another securities exchange. As it is only under Pirrong's version of a for-profit exchange that such surplus expropriation is feasible, Pirrong asserts that member homogeneity leads to a for-profit structure, whereas sufficient heterogeneity allows low-cost members to enforce a not-for-profit structure, which, under his version of a not-for-profit exchange, limits expropriation.

These models are of strictly limited use in understanding the drivers of the actual trend towards demutualized, for-profit exchanges with – at least partial – non-member ownership. The results of Hart and Moore's modelling, for example, rely on the assumption that securities exchange policies are set wholly on the basis of majority voting of the members, which is implausible in an environment where competing trading venues can and do exist.

Larger securities exchange members will clearly have greater influence because of their ability to migrate their trading activity, which is generally the primary source of a securities exchange's revenue. However, Pirrong's modelling excludes the possibility of exchanges which are not wholly owned by members, and therefore fails entirely to capture the most important feature of the demutualization movement: the separation of ownership of a securities exchange from its membership. Hart and Moore's model argue that member-owners want both low securities exchange costs and high exchange profits, whereas outside owners only want high profits. This very different incentive structure can have a significant impact on exchange policies. Pirrong's version of a for-profit securities exchange is therefore much more similar to a traditional not-for-profit mutual than a contemporary for-profit exchange with a diversified shareholder base.

The closest real-world examples of Pirrong's for-profit exchange are Deutsche Börse and the Paris Bourse prior to their IPOs in 2001. These securities exchanges were legally for-profit corporate entities, but the owners and the members were virtually one and the same. The closest real-world example of Hart and Moore's for-profit exchange, however, is UK-based Tradepoint prior to its reincarnation as virt-x. A listed firm, Tradepoint did not even have what can meaningfully be called members: users paid almost entirely on a transaction basis.

One important dimension of the link between trading automation and securities exchange governance which Pirrong's focus on member heterogeneity does capture, however crudely, is the impact of automation on the role of specialized intermediaries such as the NYSE specialist, Amsterdam Hoekman, and German Kursmakler. These intermediaries act to promote the confluence of orders and trading activity in given securities on a trading floor, but are not necessary in an automated trading environment where a computer can fill this role. Thus, trading automation has the effect of eliminating specialized intermediary functions, thereby negating a traditionally important feature of the mutual structure: precluding changes in trading rules which enable the transfer of surplus from one group to another. This also explains the observed resistance of specialized intermediaries to demutualization, which is invariably associated with a decline in their voting rights and a shift to automated trading and disintermediation. Contrary to Pirrong, however, it is the high-cost intermediaries, those with skills specific to trading floors, which typically defend the traditional mutual status, as it is their skills which are rendered obsolete under automated trading.

The focus of both the models on trader heterogeneity as the dominant explanatory variable in the governance problem is an inevitable by-product of the standard modelling technique applied, which defines the problem in terms of competitors differing along one dimension only because it is mathematically tractable in such a form. However, it is clear that such heterogeneity is itself a product of the trading technology employed and, as has been explained earlier, the traditional not-for-profit mutual structure of a securities exchange is a direct corollary to traditional floor trading. What is missing in both is the causal relationship between trading technology and securities exchange governance. This alternative model of exchange governance choice might reasonably be labelled technological determinist, as the critical independent variable is clearly the state of trading structure technology. All pre-automation securities exchanges logically begin as cooperatives, and revisit this choice of status only after trading automation makes demutualization a viable alternative. Whether a securities exchange actually demutualizes is determined largely by the state of competition, which is itself very much dependent on the confines imposed by the regulatory regime. Nevertheless, there are some exchange which demutualize because it is fashionable to do so – a kind of herding mentality common to animals and human beings.

There are three demutualization models which have been adopted by securities exchanges globally. A number of securities exchanges have undergone demutualization process with Stockholm Stock Exchanges leading the way in 1993. In 1996, the Amsterdam Stock Exchange changed its governance structure from a mutual association to a public limited firm, which acts as a holding company owning the assets of the exchange. Former members, institutional investors and listed firms own the holding company's shares. Also in 1996, the Copenhagen Stock Exchange was converted from a semi-public institution into a limited company. Its share capital was issued in a ratio of 60-20-20 to its members, share issuers and bonds issuers. The Italian and Helsinki Stock Exchanges and many others, as has already been mentioned, have also been privatised with their shares being issued to brokerage firms, banks and other financial institutions.

According to the World Federation of Exchanges by the end of 2003, over 50 percent of its member exchanges were either listed or demutualized and accounted for 50 percent of world market capitalization, whereas government-owned exchanges accounted for 12 percent of the exchanges with only 2 percent of world market capitalization. The following is a discussion of the Australian Stock Exchange, the Toronto Stock Exchange and the Egyptian Exchange (former Cairo & Alexandria Stock Exchanges), which illustrate the three different demutualization models. The ASX went public; TSE remained private after demutualization, while Egyptian Exchange, Shenzhen Stock Exchanges (SZSE) and Shanghai Stock Exchanges (SHSE) are state-owned/semi-public entities, which opted in the meantime, to remain semi-private with both members and the government being its owners.

The first model is the one adopted by the *Australian Stock Exchange*. The Australian Stock Exchange was created as a result of the merger of six provincial exchanges in Australia. It demutualized in response to technological changes and increasing competition from abroad and from ATSs domestically. Furthermore, despite growing public share ownership and a bull market, the pre-demutualization securities exchange was prohibited from paying any profits or income to members and any surplus had to be applied toward promoting the objects of the securities exchange. In addition to developing new trading platforms and mechanisms, the securities exchange determined that it had to be more responsive to the needs of market users, particularly investors and issuers, and that to accomplish such a customer focus it was no longer appropriate for individual stockbrokers to control the securities exchange.[82]

---

82 Richard G. Humphry (1995) The Future Structure of Securities Markets, ASX Perspective, 4th Quarter.

On 13 October 1998, the Australian Stock Exchange converted to a public company. In order to provide for a mechanism by which to convert membership interests to shares, the Australian legislature enacted the Corporations Law Amendment Act in record time. The new legislation also expanded the regulatory and public interest responsibilities of securities exchanges as self-regulatory organizations as well as the exchange's accountability to the Australian Securities and Investments Commission (ASIC), separated stockbrokers' rights to trade on a securities exchange from shareholders' rights; imposed a 5 percent limit on shareholdings in the exchange, allowed a securities exchange to self-list on its own exchange, and provided for the supervision of any such self-listing by the market regulator. The exchange then demutualized and on 14 October 1998, and got listed on its own board. Listing on the same exchange poses some obvious regulatory issues. However, the Corporations Law Amendment Act offered some guidance in this respect.

The legislation requires that a securities exchange enact provisions to the satisfaction of the market regulator for dealing with conflicts of interest that might arise from the self-listing. More generally, the legislation requires that such a securities exchange enters into such arrangements with the regulator as may be required for the purpose of ensuring the integrity of trading in the securities of the exchange, which may include paying the regulator a fee for overseeing the exchange's listing. Overall, the regulator is designated to be the arbitrator for conflicts of interest arising out of a securities exchange's self-listed shares. However, it had been argued earlier elsewhere that this needs to be done by a more disinterested third party entity. Either way, the exchange remained self-regulating, even with respect to its self-listing. The securities exchange has since incorporated a subsidiary to essentially take over regulator's role with respect to listings on the exchange, including its own listing. Nevertheless, critics of the move remain unsure as to whether the subsidiary, ASX Supervisory Review Pty Ltd., is far enough removed to offer effective oversight.[83]

---

83   See will ASX strike right balance? *Australian Financial Review* (10 November 2000).

The second model is the one adopted by the *Toronto Stock Exchange*. For many years, Canada housed four major securities exchanges. These four securities exchanges were streamlined into three specialized markets in 1999, with the Toronto Stock Exchange (TSE) becoming the sole senior equity market. With its more focused business strategy, TSE was ready to demutualize on 1 April 2000 and became the Toronto Stock Exchange Inc. (TSE Inc.) – a for-profit corporation. Each member of the pre-demutualization exchange received 20 ordinary shares of TSE Inc. earlier per seat held. Each ordinary share carries one vote; however, the new corporation's by-laws prohibit any person or combination of persons acting jointly to beneficially own or control more than 5 percent of demutualized exchange without the prior approval of the Ontario Securities Commission. Members who received more than 5 percent by virtue of the demutualization conversion of seats to shares have been *grand-fathered* from the provisions, but are not allowed to exercise more than 5 percent of the votes outstanding without prior approval from the market regulator.

Subject to securities legislation, the shares became freely tradable after two years, but before then, board approval or the approval of a majority of the shareholders of the demutualized exchange is required for their transfer. The distribution of pre-demutualization exchange's accrued surplus immediately before its continuance date was a serious issue in structuring the demutualization. It was decided that the surplus would be internally restricted and would remain undistributed to shareholders until winding up. The effect of the chosen demutualization structure at the exchange is that shares of TSE Inc. are held by brokerage firms that were formerly members of the pre-demutualization exchange. New participating organizations are not required to own shares in TSE Inc. However, access to trading does not entitle participating institutions to participate in the ownership or governance of the securities exchange. The demutualized exchange remains privately held although it proposed a public offering, which coincided with the expiry of the restricted transfer period, although there have been discussions regarding waiving the restricted period.[84] The regulator thereafter approved the IPO of TSX Group Inc. (TSX Group), a new holding company for TSX Inc. on April 3, 2000, as order further amended on January 29, 2002 and on September 3, 2002.

The third model is the one adopted in *Privatisation of Egyptian Exchange*. In the 1990's, the Egyptian government's restructuring and economic reform program resulted in the revival of the Egyptian securities market, and a major change in the organization structure of the Cairo and Alexandria Stock Exchanges (CASE) took place in January 1997 with the election of a new board of directors and the establishment of a number of board committees. In 1997, the exchange embarked on an aggressive modernization program, resulting in a robust and modern technology, employing a new state-of-the-art trading system, reforming the regulatory framework by implementing new listing and membership rules that are at par with global standards, promoting corporate governance and investor relations, ensuring information dissemination via publications, installing a bilingual web site and web-enabled disclosure system; and the establishment of Egypt Information Dissemination Co. to increase market transparency.[85] On 6 March 1997, the Presidential Decree No. 51/1997 re-defined the legal structure of the two exchanges and accordingly the CASE became one entity the Egyptian Exchange with two locations: Cairo and Alexandria. Both locations are managed by one Chairman and the same Board of Directors.

The second phase of the modernization program necessitated that CASE change its legal and governance structure and become privatised by converting from a fully government owned entity to a quasi-private entity. These changes have led to several crucial and compelling challenges that are facing the exchange. First, the current structure of Egyptian as a government-owned and a Self-Regulatory Organization is very rare since most securities exchanges in the world are either member-owned, member-controlled, publicly owned, or listed, including exchanges in the

---

84   Marr, G. (2001). TSE to Go Public in Next 6 to 12 Months, *National Post*, 30 May 2001.

85   See CASE (2003).

Middle East North Africa (MENA) region[86] by 2014 such as Casablanca, Damascus, Tunis and Kuwait are all fully state owned exchanges. Whereas, Amman and Iran are mutualized exchanges, Beirut, Palestine, and Abu Dhabi, Algeria, Bahrain, Doha, Muscat Exchanges are run as quasi-private companies, by their members. In addition, exchanges in the region such as Istanbul and Tehran have already started their privatisation exercises.

The EGX is the only registered stock exchange in Egypt, operating as a quasi-self-regulatory, fully government owned and unincorporated entity. The exchange is overseen by the Egyptian Financial Supervisory Authority (EFSA), established in 2009 as a result of the merger of the CMA with other financial regulators. The exchange is not very integrated horizontally but has a small stake in Misr for Central Clearing, Depository and Registry, which acts as a central depository and registry system in Egypt.

Therefore, the current structure of the Egyptian Exchange puts it in a very weak and uncompetitive position, when compared to, other world exchanges. Furthermore, the forces of change including technology, institutionalization, globalization and deregulation are affecting securities exchanges worldwide. The cumulative effect of these developments and trends pose fundamental challenges and threats to the continuance of the classical securities exchanges. Thus the survival of exchanges, including Egyptian Exchange, depends on how they transform their strategy to fit into the twenty first century. To be truly successful, securities exchanges must provide a fast, fair, transparent and low cost platform for investors to receive and act on information, companies to raise funds at attractive costs and members to trade efficiently. While structurally a SRO, Egyptian Exchange is a quasi-governmental body under the supervision of CMA. The board includes eleven members. The Chairman is appointed by the government/Prime Minister for a three-year period that is renewable. Regarding, the composition of the board of directors, 60 percent of the board members are elected from market participants (brokerage firms, fund management companies, investment banks etcetera), and the remaining 40 percent are appointed by the following entities, one from the

---

86　OECD (2014). Privatisation and Demutualisation of MENA Stock Exchanges: To Be Or Not To Be? OECD Directorate for Financial and Enterprise Affairs.

CMA, one from the Central Bank of Egypt and two from the Syndicate of banks. There are also three appointed non-voting members. The CMA must approve exchange's board decisions. Earlier the two exchanges – making up Egyptian Exchange – are governed by the same listing, trading and brokerage rules. The exchange is currently a semi-public juristic entity, as it is owned by the government. This structure is very distinct from the fully public or private structures of the above two models of *Australian Stock Exchange* or *Toronto Stock Exchange* as already described.

However, Egyptian Exchange has to fully privatise, demutualize and self-list in order to remain an important player in the MENA region, given the risk that other Arab exchanges such as Dubai, Jordan, Saudi Arabia, Qatar, etcetera. are all have taken progressive steps with regard to their infrastructure, technology, rules and regulations, services etcetera, with the main aim of competing and becoming financial centres in the region. Thus, fully demutualizing the Egyptian Exchange means that new shareholders would inject the necessary capital required to introduce new products and services, recruit qualified staff, compete on the always-expensive technology level etc. Furthermore, having private shareholders ensures that its management responds and adapts quickly to a fast-changing marketplace and are more customer-driven. Finally, becoming private gives leverage to the value of the Egyptian Exchange itself as a brand and as a business entity in ways other than trading; and later facilitates mergers/alliances with other exchanges. In the meantime, the exchange has chosen to be corporatized but remain fully owned by the government. Then, gradually the government will start selling its equity stake in CASE to financial institutions by way of private placement.

Demutualized Securities Exchanges

Demutualization as a concept is neither a very new concept nor very sophisticated. For instance, from 1802 until 1948 the LSE was operated on a for-profit basis and paid large dividends to its members.[87] Until the early

---

87   Donnan, F. (1999) Self-regulation and the Demutualization of the Australian Stock Exchange. *Australian Journal of Corporate Law*, 10: 1-33.

1990s, most financial exchanges were non-profit, mutual organizations owned by their members. Since then, the appropriateness of the mutual structure has been questioned and the first securities exchange in the world to change its governance structure was the Stockholm Stock Exchange in 1993. Several other securities exchanges have followed the footsteps of the Stockholm Stock exchange. In December 1998, the Securities and Exchange Commission (SEC) in the United States determined that a securities exchange could be registered and operated on a for-profit basis.[88]

The World Federation of Exchanges (WFE), formerly known as the *Federation Internationale des Bourses de Valeurs (FIBV)* – or International Federation of Stock Exchanges – is the trade association of publicly regulated stock, futures, and options exchanges, as well as central counterparties. The WFE is therefore the global industry association for exchanges and clearing houses. The WFE exists to serve its members – full members and affiliate members. The federation represent about 95 percent of the world market capitalization. At the beginning of 2023, the federation represented more than 250 exchanges and central counterparties of all sizes globally. The federation therefore boasts of strong membership of 250 market infrastructure providers housing 59,400 listed firms with USD122.94 trillion equities market capitalization.

The number of WFE exchanges that have privatised or listed has been increasing since the Stockholm Stock Exchange demutualized in 1993. A look at the 1999 WFE survey shows that about 22 percent of the 49 member securities exchanges responding indicated that they were demutualized, whereas perusing their documents online, only nine could be identified – plus two derivatives exchanges and never-mutualized Tradepoint – at that time. This discrepancy is consistent with an observed general preference among securities exchanges to be viewed as demutualized. A remarkable 79 percent of mutualized exchanges surveyed by BTA Consulting (2001) claimed that they would demutualize within two years, although the survey does not reveal the number of securities exchanges polled. The survey also

---

88 Securities Exchange Act Release No. 40760 63, Fed. Reg. 70844 (8 December 1998); at
    70848, 70883 (22 December 1998).

found that 49 percent of respondents indicated that they were organized as limited companies, but not demutualized; 15 percent were organized as mutual associations; and 13 percent were effectively state-controlled institutions. About 54 percent of respondents indicated that they were for-profit entities, up from 38 percent a year earlier. This included 57 percent of the limited companies and 14 percent of the mutual securities exchanges. In addition, about 78 percent of the securities exchanges surveyed at the October 2000 WFE conference said that they either had approval to demutualize or were actively considering demutualization, with several other exchanges already having stated the process.

Then Australian Stock Exchange became one of the first securities exchanges to conduct a public offering and become a listed company. The Toronto Stock Exchange demutualized in 2000, and its owner, the TSX Group, went public in 2002. Similarly, the major European exchanges, including the London Stock Exchange, the Deutsche Börse, and Euronext are now all public companies. In Asia, both the Hong Kong and Singapore exchanges are listed companies. In fact, the Tokyo Stock Exchange remains the only significant large securities exchange that has not listed its shares – although it did demutualize in 2001.

In May 2000, the Pacific Exchange (PCX) became the first securities exchange in the USA to demutualize part of its business. Also, the CME became the first financial exchange to demutualize in 2000, converting its membership interests into shares of common stock in the Chicago Mercantile Exchange Inc. that can trade separately from exchange trading privileges. The CME later conducted an IPO in 2003 and listed on the New York Stock Exchange. By early 2003, more than fifty percent of WFE members were for profit-organizations and eighty percent of the remaining exchanges planning to demutualize by 2005.[89] The restructuring of the Chicago Board of Trade (CBOT), which included demutualization into a for-profit, stock based holding company, was approved and an IPO was conducted in October 2005. By this time, about 52 percent of the WFE market capitalization was accounted for by demutualized exchanges.

---

89 See BCG (2003) Worldwide Exchanges Survey, Boston Consulting Group.

In Asia, demutualized securities exchanges including the Tokyo Stock Exchange now account for 76 percent of the region's market capitalization.

Based on WFE annual member survey of 2005 about 70 percent of the responding exchanges were already managed as for-profit entities. The proportion of this type of government structure was most dominant in the European-African-Middle Eastern (EAME) region, reaching almost 80 percent. The data shows that listed securities exchanges represented around 50 percent of total revenues and tended to outperform industry averages on financial ratios. Combining the proportions of both listed (49%) and demutualized (20%) exchanges they account for 69 percent of total revenues. Overall, 73 percent of responding exchanges operated on for-profit basis against 63 percent in 2000, and only 38 percent in 1998. These figures, however, may not add up with the situation on the ground since some exchanges may report they have demutualized just for public relations in such meetings even when in essence, they have not. In terms of operation cost, the data shows similar, but slightly lower proportions, with 43 percent of total cost occurring for listed exchanges, 16 percent demutualized, 14 percent associations, 27 percent others.

Though hatched-up little late, similar exercises have also been started in Africa. In Africa, the Johannesburg Stock Exchange was the first exchange to demutualize in 2005 and self-listing in 2006, while in Asia, the Singapore Stock exchange led the path to demutualization. In 2005 the securities exchanges of Brazil, India, Sri Lanka, Pakistan, the Philippines, and announced plans to demutualize and list their shares. The NSE then followed by demutualizing in 2010 and self-listing in 2014, with Uganda Securities Exchange completing its demutualization in 2017.

The 2018 WFE survey revealed that majority of exchanges had already undergone the process of demutualization. Almost 71 percent of the global securities market capitalization is now on publicly listed exchanges (94% America, 70% Europe/Middle East/Africa, 26% Asia/Pacific). Securities exchanges that have demutualized but not listed their shares account for an additional 19 percent (1% America, 19% Europe/Middle East/Africa, 55% Asia/Pacific). The dominance of listed exchanges is widespread across the Americas and Europe. In Asia there were only 26 percent demutualized and listed exchanges, but the total proportion of demutualized securities exchanges account for 98 percent. The remaining mutual exchanges accounted for 11 percent globally (5% America, 14% Europe/Middle East/Africa, 19% Asia/Oceania).

From the June 2020 World Federation of Exchanges survey of its 70 member exchanges which by region are located in Americas (15%), Europe/Middle East/Africa (46%), and Asian/Pacific (39%). By legal status, five (5) percent of exchanges were associations and mutual, 10 percent had demutualized, seven (7) percent were private limited companies, 51 percent were publicly listed companies, 27 percent were others. In terms of total revenue by profit focus, 17 percent of the surveyed exchanges were not-for-profit, while 83 percent were for-profit. A look at exchange revenue by legal status, seven (7) percent of surveyed exchanges were associations and mutual, three (3) percent were demutualized, one (1) percent were private limited companies, while 77 percent were publicly listed exchanges. The experiences in Nairobi and Kampala based exchange were then replicated resulting in Botswana and Nigeria securities exchanges completing their demutualization processes in 2018 and 2020, respectively. The Egyptian Exchange just privatised and remained member - and, to some extent, government-owned. Concerns for corporate governance in Africa in the last decade have also raised the need for exchange demutualization, with a number of African securities exchange having prepared detailed plans for demutualization, which are expected to be finalized by 2025.

A look at the 70 largest securities exchanges that report to the World Federation of Exchanges it is clear that the number of securities exchanges that are organized as mutuals, or are state-controlled, decreased substantially to only one (1) percent. In the same time period, the number of demutualized exchanges has significantly increased and about 80 percent of them have self-listed. Therefore, by beginning of 2021 all the major exchanges have demutualized and become public companies shows the necessity to have a structure that allows the exchange to respond to the challenges in the industry. It should be noted that almost all the major North American securities exchanges have already demutualized.

It can be concluded that over the last decade, the securities exchange industry has witnessed a wave of demutualization shifting ownership in exchanges from members and other insiders to outside investors. The demutualization of a securities exchange is a complex process that gradually takes it from being a mutual society to being a listed company. Over the course of this process fungibility of ownership increases while conflicts of interest among owners diminish. This phenomenon has been pioneered in Europe with Stockholmsborsen becoming the first for-profit exchange in 1993 and listing in 1998, and in Africa with Johannesburg Stock Exchange in 2005 and listing in 2006. Over the past decade more than forty-eight percent of the world's largest exchanges have demutualized and listed their shares publicly.

Today, demutualized exchanges control more than 80 percent of the global market for equity transactions. The foregoing demonstrates the difficulty with which this process is accomplished given the diverse interests of the parties involved. In Africa, as at June 2023 only seven (7) securities exchanges amongst the twenty-nine (29) members of the African Securities Exchanges Association (ASEA) were demutualized.

Table 3 provides a summary of recent demutualization of securities exchanges. By now, this list may have grown longer given the rapidity with which securities exchanges are restructuring their ownership and management structures.

Table 3: Demutualized and Privatized Securities Exchanges

Securities Exchange	*Year*	*Securities Exchange*	*Year*
Stockholm Stock Exchange	1993	Chicago Mercantile Exchange*	2002
OMX Group	1993	International Securities Exchange	2002
National Exchange of India	1993	Budapest Stock Exchange	2005

Securities Exchange	Year	Securities Exchange	Year
Tradepoint/Virt-x	1995[90]	SWX Zurich (Swiss Exchanges)	2002
Helsinki Stock Exchange	1995	New Zealand Stock Exchange	2003
Copenhagen Stock Exchange	1996	Bursa Malaysia Bhd	2004
Amsterdam Exchanges	1997	Philadelphia Stock Exchange[91]	2004
Borsa Italiana SpA	1997	Bombay Stock Exchange	2005
Australian Stock Exchange	1998	InterContinental Exchange*	2005
Vienna Stock Exchange	1998	Chicago Board of Trade*	2005
Iceland Stock Exchange	1999	New York Stock Exchange	2006
Simex	1999	Johannesburg Stock Exchange	2006
Singapore Stock Exchange	1999	Bond Exchange of South Africa*	2007
Hellenic Stock Exchanges	1999	Ludhiana Stock Exchange	2007
Athens Stock Exchange	1999	Bolivia Stock Exchange	2007
Stock Exchange of Singapore	1999	Caracas Stock Exchange	2007
LIFE*	1999	Bovespa Stock Exchange	2007
Pacific Exchange	2000	Sao Paulo Stock Exchange	2007
Hong Kong Stock Exchange	2000	Santiago Stock Exchange	2008
Toronto Stock Exchange	2000	Lima Stock Exchange	2008
London Stock Exchange	2000	Elsavador Stock Exchange	2008
Deutsche Börse	2000	Panama Stock Exchange	2008
Euronext	2000	Colombia Stock Exchange	2008
Sydney Futures Exchange*	2000	Lahore Stock Exchange	2008
BME Spanish Exchange	2000	Islamabad Stock Exchange	2008
New York Mercantile Exchange*	2000	Karachi Stock Exchange	2008

---

90   Never mutualized

91   PHLX became the first floor-based USA stock exchange to demutualize.

Securities Exchange	Year	Securities Exchange	Year
Oslo Exchanges	2001	Mexican (BMV) Stock Exchange	2008
Philippine Stock Exchange	2001	Nairobi Stock Exchange	2014
Nasdaq Stock Market	2001	Dar es Salaam Stock Exchange	2016
Tokyo Stock Exchange	2001	Uganda Securities Exchange	2017
Philippines Stock Exchange	2001	Botswana Stock Exchange	2018
Osaka Stock Exchange	2001	Nigerian Stock Exchange	2021

Source: Securities Exchanges' Websites, and WFE Website.

* Derivative exchanges

There have been many challenges for many securities exchanges in reconciling the powerful interests of floor traders and customers' changing demands. Their management recognizes the inherent logic in electronic trading as a means of keeping costs down, yet they still must satisfy the wishes of their members, who have paid handsome fees to trade in the pits and who fear that any move towards electronic trading could drive them to extinction. In USA, Nasdaq has been facing the threat of *disintermediation* posed by ECNs and ATS. Since 1997 ECNs like Instinet, Island, and Archipelago have provided trading platforms that can match customer orders anonymously. Such systems were developed by and for institutional investors to enable trading among themselves without the interference of middlemen. For this reason, Island had to successfully reach out to obtain retail order flow. The ECNs have handling more than 52 percent of the trading volume in Nasdaq securities.

However, Nasdaq's introduction of SuperMontage – a central limit order book – has provided it with some of the same benefits as the ECNs, and to reclaim the market share from them. ECNs have not been a major factor in Europe because most securities exchanges in Europe are electronic limit order books. And even the ECNs are not immune to industry-wide developments. The recent announcement of a merger between Archipelago and RediBook, and between Instinet and Island, suggests the beginning of a trend toward consolidation. In particular, the merger between Archipelago and rival RediBook, combines the second-and fourth-largest electronic stock trading systems and now poses a bigger potential threat to the Nasdaq Stock Market and the New York Stock Exchange.

Chapter Summary

Demutualization is the conversion of a mutual, member-owned securities exchange into a for-profit share-owned limited company. Forces such are globalization, consolidation, competition, advances in technology are responsible for the rapid restructuring of the exchange structures. In this chapter, the reason for demutualization were discussed and include the need to improve the governance structure, raise new capital for trading infrastructure development, unlocking members' equity values, capture global opportunities, countering competition and removing tension among exchange members.

It was mentioned that demutualization is one of the components of a securities exchange gearing itself up for survival in the face of the frantically paced globalization. In some circumstances domestic securities exchange reorganization like in Australia and Canada is a precursor to demutualization. Securities exchanges must get things in shape domestically as part of steeling themselves for a more global focus. Shareholder-owned market-oriented corporations are more capable of rapid change, allowing for the implementation of various steps necessary to become and stay competitive. To be competitive, securities exchanges must be transparent, fair and efficient. In addition, demutualization may facilitate the changes necessary to improve standards of self-regulation and increase investor confidence.

However, demutualization is not necessarily a panacea for poor self-regulation by an existing securities exchange. Unless the new owners of a demutualized exchange are committed to consistent and effective self-regulation, the regulatory benefits of demutualization are likely to be illusory. Thus, it may not be the whole cure to all of a securities exchange problems. Although a lot of benefits have been mentioned as accompanying demutualization, major conflicts have also been reported as shall be discussed in the next chapters. There is nothing in this world that only promises heavens, with no potential problems. In fact, as experiences are emerging, many problems will come to the fore. It is just a matter of time before we start seeing the reality of securities exchange demutualization. But all in all, so far, the benefits outweigh the problems.

Chapter Four

CHANGING SECURITIES EXCHANGE OWNERSHIP AND MANAGEMENT STRUCTURES

Introduction

This chapter discusses the processes involved in demutualization, particularly, focussing on experiences from different jurisdictions. In discussing these experiences, attention is placed on the reasons regarding why securities exchanges have demutualized, and how seats are transformed into shares. Traditionally, securities and commodities exchanges operated in the form of non-profit mutual or membership organizations. To the extent that market power was not curtailed by competition or regulation, mutual governance gave specialist or market-maker members of a securities exchange control of the price, quality and a range of services produced by the exchange. Securities exchange profits were returned to members in the form of lower access fees or trading profits. Also, securities exchanges operated as self-regulatory organizations to enforce discipline upon members. Initially, this discipline included the fixing of trading commission rates.

Nowadays, some securities exchanges have been transformed into for-profit shareholder-owned companies and many more are considering such demutualization. Some demutualized exchanges have become public firms and are listed on their own or other listing boards. Others have remained privately held firms but intend to go public in the future. In many countries securities exchanges were created by state decrees. They were organized as membership organizations from loosely connected traders who met in coffee houses or street corners. Demutualization of securities exchanges is, in fact, a response to global competition, technological innovation and other factors, as already discussed earlier, that are restructuring the securities markets. When a securities exchange changes from a mutual membership organization to a for-profit stock entity, its corporate governance is transformed and it is in a better position to raise the new capital needed for expansion and technological improvement.

The process of such transformation requires the approval of an exchange's membership and the market regulator, thus the process of turning seats into shares is complicated. Demutualization without a public offering generally is a transitional phase on the road to a securities exchange becoming a publicly owned and traded corporation. Nevertheless, because of the key role that securities exchanges play in a capitalist economy with regard to capital formation, price discovery and allocation of capital, exchanges may not develop into ordinary public corporations.

Process of Demutualization of Securities Exchanges

Faced by the trends discussed in the previous chapter, securities exchanges are responding to these forces in many ways, the most important being demutualization. They are, therefore, responding by enhancing their trading infrastructure and through reorganization for market growth and development. Thus, in a plan to undertake demutualization, the securities exchange leadership must ensure that such endeavour addresses the need to access global growth opportunities through expanding its business portfolios through market integration through mergers and other forms of strategic alliances.[92]

Table 4 below[93] depicts some of these issues and stresses one fact, that demutualization is the first line of response in addressing the most critical issues currently faced by securities exchanges globally.

---

92 Onyuma, S. O., Shem, A. O & Okumu, A. N. (2007) Reorganizing the Ownership and Management Structure of Stock Exchanges in Africa. *African Journal of Business & Economics*, 2(1):60-85.

93 Adapted from Boston Consultative Group (2003) Key Learning Related to the Demutualization of Stock Exchanges. Conference Paper, Instanbul, April 10th, Boston Consulting Group.

Table 4: Objectives and Phases of Demutualization of Securities Exchange

<table>
<tr>
<td>Goal</td>
<td colspan="2">
<ul>
<li>Improve attractiveness of market to domestic issuers and foreign investors.</li>
<li>Position better for inevitable integration and consolidation of exchanges.</li>
<li>Develop national assets and investment base.</li>
<li>Promote the growth of the financial sector especially the capital markets.</li>
</ul>
</td>
</tr>
<tr>
<td></td>
<td colspan="2" align="center">⬇   ⬇</td>
</tr>
<tr>
<td></td>
<td colspan="2">Demutualization</td>
</tr>
<tr>
<td>Phases</td>
<td colspan="2">
<ul>
<li>Separate ownership from management.</li>
<li>Separate trading rights from ownership rights.</li>
<li>Raise finance to be used to improve strategic positioning.</li>
<li>Promote flexibility to rapidly respond to competitive pressures.</li>
<li>Facilitate alliances with other exchanges and financial intermediaries.</li>
</ul>
</td>
</tr>
<tr>
<td></td>
<td colspan="2" align="center">⬇   ⬇</td>
</tr>
<tr>
<td colspan="1">
Global/Foreign Alliances
Obtain access to new products.
Increase liquidity in existing Portfolios.
Increase attractiveness as a gateway to other markets and between equity markets.
</td>
<td align="center">⬌</td>
<td>
Integrating/Merging
Acquire trading, depository technology.
Reduce system and market development risks, costs.
Cost reduction through economies of scale.
Cost reduction through economies of scope.
</td>
</tr>
</table>

In chapter 3, it was noted that the primary driver for demutualization has been to meet competition from other exchanges, including non-traditional trading markets such as ATS or ECNs. This competition has put pressure on trading profits at a time when trading volumes have increased, but technology has made trading more efficient. In order to compete with ECNs, traditional securities exchanges have had to better align their governance and business strategies to satisfy institutional and retail customers rather than the short term interests of their members.

One aspect of this realignment has been to give clearing members more influence than trading members. Securities exchanges have identified various reasons for their demutualization initiatives, and these statements are informative. The Chicago Mercantile Exchanges (CME) and PCX expressed themselves and identified objectives of their demutualization as to improve the governance and managerial structure, creating a catalyst for pursuing new business strategy, to improve the financial decision-making model, unlock members' equity values, and provide a signal and a currency for working with strategic partners.

Critical Issues to Consider in a Successful Demutualization Process
There are important issues that should be considered in the process of demutualization. This includes having inward looking assessment, strategies, operations, tactics and rewarding members by providing them with trading rights as was before demutualization. Additionally, for a success demutualization process, it is crucial to make a demutualization strategic plan beforehand. There is no single right path to follow since there still lack a rule-of-thumb for demutualization, though the lessons being learnt can be utilized by theorists and practitioners in designing a right path. However, the particular circumstances need to be taken into account before making any decision to demutualize. Irrespective of the path chosen, the following should at least be addressed if the demutualization of a securities exchange is to be successful.

Strategies
- A detailed three-five-year strategic plan and vision for the exchanges.
- A well stated and clearly defined objectives of reorganization and restructuring.

- Corporate structure must be critically considered. Possible structures may include private firm, public company listed on its own exchange, subsidiary of a publicly traded holding company. Consider also the method of listing – a private placement of members or an IPO.
- Equity allocation or ownership structure should be addressed. For instance, which entities and how much shares should they receive. Should there be limits on shareholding limits, if so, how much?
- Management restructuring needs to be considered. Critical issues include board representation, voting rights, management selection processes, their duties and rights, and methods of deciding on their remuneration.
- Qualifications of board members, their tenure, and number of executive and non-executive directors must be considered

Operations

- State the structure, role and the operating environment of the regulatory bodies.
- Possible overlap between external regulation and self-regulation. Mechanisms for dealing with conflict of interest between exchange members, as well as market regulators.
- Consider trading rights policy, for instance, who possess trading rights, and should there be any restrictions on transfer, etcetera?
- Design voting rights policy, for instance, who are eligible to vote, and what is the voting method; is it through one-man-one vote or based on number of shares held. Is proxy voting allowed?
- Retention policy must be formulated. What is the reserve distribution strategy to be followed, amount of reserves to be kept vs. distributed to owners? What is the target optimal capital structure? Does such a structure provide potential growth? Opportunities and investment requirements for the demutualized organization? Existence of flexibility and rights of management as well as shareholders.

Tactics

- A detailed stage by stage process of demutualization must be designed.
- Set also the duration of the demutualization process. Is the time frame for each stage short, appropriate or too long?
- Ensure there is right timing of the process. Is it the right time to demutualize? Are members and other stakeholders ready for the reorganization? Can the existing financial and management system contain the process?
- Assess if there is enough funding to oversee the process. Is finance to come from internal or external sources, and what is the cost?
- Put in place competent technical staff required for the process. Can the exchange afford to outsource such individuals and institutions, and at what cost?

Inward Looking Assessment. To be successful in the process, the planners must explore all advantages and disadvantages of the demutualization plan. They should narrow down to the dominant objectives and drawbacks. Demutualization should only be considered if the dominant objectives outweigh the drawbacks. Issues to consider are the required finance, systems, technology, the members' orientation, customer demand, and the challenges relating to members' resentment, regulation framework, and other conflicts of interest that are likely to emerge.

Provision of Rights to Members. Pursuant to demutualization plans, members are given trading rights that generally are coextensive with the rights held before demutualization. In addition, members and outsiders are given the opportunity to purchase capital shares. The complexity of any exchange's demutualization depends in part on how complex its membership structure was before demutualization, and what objectives the demutualization is designed to achieve. At the commodity exchanges, for example, different trading rights exist for different contracts. At some exchanges many seats are leased, and there are different economic interests between lessors, lessees and other members. For instance, the demutualization of Nasdaq and PCX, among a few others accomplished a separation of trading facilities and member self-regulation.

Sequential Demutualization Path to Follow

The process of demutualization should begin with the securities market regulations being amended to facilitate corporatization and demutualization. This should provide for the segregation of ownership and management from the trading rights of the members, restriction on voting rights of shareholders also the trading members, composition of the governing board, utilization of assets and reserves. The need for securities markets legal reform is to legally facilitate the conversion of the securities exchange into company form of organization, limited by shares. Further, this is to be followed by the reorganization of other regional exchanges, if any, through mergers. The handicaps in the process have to be removed through necessary legal amendments of income tax provisions with respect to the transfer of past profits to the new entity – particularly when the *not-for-profit* character is to be changed. Provisions in the tax laws must be addressed to exempt from stamp duty and sales tax, the transfer of the assets from the mutual securities exchanges and the issuance of shares by the new entity.

In executing a plan for demutualization of an exchange, securities markets regulator and the (independent) management of a securities exchange play a major role. A very strong role exists for both to protect against the wealthy interested parties who will buy the shares of the exchange from passing rules that help only the owners to the detriment of the development of trading and capital formation, especially in a developing country. The interests of the owners could be very different from the interest of the members or of the public. For example, if an insurance company bought a securities exchange, they could decide not to list any other insurance company, preventing any new creation of competitors that might help the society but not the insurance company. Or if the company had something embarrassing, it could change the disclosure rules so that it does not have to disclose it. The securities markets regulator must make sure that this does not occur, and that the trading of the shares of the insurance company on the exchange is on the up and up.

Given that demutualization converts a non-profit, mutually owned securities exchange to a for-profit, investor-owned corporation, the members of mutually owned exchanges – that is, broker-dealers with *seats* on the exchange – are also its owners, with all the voting rights conferred by ownership. In contrast, a demutualized securities exchange is a limited liability company owned by its shareholders. Trading rights and ownership can be separated, where shareholders provide capital to the exchange and receive profits, but they need not conduct trading on the exchange. And as discussed later, although demutualized exchanges continue to provide many, if not most, of the same services, they have different governance structures in which outside shareholders are represented by boards of directors. These dramatic changes in the organizational *form* of securities exchanges reflect major changes in their business environment – notably, the rise of global competition and technological advances and in the competitive strategies designed to respond to such changes.

Demutualization should follow a widely supported vision of making a securities exchange a national or regional leader. First, a task force should be formed to develop the vision for the exchange and examine options for the future governance and structure. At this time, the exchange is still a mutual organization. Second, the task force's recommendations of demutualization should be supported by a large majority of eligible voters to transform the securities exchange into a company requiring no link between the right to trade and ownership. Legislation should then be developed by the parliament of the country to enable the securities exchanges to demutualize, become a tax-paying entity and lose access to surpluses in the government guarantee funds or other development organizations' funds that has, in the past, been providing most of the capital for the development of its trading and settlement platforms.

The process would result in two classes of members namely, trading members and shareholder-members. Since presently as per many securities markets regulations, the term members mean the members of a recognized securities exchange – trading member only, it is apprehended that the regulation may not accommodate different categories, thus calling for legal reforms. As the third step, the membership value of the brokers is to be fixed with their exit and entry price. The dues of the exiting members may be settled with debt securities or with equity shares. There can be allowance for the existing members as either trading members or as ownership members. But as a cautious measure, brokers may be allowed to the equity participation process with a minimal holding. In LSE it is restricted to a maximum of 4.9 percent, in many others such as JSE or NSE, it is restricted at 5 percent.

Then, the exchange should cautiously move and demutualize and subsequently make a private placement of its shares to members. Next step is to put corporate governance in place with the restructuring of the securities exchange board. The self-listing of the demutualized entity should be vested in a separate listing authority, and be the next step. This should then be followed by a free public trading on the exchange where the exchange can issue shares to the public to become a full-fledged corporate firm, by performing an IPO.

There should be a wide public ownership in the securities exchange. Ultimately, the demutualized exchange should generate significant resources in the process, and formulate plans to merge with other exchanges domestically, regionally or internationally. As successful processes have shown, this process should take not less than five years. The new corporate structure should enable the exchanges to control the market efficiently as well as to gain reserves and flexibility for its future growth. Demutualization of ASX has been generally accepted as a success story. In fact, its demutualization process that started in 1997 was finally completed in 2000, a record four years. The process of demutualization therefore takes place in stages, taking different forms depending on the country specifics and orientation of former owners and management. Following Onyuma (2012), Aggarwal (2002) and BCG (2003) these stages are depicted in Figure 2.

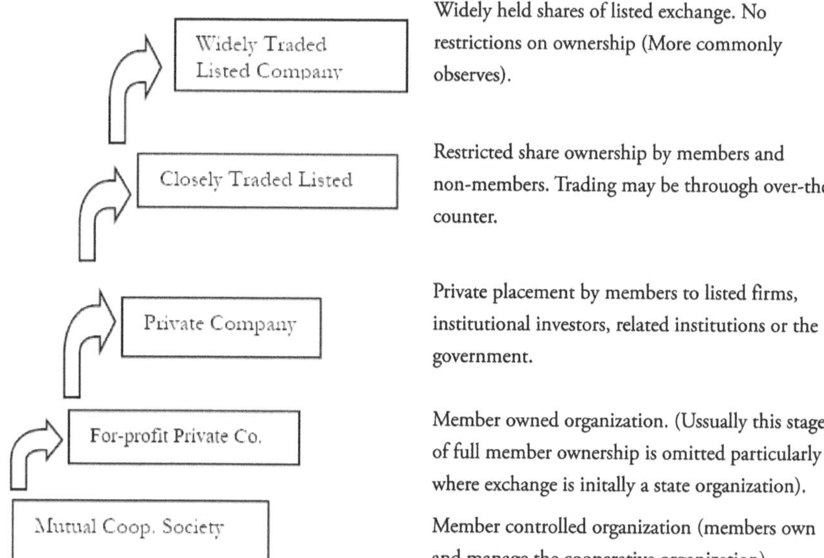

Figure 2: *Process of Demutualization of Securities Exchanges*

As summarized in Figure 2, the process of demutualization takes place in five stages and can ultimately take several different forms. In the first phase, the members are typically given shares and so become legal owners of the organization. Then, or in some cases even as part of phase one, the organization raises capital through a private placement, typically from outside investors as well as members. Having thus become a privately owned corporation, demutualized exchanges then have two basic options; it can stay private or it can list and remove all restrictions on its share trading. It should be noted that in some cases, rather than become a stand-alone company, a demutualized securities exchange can also become a wholly-owned subsidiary of a publicly traded holding company, as has been witnessed in some jurisdictions.

Listed Demutualized Exchanges

Some securities exchanges like Nasdaq and TSE, have demutualized but remain private companies. But for many exchanges, the private placement is clearly just an interim step. Others, like the ASX, JSE or NSE demutualized and became a publicly traded company with shares listed and traded on their own trading boards. The LSE, after demutualizing, completed the same transformation to public ownership – though during the interim period, trading in LSE shares was conducted through an off-market trading facility). Other securities exchanges which have been demutualized and performed IPOs, thereby becoming publicly traded companies are presented in Table 5. By now, this list may have grown longer given the rapidity with which securities exchanges are restructuring their governance structures culminating in their self-listing in their own markets.

Table 5: Listed Demutualized Exchanges

Stockholm Stock Exchange	1998
OMX Group	1998
Australian Stock Exchange	1998
Hong Kong Stock exchange	2000
Athens Stock exchanges	2000
Singapore Stock Exchange	2000
Hellenic Stock Exchanges	2001
Deutsche Börse	2001
Oslo Exchange	2001
Instinet (ECN)	2001
Euronext	2001
London Stock Exchange	2001
NASDAQ	2002
Sydney Futures Exchange	2002
Toronto Stock Exchange	2002
Chicago Mercantile Exchange*	2002
New Zealand Stock Exchange	2003
Philippine Stock Exchange	2003
Bursa Malaysia Bhd	2005
Chicago Board of Trade*	2005

Inter-Continental Exchanges*	2005
New York Mercantile Exchange*	2006
Johannesburg Stock Exchange	2006
New York Stock Exchange	2006
BM&F	2007
BME	2007
Bovespa Exchange	2007
Sao Paulo Stock Exchange	2007
Santiago Stock Exchange	2007
Lima Stock Exchange	2007
Elsalvador Stock Exchange	2008
Panama Stock Exchange	2009
Colombia Stock Exchange	2010
Nairobi Securities Exchange	2014

Source: Stock Exchanges' websites; WFE (2023), Senbet & Otchere, 2008, Serifoy, (2005); Aggrawal (2002).
* Derivative exchanges

It has already been mentioned that rather than become a stand-alone company, a demutualized securities exchange can also become a wholly owned subsidiary of a publicly traded company. For example, after demutualizing, the Swedish exchange – the Stockholm Stock Exchange – became a subsidiary (called the OM Stockholmsbörsen AB) of the OM Group, a publicly traded and listed company. Many securities exchanges continue to have some ownership or voting restrictions after demutualization. For example, ownership or voting rights for any one stockholder in many demutualized securities exchanges are typically limited to 5 percent.

Ownership and Management Structures of Demutualized Exchanges

Discussions on demutualization raise a number of important key issues relating to ownership, access rights, financial management, risk management, and corporate governance. New structural changes usually bring about many issues, and the process of demutualization raises a number of issues for consideration. As already been discussed in chapter 2 and 3, demutualization leads to changes in the ownership and management structures and as such implies changes in the methods of financing the securities exchange, and whole new types of risks never experienced before. The following is a discussion on the important issues that are likely to change the ownership and management structures of demutualized securities exchanges.

Ownership Issues in Mutual Securities Exchanges

Mutuality status of exchanges presents variety of ownership issues. The main distinguishing feature of a mutually owned securities exchange is that its owners, decision-makers and the direct users of its trading services usually are the same persons – its member firms.[94] Generally, decisions are made on a one-member, one-vote basis, and often are made by committees of representatives of member firms. The ability to influence the decisions of the securities exchange is thereby separated from the level of economic interest a member has in the exchange. Ownership rights are not freely tradable, and terminated with cessation of membership. Usually the only permitted purchasers are other member-dealers or others who qualify to become member-dealers.

Mutually owned securities exchanges are seldom able to raise capital from anyone other source other than its members. In contrast, most for-profit securities exchanges are organized, as companies with share capital under which its owners, its decision-makers and its principal customers are three separate groups. The shareholders vest decision-making power for the exchange in a board of directors who are subject to election and removal by shareholders and this power is exercised by the management of the corporation.

The voting rights of shareholders usually are commensurate with their economic interest in the exchange: one share, one vote. As for

---

94 Donnan, F. (1999) Self-regulation and the demutualization of Australian Stock Exchange. *Australian Journal of Corporate Law*, No. 10:1-12.

other companies, there may be many variations, such as multiple voting rights, golden shares, caps on shareholdings and other arrangements. The economic interests represented by shareholdings constitute property rights, which are distinct from the interests of members. As is with companies, shareholder-owned exchanges may raise new capital in a variety of ways and from various sources. As competition increases and exchanges move from mutual or cooperative entities to for-profit enterprises, new elements enter the environment. The interests of the exchange owners may diverge from those of the principal customers of its trading services. Therefore, commercial nature of the exchange becomes more evident: maximizing profits becomes an explicit objective.

The nature of the ownership issues confronting an exchange changes when it is transformed from a mutual to a for-profit status. Mutual-owned securities exchanges were created out of the need for stockbrokers to provide a means of quality assurance for individuals contemplating investment in the securities of local firms. Securities exchanges supervised the activities of brokers, and the mutual form of ownership helped to ensure that brokers were judged reasonably – by their peers – and that the livelihoods of brokers were protected.[95] There have been fundamental and universal changes in the environment faced by securities exchanges that have brought into question the continued desirability of the mutual form of ownership for securities exchanges.

Specifically, the competition faced by securities exchanges has significantly increased in the two decades. Local companies and investors are now able to switch between markets, relatively easily; and there is now a much greater and more urgent need for exchanges to think and act strategically and to adapt quickly to changing circumstances. Often, there is a large disparity in the contribution made, through trading volume, by members of a mutual, with the result that principles such as one-vote-per-member are brought into question. Irrespective of the timeliness and flexibility of decision-making, the expectations of securities exchange

---

95 Holthouse, D., (2001) The Structure of a Demutualized Exchanges - The Critical Issues. Conference Paper, manila, August 13-14, Asian Development Bank.

clients have never been higher. The control by stockbrokers for operations, as exists in mutual exchanges, means that the expectations of securities exchange's non-broker customers such as listed firms are not considered and adequately addressed.

Ownership Issues in Demutualized Securities Exchanges
The following may be viewed as the best practices for institutional framework of demutualized securities exchanges. There are a number of important ingredients that are useful in designing an appropriate governance structure of a demutualized securities exchange.[96] Such best practices are necessary in order to have an effective securities exchange activities organization and a firm that is more effective and efficient and responsive to the issues of stakeholders, and one that creates value to its owners and society at large.

The first issue relates to diversification of exchange shareholders. Traditionally in a mutual securities exchange, no one member can exert control over the operations of the exchange, and all owners are subject to an assessment of their qualifications as part of the membership approval process. Given that demutualization involves broadening the ownership structure to include others other than approved firms, two possibilities arise. The securities exchange may be controlled by one or more persons, and seen to be subject to influence by inappropriate shareholders. For example, there might be concerns if a person who had been barred from the securities industry acquired sufficient shares to elect a nominee to the board of an exchange. The acquisition of a significant ownership position by a non-financial industry firm may raise other concerns within the exchange.

In fact, the introduction of share ownership can help to address the shortcomings associated with a mutual structure noted above as it is a powerful catalyst for change but it is not, on itself, a sufficient condition to ensure that change occurs. It is, for example, possible for stockbrokers to

---

96   For more details, see FEAS (2001) Best Practices for the Development of Stock Exchanges in Transition Economies. Federation of Euro Asian Stock Exchanges/OECD/Istanbul Stock Exchange.

convert the form of ownership of a securities exchange to shares, to become shareholders, but for there to be no market for such shares. The result, inevitably, would be that little changes other than ownership by shares. Securities exchanges that are in the process of demutualizing should give careful consideration to what ownership features are most likely to address the shortcomings of the mutual structure which have been identified above and how a market with as much transparency and liquidity as possible can be established within an exchange.

Considering securities exchange ownership diversity, market supervisors and regulators should allow an appropriate diversity of ownership structure, domestic and international alliances, and technological linkages. Where a securities exchange has been established by the state and an initial amount of capital has been provided from state funds, the question of ownership may not arise. Members may own the exchange in the form of a mutual organisation, sharing in the costs through the tariffs set to absorb them. A number of securities exchanges worldwide, both developed and emerging markets have decided or are coming round to the view that they should be fully commercial entities with external shareholders. It is the best practice that securities exchanges should be free to choose their own business model, to compete for business and to set their own commercial agenda. This should be done within the regulatory framework to protect the public interest.

The second issue is aiming at specific exchange investors. There are several ownership issues specific to demutualized securities exchanges. These include whether a securities exchange intends to specifically target a particular type of investors, and if so, which ones. Usually, securities exchanges have a certain measure of influence over the types of investors that hold their securities. The types of investors can be influenced by whether the exchange seeks to list on itself, the range in which the exchange's shares trade, and the dividend policy adopted by the securities exchange. It is desirable, for public policy reasons, to encourage widespread exchange ownership, encompassing both institutional and retail investors. This can assist in reducing the likelihood of decisions being made in the interests of any one particular segment as opposed to the rest of other stakeholders.

Admittedly, there are numerous factors that could influence a securities exchange to seek to limit its ownership. These include the fact that relatively large shareholder bases are likely to impose significant on-going costs on securities exchanges arising from the need to service its owners, for example by providing them with annual reports, general meeting venues, etcetera, and where an exchange ownership is widely dispersed, investors are likely to suffer from *rational apathy* in their decision-making, with possible adverse consequences on occasions when a requisite level of extant shareholders is needed, for example where a change to an exchange's constitution is required. This problem is known in the economics literature as a public goods problem. At the time of demutualization, these mutual exchanges usually have fewer shareholders – only the broker-members – but with objective to target both institutional and retail investors as shareholders, in order to promote as wide a spread of holders as possible. The exchange later ends up with many shareholders, majority of whom are small retail investors. During 2023, the largest shareholder of demutualized exchanges had around 10 percent, with the top most 25 percent shareholders collectively hold less than half of the share registry, suggesting a large group of small holders where no single shareholder has a majority.

In addition, foreign ownership of the exchange also comes to fore. The other ownership issue that presents itself is whether, given the important role that exchanges play in capital formation, allocation and redistribution, and hence domestic employment and savings, there should be any restrictions imposed on foreign ownership. Some securities exchanges may resist any special foreign ownership restrictions being applied to them. They seem to believe that only the general foreign ownership considerations applicable to other local firms should be applied. The foreign investment requirements in most countries already provide for government scrutiny of many proposed foreign purchases of firms and properties. Most governments' shares block proposals are contrary to the national interest. In order for exchanges to survive, it may be necessary for them to enter into alliances with other exchanges globally. Foreign ownership restrictions may impede a securities exchange's ability to achieve such alliances, with the result that an exchange could find itself unable to compete realistically for listings and investment capital.

The last ownership issue faced by demutualised exchanges is whether an exchange intends to impose any form of ownership restriction, such as sectoral distribution, percentage limits or foreign ownership restrictions. The ownership restrictions are a contentious issue. In one view, such restrictions serve to fetter the market for corporate control, thereby risking inefficiencies. It can also be argued that ownership restrictions are necessary because it is undesirable on public policy grounds to allow an individual, or a small group, to control a securities exchange. In many jurisdictions with laws facilitating demutualization include a provision which limits persons and their associates to owning or controlling a maximum of 5 percent of the voting power in an exchange. The provisions reflect a securities exchange view that it is in the national interest for restrictions to be imposed on the ownership of shares in the new exchange structures.

The ownership restrictions to lower percentages may however impede future strategic alliances. Furthermore, it may provide little benefit as a means of promoting market integrity. Therefore, some securities exchange members may lobby for the ownership restriction to be increased beyond the five (5) percent. Such changes may raise a number of concerns. First, what conflicts of interest are created or increased where a for-profit exchange also performs the regulatory functions that an exchange might have, especially the primary market regulation of listing and admission of firms, the secondary market regulation relating to trading rules, and member regulation, set code of conduct? Second, a fair and efficient capital market is for public good. A well-managed securities exchange is a key part of the capital market. So, is there a need to impose a special regime on securities exchanges to protect the public interest, such as particular corporate governance arrangements or rules regarding share ownership? Moreover, will a for-profit securities exchange be run with due regard for its financial viability? Will adequate funding be allocated to regulatory functions, including arrangements designed to manage defaults? The main securities exchange function is the effective management of failures, whether market failures or defaults by market participants. This is particularly true where a securities exchange operates as the central counterparty in transactions. The emphasis on minimizing costs associated with a for-profit structure may put pressure on the exchange's ability and inclination to fulfill this function.

Evidently, majority of these questions are not new to securities exchanges, but demutualization and increased stiff competition may worsen them, calling for the need to re-look at both the issues and available regulatory responses. The most important issue is whether the commercial pressures, or the governance structure, of a for-profit securities exchange will undermine the commitment of resources and capabilities of the exchange to effectively fulfil its regulatory and public interest responsibilities to an appropriate standard.[97] The issues that arise and regulatory responses taken are somewhat interdependent. The choice of a way to address a particular issue may affect the existence or intensity of other issues. For instance, if the ownership of a securities exchange is limited to securities firms that the regulator licenses as fit and proper to do business in the jurisdiction, the potential problems regarding who controls a securities exchange may be lessened. In addition, the issues and their intensity may be affected by the form that a demutualized securities exchange takes, like whether the exchange becomes a private company comprised solely of its former broker-members or a widely held listed company, one whose share also trade on its trading board.

It is important that the structure of a demutualized securities exchange should allow for the creation of an orderly and transparent forum for the purchase and sale of securities by market participants, including member-intermediaries (in the case of a mutual structure), owner-intermediaries (in the case of a for-profit structure), other broker-dealers, investors and issuers. The securities exchange provides the infrastructure for trading securities in the secondary market. Constitutional and organisational issues that need to be addressed include the question of the exchange's legal

---

97   Australian House of Representatives, Main Committee, Official Hansard, 27 November 1997 at p.11541 (from the speech presenting legislation authorizing demutualization of Australian Stock Exchange).

status and whether it should have statutes. How should its membership or ownership structure be organised? Which organisational infrastructure is appropriate, and what amount of financial resources would be considered adequate? Which infrastructure is needed to monitor market participants? The best practise is that a demutualized securities exchange should establish membership rules as well as rules concerning the organisation and operation of the exchange within the limits of the statutory legal framework. The regulator should ensure that these exchange rules are in compliance with general laws and should monitor their enforcement.

The appropriate responses may vary depending on the nature of the activities carried out by the demutualized exchange. The need for regulatory intervention in the activities of a securities exchange may be lessened where the exchange performs few regulatory functions. There exist workable solutions available for the issues and concerns for demutualization. Many jurisdictions, after due consideration of their specific circumstances, have addressed these concerns, and the responses vary widely.[98] These solutions are discussed in the next chapter on conflict of interests in demutualized securities exchanges.

Financial Management Issues in Demutualized Exchanges
Many financial related issues exist regarding securities exchanges that are of concern to market regulators. The transformation to a demutualized securities exchange structure may have an effect on some of these concerns. These issues relate to services and fees set at a level for commercial purposes, like to build market share, unduly depleting resources of a securities exchange, and the overall issue of the public interest in the continued good financial health of an exchange. Others are the under-funding of regulatory functions, cross-subsidization between market regulatory and commercial activities, especially fees and fines generated by regulatory activities being used to fund commercial operations, and the equitable allocation of the cost of regulation across securities market participants.

---

98   See IOSCO (2001) Issues Paper on Exchange Demutualization. Report of the Technical Committee of the International Organization of Securities Commissions, June, 2001.

Funding Sources. A mutual exchange may have the power to levy assessments upon its members in order to obtain debt finance. A demutualized exchange has broader avenues open to it for raising capital, notwithstanding that, unlike the levying of mutual members, shareholders have no financial liabilities beyond their fully paid-up shares. A demutualized exchange may raise additional capital by issuing shares externally and it may be perceived as having a greater capacity to obtain debt finance. However, the availability of new equity and loan capital at a reasonable price, if required, would depend more on sustainable profits than on the current value of the exchange's net assets.

Financial Governance. A securities exchange's board is directly responsible for its financial governance. The board sets the financial policies that guide its top leadership in financial management. These policies address matters such as budgeting criteria, day-to-day financial management, safeguarding of assets, remuneration and benefits for staffs, investment practices and financial reserves. In the course of discharging its financial governance duties, the board should seek to ensure the ongoing financial viability of the exchange and the fiscal integrity of management's actions by monitoring actual performance against the board's expectation; ensure that it receives reports that provide assurance of the integrity of the financial processes, systems and reporting, and establish and manage the exchange's relationship with its external auditor – an audit committee could assist in these two last areas.

Financial Viability. The future financial sustainability of a securities exchange is an important. Being a member-owned entity, a securities exchange usually has the right to assess members and request a capital contribution. This theoretically unfettered ability of the exchange to raise finance from its members has two practical limits: the members' ability and willingness to pay rather than resign from membership and the fact that the members of an exchange, as the decision-makers, will not necessarily authorize the capital call in the first place. After demutualization, a securities exchange usually loss the right to demand that shareholders contribute additional capital. While the demutualized exchange may not have the legal right to demand further capital injection by its owners, a shareholder may opt to provide additional funding in order to maintain its investment in the exchange. In return, it gains the flexibility to raise finance from a wider array of investors, with differing investment objectives and risk tolerance. Market regulators usually deal with concerns about the financial condition of financial intermediaries by imposing capital and other prudential requirements to cushion it from dipping into financial distress.

Capital and solvency requirements serve at least two purposes. They may reduce the risk of failure of the firm by requiring that a cushion of owners' money be available to absorb unexpected losses. Capital may provide liquidity to allow a firm to continue to operate during an orderly wind down and transfer of the business. Where failure of the intermediary might have systemic implications, the emphasis is often on ensuring the firm remains solvent. Given the public interest in the continued operations of a securities exchange, capital requirements could be placed on a demutualized exchange. If such requirements are imposed, two further questions should be dealt with: what sort of capital framework is appropriate, given the nature of the businesses carried on by the exchange, and how widely these requirements should be applied? Would the capital regime be applied to the securities exchange operating company only or extended to its holding company or all related companies of the exchange? Other alternatives are to require a demutualized securities exchange to establish a reserve to address any shortfall in its capital, or for the market regulator to monitor the financial condition of an exchange and then to take remedial action if its financial condition begins to deteriorate thus affecting its operations as a going concern.

Investor Expectations. The process of demutualization and self-listing usually brings with it investor expectations concerning exchange financial management and performance. Such expectations have a major impact on the financial policies adopted by a securities exchange. Therefore, securities have to consider what an appropriate expected rate of return is and the rate of return for new activities; to what extent should activities be diversified in order to maintain a steady income despite variations in market conditions; and the appropriate dividend policy to pursue moving forward. Investor expectations and the most appropriate mix of financial policies are likely to vary from jurisdiction to jurisdiction, and even from a securities exchange to another.

Cross-subsidization. Revenue generation is a factor which exchanges do focus on post-demutualization. Even though each of the regulatory and commercial sides of the securities exchange may generate revenue, there may be an opportunity for regulatory funds to be reinvested in the commercial activities of a demutualized securities exchange. Where an exchange has the ability to set monopoly prices for trading services or for regulatory services, there may be, at least, a question of fairness if the exchange uses the fees charged to customers that use only its regulatory services, such as an alternative trading system, to fund its commercial services. This type of cross-subsidization can be viewed as distorting competition.[99] In order to assess and supervise cross-subsidization issues, the books and records of an exchange have to be separated in order to distinguish the revenues and expenses of the commercial and the regulatory activities to aid comparisons.

Sub-optimal Pricing Decisions. There exist the possibility of the exchange under-pricing its equity and services given that in the process of trying to build market share, particularly for the new shares or service, there is a risk that the price will be set at a level that will not generate sufficient revenue to fund the associated regulatory activities. There is also the possibility that the pricing decisions will be made other than in the long-term interests of the exchange and its financial viability. This may be even more of a problem in a mutual exchange, where the members benefit directly from the lower price in the short term and therefore may be less likely than public shareholders to intervene in *loss leader* pricing decisions. The appropriate internal controls of a well-run operation and the market discipline applied to a self-listed exchange should reduce these risks. A well-defined obligation to fund regulatory activities would also be of assistance in addition to avoiding potential under-pricing.

Fair Allocating Regulatory Costs. As is discussed in the chapter on market regulation, the costs of regulation should be shared equitably by

---

99 Lee, R. (2000) What is an Exchange? The Automation, Management and Regulation of Financial Markets. Oxford University Press.

those who benefit from it. If the regulatory functions are re-assumed by the statutory regulator, the costs should be spread in accordance with the funding structure of the agency, those borne by all taxpayers, those paying fees to the market regulator, or some other method. If some entity other than the statutory market regulator is performing these functions, the issue of fair allocation of costs arises and cannot be ignored.

In sum, securities exchange services and listing fees normally represent more stable, though more limited, sources of income than trading and other revenues (income from IT system sales, proceeds of financial investment, fines imposed by exchanges, and rent from securities exchange properties). To achieve this, tariffs need to be structured to equate with the market operator's expected financial objectives. As in any enterprise, proper returns on risk capital must be calculated. Forward planning must also ensure that funding for the development of the market is available when required. Some countries may wish to consider whether there should be a trust or deepening fund and capital arrangement by which additional funding can be obtained to recruit the skilled staff needed to perform impartial, unbiased regulatory work. It is a best practice that revenue flows should be sufficient to pay for operating costs and fund future development of the securities exchange.

General Management Issues in Demutualized Exchanges

In chapter 2, it was noted that one of the entities that sets codes of corporate governance in capital markets is a securities exchange. Thus, in all issues concerning corporate governance, a securities exchange – whether demutualized or not - as the body that supervises listed firms' behaviour, may be viewed as a 'standard setter' for other listed firms. It is, therefore, appropriate that a securities exchange board embody what are generally accepted to be sound principles of corporate governance. In this regard, reference should be made to local corporate governance guidelines if they exist, which provide common elements of good corporate governance. The latter principles can be adapted to reflect local economic, social, legal and cultural circumstances.[100] In many markets, such as developing ones, in addition to the governance code set by private sector governance trust organizations for use by organizations, securities exchanges have also set their own codes to be followed by their listed firms.

Need for Public Directors in Board of Directors? As a way to respond to the issue of public good, and the degree of conflict of interest in a member-owned securities exchange, it is common for securities exchanges to be required to have public directors on its board to represent the interests of the stakeholders, beyond the member-owners. These public directors generally are expected to serve as a check on conflict of interest in a self-regulatory organization and promote integrity in the board's decision-making. On the other hand, the boards of directors of most commercial firms are required to consider only the best interests of the firm and its shareholders in making decisions. The questions, which arise, are whether a widely-held demutualized securities exchange still needs to have public directors appointed to its board or has other mechanisms imposed to support the public interest. And should public directors be required, should they be given specific public interest responsibilities over and above the duties imposed on all directors of the securities exchange?

The public interest in a fair and efficient exchange continues in the demutualised environment, as does the conflict between the commercial operations and regulatory role of a securities exchange. This would argue for continuing to require public directors. However, the wider ownership of a securities exchange may bring greater opportunities for the general public interest to be represented on the board through the normal director election process. In addition, few firms, no matter how important to the economy of a jurisdiction, have similar public director requirements imposed. The main focus should be to impose statutory duties on all directors of the utility to act in the public interest, and a statutory regulator enforces these

---

100 The OECD Principles of Corporate Governance were adopted by OECD Ministers in May 1999 by member governments of OECD. These principles are non-binding and are intended to serve as a reference point for countries' efforts to evaluate and improve their own legal, institutional and regulatory framework.

duties. Some securities regulators presently impose similar duties on all directors of securities exchanges within their jurisdiction.

Need for Competent Exchange Senior Management. Traditionally, the key decision-makers in a mutual exchange are the representatives of member firms who have been elected to the securities exchange's board and the senior administrators of the securities exchange itself. Firms and their representatives are usually approved, either by the regulator or a securities exchange, as having a good reputation, sufficient resources and the necessary expertise to carry on business as securities exchange members or as representatives. But in a widely-held demutualized exchange, the key decision-makers on a day-to-day basis are likely to be the senior management of the securities exchange. Due to the market demand, a securities exchange is forced to hire as competent management as possible. However, there could be a need for direct involvement of the market regulator in these decisions so that they are seen to be adhering to the relevant regulation.

The strength of the securities exchange management team may be subject to regulatory scrutiny on the establishment or recognition of a new securities exchange, but these fit-and-proper assessments may apply to securities exchange management on an ongoing basis. Assessing the qualifications and expertise of directors and senior managers of financial intermediaries is a core principle of regulation in the banking, insurance and securities sectors. Given the public interest in an efficient and fair market, the movement from a member-run organization may suggest that some greater regulatory oversight of who actually manages the exchange might be considered. Where the regulatory functions of a securities exchange have been moved to another related entity or out-sourced altogether, the assessment of the expertise of the staff of the entity actually carrying out the regulatory functions will be particularly important in achieving this function.

Appointments to Securities Exchange Board of Directors. As has been discussed, securities exchange demutualization usually involves a fundamental change in the way that board members are appointed. As mutual structures, securities exchanges' constitutions require that a majority of directors comprise broker-appointed *member directors* and that member directors be elected by a ballot of members on the basis of one vote per member, and that the board include member-directors from each stockbrokerage firm. After becoming demutualized, securities exchanges became a company limited by shares, thus the control of the composition of the board is passed on to the shareholders, and the requirement for member-directors and restrictions regarding appointment of directors are relaxed and some also removed or thinned down.

Securities Exchange Board Committees. Worldwide, it is normally regarded as good corporate governance practice for boards to establish audit, nomination and remuneration committees, and for such committees to be comprised of a majority of independent directors, have an independent director as a chairperson, and have clearly defined terms of reference. Demutualized securities exchanges now have an audit, nomination and remuneration committees. Typically, mutual exchanges have many committees and, as was depicted in the JSE and NSE before demutualization, it is within these committees that many day-to-day management decisions are made. Achieving a timely and orderly transfer of management responsibilities from the committees to the executive is a critical issue in the successful demutualization of a securities exchange.

Trading Rules for Directors and Managers. Given a securities exchange's market position and the role that it plays nationally, even a suggestion of insider-trading by a director or staff member can do great harm to the individual as well as to the exchange itself, irrespective of whether insider-trading actually took place or is proven. It is therefore essential that a demutualized securities exchange put in place arrangements for directors, management and committee members, which govern transactions by them in the exchange's own securities. These arrangements should be made public, in order to enhance confidence in the governance of the exchange. A cornerstone of such an arrangement would be for directors of the board and other relevant people to be allowed to effect transactions in the exchange's shares only during certain periods when material information has been released to and absorbed by the market, such as fourteen days commencing two trading days after the exchange has released its financial results. There is need to introduce such share dealing rules for exchange directors and staff, which may prohibit active trading in such shares by its directors and staff. This is critical to prevent possibility of insider trading on the shares of the securities exchange.

Composition of Securities Exchange Board. A securities exchange's board should include representatives from major interest groups, such as investor and company director associations. However, this may be undesirable as it could significantly impede the decision-making processes of a board. Firm board directors should act in the interests of their company; not in the individual interests of the groups that may have nominated them. Where board directors are acting solely in the individual interests of their constituents, there is a risk that boards can become like Parliaments. Being comprised of representatives of diverse constituencies they may come to debate issues rather than to make decisions. The Boards of African exchanges before demutualization were made up of the following members: JSE (seventeen), NGX (fifteen), USE (eight), EGX (eight), Malawi (six), BSE (four), and ZSE (three). Before demutualization, NSE's board of directors, for example, as of December 31st 2012 had 12 directors including a Chairman and two Vice Chairmen.[101] During then the board was made up of a Chief Executive, Chairman, who had to be a registered member-broker of the securities exchange, 4 other member-brokers, 4 outsiders representing various interests like fund managers, bankers, insurers, pensions, etcetera, and 1 company secretary. After demutualization, the NSE Ltd now has 10 directors constituting 1-Chairman, 1 Vice Chairman, 1 Chief Executive, 4 Independent non-executive directors; 3 Non-independent directors (1 representing trading participants, 2 representing listed companies). The CEO is the executive. Board members whose backgrounds are predominantly securities broking do not constitute a majority, as only one director represents them.

The exchange board upon demutualization, therefore, should comprise of persons with complementary and diverse skills including information systems, accounting and auditing, investments, law, funds management, stockbroking and corporate administration. Members of the board should

---

101 www.nse.or.ke

bring both a global and regional perspective to the board's deliberations as well as an understanding of the external political and public policy environment.[102] They should also have extensive experience in company directorships. Non-executive directors should retire by rotation and the usual term of appointment for all non-executives, before they are nominated for re-election should they wish to continue as directors, needs to be stated, but should not be more than two years. Directors should have a maximum term in the board as well as age limit so that exchanges do not end up individuals who may not be productive on the board. The board should cater for the interests of issuers, investors and securities exchange intermediaries. There should be also some directors to represent investors. Therefore, demutualization significantly reduces the total size and the stockbrokerage representation in a securities exchange and helps reduce vested interest inherent in trading participants – the member-stockbrokers.

Risk Management Issues. The fact that operations have numerous uncertainties makes risk an unavoidable aspect of all organizational activity and therefore the characterization of organizational risks should be a key annual activity for an exchange. The board of a securities exchange should set the framework for the management of organizational risk including the level of risk allowable in certain activities or projects. To assist it in fulfilling its responsibilities, the board should consider establishing a risk management committee. A key risk that demutualized exchanges may monitor is *business risk* or threats to the achievement of its goals and to the successful execution of its strategies. They should compile an inventory of business risks and then conduct workshops to consider these risks.

Complete Accountability and Transparency of Supervisory functions. Demutualization places a spotlight on the ability of the exchange to quarantine and protect regulatory including surveillance information, to discharge its supervisory responsibilities with integrity and impartiality and to effectively manage conflicts which may arise between its supervisory responsibilities and commercial objectives. This requires a securities

---

102 Karmel, R. S. (2014). Is the Independent Director Model Broken? *Seattle University Law Review*, 37, (2). 755.

exchange to review its policies and procedures for supervisory decision-making and ensure that they promote transparency and accountability. Most demutualized exchanges have taken a number of initiatives designed to do this, including public consultation on rule development and amendments, publication of waiver and disciplinary determinations, issue of guidance materials designed to enhance public understanding and awareness of the processes and the compliance expectations, improved mechanisms, including through its website for public access to supervisory outcomes. Some have even constituted supervisory review subsidiaries to audit and report on the securities exchange's supervisory activities and challenges being experienced.

Trading System Access Rights Issues. Demutualization involves the separation of ownership rights from the customer or access to market facility rights. Complexities arise where there is more than one class of members in existence; and the trading rights are in the form of seats. Where there is more than one class of members in a demutualizing exchange it is important to value the exchange's business and determine an equitable split of shares in the demutualized entity, between classes. Where there is only one class of members, valuation is normally less of an issue as members can be offered equal shares in the demutualized entity. Where seats exist, an exchange in the process of demutualizing will need to decide whether these should continue to exist after demutualization; and if it should it be decided that seats are not to continue, what compensation should be paid to holders. The existence of seats implies that there is a restriction on the issue of new trading rights. Depending on the circumstances, this may be detrimental to market liquidity and to the commercial interests of an exchange. Where there is recent experience of trading participants paying large amounts for seats in the home market, it may be necessary, in order for demutualization to be approved by exchange members, either to continue to allow seats to exist or for the exchange to pay compensation to former member-brokers for loss of transferability of their trading rights – this may be a challenge in developing markets.

Full Continuous Disclosure Procedures on relevant and material information. Given the role they play in an economy, it is important for a securities exchange to lead in the best practice in the continuous disclosure of information relevant to the making of investment decisions in its securities. Thus, it is beneficial to put in place procedures to ensure that relevant and material information is released to the market in a coordinated and efficient way. Some securities exchanges have even appointed a continuous disclosure staff and introduced formal procedures setting out the obligations of directors and its staff relative to the disclosure of information to the market and to protect against unauthorized disclosure to the media and the public. This is testimony to their effort in satisfying their mandate for full disclosure requirements. Remember, themselves, securities exchanges require the other listed firms to fully disclose all material information to both their shareholder and the public. So being self-listed, they too must be required to do so.

The objective of such an exercise is to identify all significant business risks arising from current operations, new business initiatives and projects. The risks identified are then combined with risk data from previous years that continue to be relevant. Risks are grouped and ranked, and their containment measures identified. A risk management committee should monitor the risk management and control structure implemented by management, and advise on the need for significant changes to that structure in order to obtain reasonable assurance that exchange assets are safeguarded and that reliable financial records are maintained, and report annually on its risk management processes.

Based on the foregoing discussion, public interest requires some mechanisms to address these concerns, such as imposing limits on share ownership, requiring prior regulatory approval for ownership above a threshold percentage or giving a veto right to the regulator. The degree of regulatory scrutiny applied to shareholders in most commercial firms is fairly slight. The only obligation is that a significant shareholder of a public company must disclose that position to the company and/or the market. However, ownership restrictions and/or regulatory approval of significant shareholders in other sectors like in financial services are common. The public interest in maintaining an efficient securities exchange may suggest that some regulatory limitations or oversight of the ownership of the securities exchange may be warranted, even where the regulatory functions may be performed elsewhere.

Other Concerns Associated with Exchange Demutualization

Considering the various definitions of corporate governance and their scope, the concept of governance can be well extended to the demutualized corporate securities exchanges. But one pertinent question arises of whether demutualization ensures better governance in securities exchanges? There are several benefits of the demutualized securities exchanges and the primary driver for such benefits is the favourable governance structure associated with demutualized exchanges. Thus governance seems to be the crux of demutualization.

However, worldwide, securities exchange demutualization has been adopted by exchanges more for resource generation to meet rising capital requirements for financing infrastructure development and less for better governance. But the recent problems in many securities markets have raised the issues of governance to a new high, especially to bring independence to the risk management and surveillance function. It is apt to mention that demutualization does end neither with corporatization nor at change in board structure or with both. What is important is the demutualization of management. This is so because the role of management is to run the enterprise and that the role of the board is to see that the organization is being run well and in the right direction in a manner that creates value to owners, the exchange and market intermediaries and the wider society.

Change of mutual organization to demutualization form requires a long-term planning. The public representatives, generally not conversant with market intricacies, deal with policy issues only in a board meeting against the regular presence of the elected directors after and during trading hours. Therefore, decision-making is largely member-dependent and varies with change in office-bearers, which indicates its short-term nature. The presence of non-broker members in these organizations would perhaps crop laxity in the management. Particularly, the public representatives would not show any interest in the intricacies of the securities exchange's functioning. This will breed a different group of directors in the board and gradually the latter will be dominated by the few. This will definitely affect the quality of governance and ultimately the performance. Another conflict arises on the issue of participation of brokers in the management.

Whether the traders will be allowed to hold stake in the securities exchange is debatable. Globally, the shareholders are traders, individuals and institutions. But the conflict of owning the capital as well as trading for business would create governance problem. While keeping trading members in the board is a matter of time, but a trading member should not act as a chairman of the board. It is important to keep experienced stockbrokers in the board to facilitate policy making as well as for other members to see that brokers control the minimum functional areas. The inclusion of outside directors on board to serve as a check and promote integrity in the decision-making could reduce this risk but the market regulators may think of simultaneous imposition of statutory duties on public directors.

The literature on member's heterogeneity and governance problem do not provide any unique solution. More heterogeneity favours a not-for-profit structure and does not favour separation of ownership from membership, thus disclaims demutualization. At the same time, the separation of ownership from membership may entirely favour demutualization since member-owners want both low exchange costs and high exchange profits, whereas outside owners only want high profits. This very different incentive structure can have a significant impact on the securities exchange policies. But this may relate more to a traditional not-for-profit mutual than a contemporary for-profit exchange with a diversified shareholder base.

One way to resolve this structure conflict is to allow the traders to hold small chunk of shares with a restriction to hold important office. This will help the securities exchange board to capitalize on the stockbroker's experience. However, if the securities exchange were to be owned fully by private shareholders, the chances of slackness in regulatory action due to the fear of its impact on business and profitability would arise. In order to avoid the conflict of ownership, a public representative should be the chairman of the board, as is the global practice, with some representation from traders baring important offices. Public representatives should be appointed for a longer term and should get proper exposure to the intricacies of the functioning of securities exchanges through familiarization training programmes.

The governance problem can also arise due to the conflict on the issues of self-listing and self-regulation.[103] While listing of a demutualized exchange either can be done in itself or in other securities exchanges, the problem of governance particularly lies with the former. Securities exchanges as self-regulatory organizations have to carry out functions like, listed company governance and disclosure; surveillance and discipline of their markets and specialists, floor brokers and market makers; member firm financial and operational compliance; and fair and equitable treatment of customers. As these functions need to be carried out effectively in any securities market, it is important to consider carefully whether demutualization implies that a securities exchange will be less motivated or less able to manage them.

Conflicts arise because the securities exchange members are being asked to: set rules in the public interest that may negatively affect their own commercial interests; and monitor and enforce these rules against each other. The offsetting benefit to these conflicts lies in the expectation that self-regulation produces better rules as industry participants have the most expertise in and knowledge of their industry. The members are also more likely to follow rules that they have participated in developing. In a member-owned exchange, the members share the financial and reputational risks of a failure to regulate appropriately. Finally, the bulk of the cost of regulation is likely to be borne by the regulated industry and the participants in that industry. But, can a self-regulating securities exchange reprimand itself after finding that it has violated its own set rules?

In terms of ownership, most demutualized exchanges have allowed control of the securities exchanges to still remain with the former members. However, Malaysian Stock Exchange distributed its ownership equally – 30 percent – amongst the brokers, government, market development fund, and 10 percent to other intermediaries. Consequently, the demutualization

---

103 This problem of conflict of interest within a demutualized securities exchange and between the securities exchange and securities market regulator is discussed in details in chapter five.

of securities exchanges should be poised to envisage such structure. But, a problem is likely to emanate upon the demutualization, since the securities exchange has been a brokers' private enterprise, with government having contributed no monetary assistance in its development. This has the potential of stifling further growth and development of the exchange since governments are known to be messy in most enterprises where they have control in decision-making.[104]

There are, however, ways of resolving these conflicts, like functional separation of the commercial activities of the exchange from its regulatory functions by establishing a separate legal entity or transfer of some or all regulatory responsibilities to the securities market regulator or another body. However, questions can be raised on the regulator's jurisdiction over the entity assuming the tasks; the need to assess the resources, experience and reputation of that entity; the continuing degree of responsibility that the exchange may have for its contractor; how to structure the oversight activities of the regulator; and other issues where the contractor is now performing these functions. Thus striking a perfect balance between the commercial and these regulatory roles shall determine the future success of the demutualized securities exchanges. All the above concerns are discussed in details in chapter five.

Chapter Summary

The growing competitive pressure from ATS, ECNs and among securities exchanges has triggered a wave of restructuring through the demutualization process, and mergers and alliances among securities markets to maximize economies of scale, accessibility and market reach, while providing global trade facilities through a round-the-clock trading. Most of these exchanges are already reforming their ownership and management structures by demutualizing. Demutualization of exchanges is accomplished by a separation of trading facilities and member self-regulation. A successful

---

104 In Kenya, the government had vowed to take ownership in the demutualized Nairobi Securities Exchange, even when it was public knowledge that it had neither had any interest in the exchange's ownership nor contributed anything material towards its development.

demutualization process calls for the need to explore all reasons and disadvantages of such transformation. Securities exchanges should narrow down to dominant objectives and drawbacks, and demutualization option should only be considered if dominant benefits outstrip drawbacks.

Demutualization should follow a widely supported vision of making a securities exchange a national or regional leader. First, a task force should be formed to develop the vision for the exchange and examine options for the future governance and structure. Second, the task force's recommendations should be supported by a large majority of eligible voters to transform the exchange into a company requiring no link between the right to trade and ownership. Legislation should then be developed to enable the exchange to demutualize and become a tax-paying entity and lose access to funds from the state or donors. Moving cautiously, an exchange should move to demutualize and subsequently make a private placement of its shares to its members. Then share should freely be traded to the public.

Finally, there should be a wide public ownership in the demutualized exchange. However, a thorough consideration must be placed on financing, systems advancement, technology development, members' orientation, customers' demand, and challenges relating to members' resentment, regulation framework, and other conflict of interests that will emerge. The exchange members should be given trading rights that generally are commensurate with the rights held before demutualization. In addition to members, other outsiders should be given the opportunity to purchase issued shares of the exchange. The complexity of any demutualization depends on how complex a securities exchange membership structure was before demutualization, and what objectives such demutualization is designed to achieve.

The ownership and management issues of securities exchange demutualization calls for best practices for the institutional framework in terms of constitution and organisation, ownership and business model, and financing. The transformation of exchanges from mutual to demutualized structure involves two key features: a change in the ownership structure, and a change in legal as well as organizational form. Adequate safeguards to ensure appropriate governance and financial sustainability should accompany these features. Depending on the nature of ownership and management forms adopted, a demutualized exchange, given their corporate model and facing growing competitive pressures, lends itself to focusing on evolving strategic positioning which, depending on a number of conditions, could involve greater market consolidation, vertical integration and product diversification. The transformation from the mutual member-based to demutualized exchange involves issues of transferability of ownership from members to non-members. In many demutualization cases, securities exchange members have opted to retain their share ownership. The listing of shares facilitates the unlocking of the members' equity, buy-out of the interest of the traders, and assignment of monetary value to the members' seats.

There are many issues that present themselves when exchanges consider the most appropriate post-demutualization structure. These includes whether an exchange should target any particular type of investors, any ownership restrictions like percentage limits or foreign ownership caps, the composition of the board and creation of board committees, type of the share-dealing rules and policies for directors and managers, and treatment for different classes of members and seats. Other issues relate to how the board should monitor risk management, types of risks to focus on, how to meet the investor expected returns, and the role of the board on financial governance.

To maximize the benefits of demutualization, a securities exchange should consider these issues in light of its own environment since it is unlikely that one set of solutions will suit all exchanges. Securities market regulators often place restriction on ownership by one holder or a group of holders to non-controlling stakes of between 5-10 percent. Limits on ownership stakes could affect potential takeover by other exchanges, as has been witnessed in America, Asia and Europe. Such takeovers could have merit in terms of efficiency and economies of scale of the market especially where more efficient participants acquire inefficient ones.

Securities exchanges should establish membership rules as well as rules concerning the organization and operation of the exchange within the limits of the statutory legal framework. Market regulators should also ensure that such rules are in compliance with general laws, and they must monitor their enforcement. Securities exchanges should be free to choose their own business model, to compete for business and to set their own commercial agenda. This should be done within the regulatory framework to protect the public interest.

Lastly, the revenue flows from a demutualized exchange should be sufficient enough to pay for operating costs and finance its future development. In the next chapter, we now turn our focus to the possible conflicts that may arise during and after a securities exchange has transformed its trading, ownership and management structures, and how securities exchanges can deal with such conflicts.

Chapter Five

CONFLICT OF INTEREST IN DEMUTUALIZED SECURITIES EXCHANGES

Introduction

Having discussed the process of demutualization and the organizational and management issues that are likely to present themselves when a securities exchange demutualize, this chapter narrows down to the possible conflict of interest that are created during that process. It was noted that the organizational structure available for securities exchanges differs from one securities exchange to the other. These structures were discussed in depth in chapter two and three and the resultant ownership and management issues inherent in each provided in chapter four.

The two organizational structures of securities exchanges – mutualized and demutualized – are again revisited to depict the possible conflict of interest should a securities exchange transform from mutualized to demutualized structure. The conversion process itself poses many conflicts, particularly in the setting of rules to govern the exchanges owners, management and its operations. Some owners may be listed firms and trading intermediaries, some of which were the once being regulated by the securities exchange itself. It is interesting, as we are going to see, how a securities exchange oversees and supervises itself and the listed firms, and how it relates to the securities market regulator.

In trying to clarify the meaning of demutualization, it is important to clarify the sources of conflict between the role of a securities exchange as a commercial enterprise, acting in the interests of its owners and its role as a quasi-regulatory entity. Government market regulators around the world have expressed concern about the effect of securities exchange ownership and governance reforms on the ability of these exchanges to meet the self-regulatory obligations devolved to them. Mutuality and self-regulation in the public interest are typically seen as going hand-in-hand. It is this misapprehension that lies at the heart of many concerns directed at demutualization of securities exchanges. Regulatory failures are inevitable any time self-regulatory obligations imposed on a securities exchange appears to be in conflict with the commercial interests of the securities exchange owners. Such commercial interests are no less powerful for a mutualized than for a demutualized securities exchange.

Mutualized and Demutualized Structures

It has been noted in the earlier chapters that the legal forms that traditional securities exchanges have commonly adopted is that of a company limited by guarantee or company limited by shares.[105] Even in those cases where the legal form of an exchange is that of a company limited by shares, the essential character of the organization and operation of the exchange typically resembles that of a cooperative or mutual enterprise. The distinguishing feature of a mutually-owned exchange is its cooperative structure of governance. The owners of the securities exchange, its decision-makers and the direct users of its trading services are the same persons – the member-broking firms. Decisions are usually made on a one-member, one-vote basis, and often are made by committees representing the interests of member firms. In a true mutual, ownership rights are not freely transferable and may terminate with cessation of membership. Where a shareholding structure is used, the exchange is typically non-public and share ownership is confined to a small group, usually stockbrokers.

From time to time, a number of independent or public representatives are appointed to the board to offset the self-interest of the members.[106] Within these traditional structures, the exchange is expected to perform

---

105 See IOSCO (2001) Issues Paper on Stock Exchange Demutualization: IOSCO Technical Committee, June .

106 William Pearson, Director, Corporate Finance, Securities and Futures Commission, Hong Kong, China.

regulatory functions such as listing, and conduct prudential regulation of its broker-members. The securities exchange is in turn regulated or supervised and overseen by a government statutory markets regulator. In contrast, most for-profit enterprises are organized, as corporations with share capital under which the owners of the exchange, its decision-makers and its principal customers are three separate groups. The shareholders vest decision-making power in a board of directors who are subject to election and removal by shareholders. The day-to-day decisions are made by the management of the firm. The voting rights of shareholders are generally commensurate with their economic interest in the firm – one share, one vote. Companies limited by shares may raise new capital in a variety of ways and from various sources. These sources are well discussed in many textbooks for business finance or financial management.

As a result, many exchanges have been recently changing from not-for-profit member-owned into for-profit shareholder-owned organizations. This is known as demutualization without strict regard to whether prior to conversion the exchange was truly mutual or cooperative in nature, or a company limited by guarantee. The restructuring involves moving from an entity in which ownership of a share or seat in a securities exchange confers a right to trade on, and have some influence over, the management of the exchange, into an entity where ownership rights and trading rights are separate, and where the right to trade confers no ownership or management right. The trend to demutualize an exchange is being driven largely by changes in technology and increased competition.

Trading and depository technologies are developing rapidly and they are also expensive to install and maintain. Competition from ECNs and other ATS offering anonymity and alternative or lower cost structures is drawing trading volume away from traditional securities exchanges. These developments are forcing traditional securities exchanges to become more efficient in all activities, including in their decision-making processes. The conventional rationale to public companies limited by shares is profit maximization. It has been said that the single overriding objective shared by all listed public firms, whatever their size or type of business, is the preservation and the greatest practicable enhancement over time of their shareholders' investment.

A public company is able, under some pressure, to distribute profits to its owners. For-profit enterprises are said to respond to a changing environment quickly, and engender a proprietorial sense in shareholders and holders of stock options, such as management. They are disciplined by competition from other firms and it is this competition which forces the creation of mechanisms to efficiently monitor the performance of management. Ownership is seen as a key factor in determining the ability of a firm to respond to market and regulatory developments. Under a mutual governance structure, a securities exchange is focused primarily on how its operations affect its staffs, commercial interests of its member stockbrokers.

Outside ownership of a public for-profit exchange enables it to focus on the requirements of the exchange as a business and increase its capacity to make the difficult business decisions required by changing markets, technology and international and domestic competition. Therefore, demutualization is seen as facilitating a response to market and regulatory developments by separating rights of ownership from rights to trade and rights to manage; removing certain inefficiencies and conflicts of interest which impaired the decision-making process; and facilitating capital raising and alliances or mergers between securities exchanges. The decision to demutualize has far-reaching consequences both for the securities exchange and the traditional manner of its operation, and for the regulatory framework for markets both for futures and stocks.

Demutualization and self-listing by a securities exchange places a spotlight on the management of potential conflicts of interest. This chapter therefore explains the nature of these conflicts, and the means by which some have been addressed by some demutualized exchanges. The incidence of conflict or potential for conflict is not unique to a demutualized exchange. However, a key consideration in preparing for a demutualized environment is the need to demonstrate that effective mechanisms exist to address potential conflicts of interest arising from an exchange's profit motive and the supervisory function that a securities exchange performs.

Potential Conflicts of Interest Upon Demutualization

Demutualized securities exchanges raise greater concerns about conflicts of interest than mutual exchanges. Mutual securities exchanges answer to their members, but once demutualized, exchanges must protect their owners' interests. Although a securities exchange members initially may be its owners, they eventually may choose to sell their ownership interests in the exchange. The new owners may have no interest in trading and may be disinterested in the exchange beyond reaping returns on their investment. While this divergence of interests may exist regardless of whether such an exchange is privately or publicly owned, the divergence would be greater in the case of a publicly self-listed and traded exchange because its shareholders are less likely to be market participants. In addition, shareholder interests may be protected by shareholder derivative litigation or shareholder class actions, at the expense of market participants. A securities exchange, however, must continue to maintain an effective program of self-regulation. A conflict of interest may arise if an attempt to fulfil self-regulatory obligations negatively affects the profitability of a demutualized exchange. A conflict may also arise in disciplinary proceedings involving securities exchange participant who is the owner, or a significant shareholder, of a competing securities exchange. The securities markets are also facing another complication of exchanges listing their own shares on their trading boards – a phenomenon known as self-listing.

However, in the case of futures markets, exchanges begin to offer contracts on single equities, the market regulator does not yet share analogous concerns. Conflicts of interest inherent in self-regulation manifest equally, but differently, in demutualized and mutualized entities. After all, traditional securities exchanges are run by members interested in making money and enhancing value through trading and maximizing seat value. Furthermore, securities exchange disciplinary programs where members sanction fellow members can affect the rigor of an exchange's self-regulatory program. Even if conflicts are heightened in a demutualized environment, securities exchanges would continue to have a vested interest in preserving their reputations for providing fair and efficient markets.

These exchanges ultimately would bear a heavy price in sacrificing good will and their reputations in the interest of short-term profits – a habit common in human beings.

Basically, there are six main types of conflict that present themselves under these circumstances. First, is the resources conflict relating to whether a for-profit exchange can devote sufficient resources to regulatory activities. Second, the executive time conflict relates to whether senior executives of a securities exchange would devote sufficient of their high-powered time to regulation compared with profit making. Third, the listings supervisory conflict relates to whether the listings department in a securities exchange would ease up on scrutiny of new listings, grant listing rule waivers more readily and subject existing listed firms to less intense scrutiny. Will the listings department be too tough in applying listing rules to listed competitors, or give favoured treatment to any listed firm with which the exchange conducts business? Moreover, the broker supervisory conflict relates to whether the compliance department would ease up on its scrutiny of brokers because they are now viewed as paying customers.

The demutualization of securities exchanges raises other contentious issues, for example self-regulatory conflict, arising between shareholders and members that could lessen the ability of exchanges to engage in effective self-regulation. A potentially more serious conflict is the regulation of an ATS market by an exchange. Also, securities market service firms are concerned about increased costs if several ATSs becoming exchanges and begin to engage in self-regulation. Therefore, some financial services industry participants argue in favour of a single self-regulatory organization (SRO) for exchanges and member firms.

Moreover, there are ongoing power struggles amongst SROs and between the SROs and the state market regulator.[107] Conflicts arise because exchanges set rules in the public interest that may negatively affect the commercial interest of its members, and monitor and enforce rules against the members. Some critics have argued that demutualization may reduce

---

107 See Karmel, R. (2000). Turning Seats into Shares: Implications of Demutualization for the Regulation of Stock and Futures Exchanges, at 57 (December).

SRO conflicts. The interests of owners in a demutualized exchange may act as a constraint on actions that benefit only member firms. A reputation as a fair and efficient market is a competitive advantage for a securities exchange, and a for-profit exchange may have more resources to devote to the regulation that enhances its reputation. However, the more commonly expressed concern is that the for-profit structure increases the scope and intensity of conflicts because revenues must meet expenses and generate a rate of return for exchange investors.

We have recently witnessed cases where some securities exchanges resolve to subsidize their regulatory arms. The benefits of good regulation are hard to quantify and therefore a for-profit exchange may be unwilling to devote sufficient resources to enforcement. Further, since a regulatory function imposes additional costs, having a regulatory arm makes a firm a less attractive candidate for an initial public offering (IPO). In preparing for an IPO a securities exchange will seek to minimize costs and emphasize its potential for earnings. Spinning off the regulatory arm does that. A for-profit securities exchange may enter new businesses, increasing further the opportunities for conflict. If a securities dealer that operates an ATS is also a member of the exchange, conflicts of interest may arise in the exchange regulating the dealer providing a competing service. Conflicts include denial of access to particular activities or failure to make changes to accommodate an entity providing a competing service.

Under the SRO model, an exchange assumes the role of co-regulator with the designated regulatory authority to ensure that the securities market is fair, well-informed and efficient. The state should pass a law clarifying the responsibilities of a securities exchange as an SRO, and its accountability to the market regulator and the government in carrying out its SRO responsibilities. It has to impose a duty on the exchange to do everything necessary to ensure that the market it conducts is an orderly and fair market and that the self-regulatory functions are carried out on an ongoing basis. It should oblige the exchange to notify the market regulator of the particulars of the situation in a variety of circumstances like when it fines or disciplines a stockbroker.

Moreover, if a securities exchange believes that a person has committed or is about to commit a serious contravention of its business or listing rules or the law, it must notify the market regulator. When a securities exchange makes available to the market information about a listed company, it must also provide that information to the regulator. If a securities exchange becomes aware of any matter which adversely affects a stockbroker's ability to meet its obligations under the law, it must notify the regulator of the details. In sum, a market regulator has statutory regulator roles and the demutualized securities exchange is an SRO which has responsibility for the day-to-day running of the securities market. Among these responsibilities include the maintenance of market integrity, fair trading systems, guarantees of trade completion, clearing, settlement and transfer systems and information about securities that are traded in the market through its trading system.

Self-Regulatory Roles

Securities exchanges, whether mutual or demutualized, have multiple roles to play. First, a securities exchange is a *commercial entity* carrying on the business of running a trading platform and seeking to protect and promote its business. Second, it plays a critical role in ensuring the *integrity and efficiency* of capital markets by setting and enforcing rules to regulate its market. The commercial role of an exchange is to provide services and generate revenue. The exchanges generate revenue from listings, trading services, settlement fees, market data and information fees, and membership fees. The revenue is derived directly from those who use or purchase services or information from a securities exchange, inkling the stockbrokers, intermediaries, listed issuers and information vendors, and indirectly from the investing public. In performing their role in the capital markets, securities exchanges are usually viewed as performing public functions and are subject to oversight by the statutory regulator or government. They are further vested with self-regulatory functions involving regulation of listed firms and member-brokers.

The typical self-regulatory functions of exchanges are the regulation of trading and listing on the exchange and the regulation of the conduct of member brokers. Regulation of trading includes admitting new users to the exchange trading system, devising rules for trading and enforcing such rules.

Regulation of member-brokers includes monitoring financial resources as well as their conduct. Regulation of listing includes screening to determine qualifications for listing, approving new applicants and monitoring listed issuers' ongoing compliance with the listing rules – including continuous disclosure of material information to the market. There exist numerous advantages and drawbacks of self-regulation, as discussed in other sections in this chapter.

Objectives of Public Policy Market Regulation
The public policy objectives of securities market regulation are generally common to most jurisdictions. The objectives and principles of Securities Regulation of the International Organization of Securities Commissions (IOSCO) succinctly state these objectives to be the protection of investors, ensuring that markets are fair, efficient and transparent, and the reduction of systemic risk. It therefore follows that the underlying objective of securities market regulation is ensuring market integrity such that users will have confidence in using the markets. This means adopting those processes that result in markets being transparent, users being treated fairly, the price formation process being reliable, transparent and securities market being free of misleading, manipulative or abusive conduct.

An investigation by NASD and NASDAQ Stock Market (NASDAQ) in USA, for example, contains the SEC's view of the standard for a self-regulatory organisation. The investigation uncovered a number of matters of fundamental concern about the operations and structure of the NASD and the Nasdaq market that warrant serious changes. It noted that while self-regulation benefits from the knowledge, insight and expertise brought by industry participants, it must give primacy to the fundamental purpose of regulation of the securities markets, the protection of investors and the public interest.[108]

---

108 Securities Exchange Act of 1934 - Release No. 51163 / February 9, 2005. Report of Investigation Pursuant to Section 21(a) of the Securities Exchange Act of 1934 Regarding The Nasdaq Stock Market, Inc. as Overseen by Its Parent, The National Association of Securities Dealers, Inc. https://www.sec.gov/litigation/investreport/34-51163.htm.

Given its regulatory duties, NASD's most important constituency was the investing public, not listed firms or broker-dealers. The report states that there is a tendency for a regulated industry to influence its regulator to protect the industry's proprietary interests. A securities exchange must therefore guard against the efforts of any one segment of its membership to assert undue influence over its regulatory functions and processes. The public interest must be the predominant concern. Failure of an exchange to take appropriate action in circumstances where some action is dictated by the facts must constitute a failure by an SRO to meet its statutory obligations and its public interest mandate as an SRO. The characteristic mode of the regulation of securities and futures markets that has emerged to overcome the weaknesses of self-regulation is a system of co-regulation. Under this system SROs generally assume the role of co-regulator with the government regulatory authority to protect investors and the public interest, promote just and equitable principles of trade and prevent fraud and manipulation. The government market regulator oversees the SRO and exercises statutory powers, often including, among others, its own rule making, powers to compel testimony and production of documents, and sometimes prosecution – all meant to force the SRO to toe the line.

Possible Self-Regulatory Organization Conflicts
Securities exchanges, which have historically operated as self-regulatory organizations, are subject to conflicts of interest. Conflicts arise because the exchange members are asked to set rules in the public interest that may negatively affect their own commercial interests and monitor and enforce rules against each other. A major weakness of self-regulation is the inherent potential to favour the interests of the member- brokers over those of the investing public. Because SROs are left directly in charge of the implementation of a program of the state and public policy, and are themselves owned or controlled by the industry participants who are the objects of regulation, self-regulation raises the distinct possibility of inadequate enforcement of rules and standards, and concerted anti-competitive conduct in opposition to the public policy goals.

Indeed, the SRO may, in ways that are not readily apparent to outsiders, subvert the regulatory goals to its own business goals and, by establishing a façade of self-regulation, give the impression of a properly regulated industry. Demutualization may lessen some of the SRO conflicts. Where demutualization leads to a separation of the owners of a securities exchange from its users, the interests of the owners may act as a constraint on actions that would benefit the interests of the member firms. The more the shareholder base looks like the public as a whole, the greater this effect is likely to be, as the shareholder interest and the public interest will arguably tend to converge. Furthermore, where a reputation as a fair and efficient market is seen as a competitive advantage, or the lack of one as a significant disadvantage, a for-profit securities exchange may have a greater incentive to devote more resources to activities that enhance that reputation. In fact, demutualized exchanges may experience greater conflicts of interest. Becoming a listed firm permits the raising of capital from the public, but brings with it enhanced duties and obligations enshrined in the Company Law and Listing Rules and greater responsibilities to shareholders.

Seemingly, these influences combine to accentuate the competitive and profit-making motive. The risk is that a fair and orderly market remains a goal only if it passes a commercial cost - benefit analysis. These possibilities are greater still where the SRO is a monopoly with little or no domestic competition. The possible conflicts of interest are generally created or increased where the for-profit entity also performs regulatory functions. This is especially the case where the regulatory functions are a cost centre rather than a profit centre. While not all such possible conflicts are new, demutualization may exacerbate some of them calling for the need for the re-examination of the specific issues and regulatory responses which should emerge. It is necessary to consider carefully whether the commercial pressures and corporate structure of a for-profit entity may undermine the commitment of resources and capabilities of the exchange to fulfil its regulatory and public interest responsibilities to an appropriate standard. It must, however, also be accepted that commercial considerations are proper considerations for an exchange. Self-regulation is an expensive undertaking, which has considerable public benefits and a securities exchange must be able to fund the costs of this activity and its aftermath. This is a serious issue that must be considered if demutualization process is to be a success.

Regulatory Concerns Upon Demutualization

There trepidations that securities exchange demutualization may bring to the fore some regulatory concerns in a number of areas, given that cost cutting on regulatory functions can affect the ability to properly perform the relevant function. A securities exchange competes with other operators providing similar services but who may not carry out regulatory functions. These pressures may affect the proper performance of self-regulatory functions, to the detriment of the market and public interest. In the cost versus benefit equation of *good regulation*, the costs are easier to determine than the benefits. It is not difficult to envisage a securities exchange being confronted with decisions involving a choice between expenditure on regulatory infrastructure, such as market surveillance or enforcing disclosure of price sensitive information, and financial returns to shareholders. Lowering of standards to increase business and revenue leads to a race to the bottom. Particularly, a for-profit securities exchange may wish to lower listing standards in order to attract more companies and increase its fee income; or it may be less willing to take enforcement action against users who are a source of revenue for the exchange. In addition, a securities exchange may seek to use its regulatory powers more vigorously to increase its competitive position, a race to the top, or its revenue. This may include a tendency to apply higher standards or take greater enforcement action than before to generate revenue from fines.

Securities exchange demutualization may lead to increase in other possible conflicts of interest. First, those arising between the interests of the exchange and the interests of users, which are regulated by it, especially where the user may be in competition with the securities exchange business. There is a risk that the exchange may seek to use its regulatory powers against competitors, which are listed firms or trading members in a way that adversely affects the competitors' business interests. Conversely, the exchange may be tempted to treat more leniently a regulated user, which is a business associate. Competition laws may not adequately address these situations, unless such laws are reformed.

Second, there may exist a conflict between the interests of the exchange and interests of the public. In the context of securities exchanges listing on their own markets, it is widely acknowledged that the public interest is not well served by allowing an exchange to supervise itself. The exchange is likely to face conflicts of interest in screening and admitting itself to listing, monitoring its on-going compliance with listing rules, monitoring the trading in its securities and taking necessary enforcement action, should it find itself in violation. Also, a securities exchange which is successful in attracting new listings may find its own market capitalization increasing. The exchange may try to increase the value of its securities by seeking to be included in one or more index funds on the basis of its market capitalization. This is especially problematic if the exchange creates its own index fund and becomes a constituent member. Remember, virtually all securities exchanges do compute and maintain at least one market index.

Furthermore, more conflict may arise between the interests of the securities exchange and the interests of its board members, who are associated with some regulated users. In the past, concerns have arisen from the fact that representatives of market participants or listed issuers are elected to the board of an exchange. In fact, there is a serious risk that these officers take action on behalf of the exchange, which serves their own business interests. Undeniably, these conflicts may be greater where a securities exchange is a profit-making firm, which competes with those business interests. Moreover, there is likely to be a conflict between duties of board members who are representatives of the public interest, and their duties to the exchange shareholders. Public interest board members may find that they face a conflict between actions, which are in the public interest but may not be in the interests of shareholders or sometimes even the management.

Finally, securities exchange member-brokers have been found to resist corporate restructuring of ownership and management structures of their exchanges fearing that such process will either drive them out of business or reduce their revenue and control of the exchange. Imagine being asked to let go the goose that has been laying you the golden eggs, yet you are the one to make that decision. So from the onset of demutualization process, member-brokers are already conflicted. In sum, these conflicts of interests are serious and would affect the integrity, fairness and transparency of operations of demutualized exchanges.

Responding to Conflict of Interest Upon Demutualization

Globally, how have securities markets regulators responded to concerns arising about conflict of interest during and after demutualization by securities exchanges? In an effort to address the inherent conflict of interest, there have been varied regulatory responses to such issues arising from demutualization, depending on jurisdiction since they depend upon the prevailing legal framework and regulatory philosophy. Some consistency has, however, existed in dealing with the issues which arise, and the general approach has tended towards retaining the self-regulatory function for the time being and transferring some regulatory functions to the state market regulator. While there are no examples where demutualization has led to the removal of all self-regulatory functions, the United Kingdom has tended to move closer to that end.

A closer look at the existing experience, the regulatory responses can be divided into three. The first one relates to changes to the corporate structure to ensure that the regulatory function continues to be performed and is adequately resourced. The second one is creating new independent supervisory committee to oversee the self-regulatory functions. The third is making changes to the governance structure to ensure that the public interest is safeguarded and prevails over commercial interests of the exchange. Finally, is making changes to the regulatory framework to address the possible conflicts of interest which arise between the exchange upon its self-listing and between the exchange and individuals dealing with it in the course of its operations.

Changing the Governance Structure. It is accepted that whether mutual or a for-profit entity, the governance structure of a securities exchange has an important bearing on its regulatory and commercial performance and on its ability to reconcile the competing interests of its managers, owners and users, and potential users of its services. The structure may affect the delivery of the self-regulatory functions. A failure in this respect may have an adverse impact on the market as a whole and on the capacity of securities exchanges to deliver the public policy objectives set for them by the state. Given the additional pressures that arise upon demutualization, the statutory market regulator or the state may provide, for example, that there be individuals to represent the public interest on the board of directors. In some cases, the state is empowered under legislation to appoint a majority of directors. Furthermore, to overcome the potential conflict such directors may face between reconciling the interests of the public and their duties to the exchange shareholders, it may be appropriate to provide a statutory remedy.

For instance, in some jurisdictions, the demutualization legislation imposes an express duty on a securities exchange to ensure an orderly and fair market in securities or futures contracts traded on or through a securities exchange. In discharging this obligation, the exchange is required to act in the interests of the public, having particular regard to the interests of the investing public. Where these interests conflict with any other interests that the exchange is required to serve under any other law, the former must prevail. Since this obligation applies to the exchange, all directors – not only those appointed by the state – are placed in the same position. Furthermore, statutory indemnity could be provided for a securities exchange and its officers to remove any potential liability they may have as a result of giving priority to the public interest as required by the law.

Different ways exist that can be used to control the abuse of any monopoly position, including the requirement that changes to fees imposed by an exchange should be subject to approval. Such law may require that in considering any changes to fees or commissions the market regulator must have regard to the level of competition for the matter for which the fee is imposed, and the level of fees imposed by any similar body in or outside country for the same or similar matter. Oversight by a statutory market regulator or by a parliamentary committee may be provided. In fact, exchanges need to file a report each year and answer questions in relation to its operations. Share ownership may be limited, with or without scope for a waiver of those limitations by the statutory market regulator. In many jurisdictions, legislations provide that no person and their associates may have more than 5 percent of the voting rights in a demutualized exchange unless authorized by the market regulator.

Authorisation is likely to be given in the context of share issues for the purpose of entering into alliances. To ensure that any holding company of an exchange does not dispose of some or all of its shareholding to a third party, it should be a legal requirement that prior regulatory approval be obtained from the market regulator. Indeed, these are some of the checks and balances to be put in place to address the conflicts of interest, which have been reported in some markets.

Changing the Corporate Structure. The other means of addressing the possible conflict of interest upon demutualization is that changes may be made to the corporate structure of an exchange to ensure that the regulatory function continues to be properly performed and adequately financed. This means that such functions are carried out independently from, and is not compromised by, the exchange's commercial operations. These actions often involve transferring some or all of the regulatory functions to a separate entity, such as another group company with an independent governance structure and budget; another self-regulatory organization, or giving the choice to contract out the performance of the functions to another SRO or retaining it in-house but securing its performance in various ways; or transferring the functions to the statutory market regulator.[109] In the second case, an assessment must be made of the capacity of the company and its officers, to which the functions are transferred, to properly perform them.

Nevertheless, all these options require an assessment of various factors, including whether the entity in question has adequate arrangements in place to operate the market and settle and clear trades; supervise the market; protect retail investors including providing compensation funds, and has sufficient resources generally to adequately carry on each of these

---

109 See SIA (2000) Reinventing Self-Regulation, White Paper for the Securities Industry Association's Ad Hoc Committee on Regulatory Implications of Demutualization, 4 January.

functions. Even in jurisdictions where the commitment to self-regulation is strong enough to ensure that there is presently no urge to transfer the regulatory functions to the statutory regulator, it is important to ensure that any restructuring is seen to achieve true independence. Unless the public perception is one of genuine independence then the solution is unlikely to last and pressure will mount for a complete transfer of responsibility to the statutory market regulator. Ensuring adequate sourcing of the regulatory function may also involve imposing capital adequacy requirements or requiring the establishment of reserves, much as for financial intermediaries. There is commonly no requirement for a securities exchange simply to have sufficient financial resources to conduct its regulatory functions in an efficient manner. Such a requirement is desirable and market regulators should direct the expenditure of sufficient resources to particular areas of regulation if this is to be achieved.

Launching New Supervisory Committee. Given the multiple roles of securities exchanges, issues are likely to arise questioning the role of an exchange as a regulator. Recall that exchanges operate both as market supervisors and independent entities. Once demutualized, an exchange is likely to focus more on profit rather than regulation. There is need therefore to launch a supervisory review committee to monitor the exchange's regulatory performance and oversee the supervision of listed firms with which the exchange either does business or competes. This is necessary to manage the trading due to the tension likely to arise from the exchange's role as the market regulator and a market participant.

Over-Regulating of Exchange Users. Due to the obvious conflicts of interest involved on demutualization, it is now generally accepted that it is not appropriate for a self-regulatory exchange to be responsible for its own listing or supervising its own compliance with the listing rules and the trading in its securities. It is less obvious what should be done with conflicts arising between the exchange and other users of the exchange. However, these may involve treating a business competitor like a listed firm or stockbroker setting up a new trading or clearing system, more harshly or a business associate more leniently than would otherwise be the case. In such cases, powers may be needed to step into the shoes of a securities exchange and discharge the relevant regulatory function. Therefore, a demutualization legislation should provide that whenever a statutory market regulator is satisfied that a conflict of interest exists or may arise, or has existed and may be repeated, between the interests of the exchange and the interests of the proper performance of a regulatory function, such regulator may by notice direct the exchange to take steps specified in the notice, including those relating to any of its affairs, business and property, for the purposes of remedying the conflict or the cause of the conflict. Nevertheless, such power should not be abused by a market regulator.

It can be presumed that in such instances of conflict, any third party, who feels it is being prejudiced, will make this known to the statutory market regulator. However, it can also be assumed that a business associate of a securities exchange being given a good deal by the exchange will not be so quick to announce it. Furthermore, there may be some concern that users of an exchange will be tempted to complain too readily that conflicts of interests arise and that the exchange becomes increasingly unable to exercise its normal regulatory and disciplinary functions. While responsibility for stepping into the shoes of the SROs and exercising relevant functions may be assumed by the statutory market regulator, it is possible for such regulator to appoint another entity to undertake this function on its behalf.

Dealing with Conflicts of Interest Upon Demutualization

How can securities exchanges as well as state market regulators manage and deal with the inherent conflict of interest during and after demutualization? Conflicts brought about by demutualization, as has been discussed, have the potential to ruin the integrity and fairness in securities markets. Nevertheless, the main challenge for exchanges is to create an environment in which conflicts are recognized, minimized and managed. Such an environment involves corporate governance requirements like the need for public directors; a clear statutory statement of the obligation to provide a fair and efficient public trading market; rigorous regulatory oversight; and enhanced transparency through requirements to publish rules and decisions.

Such environment should also have mechanisms to enhance exchange accountability to the state market regulator and the public; separation of the commercial activities of a securities exchange from regulatory functions; and dividing lines of authority and accountability within a single firm to establishing a separate legal entity or transferring some regulatory responsibilities, like regulation of an exchange as a listed firm, to the government market regulator. A member-owned exchange has the right to assess members and request adequate capital contribution. A demutualized exchange loses the right to demand that shareholders contribute additional capital, but gains the flexibility to raise capital from public or other private sources. Capital and solvency requirements serve to reduce the risk of failure of a financial market related firm by requiring a capital cushion to absorb losses. Capital also provides liquidity to permit a firm to operate during an orderly wind down.

Many market regulators have raised the issue of whether capital requirements should be imposed on a demutualized securities exchange. Demutualized exchanges may also be required to establish a reserve to address shortfalls in capital, or for the regulator to monitor the financial condition of an exchange and take remedial action, if appropriate. New business lines of exchanges may reduce financial risks by diversifying the exchange's sources of income. A regulator could require segregation of core and non-core activities, firewalls to protect the resources necessary to run the exchange's core activities or impose a requirement for prior regulatory approval. A mutual securities exchange is governed by consensus, so no one member exerts control over the decisions of the exchange. With demutualization, ownership is broadened to include non-member investors.

Concerns may arise if an exchange is controlled by one or more persons. An issue arises, whether the public interest requires a limit on share ownership or prior regulatory approval for ownership above a threshold percentage. So that no person or combination of persons acting jointly or in concert may beneficially own or control more than five percent of the outstanding shares without the prior approval of the market regulator. Moreover, persons who hold more than five percent immediately following demutualization may need to be *grandfathered* from these provisions, meaning such persons may not vote in excess of five percent without the prior approval of the market regulator. A requirement should be put in place requiring that in the first two years following the continuance of a securities exchange as a for-profit corporation, the transfer of shares is restricted, and any transfer must require either the majority consent of the Board or the majority vote at a annual general meeting of shareholders.

However, the state market regulator, in consultation with the head of national treasury, may give approval to a person to hold more than 5 percent if it can be demonstrated to be in the interest of the investing public.

Such restrictions on the shareholding limits is due to the fact that securities exchanges have a critical role to play in the national economy and thus it is in the national public interest not to allow any one party to gain control of the Exchange, and such a limitation encourages diverse ownership of such exchanges. The 5 percent shareholding limit results in a prohibition on hostile takeovers of a securities exchange thereby removing a disciplinary tool on management. Economists argue that a healthy take-over market works efficiently and effectively to control costs imposed by the managers on the owners of the firm. The threat of take-overs forces the management to focus on performance and use capital efficiently in a manner that creates value to all the stakeholders, including the society

Nevertheless, the fair and efficient functioning of an exchange is of significant benefit to the public. An exchange provides liquidity and price discovery that facilitates efficient raising of capital for businesses, benefiting the wider corporate sector and the economy as a whole. In recognition of the role of a securities exchange and the degree of conflict of interest in a member-owned exchange, securities exchanges are commonly required to have public or independent directors on the board to represent the interests of the community. Public directors monitor conflicts of interest in an SRO and promote integrity in decision-making. But should demutualized securities exchanges still need to have public directors and if so, should they be given specific public interest responsibilities? Since the public interest in a fair and efficient securities exchange continues in a demutualized exchange, the need for public directors continues. The directors of a for-profit securities exchange must take into account the interests of all of its stakeholders if the exchange is to function effectively and to be of benefit to the wider society.

In fact, these exchange stakeholders are its customers (firms that list on the exchange and the securities information processors), its members that have trading privileges (broker-dealers), its owners (shareholders) and the investing public (the society). Thus, while a corporation exists to make profits for its owners, it is imperative that the investing public should not lose confidence in the integrity of the stock exchange. In a demutualized exchange, the senior management of the exchange are likely to be the decision makers on a day-to-day basis. Market demands will push such a securities exchange to hire as competent people as possible. Is there a need for direct involvement of the state regulator in hiring decisions? Apparently, MOUs are used to define the regulatory relationship between institutions such as MoUs for companies matters covering exchange's supervision of listed entities; for transfer of Information through provision of documents released to the market by listed entities; for self-listing detailing arrangements for an exchange to be listed on its own market and supervised as a listed entity; for referral to market regulator matters detected by an exchange in its supervision; for an exchange's responsibility for supervision of brokers and broking firms; and for a securities exchange to regulate conflicts of interest that may arise.

Therefore, on demutualization, securities exchanges may face the four major conflicts of resource, executive time, listing supervisory, and broker supervisory conflicts. There are a number of ways in which these exchanges may deal with these conflicts. First, is the removal of activity option, which removes certain activities from the relevant division of a securities exchange. Second, is the separation option separating the business activities of an exchange from its regulatory activities. Third, is the external oversight option, subjecting the regulatory activities of the exchange to external oversight. Fourth, is the disclosure option meant to disclose how a securities exchange has dealt with regulatory issues, for example in an annual report meant for an AGM. Restricting ownership or involvement option, limiting those who could control or influence exchange activities.

These options are not always mutually exclusive for a given activity as it is possible to adopt different options for different types of activities. Some securities exchange may adopt elements of each option across their business lines. For example, the removal of activity option can be adopted in relation to the oversight of an exchange's own listing. This can create a separate investigations and enforcement unit. Prior to demutualization this role could have been blended with membership administration. The law can then be amended to clarify the continuing obligations of an exchange and to ensure accountability to the state market regulator in carrying out these responsibilities. Reporting requirements and audit and direction powers concerning compliance with these ongoing requirements have to be introduced. The external oversight mechanisms in the law should further be enhanced under the capital markets legal reforms by conferral of direct audit powers upon the securities market regulator, who should then take initiatives to enhance transparency of its supervisory policies and procedures.

This should include public consultation for rule development proposals, publication of waiver and disciplinary determinations, the issue of guidance notes about the procedures and compliance expectations and improved mechanisms for public access to supervisory outcomes. This also calls for creation of a supervisory review committee which, among other things, reviews and separately reports on the exchange's supervisory activities. Such amendments must be accompanied by the introduction of a fit and proper person requirement in relation to those involved in the securities exchange. Whichever model is chosen, it is important to regularly review existing arrangements to help ensure that a securities exchange builds for itself a reputation for integrity, efficiency and transparency. In view of the increasing globalization of markets, there is also a need to monitor international developments in governance of supervisory activities and to assess whether the model chosen best equips a securities exchange to embrace international alliances and other forms of cooperation among exchanges. This necessary given that demutualized exchange have been found to grow their activities through mergers, acquisition and other forms of strategic alliances targeted at other exchanges.

Regarding the issue of regulation upon exchange self-listing, if an exchange is to remain credible in its oversight of public firms, it must ensure that, in relation to its own listing, it adheres strictly to the highest standards set for other companies. In most countries where demutualization has taken place, company law has been amended to provide that a securities exchange may be included in its own official list and its securities granted quotation. If a securities exchange has entered into such arrangements, securities regulators require for dealing with possible conflicts of interest that might arise from the securities exchange quoting its own securities on itself and the purpose of ensuring the integrity of trading in securities of the securities exchange. To complement this change in the law, exchanges and their regulators can enter into an MOU setting out the way that the exchange and the securities regulator would relate to each other in the monitoring of the exchange's compliance as a listed entity with the listing rules, the settlement rules and the company law, and of regulator's supervision of the exchange as a listed entity.

A key objective of the exchange and securities regulator in negotiating such an MOU should be to ensure consistency of outcomes and timing between the exchange in the administration of the listing rules for other entities, and the regulator in its administration of the listing rules for the exchange. Under such an MOU, the regulator should be responsible for supervising the exchange's compliance with the listing rules. It should receive the exchange's application for admission to the official list of an exchange. In relation to the continuing regulation of exchange as a listed entity, the regulator should be responsible for exercising the powers and functions that an exchange has as a securities exchange in relation to other listed entities. Such exchanges are not bound to monitor or enforce the listing rules in relation to themselves. If an exchange wishes to apply for exemption or declaration in relation to a modifiable provision of the company law, or a waiver of the listing rules it may apply to the regulator. Listed exchanges should pay the fees required by the listing rules to the market regulator.

However, listed exchanges should make their own announcements to the market regulator in the same way that other listed companies do. The exchanges set appropriate parameters for generating surveillance alerts relating to dealings in their own securities. Such a structure is designed to allow independent supervision of an exchange's compliance with its listing rules, while at the same time utilizing the same platforms and mechanisms that the exchange has established practically to accommodate supervisory activities. But the structure should operate effectively and efficiently in order to cultivate a harmonious relationship between an exchange and market regulator.

There is also the need to review the supervisory functions of securities exchanges. Upon demutualization and self-listing, one of the issues that may arise is that the exchange operates both as a market supervisor and a listed company. Such an exchange would be focusing on profiteering rather than regulation. Some exchanges have responded to these concerns by launching a supervisory review subsidiary to monitor the exchange's regulatory performance and oversee the supervision of listed companies with which the exchange either does business or competes. This was necessary to manage the trading due to the tension likely to arise from the exchange's role as the market regulator and a market participant. The role of the subsidiary is to review policies and procedures, including the resources; provide reports and opinions to the exchange's board about standards and resources; provide assurance that the exchange adequately complies with its responsibilities, conducts itself ethically and responsibly and has appropriate controls against conflicts; oversee supervision of 'conflicted' entities; and makes reports available to securities regulator.

There is also the need to address the issue of supervision of the other listed firms. Another issue that usually arises is whether a for-profit exchange should ease up on its supervision of listed companies. There are strong commercial reasons for exchanges to maintain a high level of supervision: if they do not, a fall in investor confidence is likely. Where there is a loss of confidence, investors will almost certainly withdraw from the exchange's market and go elsewhere to make their investments. The consequentially reduced market activity will have a direct negative impact on an exchange's profits. In addition to this commercial discipline, there are usually significant regulatory controls on exchanges that collectively serve as a strong deterrent to inappropriate supervisory decisions.

Similarly, there is also the need to relook at overall supervision of market intermediaries by a demutualized exchange. When an exchange is mutualized, it has a membership department that is responsible for monitoring and enforcing compliance with its business rules, as well as acting as the central point of contact for members regarding exchange enquiries. When it is demutualized, it separates its supervisory functions associated with brokers from its customer relations' functions.

Exchange Profit Objective Versus Supervisory Functions

There are a number of issues relating to market and regulatory *controls* and supervision activities.

Market and Regulatory. In many jurisdictions, the regulatory framework governing supervision of exchanges and prohibiting anti-competitive behaviour provides powerful incentives to an exchange and its board of directors and senior management to behave ethically and responsibly. So do the commercial interests of an exchange in promoting public confidence in, and therefore custom to, its markets.

There are numerous checks and balances to ensure an appropriate level of accountability by exchanges in respect of its market supervision obligations. These include, first, a clear and continuing obligations imposed on an exchange as a market operator under the company law. Second, is the transparency of processes, by their embodiment in rules, which are available for public scrutiny and comment. These rules are subject to informal regulator's approval processes and ministerial disallowance procedures. The other issue relates to the structural arrangements, which enable the quarantining of the supervisory decision-making and the hearing and appeal rights afforded to customers. In addition, there should be a public register of listing rule waiver decisions and of business rule disciplinary determinations. Also, there is the need for the publication of the bases upon which the exchange exercises discretion under, or grants relief from, business rules. Finally, there should be a requirement to lodge a compliance report annually with securities market regulator.

Usually, securities regulators have the power to prohibit trading in the securities of any listed company, and may also require an exchange to enforce its rules. Therefore, there should exist the requirement to lodge particulars of disciplinary action and serious contraventions of the law/rules with the regulator and the obligations imposed by exchange's MOUs with the regulator. Such MOUs with the regulator may be meant to further refine and ensure that the exchange properly implements and carries out its supervisory responsibilities. These MOUs, dealing with markets, membership matters, company matters and transfer of information, place responsibilities on an exchange which expand on and complement its supervisory responsibilities under the company law, the committees and tribunals which assist an exchange in the performance of its supervisory responsibilities; these committees and tribunals consist of people external to an exchange; and prohibitions on anti-competitive behaviour or misuse of market position contained in trade practices law. These issues have already been espoused.

Supervisory Activities. Where there is discontent with a supervisory outcome, commentators may try to attribute this to an exchange's for-profit status. Demutualized and listed exchanges have been very careful to ensure that their internal structures best complement the legislative framework designed to ensure the fair and efficient conduct of the market. Most of them have committed significant financial, human and technological resources to ensure the highest standards of integrity. They also work closely with the market regulator in the implementation of their supervisory responsibilities. The crucial market integrity activities undertaken by such exchanges include surveillance of market activity, identifying unusual trading and preliminary investigation of unusual trading, and where necessary, making referral to the regulator or relevant exchange departments. The setting of standards for participants, include prudential and systemic risk management through business rules, supervising and encouraging compliance with business rules and relevant provisions of the Company law, including education, administration of self-assessment procedures, inspections, as well as formal investigations. These are also the investigation of breaches and presenting appropriate cases for disciplinary action and adjudication and appeal of disciplinary matters, and powers to restrict or suspend access, in addition to the referral or notification to the regulator.

The demutualization and listing of exchanges has also led to the setting of standards for listed entities through the exchange's listing rules; supervising and encouraging compliance with the listing rules; implementation of trading halts, and the suspensions and removals of some rules. Moreover, there has been the establishment of standards for the testing and authorization of designated trading representatives, maintaining trading parameter settings and access passwords, gauging compliance with trading rules and procedures and reporting incidents to relevant exchange departments. Similarly, some standards have been set to oversee the provision of fair, orderly and transparent systems for trading, settlement, clearing and dissemination of company information, in addition to, those for guaranteeing trade completion; and risk management. These issues have already been explained in details.

Public Interest Versus Exchange's Commercial Interest

Worldwide, there exists a high level of public interest surrounding the affairs of a securities exchange. Given that exchanges have commercial objectives; the issue arises whether an exchange might put its commercial interests ahead of public interests. The potential conflicts are generally regarded as greater where exchanges are structured as for-profit bodies. There is a very high correlation between what is in the public interest and what is in an exchange's interests. For example, it is a commercial imperative for any securities exchange to engender confidence among investors in the operation of the exchange's market(s). This is achieved by providing a fair and efficient marketplace in which investors may buy or sell their securities. Another commercial imperative for securities exchanges is to operate a listings business and to encourage listings by providing an environment where firms are able to lower their costs of raising capital.

In addition to the alignment of such interests, there are also a variety of controls on securities exchanges that help to reduce the possibility that they will act in a manner contrary to public interest. Exchanges are typically subject to some form of regulatory approval process that includes an assessment of whether an exchange has paid due regard in its rules to the interests of the public. Other controls include anti-trust legislation which prohibits anti-competitive behaviour or misuse of market position; and a requirement that there be transparency in processes. This encompasses the embodiment of processes in rules, rule changes being made available for public scrutiny and comment, and government oversight of rule changes.

Consider incidences where a securities exchange expands its business lines, it may find itself in collaboration or competition with listed firms that it supervises. Such a relationship might develop, because an exchange decides that there are strong commercial imperatives for it to enter into a joint venture with another listed firm. In the absence of special arrangements, this may put the securities exchange in a position where it could favour that firm. Conflict may also arise when the exchange is in competition with another listed company. The exchange could, conceivably, in the performance of its supervisory functions, discriminate against the other listed firm. One way of addressing this potential for conflict is by ensuring the transparency and accountability of the supervisory decision-making process. A mechanism to counter this is to introduce an oversight role in relation to supervisory decision-making concerning entities with whom there is potential for conflict of interest. Such a model has been adopted in some demutualized exchanges where there is both a general oversight of the supervisory activities of securities exchanges; and specific oversight of the exchange's supervision of those of its listed entities who have special identified conflicts. The latter oversight function encompasses consultation on each supervisory decision involving the exercise of discretion. This model may be preferred by securities exchanges to the removal of supervision responsibility for such parties to another entity. In fact, it seems to work for such exchanges.

Therefore, in considering what appropriate arrangements to handle conflicts are, it is important to remember why markets around the world have tended to favour a co-regulatory model in the first place. Co-regulation is designed to achieve a productive collaboration between the government regulator and the self-regulatory organization with its special expertise and close proximity to the market. The proximity of the market operator to the market and its participants allows it to respond quickly and effectively to supervisory issues. If the market operator outsources part of that function for particular entities with which there may be potential for conflict, there is a risk that the distance and isolation of the alternate supervisor will produce less effective supervisory responses or result in a disparity of outcomes and timing of supervisory responses. But these are options which exchanges could consider.

Exchange Self-Listing

Most securities regulators in demutualization jurisdictions' experience with conflict of interest issues derives from their regulation of listed demutualized exchanges. Upon demutualization and listing, market regulators experienced for the first time that shares in an exchange anywhere in the world traded on a market operated by the exchange. They had to reform the law to allow an exchange to self-list and at the same time operate as a market for listed firms. Such provisions should be enacted at the time the exchange demutualize in order to overcome conflicts of interest, which might arise because such an exchange becomes both the securities exchange and a listed entity.

These adjustments in security laws can enable the market regulator to require an exchange to enter into arrangements designed to address the potential for conflicts of interest that might arise from the quotation of its securities on its own market. These arrangements should be entered into at the time that securities are granted quotation on a securities exchange.

Nevertheless, such provisions need to be restricted to possible conflicts arising only from the quotation and trading of an exchange's securities on its own market. Potential conflicts of interest which may arise in an exchange's administration of the listing and business rules are not dealt with since they relate to the exchange's corporate objectives and business interests and not directly to the trading of the exchange's securities. The limitations in most provisions have been revealed in several recent situations involving exchanges as they pursue business opportunities in many directions and concerns of possible conflicts of interest have been addressed on an interim basis.

In order to provide administrative flexibility, there should be a hierarchy of responsible officers from the market regulator to administer the self-listing arrangements, which mirrors the securities exchange structure of responsibilities for monitoring and enforcing compliance of the listing rules by all other listed entities. The types of matters to be dealt with at the operational level include monitoring compliance by the securities exchange with continuous disclosure and other obligations in the listing rules, referring any share trading anomalies, approving for release market announcements, assessing waiver applications and reviewing notices of meetings. Matters such as significant waivers from the listing rules should be passed to more senior staff within the regulator based on their regulatory significance. Such arrangements are working well in Australia where exchanges introduced a specific chapter in their listing rules that apply solely to it as a listed entity and is meant to provide a substitute for the ordinary listing arrangements reflected in the listing rules for all other listed firms.

Exchange Mergers, Acquisitions and Hostile Takeovers
As we have seen, securities exchanges' retention of the listings function on demutualization and self-listing sometimes give rise to the potential for other conflicts of interest that are usually not covered by the comprehensive arrangements during demutualization. The only conflict the law usually deal with is about securities exchanges themselves as listed entities, not as commercial rivals of another listed firm. There have been cases of demutualized exchanges bidding to merge, acquire or takeover other exchanges. In Australia, ASX once placed a bid for the Sydney Futures Exchange (SFE) in 1998. Five months later, Computershare Limited, a firm listed on ASX, announced a rival bid for SFE. Computershare has a major business in supplying market technologies and a substantial part of the share registry services business. The question confronting the market regulator then was what arrangements should be put in place to ensure that the supervision of Computershare as a listed firm was not seen as tainted by the obvious conflict between the securities exchange's role as a market supervisor and its interests as a competing bidder for SFE. In response, the market regulator instructed that until the issue of the rival bids was resolved, the securities exchange as market operator would not make any substantive decision about Computershare without first consulting and acting in accordance with advice provided by

the market regulator. The agreement was made public and details released to the market, an attempt that led to all bidders failing, and SFE proceeded with its demutualization independently.

In a similarly move, the Deutsche Bourse mooted a bid for the acquisition of the LSE, an attempt that failed in 2006. A more serious bid in the history of LSE was its hostile takeover bid by the Nasdaq. Following the LSE's demutualization, Nasdaq acquired 28.75 percent share through share purchase from the market and convincing the shareholders to sell to it their shares at $24.35. This effort also yielded a paltry 0.41 percent of the shares, making a total of 29.16 percent shareholding, short of the 50 percent requirement. Since 2004, several exchanges and other financial institutions had wielded four failed takeover bids for LSE. These include, Deutsche Boerse AG, Macquarie Bank Ltd of Australia, Euronext (operator of Lisbon, Paris, Brussels and Amsterdam exchanges). Following its demutualization, Euronext merged with the NYSE in April 2007 creating the world largest stock market.

Competition with Financial Intermediaries

Self-listed securities exchanges have pursued a number of other business opportunities following demutualization. This demonstrates the broad scope for possible conflicts between an exchange's role as a market regulator and its role as a commercialised entity able to undertake a variety of business projects. Demutualized securities exchanges may compete with financial market service providers generally, and specifically with the intermediaries who trade on its markets, such as stockbrokers, stock dealers and investment bankers.[110] They may therefore, have commercial interests which may result in conflicts with entities listed on them since they no longer have the close ties of ownership and membership with those who trade directly on their markets.

As a result, securities exchanges have responded to concerns about the conflicts issues by forming special purpose subsidiaries with purpose

---

110 See Onyuma S. O. Paradigm Shift in Securities Exchanges: Automation, governance, Competition, Integration & Regulation of Securities Markets (forthcoming).

of providing assurance that the exchange, and its group of enterprises, adequately complies with its obligations as market operator and a clearinghouse. The implication is that conflicts can arise very quickly without any prior warning, and that they need to be dealt with immediately when they arise and must be dealt with as soon as the security regulator can manage. In this case the very announcement of merger, acquisition or takeover bid is a first test, as it has to be released to the market over the firm's announcement platform managed by the same securities exchange. In fact, this has to be done since market regulators are always on the lookout for any violation of the relevant regulation.

Chapter Summary

This chapter has discussed in details, the possible conflict that may arise upon exchange demutualization. It was mentioned that following demutualization and possibility of self-listing, several new regulatory issues arise when an exchange demutualize. Among other things, it is necessary to review the self-regulatory functions, which are performed. There are good reasons for exchanges to continue as SROs, but some changes need to be made to the corporate and governance structure of the organization to ensure that the self-regulatory function continues to be properly performed and that the public interest is safeguarded. While self-regulation is accepted as a primary mechanism for the regulation of the securities industry, it also poses risks for the implementation of public policy objectives in the industry. There is the risk of uneven enforcement, the capture of the regulators by the regulated industry and the creation of barriers to entry or competition. These concerns are not necessarily resolved where a demutualized securities exchange decides that it is no longer willing to continue to perform all or some of the SRO functions. If an entity qualifies to assume such functions, the state may have to refuse such a plan. This calls into question the exchange's commitment to perform the functions to the same standard, as before, implying that demutualization of a securities exchange may be incompatible with self-regulation.

The ability of the exchange to meet the standards set for it and deliver key regulatory and public interest objectives depends on a range of factors including the overall regulatory framework, the exchange's obligations under the law, the formulation, administration and enforcement of its listing and trading rules, its formal and informal arrangements with the statutory market regulator, its management structure, the transparency of its decision making processes, its allocation of resources for particular regulatory functions and the experience and quality of its staff. Arguably, the capacity and the willingness of the statutory market regulator to perform its supervisory role is key to the success of the regulatory framework.

The chapter also espoused on the main types of conflict that can arise for demutualized exchanges. Many of these conflicts also arise in the case of mutual exchanges, but they are brought into sharper focus when a securities exchange demutualizes. Several ways exist for addressing these potential conflicts were discussed in details. The fundamental fact is that it is in the commercial interests of each securities exchange to ensure that there are appropriate controls in place for comprehensively addressing these areas of potential conflict in order to retain public confidence in the integrity and efficiency of the markets operated by the exchange. The chapter concluded with a discussion on the nature and remedies for conflicts arising from securities exchanges pursuing profit objective versus supervisory functions, public interest versus commercial interest, mergers and hostile takeovers, and exchanges competing with other financial intermediaries.

Chapter Six

REGULATION AND OVERSIGHT OF DEMUTUALIZED SECURITIES EXCHANGES

Introduction

In this chapter, the issues relating to financial market regulation to enable the understanding of the purposes and strategies of financial regulation, and the principles for determining whether, where and how such regulation should be applied are discussed. The discussion on the principle of financial regulation is meant to set the stage for the discussion on the regulation of demutualized exchanges. In order to understand demutualized exchanges, there is need to explore self-regulatory issues upon demutualization. An overview of the regulation of demutualized exchanges is presented and the changes created by recent legislation with regard to new types of securities markets highlighted. The chapter focuses on the regulators oversight authority over regulated exchanges, and identifies some issues raised when a securities exchange chooses to demutualize and even self-list. These issues are discussed in light of the recent market regulators' regulatory experiences in America, Europe, Asian Pacific and Africa, and factors that regulators have considered in adapting the securities regulatory framework in response to changes in the ownership and management structures of securities exchanges.

Philosophy of Financial Markets Regulation

The free and competitive markets can produce an efficient allocation of resources and provide a strong foundation for economic growth and development. States also play a vital role in maintaining a healthy economic and social environment in which firms and their customers can interact with confidence. The general case for financial regulation is founded in market failure. This occurs when factors are present that prevent efficient market outcomes. The potential for market failure is a necessary but not sufficient condition for state intervention. One of the most complex issues facing states is identifying the appropriate level and form of intervention. Regulatory efficiency is a significant factor in the overall performance of the economy and the enterprises therein. Financial market inefficiency ultimately imposes costs on the economy through higher taxes and charges, poor services, uncompetitive pricing or slower economic growth. The best way to control these costs and ensure the effectiveness of financial regulation is to place it within a consistent framework. To do this, it is necessary to establish clearly what needs to be regulated and why, as well as to define the principles for effective and efficient financial regulation.

Why do we Need Financial Regulations?
There are numerous purposes for financial regulation. Regulation of all markets for financial services can be categorised according to three broad purposes. The first purpose, which applies in all sectors of the economy, is to ensure that financial markets work efficiently and competitively. Regulation for this purpose includes rules designed to promote adequate disclosure, prevent fraud or other unfair practices and to prohibit anti-competitive behaviour such as collusion or monopolisation. This type of regulation does not materially alter or prescribe the nature of financial products or services, but simply aims at ensuring that they are traded in fair and efficient markets. The second purpose, which applies less generally, is to prescribe particular standards or qualities of financial service (or to prohibit certain financial products or services). This form of more intensive financial regulation is restricted to areas where the dealing in financial products or services carries risks, so that safety is a focus of concern. Of more importance, this regulation may also aim at promoting financial investment safety.

The third purpose of financial regulation, which is applied more rarely, is to achieve social objectives. This includes regulation conferring subsidies on one group of market participants in preference to others. Regulations of this kind are often referred to as *community service obligations,* and typically take the form of price controls. Each of these regulatory purposes is considered in the context of the financial system. A philosophy is set out for determining whether, where and how such regulation should be applied and provides a foundation for the recommendations set out in subsequent sections. Finally, a broad conceptual analysis of financial contracts, markets and institutions is set out which together constitute the financial system.

In developing a philosophy of financial markets regulation, the starting point is to identify the core characteristics of the financial products, markets and institutions, which may be subject to regulation. There is also the need to examine the economic function of financial markets and institutions in facilitating the exchange of financial contracts. *Financial contracts* play a fundamental role in the efficient functioning of commerce, facilitating the settlement of trade and channelling resources efficiently across time and space. The basic elements of financial contracts are *promises:* to make payments at specified times, in specified amounts and in specified circumstances. Financial arrangements, which take the form of trust relationships also, involve promises to manage assets in the best interests of beneficiaries.

Financial promises are among those financial products and services, which incorporate risk, including the risk that the promise will not be kept. The financial system provides the framework within which these promises are created and exchanged. Unlike the markets for most other goods and services, the exchange of many financial contracts takes into account both the explicit contractual promise and the varying risk that the promise will not be kept. Identifying, allocating and pricing risk is a key role of the financial system. The exchange of promises can take place directly between parties. This is feasible where the parties have efficient means of conducting transactions and access to the information necessary to make informed judgments, especially about risks inherent in financial promises.

However, imperfections arise in financial markets, especially in capital markets, because information is not complete, and transactions and information are not costless. In the presence of such imperfections, financial institutions have developed ways to supply information and transaction services, including the management of risk, wherever financial markets have been unable to do so directly. Two forms of financial institutions have evolved, first, intermediaries, including commercial banks and insurance firms, which transact with promisors and promisees on their balance sheets; and second, stockbrokers and dealers, investment bankers, fund managers and other agents, who act to bring promisors and promisees together in securities markets. Financial regulation targets the performance of both financial institutions and financial markets in meeting the underlying promises contained within financial contracts.

Characteristics of Financial Securities and Promises
While financial promises vary in many ways, the most important differences relate to the risks of possible breach of promise. Different promises can be distinguished according to three main characteristics. These differences in financial promises have profoundly influenced the development of financial institutions and financial markets – both money and capital markets, and also strongly influences the objectives of, and the approach to, financial markets regulation. The first characteristic is the difficulty in assessing creditworthiness, particularly whether or not an institution making a financial promise can be trusted to keep it. Creditworthiness therefore, depends on the honesty, financial standing and operational systems of the promisor. It is easier to assess creditworthiness in some cases than in others. For example, the creditworthiness of a treasury bond is highly transparent. However, the creditworthiness of a small business planning to issue shares or bonds can be much more difficult to assess, because the business cannot provide reliable financial information or lacks a track record in capital markets.

Assessing the creditworthiness of borrowers is a specialised task which can consume considerable resources, time and expertise, and can be undertaken within a financial institution or outsourced to specialist firms, such as rating agencies. The ease of assessing the creditworthiness of financial institutions can also vary. For example, a unit trust holding only cash and treasury securities is highly transparent. In the absence of fraud or gross negligence, the creditworthiness of its promises to unit fund holders is closely linked to the creditworthiness of the underlying government securities. In contrast, it may be very difficult to assess the creditworthiness of an insurance company underwriting long-term mortality or disability risks. The difficulty of assessing credit risk is exacerbated by information asymmetry, whereby promisees cannot make a reliable judgment about risks, no matter how much information is made available to them.

Second, there is adversity caused by broken promises because, not only are some financial promises intrinsically difficult to assess, the consequences of breach can also be more or less adverse. These consequences fall into two broad categories. The first category relates to systemic or third party, risk. For example, a stockbroker failing to honour its promises could trigger a general panic as stock investors fear, even without justification, that similar promises made by other brokers may be dishonoured. For market efficiency reasons, financial regulation must also take account of the risk that some financial failures may have onerous consequences for financial markets stability and hence the real economy. The second category relates to the consequences for specific individuals of breaching a financial promise. Where such consequences would be highly adverse, promisees often seek the security of a low-risk safe haven.

There is also the difficulty in honouring promises since the least onerous financial promise is a commitment to make a payment only if circumstances allow, and then only in strict proportion to some measure of underlying value – more common in securities markets. This type of promise is made by the issuers of equity instruments like listed shares. A more burdensome promise is assumed by the corporate issuers of debt instruments as pure debt promises involve a commitment to make specified payments, often fixed in nominal terms, at specified intervals in all circumstances. Failure to make payment in full at the agreed times constitutes default and often leads to bankruptcy. Pure equity and pure debt promises can be combined to yield hybrid securities like convertible notes, preference shares and subordinated debt. The burden implicit in such hybrid promises vary according to the elements of debt and equity they contain. The more burdensome the promise, the more it resembles debt.

Promises which commit the promisor to make specified payments in specified circumstances, regardless of time, are known as pure insurance. This refers to a contract where particular events trigger payment, such as a fire insurance policy or an option contract. The more that the performance of a contract is contingent upon a particular event, the more it resembles pure insurance. The intrinsic difficulty in honouring promises can also vary within these broad categories of promises. A corporate bond promises to make a payment at the sole discretion of the promisee, on demand, is more burdensome than an obligation to pay only at a fixed future time. The promisor may be called upon to fulfil an on-demand promise at any time regardless of circumstances, for example, ordinary at-call deposit account held at deposit taking institutions. Many of these financial products provide the store of value used to make payments through instruments such as cheques. The holders of such accounts demand certainty of payment and are expected to be close to riskless.

Characteristics of Financial Services

The financial system provides the framework for the exchange of financial promises. Financial institutions effect the exchange of financial promises by providing a set of financial services, which can be grouped into seven categories. The first characteristic of financial services is *maturity transformation*. There is a natural mismatch between the maturity preferences of providers and seekers of capital. Lenders and investors generally wish to commit resources for shorter periods than borrowers need. Economies of scale and scope enable financial institutions to assume the maturity mismatch by increasing the turnover of liabilities needed to support long-term assets. Second, promisors often find it costly and inconvenient to divide their claims into the range of denominations, both large and small, that promisees may desire. Financial intermediaries can break up large denomination claims and aggregate small denomination claims into infinite sizes. These economies enable financial institutions in capital markets to tailor both assets and liabilities to meet the needs of borrowers and lenders.

Third, by pooling the resources of investors, financial intermediaries can use diversification to lower risks to a greater extent than is usually available to an individual investor. Scale economies enable financial intermediaries to incur lower transaction costs, to overcome problems of indivisibility and to process information more efficiently in seeking to reduce risk through diversification. Forth, in any financial system, a limited range of financial claims can be used as a means of payment to settle transactions. To serve as an effective means of payment, a claim must have a highly stable capital value, be widely accepted in exchange and be linked to the arrangements for ultimate settlement. The deposit liabilities of banks, mobilised by instruments such as cheques, have provided one of the traditional stores of value upon which payments services are based. Payment services can also be provided through notes and coins and through credit cards backed by lines of credit. Fifth, information is costly to access and process calling for a need to reduce information costs.

The sixth characteristic relates to liquidity, which is the ease with which a financial claim can be exchanged for cash without a significant lose in value. Liquidity in this sense is not equivalent to predictability of value. For example, some listed equity instruments are highly liquid but exhibit volatile prices. One of the traditional roles for banks is to transform illiquid assets (loans) into liquid liabilities (deposits). Finally, resolving information problems is another characteristic of financial services. Borrowers are often unwilling to provide lenders with sensitive information about their financial situation; unless they are assured that the information will not be used to erode their competitive position in the market. By specialising in finance, financial institutions provide the confidentiality and assurance needed by borrowers to induce them to reveal the information necessary to manage the risks involved in the promise.

The Role of Financial Institutions

Financial institutions facilitate the exchange of promises by providing the financial services of intermediation and market facilitation. Financial intermediaries interpose their balance sheet between the parties involved in exchanging financial promises. At one end of the spectrum, deposit-taking intermediaries provide a full range of services. They offer liabilities that serve as means of payment, transform longer-term illiquid assets into shorter-term highly liquid liabilities, provide claims in divisible quantities, diversify risk and efficiently manage information needs. The depositor receives the full range of financial services, while the borrower enjoys the benefits of maturity transformation and informational efficiencies. At the other spectrum, life assurance firms offering market linked investment policies primarily provide divisibility and risk pooling services. In the case of deposit taking intermediaries, the process of transforming promises includes an implicit guarantee of the promises made by ultimate borrowers, as the intermediary absorbs the price and credit risks involved. The transformation is much more limited for a life company investment policy where most of the ultimate risks are passed through the life company to investors.

Funds managers and other agents, such as investment advisers and stockbrokers, act to bring promisors and promisees together in securities markets. They offer a more limited package of financial services and leave the ultimate risk with investors, through market facilitation, and do not transform financial promises by interposing its balance sheet between promisors and promisees. Such financial advisers and brokers primarily facilitate the exchange of financial promises by addressing information problems.

Regulation of Financial Markets

It has been mentioned that financial regulation may be applied to facilitate the general operation of capital markets, to enhance safety or to pursue social objectives. It is important to provide a basic framework for considering whether and, where and how each of these purposes of regulation should be applied in the financial system. All financial markets, financial face potential problems associated with the conduct of market participants, anti-competitive behaviour and incomplete information. These common forms of market failure have justified at least a minimum level of regulatory intervention in markets on an economy wide basis. Such intervention generally takes the form of, one, conduct regulation such as criminal sanctions for fraud and prohibitions on anti-competitive behaviour; and two, disclosure regulation such as general prohibitions on false and misleading statements contained in fair trading laws. There are some markets where this minimum level of economy-wide regulation is considered to be inadequate. These markets, or their products, have characteristics which warrant more specific disclosure and conduct rules than apply in other industries. In many cases, it is also considered necessary to establish a separate regulatory agency to conduct such specialised regulation, as we seen in chapter four.

Financial Market Integrity. It is important to ask whether the conduct and disclosure regulation of financial markets should be best left to general economy-wide arrangements and where are more specialised regulations required. As a rule of the thumb, greater regulatory consistency and efficiency will result from economy-wide regulation. This should always be preferred unless a clear case for sector-specific arrangements can be demonstrated. Specifically, securities market integrity regulation aims at promoting confidence in the efficiency and fairness of these markets. It seeks to ensure that securities markets are sound, orderly and transparent. Usually, securities market prices can be sensitive to information, and this raises the potential for misuse of information. For this reason, securities markets regulators globally impose specific disclosure requirements, like IPO prospectus rules, and conduct rules, like prohibitions on insider trading by securities market participants. The complexity of financial products and markets, their intrinsic risks including those due to limited information and the detailed knowledge required to deliver efficient regulation in this area argue strongly for continued specialised regulatory arrangements.

Investor protection is the form of regulation aimed at ensuring that retail investors have adequate information, are treated fairly and have adequate avenues for redress. There are close links and no clear dividing line between investor protection and market integrity regulation in retail securities markets since both use the same regulatory tools, namely disclosure and conduct rules. For instance, IPO prospectus requirements can promote both investor protection and confidence in the efficiency and fairness of overall securities markets. Specialist investor protection in the securities markets is justified on two grounds. First, the complexity of financial securities increases the probability that financially unsophisticated investors can misunderstand or be misled about the nature of financial securities, particularly their obligations and risks. This, combined with the potential consequences of dishonour, has led most countries to establish a disclosure regime for financial securities that is considerably more intense than disclosure rules for most non-financial products. Secondly, financial complexity also increases the incidence of misunderstanding and dispute. Given this, and the high cost of litigation, a number of jurisdictions have imposed specific regulation of financial sales and advice and established low-cost industry complaint schemes or tribunals for resolving disputes.

Competition regulation relates to laws, which ensure that all capital markets are competitive. Two main areas of concern are market concentration and collusion, which can lead to overpricing of financial securities and under provision of services essential to economic growth and welfare. While financial securities are complex and any assessment of competition requires detailed analysis of the market, the key features relevant to competition assessment in this sector are not unique. The application of economy wide competition regulation to securities exchange and overall securities markets ensures regulatory consistency. Anti-competitive behaviour is not unique to securities exchanges, and it is preferable to establish both the bounds of acceptable competitive behaviour and rules for mergers and acquisitions, which are common to all industries. The case for specialised arrangements in this area is relatively weak.

Regulation for Financial Safety. A further case for financial regulation arises from the risks attached to financial securities. While in some other industries safety regulation aims to eliminate risk almost entirely (for example, to eliminate health risks in food preparation), this is not an appropriate aim for most areas of the financial markets. One of the vital economic functions of the financial markets is to manage, allocate and price risk. However, there are some areas of the financial markets where government intervention is aimed at eliminating or reducing risk. One of the most difficult tasks facing those charged with designing financial market regulations is that of defining the aims and boundaries of regulation for financial safety.

Some capital markets securities have characteristics that warrant much higher levels of safety than would otherwise be provided by financial markets, even when they are subject to effective conduct, disclosure and competition regulation. These characteristics include the inherent difficulty of honouring promises; the difficulty in assessing the creditworthiness of promisors; and the adversity caused by breaching promises. As a general principle, financial safety regulation will be required where promises are judged to be very difficult to honour and assess, and produce highly adverse consequences if breached. The promises which rank highly on all three characteristics are referred to as having a high *intensity*. The higher the intensity of a promise, the stronger the case for regulation to reduce the likelihood of breach.

Causes of Financial Market Failure

The underlying reason for regulating intense promises is that financial markets are more likely to fail where more intense promises are being exchanged. In markets with intense financial promises, two sources of potential market failure have long been recognised, first, the risk of third party losses due to systemic instability; and second, the problem of information asymmetry facing most investors, which means that they cannot reliably assess risk, particularly the creditworthiness of the securities issuer. The first case for regulation to prevent systemic instability arises because certain financial securities have an inherent capacity to transmit instability to the real economy, inducing undesired effects on price inflation. The more sophisticated the economy, the greater its dependence on financial promises and the greater its vulnerability to failure of the financial markets. The most potent source of systemic risk is financial contagion. This occurs when financial distress in one market or institution is transmitted to others and, eventually, engulfs the entire financial markets. This was recently witnessed in 2008 when the failure in mortgage market is USA led to contagion in other capital markets globally – leading to global financial crisis.

The second case for regulation relates to the need to address information asymmetry. In a market economy, investors are assumed, for the most part, to be the best judges of their own interests. In such cases, disclosure requirements play an important role in assisting investors to make informed judgments. However, disclosure is not always sufficient.

For many financial securities, most investors lack (and cannot efficiently obtain) the knowledge, experience or judgment required to make informed investment decisions. This is known as information asymmetry- a situation where further disclosure, no matter how high the quality or how comprehensive, cannot overcome securities market failure. In these cases, it may be desirable to substitute the opinion of a third party for that of the investors themselves. In effect, the third party is expected to behave paternalistically, looking out for the best interests of investors when they are considered incapable of doing so alone. Such third party information can be supplied in a financial market by the rating agencies. However, for many years the practice in all countries has been for state prudential regulators to take on much of this role.

In altering the risks that would otherwise attach to financial securities, financial safety regulation effectively provides a degree of assurance to investors. The need for *safe havens* in key financial services does not mean that all financial services should be subject to financial safety regulation. If regulation is pursued to the point of ensuring that financial promises are kept under all circumstances, the burden of honour is effectively shifted from the securities issuer to the market regulator. All securities issuers would become equally risky (or risk free) in the eyes of the investing public. Regulation at this intensity removes the natural spectrum of risk that is fundamental to financial markets. If it were extended widely, the community would be collectively underwriting all financial risks through the tax system, and all financial markets would cease to work efficiently. Thus, financial regulation cannot and should not ensure that all financial promises are kept. Indeed, the state should not provide an absolute guarantee in any area of the financial markets, just as it does not do so in other areas. Primary responsibility should remain with those who make financial promises. It would be inequitable for the state to underwrite some financial promises but no other promises made by participants in the broader economy.

How intensively, then, should financial safety regulation be applied? How much regulatory assurance should it provide in the various areas of the financial markets like in banking or securities markets? The intensity of financial safety regulation should be proportional to the intensity of financial promises. The most intense financial promises are those which provide payments services. Such promises are intrinsically difficult to honour. Those who use them rarely have the time, motivation or resources to assess the risks, and any breach would have potentially highly adverse consequences for the efficient conduct of commerce in the whole economy. The most intense financial safety regulation should therefore apply to the provision of means of payment, to the point of securing their safety at the highest possible level, short of an outright government guarantee.

Beyond this, the extent of financial regulatory assurance is a matter of judgment. Where systemic risk and information asymmetry are greatest, financial regulation should at least strive to minimise the risk of promises being dishonoured. If financial regulation falls short of providing a guarantee against failure, it must provide speedy and efficient mechanisms for resolving financial distress when it arises, so as to minimise the danger of loss or contagion across capital markets. This requires, at least, that the securities market regulator have unambiguous powers to intervene in the operations of institutions making such intense promises. A financial instrument which provides investors with a risk exposure rather than a payments service is a less intense promise requiring less intense financial safety regulation. Securities markets regulation should seek to ensure that, while risk remains, firms issuing securities making promises ensure that risks are appropriately managed in accordance with the reasonable expectations of their investors. This may involve varying degrees of regulatory intensity with greater regulatory intensity being appropriate for an annuity product involving both investment and mortality risks than for a market-linked investment like shares or bonds.

The application of this general principle to determine the degree of regulatory assurance may require adjustment to take account of two additional factors, which may have a significant influence. These may include the implications of compulsory contributions and tax assistance for superannuation. These combine to imply that the state should provide greater regulatory assurance in relation to superannuation than would normally apply to securities market-linked investments. Second, there are other pragmatic considerations resulting from the structure of capital markets and institutions. It is sometimes difficult to separate some classes of financial promises from others where they are made by the same entity subject to institutional regulation. Thus, the practical course may often be to broadband financial regulatory interventions, applying them across a wider spectrum of promises, not strict adherence as the general principle may otherwise suggest.

The most common form of preventative regulation to promote financial safety is *prudential regulation*. At the high-intensity end of the spectrum, prudential regulation involves the imposition of prescriptive rules or standards governing the prudential behaviour of institutions making certain types of securities or promises. These rules may be directed at specific areas of concern, such as minimum liquidity standards for institutions with liquid liabilities. Alternatively, they may be directed more generally at minimising the risk of failure, like minimum capital requirements and risk management standards. Prudential regulation in part substitutes the judgment of market regulators for that of regulated financial institutions and their customers or investors. To the extent that the market regulator absorbs risks, which would otherwise bear upon financial institutions and their customers, it faces the twin problems of *adverse selection* and *moral hazard*. In this respect, the prudential market regulator acts like an insurer. When an insurance firm sells fire insurance, it immediately attracts those people whose properties are more likely to be destroyed by fire. After all, those whose premises are fireproof have no need of insurance, the problem of adverse selection.

Similarly, once a person has obtained insurance against property fire, the incentive to be vigilant against such fires can be reduced. The tendency for insured parties to alter their behaviour in ways, which increase the risk of loss, is known as moral hazard. The incentive problems associated with adverse selection and moral hazard explain the particular approaches that prudential market regulators normally adopt to different aspects of prudential oversight. The problem of adverse selection leads an insurer to discriminate carefully among risks, and to refuse risks, which it cannot clearly discern. Similarly, a prudential regulator may seek to maintain strict entry criteria, thereby screening out riskier customers or participants and reducing the likelihood that a supervised institution will fail. While this is an understandable response on the part of a prudential regulator, it reduces competitive pressure on regulated financial institutions, and is a source of efficiency loss. The problem of moral hazard leads an insurer to grant insurance on condition that it can monitor its risk exposure during the tenure of the insurance contract. Moral hazard dulls the incentive of a regulated financial institution to monitor risks incurred in its operations. As a result, the prudential regulator insists on supervising and limiting the behaviour of regulated financial institutions in order to limit the regulator's exposure to failure. Such rules carry efficiency costs by limiting the scope for commercial judgment by financial institutions, calling for the appropriate balance between prudential and efficiency objectives.

Instability arising in that part of the financial market, which is subject to prudential regulation, is only one of a series of potential threats to systemic stability – a variety of financial and real economic shocks can strike any economy. Prudential regulation, even in its most intensive form, cannot guarantee that systemic instability will not occur. In the event of such instability, the task of restoring stability falls to the money market regulator – central bank, in the first instance, through the provision of liquidity and other means though in extreme cases, the state may also play a role, like was seen in USA following subprime mortgage crisis of 2007/2008 or in Europe following sovereign debt crisis in 2011/2012. Thus, a central bank has the primary responsibility for systemic stability in an economy, irrespective of who has responsibility for prudential supervision. An important judgment in developing financial market regulatory arrangements is to decide the balance between prudential supervision, acting on a preventative basis, and central banking, maintaining stability with both preventative and response strategies. This calls for a need for financial market stability.

The last case for financial regulation is sometimes made on the grounds that financial institutions and markets have *community service obligations* to provide subsidies to some customer groups. Financial institutions are urged to deliver certain services free of charge or at a price below the cost of provision. This is the least persuasive case for intervention. Financial institutions, like other commercial entities, are designed to produce wealth, not to redistribute it. This is not to say that their creation of wealth should ignore the claims of social and moral propriety. But it is another thing altogether to require financial institutions to undertake social responsibilities for which they are not designed or well suited. Obliging financial institutions to subsidize some activities compromises their efficiency and is unlikely to prove sustainable in a competitive financial market. If there is a social concern about imposing the real cost of financial services on certain groups, this is more efficiently dealt with through direct government funding, transfer payments or provision of services. This approach is used to fund most other services required by disadvantaged groups. If access to financial services is as important as access to transport or medicines, this should be recognized explicitly and funded in the same way.

Principles of Financial Regulation

Having set out a broad philosophy for regulating the financial markets, it is important to note that financial regulation has great potential to impose costs and should be designed to meet its purposes while minimising such costs. Thus regulation requires that a careful balance be struck between effectiveness and efficiency. The focus should be directed at reducing the costs of financial markets regulation, both the direct costs of regulation and the broader costs arising from rules which restrict economic activity. Having considered the arrangements for financial regulation, a more effective and streamlined framework becomes imperative. There seems to be a general view that there is considerable potential to improve financial markets efficiency through a broad range of reforms. In recommending these reforms, this book has regard to the following regulatory principles.

The regulatory agencies operating in the various financial markets should operate independent of sectional interests and with appropriately skilled staff. The regulatory structure must be accountable to its stakeholders and subject to regular reviews of its efficiency and effectiveness. If there is a general perception that a particular group of financial institutions cannot fail because they have the cover of government, there is a great danger that perception will become reality. Transparency of financial markets regulation requires that all guarantees be made explicit and that all purchasers and providers of financial products and services be fully aware of their rights and responsibilities. It should be the top priority of an effective financial regulatory structure that financial promises, both public and private, be understood. Moreover, one of the most pervasive influences over the continuing evolution of the financial markets will be technology. While it is not possible to forecast with any certainty the precise impact that technology will have on the shape of financial services and service delivery, it is certain that the impact will be considerable particularly, for banks and securities exchanges.[111] These developments make flexibility in securities exchanges ownership and management structures critical. The regulatory framework must also have the flexibility to cope with changing institutional structures of these financial institutions and markets without losing its effectiveness.

Furthermore, competitive neutrality requires that the regulatory burden applying to a particular financial commitment, apply equally to all who make such commitments. It requires further that there be minimal barriers to entry and exit from capital markets; no undue restrictions on institutions and the financial products and services they offer; and markets open to the widest possible range of participants. The cost effectiveness is one of the most difficult issues for regulatory cultures to come to terms with. Any form of regulation involves a natural tension between effectiveness and efficiency. Financial regulation can be made totally effective by simply prohibiting all actions potentially incompatible with the regulatory objective. But, by inhibiting productive activities along with the anti-social, such an approach is likely to be highly inefficient.

In sum, the underlying legislative framework must be effective, including fostering compliance through enforcement in cases where participants do not abide by the rules. However, a cost-effective regulatory

---

111 Compare the already felt profound impact of mobile money as well as block chain technologies leading to cryptocurrencies, which has threatened to revolutionize currencies or money as we have traditionally known them.

system also requires a presumption in favour of minimal regulation unless a higher level of intervention is justified; an allocation of functions among financial markets regulatory bodies which minimises overlaps, duplication and conflicts; an explicit mandate for regulatory bodies to balance efficiency and effectiveness; a clear distinction between the objectives of financial regulation and broader social objectives; and the allocation of regulatory costs to those enjoying the benefits. These principles set here are going to be applied in the next section where we are going to see how demutualization of securities exchanges may pose regulatory challenges for capital markets regulators.

Regulating Demutualized Securities Exchanges

The regulatory responsibilities of securities exchanges include developing trading rules and enforcing them; setting listing standards and ensuring continuous disclosure of material information by listed firms; adopting and enforcing rules of conduct for broker-members of the exchange; setting qualification and financial standards for industry professionals; conducting surveillance of the market and its participants and investigating violations of securities exchange rules and disciplining violators; and monitoring and regulating daily trading and the operation of the securities market to ensure its integrity. Not all securities exchanges are responsible for the regulation of the business affairs of its broker-members and their dealings with customers. Since demutualization of a securities exchange involves the conversion of a not for-profit member-owned organization to a for-profit shareholder-owned corporation, a government market regulator of a demutualized securities exchange must balance the interests of the profit motive of the demutualized securities exchange with that of investor protection.

The practice has been for the securities markets regulators to reform their laws to fit in the new environment. Such new provisions create a new array of possibilities and greater responsibilities for securities markets. Securities exchanges therefore face a challenging business decision that demands resolution with greater expediency, but bear increased self-regulatory responsibility. Without the restrictive market regulations, securities markets will be challenged to develop more creative solutions and will be required to answer to a broader constituency than the traditional collective of securities exchange members. Securities markets now have a wide range of choices: trade cash, futures, options, over-the-counter derivatives, bonds and equity securities; link or form alliances; acquire or be acquired by other entities; form new subsidiaries or holding companies; branch out or establish other businesses. As regulatory restrictions loosen and technological capability expands, securities markets also face an ever-widening range of competitors.

Remember, demutualization transfers the ownership structure of securities exchanges from mutually owned (not-for-profit, broker/dealer-owned) to demutualized (for-profit, shareholder-owned). This ownership transfer allowed securities exchanges to access new financing, enabling technological advancements. It also separated the management from members/stockbrokers, making faster decision-making possible.

The available literature has explored the association between demutualization and aspects like securities exchange values, liquidity, technical efficiency, and additional investment in software and derivative trading. However, while analysts consider it a potential issue, the relationship between the for-profit focus of demutualized securities exchanges and their monitoring and oversight of listed firms has largely remained unexamined. Taken together, whether and how securities exchange demutualization influences securities exchanges' monitoring efforts therefore remains unaccounted for, and this chapter is intended to bring more clarity on this important debate.

It is a well-known fact that securities exchanges play a critical role in their domestic markets. While exchanges seldom make the primary rules of these markets, they significantly impact the regulation and oversight of listed firms. Securities exchanges influence national regulations through lobbying and shape company abidance through voluntary regulations like corporate governance codes. Moreover, using their autonomy, securities exchanges can set their own rules ranging from financial disclosure to governance practices, decide whether to cooperate with agencies supervising the market, and opt to create segments with different levels of regulatory requirements and oversight. Given the important role securities exchanges play in regulation and oversight, a change in their incentives due to an increase in their for-profit focus following demutualization is likely to affect their monitoring efforts.

On one spectrum, demutualization may weaken the exchanges' monitoring efforts, as effective oversight is costly. Under the for-profit model, the managers of demutualized securities exchanges, who also supervise regulatory functions, are compensated in part based on the exchanges' financial performance, which inevitably leads to conflicts of interest. Thus, the for-profit exchanges may decrease spending on the human and financial resources needed for regulation and oversight to save costs. Furthermore, exchanges largely earn revenues from trading fees. Many market-abuse strategies lead to higher trading volumes and hence higher trading fees. This relationship, in turn, decreases securities exchanges' incentives to cooperate with agencies that supervise securities markets.

On the other spectrum, demutualization may instigate a stricter regulatory environment for listed firms. To improve profits from trading fees, securities exchanges must encourage investors to participate in the securities market. However, lack of trust in the fairness of the securities market can deter individuals from participating. Evidence from a study using USA household data[112] illustrate that residents in states with more corporate scandals have a lower tendency to invest in the securities market. Thus, demutualized exchanges' for-profit focus may incentivize improved monitoring of listed firms thus boosting investors' confidence in the securities market.

It is evident that increasing globalization and rapid technological development in recent decades have caused many securities exchanges to change their ownership structure from mutually owned (broker/dealer-owned) to demutualized (for-profit, shareholder-owned). Nevertheless, increased for-profit focus could weaken securities exchanges' monitoring incentives. Research using multiple metrics for the quality of listed firms' mandatory financial disclosure to capture securities exchanges' monitoring

---

112 Giannetti, M. & Wang, T. Y. (2016). Corporate scandals and household stock market participation. *The Journal of Finance*, 71, 2591-2636.

efforts, have found that securities exchanges' monitoring declines post-demutualization. This has been attributed to changes in oversight by securities exchanges.[113] However, such could be possible in weak regulatory regimes.

In addition, the SEC also found deficiencies in the self-regulatory efforts to enforce their rules or to exercise the self-regulatory oversight required by the securities market regulation that stem from the competing interests behind the operation of the securities exchanges. This phenomenon was observed in the 2005 NYSE case regarding specialists, the 2005 Nasd and Nasdaq report involving MarketXT, and the 2003 enforcement action against the Chicago Stock Exchange. In each of these cases it appears that regulation may have taken a back seat to business concerns. This emphasizes the significance of strong and independent national-level regulatory organizations in monitoring demutualize securities exchanges.

Regulatory Questions Upon Demutualization

In considering how to adapt the regulatory framework to a demutualized securities exchange, securities market regulators consider a number of issues. These include, first, whether conflicts of interest are created or increased if a for-profit entity also performs the regulatory functions of a securities exchange such as primary market regulation (listing of issuers), secondary market regulation as well as member regulation. Second, fair and efficient capital markets are public goods. Should particular corporate governance arrangements or rules regarding share ownership be imposed to protect the public interest? Moreover, will a for-profit securities exchange allocate adequate funding to regulatory functions? Finally, what incentives should a regulatory framework and environment for a demutualized securities exchange provide? Are the incentives different from those provided by regulation governing a mutual exchange? Arguably not, since at the end of the day, regulation is designed to promote the efficient functioning of the securities market and the protection of the investor.

---

113 Huang, S. X., Kim, M., Rykaczewski, M. & Vulcheva, M. (2022). Regulation Takes a Back Seat to Business Concerns: Evidence from Stock Exchange Demutualization. http://dx.doi.org/10.2139/ssrn.3525501.

The potential for conflicts of interest that may arise if the SRO functions are enmeshed within a for-profit corporation must be defused. At the very least, strict corporate separation of the self-regulatory role from the marketplace it regulates is a minimum for the protection of investors in a for-profit securities exchange structure.[114] Markets do not solve all the problems generated by economic activity within the financial system. Consequently, market regulation is necessary to correct the problems generated by economic activity but the regulation should be responsive to changes in market conditions so as not to stifle innovation. Regulation in the securities market is necessary for primarily three reasons. First, incomplete contracts can prevent securities markets from working by increasing to prohibitive levels the costs of transacting in the market. Second, there may be severe problems with enforcement of rules in the absence of some centralized regulation. Third, there may be effects on third parties or externalities that arise in the functioning of these markets.

Self Versus Sate Regulation

The three main objectives of securities market regulation as expressed by the IOSCO[115] are the protection of investors, ensuring that markets are fair, efficient and transparent, and the reduction of systemic risk.[116] In countries with multiple developed and sophisticated securities markets, another objective of market regulation is enhanced competition. Competition between securities exchanges in the delivery of their products is good because the competition forces securities exchanges to innovate and become more

---

114 Fried, L. (1999) Plans Debated for Stock Markets' For-profit Conversion, New York Law Journal, 80, September.

115 The objectives of IOSCO include: to cooperate in developing, implementing and promoting adherence to internationally recognized and consistent standards of regulation, oversight and enforcement to protect investors, maintain fair, efficient and transparent markets and to mitigate systemic risks; to enhance investor protection and promote investor confidence in the integrity of securities markets, through strengthened information exchange and cooperation in enforcement against misconduct and in the supervision of markets and market intermediaries; and to exchange information at both global and regional levels on their respective experiences to assist the development of markets, strengthen market infrastructure and implement appropriate regulation.

116 See IOSCO (1998) Objectives and Principles of Self-Regulation (September), IOSCO.

efficient in the delivery of their products. The reasons for each of the three main objectives overlap to some extent, reinforcing the importance of each to the foundation of a sound financial system. For example, the first objective is based on the theory that securities investors need to be protected from misleading, manipulative and fraudulent practices. To achieve this objective, securities markets should not favour some market users over others and therefore must provide full and timely disclosure of relevant information.

Furthermore, the protection of investors can only be achieved if regulation aims at reducing the risk of failure of a participant in the financial system or seeks to reduce the impact of that failure and isolate the risk to the failing institution. The need for efficiency and transparency is also driven by market forces as issuers and investors demand liquid, transparent, well-informed markets with low transaction, including regulatory, costs and high integrity. If securities markets and intermediaries do not satisfy these requirements, transactions can easily flow elsewhere. It is not necessary that the responsibility for all aspects of the enforcement of securities market law be given to a single body. There are several effective models in which responsibilities are shared between several state or quasi-state agencies or where responsibility is shared with SROs.[117]

Some of the advantages of a government regulator delegating responsibility for oversight of the market to SROs are the ability to utilize industry expertise; the potential for higher standards than may be imposed by law; potentially greater compliance with mutually agreed rules set by peers than with externally imposed requirements; and greater flexibility and responsiveness.

Nevertheless, the financial services industry indirectly regulates itself through little discussed, scandal-prone, and structurally-entrenched self-regulatory organizations.[118] Securities exchanges and their lobby group – such as in Kenya (Kenya Association of Stockbrokers and Investment Banks), the most prominent of these self-regulatory organizations, makes

---

117 Karmel, R. S. (2007). Is the Financial Industry Regulatory Authority a Government Agency? Brooklyn Law School, Legal Studies Paper No. 86. Brooklyn.

118 Edwards, B. P. (2017). The Dark Side of Self-Regulation. University of Nevada Scholarly Works, 1117. https://scholars.law.unlv.edu/facpub/1117.

regulations and sets enforcement policy that directly affect public welfare. As with other self-regulatory organizations such as microfinance institutions, securities exchanges' structure poses a continual risk that industry members will subvert its processes to act like a cartel, promoting industry interests at the expense of the public and contributing to the excessive rents collected by financial intermediaries. Although this dark side to self-regulation poses a constant danger, structural reforms may increase the likelihood that securities exchanges and other self-regulatory organizations will take the public's interests into account.

Whereas others have discussed how self-regulatory organizations increasingly resemble a fifth branch of the government, this chapter shifts the focus to how the public actually exercises its voice within securities exchanges as a self-regulatory organization. The chapter examines the purportedly public representatives serving on securities exchanges' Board. In fact, these public representatives often simultaneously serve on the boards of corporate financial intermediaries (like listed banks and insurance firms, pension scheme, etcetera), giving rise to conflicts of interest between loyalties to market participants and industry lobbying groups and their roles as protectors of the public interest. To amplify the public's voice within these organizations, there is need for a different appointment process for the public representatives serving within self-regulatory organizations, calling for increased transparency and improved oversight.

In addition, self-regulation also has a number of risks arising from the conflict between the interests of the members and the public. These risks may include, first, operational failures resulting from lack of resources or commitment, such as the application of inconsistent standards or arbitrary penalties or the failure to respond promptly to problems. The second risk is the anti-competitive behaviour like the entry barriers and sub-optimal market structure, which favours the interests of members over those of investors. In addition, there is the risk of the heightened possibility of *regulatory capture*, through control of the information necessary to regulate properly and increased regulatory dependence on the SRO for policy input and expertise. Finally, there is the self-serving regulation generally, and the chilling effect on dissent that may result from a well-organized interest group. The need for government supervision of SROs is therefore important because the government must be assured that the SRO actually performs its regulatory functions and that the government must seek to reduce impairment of competition. Industry members know that unless conduct is effectively policed, securities investors will incur losses and complain to government about inadequate regulation.

Regulatory responsibility is shared between the SRO, as regulator, and the state, as supervisor. Inadequacy of the regulation will generally be the fault of both the SRO and the government and will result in less SRO regulatory power and more state supervision, a situation that industry seeks to avoid. The key to successful state-SRO regulation is to establish increased competency in each regulator, effective arrangements for information exchange and coordination and appropriate oversight of the SRO by the state regulator. Therefore, two must each commit to promote an improved understanding of the roles, powers and responsibilities of each regulator; exchange of expertise; consistent implementation of regulatory standards; access by each regulator to the information necessary to fulfil its responsibilities; and communication lines that will maintain and enhance each regulator's ability to react to market activities in a timely manner.

Oversight Over Listings

Another concern is that the conversion of a securities exchange to a for-profit corporation would precipitate a *race to the bottom* in which to compete successfully with each other for listings. Securities exchanges would lower their listing and reporting standards in order to allow more firms to list in order to obtain more listing fees and transaction fees for such exchanges. While competition among securities exchanges would probably result in a lowering of fees and other costs related to listing for firm, the competition would be accompanied by a loosening of listing standards which would undoubtedly undermine the investing public's confidence in the strength and quality of the capital markets in general. However, a reply to this argument is that while some securities exchanges may choose to lower their listing standards in order to be more profitable for their shareholders, other exchanges will in fact put in place more stringent and rigorous standards in order to distinguish themselves and the service they are offering from other exchanges. The NYSE has adopted such a strategy to distinguish itself from other exchanges. In fact, firms seek to list on it because of the reputational capital that comes with listing on this world's premier securities exchange since it supplies reputational capital to the firms that list on it.

A securities exchange listing on itself presents a more fundamental conflict of interest than those inherent in an SRO. In addition to the issue of whether a securities exchange can function as its own regulator is the issue of whether self-listing increases the conflicts of overseeing competing entities that are also listed on the exchange. Two factors that act as controls against discriminatory treatment of competitors, are first, competition for listings among exchanges; and second, the risk to the exchange's reputation. Potential conflicts are lessened by the state market regulator assuming regulation of the exchange as issuer. When the Stockholm and the Australian exchanges went public, the state was assigned the task of overseeing exchange disclosure to shareholders. For instance, such regulators supervise exchange's listing and undertake the day-to-day supervision of its compliance with the listing rules to ensure that the exchange is subject to independent scrutiny.

Securities Exchanges as Self-Regulatory Organizations

The ability of securities exchanges to meet the self-regulatory obligations devolved to them is a serious problem which exchanges must grapple with. Mutuality and self-regulation in the public interest are typically seen as going hand-in-hand. It is this misapprehension that lies at the heart of many concerns directed at demutualization. Regulatory failures are inevitable any time self-regulatory obligations imposed on a securities exchange conflict with the commercial interests of securities exchange owners. Such commercial interests are no less powerful for mutualized securities exchanges than for demutualized ones.

The model always chosen by securities exchanges has been a self-governing one reflecting an enlightened self-interest on the part of participants. Securities markets would not be successful if participants did not have confidence that they would be treated fairly and honestly by their stockbroker and that the market itself operated fairly. Securities exchanges restrict access, set rules and regulations governing the business conduct of their broker-members and set rules or procedures designed to ensure that bargains would be honoured, the credit-ring. Even today, the requirements for new applicants for membership on virtually every securities exchange boils down to two essential characteristics, demonstrating that the applicant is *fit and proper* and creditworthy as has been discussed above. There are therefore both advantages and disadvantages of self-regulation.

A major problem with demutualization is that of conflict of interest and regulatory oversight. Securities exchanges tend to shy away from taking enforcement actions against their own customers who are a source of income. There is a potential commercialization of services; data and trade information that traditionally is offered freely is now sold. Listing standards and oversight can be compromised by a securities exchange concerned. To solve these problems self-listing arrangements can be implemented. For instance, in Singapore, the Singapore Stock Exchange SGX (holding company), the SGX-ST (Singapore Stock Exchange Security Trading) and the monetary authority have a regulatory arrangement whereby SGX-ST is the frontline regulator for listed firms on the SGX and the SGX itself is subject to the same rules applicable to other firms, and the Monetary Authority is the overall overseer.

Advantages of Self-Regulation

There exist numerous advantages that securities exchanges stand to gain through self-regulation. These may include:

- *Trading Environment Knowledge.* Self-regulatory rules can be more effective because of the SRO's intimate knowledge of the trading environment and market practices compared to state officials and the judiciary. Securities exchange management and regulatory staff are closer to the market activity and are likely to be better placed to understand what may be going on. Under self-regulation, it is not sufficient merely for an SRO to have knowledge of the regulated activity. It must be prepared to act on its superior knowledge in the public interest. Thus benefits of self-regulation can be realized only if, among other things, the SRO fully informs itself of the nature and purposes of the full range of activities occurring in the market.

- *Member Surveillance.* The SRO is in a better position to vigilantly surveil and investigate the activities of market participants and take appropriate action as warranted under the facts and as required by law. Market participants may have a strong interest in maintaining the integrity of the securities markets on which they trade. They stand to lose most if market misconduct leads to lower turnover and causes a migration of liquidity and trading activity to other markets.

- *Checks and balances.* Self-regulation has a built-in system of checks and balances. The persons and organizations which must comply with the regulations, such as firms who list their securities, members and investors who do business on the securities exchanges, are less reluctant to make their views known to the SRO with whom they have a business relationship.

- *Efficient Resource Use.* Self-regulation may result in cost saving for the state if the supervision of the regulated industry requires fewer resources than direct regulation, and less costly regulation overall.

- *Capacity Building.* The presence of market practitioners as self-regulators enhances the knowledge, expertise and experience of the regulatory authorities and the relevance of regulation. Moreover, market practitioners learn about the regulatory process by participating in it and thereby enhancing their firms' internal compliance with their regulatory duties. Various rules imposed by industry peers carry more legitimacy with market participants than those imposed by an external regulator.

- *Rule Compliance.* Self-regulation results in better compliance because self-enforcement is more effective and more readily accepted by the regulated entities. Industry participants bring to the task expertise and intimate knowledge of the complexities of the industry and can respond more quickly to regulatory problems. The rules are likely to be tailored to the conditions of the regulated industry and accepted as being more reasonable compared with prescriptive rules issued by a state agency.

- *Acceptability.* Self-regulation operates in an environment where there is a willingness to accept regulations promulgated by professional peers as the necessary and appropriate action for the common good of the group. It is not limited to the SRO, but extends to firms and other users. The credibility of the SRO staff, as well as the opportunity to participate means that changes that impact on business are more likely to be accepted than rules issued by a state agency.

- *Prescriptive Regulation.* Usually, it is difficult for statutory regulators funded by public revenue to pay the same wages or attract the same calibre of people as private sector regulators funded by the market. Self-regulation seeks to avoid prescriptive methods of regulation. Prescriptive and legalistic rules limit discretion and are criticized as being largely ineffective particularly when compared with their costs.

- *Political Interference.* The policies determined by self-regulation may be less susceptible to political influences than those determined by a government regulator.

- *Monitoring Conduct.* Self-regulation is best suited for monitoring conduct, which lies beyond the practical reach of the law. Trading is a fluid activity and rulebooks need to deal with matters and concepts, which do not lend themselves to statutory language and formal principles of statutory interpretation.

- *Rule Reform.* Under the pressure of competition, SROs have a strong incentive to keep their rules current and cost effective, while taking advantage of their position in the market.

- *Ethical standards.* SROs have the ability to impose ethical standards, which go beyond those, which can be imposed by statutory laws. This is because they are in touch with their members and get to know quickly those with deviant behaviours.

- *Accountability.* Self-regulators are directly accountable to their members, and to the state, for actions taken or not taken. Thus, the SRO system carries a built in motivation to take the regulatory course, which is the most effective and least disruptive to market efficiency.

- *Sensitivity.* Self-regulators have the business sensitivity to know when a regulation will be workable and beneficial to the investors and users of the securities markets.

- *Participation.* The opportunity of persons and organizations that are subject to the regulations to participate at all levels of the self-regulatory process makes it easier to accept new regulations which often mean restrictions or impediments to legitimate business activities.

- *Responsiveness.* Self-regulators are able to identify and comprehend complex problems at an early stage and can respond with a solution or approach to meet the specific development or problematic situation. This ability to respond to developments as they are occurring often can ameliorate or lessen potential problem situations before they reach a crisis stage. They are therefore, able to modify their rules quickly in response to developments in the market environment. The bureaucratic structures of state agencies and rigid, formal requirements for rule making and enforcement inhibit innovation and quick responses to sudden changes in the environment.

- *Expertise.* Self-regulators also have a reservoir of expertise in the offices and staff of their members, which can be drawn upon at different levels, and stages of the self-regulatory process. It is often more efficient for the state to rely on the SRO's knowledge and expertise than try to reproduce it at a state level. Thus, SROs have a closeness to, and familiarity with, the field of financial activity to be regulated.

- *Cost Effectiveness.* Self-regulation, which often operates as a part of a voluntary membership organizational structure, has a built in incentive to minimize the cost of regulation to investors and users of the markets.

- *Effective use of State Resources.* Self-regulation permits the state to devote its resources to activities, which cannot be adequately served by self-regulation, such as criminal proceedings, legal actions on insider trading and manipulative practices by non-members.
- *Good Business Sense.* Self-regulation makes good business sense for those concerned about investor protection and those subject to the regulation.

Disadvantages of Self-regulation

Although many benefits accrue from self-regulation, there also exist some potential problems of self-regulation by securities exchanges. These may include the following:

- *Enforcement Powers.* It is true that exchanges do not have adequate statutory enforcement powers, which may be reserved for the statutory regulator, thus losing some credibility in exercising enforcement powers. They may be ineffective in regulating cross-border activities such as cross-border listing by listed firms.
- *Conflict of Interest.* Like other SROs, securities exchanges have to serve the interests of various constituencies like members, customers and the general public, and reconciling their often-conflicting interests can be difficult and lead to inefficiency.
- *Efficiency of* Regulation. Furthermore, the composition of a securities exchange membership itself, and their role in the governance of securities exchange may give particular constituencies undue influence over critical aspects of the exchange operations, such as oversight of trading and enforcement of rules and regulations, and lead to deficiencies in the performance of these functions.
- *Monopoly Interest.* SROs like securities exchanges are often in a monopoly position and may seek to preserve and enhance that position to the detriment of members, customers and the general public. Alternatively, as membership organizations, they may regulate the market they operate to their own advantage and contrary to the public interest. An SRO may use its regulatory power to impose purely anti-competitive restraints as opposed to those

justified by regulatory needs. Similarly, the SRO may resist change in the regulatory pattern because of vested economic interests in its preservation or insufficient knowledge of newly developing market conventions or investor needs.

- *Overstretching Arm.* Securities exchanges may be required to supervise intermediaries such as investment advisers who are not licensed to trade on the exchange who have no interest in the markets the SRO operates. This again, results in conflicts of interest between those persons and intermediaries who are members of the exchange. This may also give rise to arguments as to the proper apportionment of costs between different classes of intermediaries.

- *Duplicating Regulatory efforts.* The structure of government regulation plus those of SROs is duplicative and costly. If there are several SROs with overlapping jurisdictions, their independent licensing, market surveillance and enforcement activities may further duplicate each other and force market participants to incur unnecessary time and costs in complying with different regulatory regimes. Competition and innovation may be stifled if every securities exchange, as an SRO is expected to perform the full range of SRO functions. Performance of all functions may be uneconomic and irrelevant for smaller niche markets. However, not to require full SRO functions in every case creates inequality and increases the administrative burden of the statutory regulator in discharging its monitoring and supervisory functions.

- *Members vs Listed Firms.* Regulation of listed firms came later than regulation of members. By itself, regulation of the listed firms is not, strictly speaking, self-regulation as securities exchanges are not organizations of public firms. The jurisdiction over listed firms is contractual, based on the listing agreement pursuant to which the firms agree to comply with applicable securities exchange rules. Originally, the concept of listing did not exist for many exchanges, which traded any and all financial instruments.

- *Conflicting Goals.* The combination of fulfilling self-regulatory and commercial goals splits the SRO focus such that it excels at neither. The potentially conflicting goals also inhibit the SRO ability to raise capital. As such therefore, securities exchanges, just like other SROs have limitation in terms of the required financial resource to execute effective regulation of listed firms and market intermediaries.

Is Self-Regulation Inconsistent with Demutualization?

Former USA Securities and Exchange Commission (SEC) Commissioner - Roberta Karmel identified four areas in which the NYSE and Nasdaq carry out self-regulatory functions:[119] listed firm governance and disclosure; surveillance and discipline of their markets and specialists, floor brokers and market makers; member firm financial and operational compliance; and fair and equitable treatment of customers. As these functions need to be carried out effectively in any securities market, it is important to consider carefully whether demutualization implies that a securities exchange will be less motivated or less able to manage them. Let us consider each of these functions in turn.

Listing and Disclosure

Securities exchanges typically perform functions wholly unrelated to the actual trading of securities, and indeed are frequently required by national law to perform such functions. The most significant one is listing a firm's shares to be traded on a securities exchange. The 2001 IOSCO Technical Committee specifically refers to listing as – a regulatory function.

Indeed, listing is fundamentally a quality control function, designed to ensure that firms admitted to a given segment of the securities market – for example large cap or small cap – meet disclosure requirements appropriate to their size and age. Its role in the equity markets is comparable to that of ratings in the bond market, even if the mechanisms of being listed and rated are very different. But just as bond rating agencies have a strong incentive to rate bonds more accurately than their competitors, listing agencies

---

119 Karmel, R. S. (2007). Is the Financial Industry Regulatory Authority a Government Agency? Brooklyn Law School, Legal Studies Paper No. 86. Brooklyn.

should have strong incentives to set listing requirements for publicly traded firms neither too low nor too high. If disclosure requirements are excessive for the size and age of the firms wishing to be publicly traded, then the agency will unnecessarily sacrifice listing revenues. If they are set too low, however, investors are more likely to be harmed by unexpected events, like profit warnings. Investors will therefore shun such stocks, and the agency's reputation and pricing power in the listings market will suffer severely.

It is an unfortunate historical legacy, however, that in much of the world governments have treated listing as a self-regulatory function to be performed by the monopoly national securities exchange. As a matter of logic and history, however, listing should never have been considered an obligation that needed to be imposed on securities exchanges. In fact, the board of the NYSE began imposing formal listing standards in 1856, and did so wholly of its own accord and in consideration of its own interests. The main reasons for the development of such standards would appear to have been the protection of members trading on their own account and the incentive to listing provided to firms from the public signal of financial soundness and stability.

Whereas listing is clearly a valuable market function, it is important to recognize that there is no logical reason why trading system operators such as securities exchanges should necessarily be the ones to carry it out. It could just as easily be performed by accounting firms or rating agencies, and done on a competitive basis. Competition for listing standards should help both to drive down listing costs and to discover the optimal listing standards for firms with different characteristics. Remember, one of the barriers to undertaking IPOs by many firms, both small and large, is cost of listing.

This incentive is reflected in the fact that securities exchanges typically extract a significant proportion of their annual revenues from listing activities – 23 percent generally according to the 2023 WFE member survey. Any assumption that listing standards will always be set too low if established on a purely commercial basis is clearly faulty. Neuer Markt – a Germany's small cap market operated by Deutsche Börse – once concluded that a 70 percent year-on-year decline in its listed share prices needed to be at least partially ascribed to a lack of investor confidence in listed firms' disclosure following a string of profit warnings, insider dealing investigations, and insolvencies. Consequently, exchange implemented new rules to mandate more comprehensive and standardized firm financial reports and revelation of directors' share dealings. Offenders were made subject to new punitive actions and publication of their offenses on the internet. These actions were taken wholly on the basis of the exchange's evaluation of its commercial self-interest. The trend reversed.

Securities exchange demutualization is therefore certainly no less consistent with the development and enforcement of appropriate corporate listing and disclosure standards than is mutualization. Indeed, market regulators should welcome the entry of non-exchange entities into the listing business as a means of driving down capital costs through lower listing fees and the development of better listing standards.

Trading Surveillance

Karmel, in referring to the surveillance of specialists, floor brokers and market makers, identified specific features of the NYSE and Nasdaq trading environments; features which either do not exist or play only an ancillary role in automated trading structures.[120] Financial markets where human intermediation is built into the basic trading mechanism do require a level of active monitoring and policing which exceeds that which is necessary in markets where the matching of investor orders takes place in a computer according to a pre-specified algorithm. Human discretion breeds error, inconsistency, and malfeasance.

Evidence has shown that at one time, SEC issued an administrative order which found that the NYSE had failed, without reasonable justification or excuse, to enforce federal laws and NYSE rules against unlawful proprietary and discretionary trading by NYSE floor brokers. The nine floor brokers pleaded guilty in 1998 to reduced criminal charges surrounding systematic front-running of customer trades – a practice which had been widespread and known to NYSE officials.

---

120 Karmel, R. S. (2007). Is the Financial Industry Regulatory Authority a Government Agency? Brooklyn Law School, Legal Studies Paper No. 86. Brooklyn.

Floor brokers are prohibited by law from trading for themselves or sharing in the profits generated by their own trading. The floor brokers in question were charged with an illegal form of trade front-running known as intraday trading or flipping. This involves the rapid buying and selling of shares at prices between the quoted sale and purchase prices. This practice had been ruled as illegal when traders take a share of the profits. The floor brokers in question were charged with flipping based on knowledge of large orders on the floor and splitting the profits with Oakford Corp. - a now-defunct brokerage firm. Revelations from more recent investigations suggest that NYSE officials not only knew of such activities, but took active steps to keep them hidden from the SEC and the public at large.

In the case of Nasdaq, the SEC published report concluded that Nasdaq market makers had engaged in collusion and other illegal behaviour in order to keep publicly quoted bid-offer spreads artificially wide, and that the Nasd had systematically failed to enforce its own market rules. These are just but only a few cases of major failures of self-regulatory organizations trading surveillance in USA. There is a long and inglorious history preceding them as well as many similar cases in other jurisdictions.

There is nothing about mutuality that lends itself to an effective partnering with SRO trading surveillance obligations. Whether a mutualized securities exchange is run on a not-for-profit or for-profit basis is immaterial. A mutualized securities exchange exists to serve the interests of its members. This is what it is established to do, and if it fails to do so effectively, it will inevitably be reformed or dissolved. A demutualized securities exchange is not faced with any greater conflict of interest merely because some portion of its ownership is not trading members of the securities exchange. Indeed, the scope for such conflict of interest should be less for demutualized securities exchanges or proprietary trading system. Also known as prop trading, proprietary trading occurs when a trader such as a bank decides to trade stocks, bonds, currencies, commodities, their derivatives, or other financial instruments with the firm's own money – instead of using depositors' money – in order to make a profit for itself.

Proprietary trading can create potential conflicts of interest such as insider trading and front running. Proprietary traders may use a variety of strategies such as index arbitrage, statistical arbitrage, merger arbitrage, fundamental analysis, volatility arbitrage, or global macro trading, much like a hedge fund. In fact, large banks purposely leave ambiguous the proportion of proprietary versus non-proprietary trading, because they believe that proprietary trading is riskier and results in more volatile profits. It is worth noting that proprietary trading system is a generic term referring to non-member-based trading systems owned and operated outside the legal entity of a securities exchange.

Member Financial and Operational Compliance
Mutualized securities exchanges have a formidable interest in ensuring the credit worthiness of all members. Each member wants assurance that the counterparty on a given trade can meet its obligations. Securities exchanges often institute highly-rated central counterparties to guarantee performance on all trades, and the cost of establishing and operating a central counterparty will itself depend upon the financial viability of the participating members. Therefore, ensuring that members complete transactions with other members in a timely and secure manner is hardly a self-regulatory obligation of a securities exchange. In fact, it is a prerequisite for effective operation in the interests of its members.

Demutualized securities exchanges or proprietary trading systems have no less an interest in ensuring the inviolability of a transaction. Instinet, for example, operates as a central counterparty for all client trades so that clients do not have to be concerned about the reliability or financial condition of other Instinet clients. Instinet, in turn, has a strong financial interest in vetting its clients, and in not doing business with those which could expose it to trading losses. Nevertheless, securities market regulator in USA concern that systems such as Instinet are closed, rather than public, is misguided along two dimensions. The floor-based securities exchanges are no more publicly accessible than Instinet. In fact, they are less so, as they, unlike Instinet, allow only a strictly limited number of members. Also, obliging Instinet to extend access to its clients' bids and offers to non-clients exposes Instinet to credit risk which it cannot control. This is neither in the interests of Instinet nor its clients. These issues are bothersome not only to regulators but also securities exchanges as well as their trading members.

Fair Treatment of Investors

In terms of fairness in treatment of securities investors – the area of investor protection – where mutualized securities exchanges operating as SROs suffer from the most salient conflict of interest. Securities exchange members are never going to want interference in their customer relationships from a securities exchange which they own, and which was created to serve their interests. A demutualized securities exchange or proprietary trading systems with minority broker ownership will be concerned with ensuring the satisfaction of those with the ultimate power to direct order flow to its trading system. This will frequently be the actual investor and mostly institutional, rather than a broker which may or may not act as a conduit between the investor and the system.

Taking Excessive Financial Risks

Are demutualized securities exchanges more likely to take excessive financial risks? There is some concern that the profit-seeking actions of a demutualized exchange may provide further encouragement to enter businesses other than those directly ancillary to its traditional trade execution functions. This entails new financial risks for a securities exchange that may merit regulatory intervention, such as the imposition of firewalls to protect the resources necessary to run the exchange's core activities. As a matter of logic and actual market behaviour, these concerns appear to be illogical. Why? One, because mutualized securities exchanges, both for-profit and not-for-profit, have displayed a more than healthy appetite for expansion of their activities, like buying CSDs (Deutsche Börse pre-IPO), investing in international joint ventures (Swiss Exchange), buying derivatives exchanges (Johannesburg Securities Exchange, Paris Bourse pre-IPO), or buying other domestic and foreign exchanges (Nasdaq). Bull markets tend to increase securities exchanges' cash surpluses, inciting those not explicitly disciplined by the exigencies of share price maximization to pursue outlets for business expansion. Exchanges appear to be operating a far more disciplined, targeted and incremental approach to business expansion after demutualization and self-listing.

Two, demutualized securities exchanges do not appear to exhibit a greater propensity to invest in ancillary services than mutualized exchanges. Data from WFE shows that in 2023 demutualized securities exchanges generate less than 31.7 percent of revenue from services such as membership, clearing, settlement, depository, and data dissemination, compared with 29.3 percent for mutual associations and 34.6 percent for limited companies owned by the members. However, demutualized exchanges generated about twice as much of their service income (81.7%) from market data dissemination than did traditional exchanges. The latter were more reliant on membership fees, not surprisingly, as demutualized securities exchanges tend to have more competition for their members' order flow. Demutualized exchanges also derive other revenues from investment in other institutions locally as well as globally.

If one accepts that demutualized exchanges are not more likely than mutual ones to engage in risky business expansion, then there would appear to be less reason for concern about their investments. This is because their investments have been far more profitable. So if market regulators still fear excessive risk-taking by securities exchanges, mutualized or demutualized, they can impose capital requirements, as they do with commercial banks, to reduce the probability of insolvency and eventual liquidation.

Emerging Lessons Learnt
Experience gained so far shows that demutualized exchanges have developed different regulatory arrangements and controls. Most exchanges recognize that a publicly traded securities exchange cannot afford to risk its reputation and market integrity given the implications for business and revenue stream or profits. To address the issues and challenges they face, demutualized securities exchanges have evolved governance structures to lessen the emerging conflict(s) and are adopting a set of regulatory responses. The demutualized securities exchanges have been observed to pursue different options. Some are entirely self-regulatory organization, some are a hybrid of external and self-regulation. For instance, in Australia, securities market regulation is based on a co-sharing regulatory model

that involves a combination of statutory oversight provided by the capital markets regulator and by the stock exchange supervisory review to oversee the operations of exchanges.[121]

The common approach has been to lay down a credible approach and proper regulatory standards to avoid conflict of interest at securities exchange level in relation to its own prospective listing. Generally, the securities markets regulators have all the powers and functions that exchanges' have in relation to listed issuers except for their powers to make listing rules. The listing standards for securities exchanges have to be the same as for other listed firms and the listing fee for the securities exchange has to be determined and sometimes collected by the securities market regulator. Although securities exchanges serve as the front line regulators, they are obligated to take action as required by the securities market regulations guiding admission, suspension or removal of listing on securities exchange; and to put in place procedures to deal with the conflicts of interest that may arise, and to ensure complete disclosure of listing. Securities exchange demutualization has therefore triggered extensive debate on the merits of self-regulation. Questions have been raised on inherent conflicts of interest that SROs, which in some cases could be stock exchanges, face in their dual roles as market operators and regulators. On the part of securities exchanges, there have been concerns regarding the direct costs, to the securities exchange, of implementing the supervisory framework, and the indirect costs associated with a perceived lack of flexibility and management of authorization and approval process.

Stern critics outside exchanges raise doubts regarding the ability of SROs to regulate members with whom they compete and there are perceptions that SROs might abuse its regulatory authority, like through rule making processes, disciplinary actions, and use of in proprietary information and unfair practices vis-à-vis the competitors it regulates. Market participants have also complained of regulatory inefficiencies that have emerged because the broker-dealers are subject to the multiple SROs that have different rules and examination standards.

---

121 See ASIC Regulatory tracker 2023 – https ://asic.gov.au/regulatory-resources/find-a-document/regulatory-document-updates/regulatory-tracker/regulatory-tracker-2023/

Despite inquiries on these fronts, self-regulation, though riddled with issues of perception, continues to be a preferred mode of oversight as the exchanges or its specialized subsidiaries have the advantage of: proximity to market participants and an understanding of the supervision of a complex industry, products and market; developing rules and supervisory arrangements that reflect market needs, adopting flexible and effective enforcement and monitoring; keeping costs of regulation manageable given that exchanges may lose the competitive edge; and having experienced, well-funded, independent experts who regulate better than the state regulators with little or no experience. Self-policing is critical as the exchange's key business asset is its reputation for integrity and efficiency and is not one that could be compromised without threatening the value of its own business.

Issues to Consider in Regulating Demutualized Exchanges

Some of the main areas of difficulty, which have been encountered during demutualization in Asian Pacific, Europe and Oceania, and USA provide some lessons, which may arise in other jurisdictions like Africa and recommendations on issues to be considered during the demutualization process. Consider the competition laws, the competitive environment of exchanges, the scope of approval if applicable and factors to consider for approval, and control over an exchange's budget. In a freely competitive market with a competition authority, regulatory involvement may be unnecessary. But where a country lacks a competition authority, securities exchanges have exclusive rights to operate a securities market in the country, there is a need for regulation. In fact, practices of private or mutual bodies are likely to raise or reveal many issues. It is necessary to begin the work early to avoid surprises and resolve issues well ahead of listing. In jurisdictions with no legal mechanisms for the conversion of a company limited by guarantee, the corporate structure of securities exchanges before their demutualization, to a company limited by shares. This should be addressed in by either legal reform or setting new statutory provisions.

There is a need to consider state and public interest duties. Consider whether any pre-existing public interest duties should be expanded. The exchanges' duties can be expanded to a holding company level. Changes need to be made to the governance structure of the exchange. There will be some concern over achieving a diverse shareholder base leading to the thinning down of the number of exchange board members; this can be phased out over time. Consider the need for increased regulatory involvement and maintaining value added participation by market players. The market regulator may wish to have a say if there is any proposal to vary risk management reserves. The new governance structure may exclude market participant specialists who are themselves at risk to the securities exchange operations and have a strong self-interest in maintaining state of the art risk management.

Should there be a statutory regulator making all listing decisions where a securities exchange or holding company self-lists or an affiliate? The possible conflict of interest should be considered, particularly conflicts of interest of the listed group where it may make decisions affecting its competitors or business associates including listing, admission, service provision, and pricing. New provisions may be appropriate depending on the competitive environment, adequacy of competition laws and pre-existing regulatory powers. An MoU is important for conflict identification, recording, auditing, and resolution, and can enable the statutory market regulator to make decisions in time.

Should the demutualized exchange continue to have a commitment to any pre-existing self-regulation and if self-regulation is to continue, are new arrangements necessary to reinforce this? If regulatory functions are to be reallocated, there is a need to consider an MoU and begin work early to ensure a smooth transition. But, will the demutualized securities exchange be willing to give up a function if it means giving up control over a material source of income? There may be a need to consider whether ownership restrictions should apply to the listing body or its exchange affiliates, and this is likely to affect valuation and have governance implications. The auditing financial status of an SRO requires that if financial intermediaries are routinely audited, then a securities exchange should be required to meet specified capital or other financial requirements.

In sum, internationally, the regulatory relationship between the statutory market regulator and a securities exchange is continuously evolving. There is no single model that is appropriate for all countries. With the demutualization and listing of a securities exchange, the division of regulatory responsibilities between the market regulator and the securities exchange has to be explicitly defined. The market regulator has to ensure that arrangements for the regulation and supervision of the securities and futures markets between itself and the self-listed exchange are in place, with an enhanced oversight responsibility and powers to pursue civil prosecution, will prove robust. However, given the rapid changes in the capital markets brought about by globalization and technological advances, the arrangement can be expected to evolve over time. This model has been witnessed in Singapore and Canada. Alternatively, the regulatory function can be shared between the demutualized securities exchange and the market regulator. The listing and operation of firms is, in some cases, regulated by the capital markets regulator and the operation and listing of the exchange itself, is also regulated by such regulator. This model exists in United States and Hong Kong. In others jurisdictions, the securities exchange regulates its own listing and that of other listed firms, like in the case of the few African Exchanges which have demutualized. Therefore, the regulation of demutualized securities exchanges in different jurisdiction such as in America (USA and Canada), Europe/Oceania (Australia), Asian Pacific (Singapore and Hong Kong), and Africa/Middle East fall within these models.

Chapter Summary

Traditionally, mutual securities exchanges enjoyed a monopolistic role in their jurisdictions. However, this role was disrupted in the 1990s due to rapid technological advancement and increasing globalization which promoted domestic and international competition. Also, securities exchanges saw the opportunity to expand by accessing foreign investors, offering new products, and improving trading systems' efficiency. To address the emerging competitive threats and in order to take advantage of growth opportunities, securities exchanges started demutualizing. Demutualization transform the ownership structure of securities exchanges from mutually owned to demutualized. It has been noted that this ownership transfer allowed securities exchanges to access new financing, enabling technological advancements. It also separates the management from members-brokers, thus making faster decision-making possible.

This chapter has espoused on the relationship between the for-profit focus of demutualized securities exchanges and their monitoring and oversight of listed firms as well as the general market regulation. It was argued that securities exchanges are pure self-regulatory organizations, yet they are also regulated by the state capital markets regulator. We have seen that whereas securities exchanges rarely make the primary rules of these markets, they significantly impact the regulation and oversight of listed firms and influence national regulations through lobbying and shape company abidance through voluntary regulations like corporate governance codes. Given their autonomy, securities exchanges can set their own rules ranging from financial disclosure to governance practices, decide whether to cooperate with regulatory agencies supervising the market, and opt to create segments with different levels of regulatory requirements and oversight. Given the important role that these exchanges play in regulation and oversight, a change in their incentives due to an increase in their for-profit focus following demutualization can influence their monitoring efforts. It can weaken their monitoring efforts or make them instigate a stricter regulatory environment for listed firms.

There are therefore certain changes and needs resulting from demutualization and merger of securities exchanges, which should be noted. For instance, the separation between the trading-access and the decision-making power. The trading access and the others services provided by the securities exchange are, generally, separated from the ownership of shares. The decision-making power now belongs to the shareholders – that will not be, necessarily, if the former brokerage houses or the former members were the only decision makers. Also, there is need for corporate governance reinforcement and strategy. For-profit corporation, the management will be more competitive. There is the adoption of a commercial model by securities exchanges. This calls for some regulatory changes in the changes self-regulation model after the demutualization. There are also the jurisdiction conflicts in the exchange merger process.

Trading access models adopted also needs to be considered. There is the issue of trading access licenses automatically granted to the former owners of the membership certificates. There is need to facilitate entrance possibility to the new intermediaries, since they are properly qualified for that, as was done in NYSE. Exchanges contemplating demutualization should consider also the issue of shares with different classes, like voting right class and trading access right class, like happened at CME and NYMEX. The other regulatory issues are jurisdictional conflicts relating to anti-trust issues and difficulties to conciliate the regulators' requirements in the regional exchanges involving international mergers and takeovers. The other issue is self-regulation function of the securities exchange. As a commercial entity, for profit organization, can a securities exchanges keeps satisfactorily its self-regulatory function? This is so as the exchange's objective will be split between profit maximization as well as fair market operating.

In attempt to address these regulatory issues, securities exchanges can adopt any of the following three alternatives of self-regulation. One is where the securities exchange keeps the self-regulatory activities. If the securities exchange acts in a relapse way regarding its regulatory activities, it can cause damage to its commercial image. The securities exchange has a better display to perform the trading supervision as well as the compliance of the public firms. It is its task to provide a regulated market. The second one is where the exchange ensures there is dissociation between the commercial activities and the regulatory activities inside the demutualized securities exchange. It can undertake a launch of a non-for-profit entity to take care of the regulation activities, under the same holding, but constituted by an independent board and an independent management.

Lastly, there can be the outsourcing of the regulatory activities to a third party. Again, it can undertake the launch of a non-for-profit entity, fully disentailed and constituted by members that do not have entails with it or interest in the securities exchange activities. In this case, the regulatory activities are fully attributed to a governmental body. There is no one-size-fits-all model that can be said to be appropriate for all countries as long as the market is transparently and fairly regulated with no regulatory gaps and loopholes.

Chapter Seven

POST DEMUTUALIZATION OF SECURITIES EXCHANGES: LESSONS FOR AFRICAN MARKETS

Introduction

Globalization, institutionalisation and technological advancement are changing the way securities exchanges operate and compete. Securities exchanges today face competition from proprietary trading systems, such as ECNs, especially ATSs, and investors are more sophisticated and demanding as they seek to execute trade directly, want convenient low-cost access, and look for a variety of cash and derivative instruments. These challenges are forcing securities exchanges to be more commercial, which in turn is causing them to consider their constitutional structure. Often, they are deciding that the mutual structure does not provide the flexibility to meet these challenges because it is geared toward maintaining members' interests. On the other hand, demutualization allows trading rights to be separated from ownership and therefore allows securities exchanges to be driven as commercial entities. Listing, a separate decision, takes these issues a step further by speeding up the process of separation and sharpening the focus on shareholder value. However, for a securities exchange to reap the benefits of demutualization, it must plan the appropriate organization structure, risk management strategy, corporate governance model, commercial model, and ownership structure.

The experiences of demutualized securities exchanges provide experiences and lessons but different exchanges have different issues to be addressed. Therefore, the answer is not to be found in a single model, but in a range of responses which take into account the history of the exchange, its place in the economic structure of the country, the state of market development, the existing ownership position, the intended goals, and public policy. The state, statutory regulator and the securities exchange each have a role to play in the decisions. Most of these issues are found in discussions in the previous chapters on demutualization in Europe/Oceania, America and Asian Pacific, and which African securities exchanges can consider. There are some commonalities and variations found in the lessons learnt from the different justifications. Many securities exchanges have increased their resource availability upon demutualization. Majority of them have acquired, merged with or taken-over other exchanges. New regulations have been enacted that encourage securities exchanges, especially in developed markets, to integrate their shares, cash, bonds and derivative trading under one roof. Share prices of shares issued by demutualized and integrated securities exchanges, as we are going to see, have also improved in value.

Resource Availability and Commercial Focus by Exchanges

Demutualization and subsequent self-listing have increased the resource availability for, and enabled a more commercial focus by securities exchanges. Considering the post demutualization status of securities exchanges, a number of issues are evident. Demutualized exchanges are able to pursue commercial initiatives quickly, opportunities can be grabbed faster and market threats identified before they become severe. Such securities exchanges are therefore more able to act and respond quickly to competitive market forces. Since their main focus is profiteering, they have been able to pay dividends to their shareholders and increase reserves for investments in systems and technology. IPOs by exchanges have also provided an opportunity to finance takeovers of, and mergers with, other exchanges. Securities exchanges have therefore been able to increased value to be utilized in mergers, joint ventures and other strategic alliances – initiatives that can now be pursued quickly and with necessary speed. Securities exchanges have also become more commercial and service focused in their operations. Through demutualization, securities exchanges have reorganized themselves to facilitate evolution from public duty culture to more customer and market-focused culture.

Majority of demutualized securities exchanges have also developed user friendliness of services and their public relations have improved dramatically. Some like ASX have even established an Index Advisory Panel to publicly explore customer concerns, and as a result increased customer confidence, increased listings, volumes and the share of stocks and mutual funds in investors' portfolio. The demutualized securities exchanges have also become more profit and value focused with management becoming more accountable, transparent, and focused on profit-centre basis. Some of them are even levying fees for their index service and other exchanges services usually offered to the public freely. These exchanges have ventured into rationalization and reorganization of their structures and physical operations, with others closing their under-utilized investor centres. In terms of strategy, demutualized securities exchanges have assumed a more strategic focus with deputy manager position created for strategic planning to strategically focus the exchange more. They have even included welfare issues in their operation with value created passed to affected market participants.

Mergers and Acquisitions of Securities Exchanges

There are many ways in which both demutualized and mutual securities exchanges can cooperate with each other[122] including effecting a linkage, forming a joint venture, an alliance or merging with others. The various functions undertaken by two securities exchanges like marketing, listing, order-routing, marching and execution, dissemination of information, clearing, settlement, and administration services can be shared to remove duplicity. There are also different contractual procedures by which shared delivery of these services can be implemented like one securities exchange can purchase the services form another, both exchanges may agree to sub-contract delivery to a third party, or one securities exchange can buy from

---

122 Onyuma, S. O. (2005) Integration of Stock Markets in Africa. 8th OSSREA Conference, Addis Ababa, Ethiopia, Nov. 21-13.

the other exchange. The first form of integration is a cross-border merger or joint venture (any type of mixed integration using some common vehicle), where the parties (exchanges, clearing houses, or technology providers) to the deal are located in different countries, and which leads to the same trading system. Secondly, a domestic merger or restructuring is where exchanges in a country, vertically or horizontally, merge their internal activities like trading, and clearance and settlement facilities to enjoy economies of scale and scope. This form has been conducted by the Deutsche Bourse, Amsterdam, Brussels, Singapore, and Helsinki securities exchanges.

In addition, a cross-remote membership is where a securities exchange gives access to its trading engine to brokers of another exchange even if they are not located physically in the same country. It is a much easier and feasible form of cooperation as it provides wider access to other markets. Moreover, cross-border listing is where firms cross-list their stocks to allow domestic investors to trade in a foreign firm's stocks. Firms are able to raise more capital, diversify their shareholder base, allow for a broader investor exposure, and enhance the image of the firm in other markets outside its home country. But, the bulk of trading usually occurs at the domestic market, although the reverse could occur and the market liquidity driven out of local smaller, to larger and more liquid, exchanges. This has been witnessed in the case of NYSE and Buenos Aries Stock Exchange. Lastly, an implicit merger, a hybrid of cross-membership and cross-listing, is an agreement between two exchanges, where stocks originally listed on one securities exchange are listed by the other, and remote access is reciprocally offered to stockbrokers of both securities exchanges.[123] This can lead to higher profits for both exchanges due to cross advantages of marginal costs, as one securities exchange may have a lower marginal cost in trading and the other lower listing cost.

---

123 For a detailed discussion on these models, see Onyuma, S. O. (2006). Regional Integration of Stock Exchanges in Africa. *African Review of Money, Banking & Finance* (Supplement Issue) December: 99-124.

After being demutualized, most securities exchanges have revisited their commercial strategy to improve viability and enhance commercial prospects. These securities exchanges have opted to consolidate, merge and/or integrate their domestic markets; build alliances by establishing cross-border linkages with other exchanges within or outside the region; and merge with other exchanges – a phenomenon more predominant in Europe. In Asia, the exchanges have by and large opted for the first two, while in Africa securities exchanges are exhausting benefits of the second model. Generally, emphasis has been largely to re-group businesses to broaden the markets, and to offer securities issuers and investors better distribution networks and improved liquidity. Predominant domestic mergers or restructuring have taken place in markets in the United States, Singapore, Hong Kong, Australia, Japan, and United Kingdom. The same integration form was applied in the merger of the Kuala Lumpur Stock Exchange and MESDAQ.

Domestic restructuring of exchanges has taken many forms. First, a merger of two or more exchanges into a single viable national level firm, which would be of sufficient scale to be an interesting partner for other – foreign – securities exchanges, and as a listed firm for investors to consider. While these mergers lead to synergy effect on the cost side, they tend to reduce possible competition on the domestic market. Thus, the effect of the merger can in some cases nurture monopolistic behaviour, at least until new entrants appear or until domestic firms can be traded on securities exchanges domiciled in other jurisdictions. Second, a consolidation of same-market exchanges, whether domestic or regional, is part of a global trend where the minimum economic scale of the securities exchange increases as the trading fees decreases with competition. The lower the fees a securities exchange can charge, the higher the necessary trading volume needed to stay profitable.

Moreover, a vertical integration of the clearing, settlement and depository institutions with a securities exchange helps to guarantee the availability of those functions in-house and provides for an alternate source of revenue, while supporting cost reductions that lower the overall transaction cost to the investors. This integration could potentially reduce the competitive threat by attempting to restrict access to the clearing functions in the country to any potential new entrants. Lastly, a merger of different types of markets such as the derivatives and cash markets or equity, bond, derivatives, and commodities markets have led to economies of scale. Mergers of this nature have been driven by a combination of factors, including economies of scale, cost cutting in administrative functions, *one-stop-shopping* for investors and stockbrokers, as well as product development potential.

After demutualization, some regional exchanges such as the SGX and HKEx have taken a wide range of initiatives. For instance, SGX has developed cross linkages with Japan, Nasdaq and Australia, and has also provided global access to the Singapore Exchange Derivatives Trading Ltd. (SGX-DT) electronic trading system to provide on-line access for both trading of domestic and international securities, offered Exchange Trade Funds and effectively integrated the settlement infrastructure to the central depository to facilitate straight through processing. The SGX has also offered a new real-time multi-level data system that allows investors to access the full order book information on the SGX securities market, on a subscription basis. The greater transparency and the enhanced price discovery process offered by the system currently enable investors to make better-informed decisions. In order to remain competitive, securities exchanges need to continually restructure and upgrade themselves based on the latest technological advancements in trading and information dissemination technology. Members of mutual exchanges have been unable or unwilling to commit themselves to such investments. A profit-seeking securities exchange with transferable and self-listed shares has access a broader investor base for such funds.

While the wave of demutualization and self-listing of securities exchanges seems to have run its course, it may well be followed by an era of consolidation of exchanges both geographically – as illustrated by the NYSE-Euronext merger and the aggressive pursuit of the London Stock Exchange by Nasdaq – and across products like in the merger of the Australian Stock Exchange and the SFE Corporation, which trades derivatives. Advances in technology allow the trading of stocks, cash, bonds, and derivatives on a single trading system. This ability of adding more trades to an electronic trading system at close to zero cost is seen as the main driving force behind the consolidation wave in the securities exchange industry. Recent developments in Europe have broadened the appeal of cross-border trading. As a growing number of European countries have adopted the euro, intra-European currency exposure – the risk associated with an unexpected change in exchange rates – has diminished, making cross-border investment more desirable. Significantly, the increased use of the euro has been accompanied by the removal of some regulatory restrictions on intra-European capital flows.

Securities exchange groupings and consolidations – mergers, acquisitions, takeovers – in the European region are the Euronext, BME (Spanish Exchanges)[124] and OMX.[125] Globally, the most notable merger activities include the Euronext merger, the NYSE merger, the OMX merger, ICE acquisition of the NYSE-Euronext, Nasdaq's interest in the London Stock Exchange, attempted acquisition of Deutsche Borse by NYSE-Euronext, and attempted acquisition by Deutsche Borse of London Stock Exchange.

Euronext Group

Euronext is the leading Pan-European exchange that connects local economies to global capital markets, to accelerate innovation and sustainable growth. It offers various trading and post-trade services, with traded assets including regulated equities, exchange-traded funds, warrants and certificates, bonds, derivatives, commodities, foreign exchange as well as indices. Its multi-asset offering therefore meets the needs of firms and investors worldwide. It connecting European economies to global capital markets, to accelerate innovation and sustainable growth. The listed firms are worth €6.6 trillion market capitalisation at end March 2022. As Europe's centre for raising capital, its federal model remains a core strength,

---

124 BME is the holding company of Barcelona, Bilbao, Madrid and Valencia Stock Exchanges.

125 OMX started its consolidation process in 2004, and the Group includes the Copenhagen, Helsinki, Iceland, Stockholm, Tallinn, Riga and Vilnius Stock Exchanges.

while new asset classes drive international expansion. Its new Strategic Plan – Growth for Impact 2024 – sets out the group's ambition to build the leading market infrastructure in Europe.

From the first 17th century marketplace to providing tomorrow's sustainable growth products, Euronext has been financing the European real economy for over 400 years. Building the leading market infrastructure in Europe, Euronext has a strong Pan-European presence giving it access to regulated markets in Amsterdam, Brussels, Dublin, Lisbon, Milan, Oslo and Paris. Having acquired these exchanges, Euronext also owns the London International Financial Futures Exchange (Euronext-Liffe). Offices spanning three continents serve clients of its global products and services, thus drawing on each local market's strengths while providing scale and reach.

Euronext recently acquired Italian Stock Exchange, Nord Pool, and VP Securities. Nord Pool is a Pan-European power exchange which runs the leading power market in Europe and offer day-ahead and intraday markets its customers. The Oslo based institution celebrated its 30th anniversary in 2023 priding itself with the following subsidiaries: Nord Pool Finland Oy, Nord Pool AB, European Market Coupling Operator AS. VP Securities is a Copenhagen based central securities depository, which offers local knowledge of the Nordics along with cross-border securities transactions and services that match the new European environment. Its range of services includes secure issuance, clearing & settlement and safekeeping of securities to facilitate the requirements of the financial industry efficiently and reliably. It became part of Euronext in August 2020.

The Nasdaq Group

Created in 1971, Nasdaq is an exchange company with over 3,900 listed firms and delivers trading, exchange technology and public company services across six continents. In 2007, the Chicago Board of Trade merged with the Chicago Mercantile Exchange, while late in 2007, Boston Stock Exchange was acquired by Nasdaq and renamed to Nasdaq OMX BX. The securities exchange acquisition pursuits continued and in 2008, the Philadelphia Stock Exchange was acquired by NASDAQ, and to Nasdaq OMX PHLX.

NASDAQ OMX offers multiple capital raising solutions to companies around the globe, including its USA listings market; the OMX Nordic Exchange, including First North; and the 144A PORTAL Market. Nasdaq has made 13 acquisitions and 22 investments. It relentlessly reimages the world of tomorrow – one that is built on innovative technology, fuelled by market-moving insights and driven by forward thinking. It aims to set the pace for rethinking capital markets and economies anywhere and everywhere. Nasdaq has acquired 29 companies, including 8 in the last 5 years. A total of 7 acquisitions came from private equity firms. Nasdaq has done acquisitions in 9 different US states, and 8 countries.

The Nasdaq's most targeted sectors include financial services (21%) and business services (18%).These acquisitions include the recent acquisition such as the 2022 of Metrio in Monreal, Canada; the 2021 of Puro.earth in Helsinki, Finland; and the 2020 of Verafin in St. John, Canada – its largest acquisition to date for $2.8B. Others are Sybenetix in London; Cinnober in Stockholm, the 2016 of International Stock Exchange (ISE) in New York City, eVestment in Marietta in 2017, and Boardvantage in Menlo Park, thus spending slightly over $ 4.98 billion for the acquisitions. Nasdaq has invested in multiple sectors such as Investment Tech, GRC Software, Banking Tech and more. It has also divested 7 assets, with Its largest disclosed sale being the 2018, when it sold Nasdaq - Public Relations Solutions and Digital Media Services Businesses to Intrado for $335M.

ICE Acquisition of NYSE Euronext

In December 2012, the boards of directors of both Intercontinental Exchange (ICE) and the NYSE Euronext approved an $8 billion acquisition of NYSE Euronext. Under the terms, shareholders of NYSE were to receive either $33.12 in cash for each share or 0.2581 ICE shares, or a combination of $11.27 in cash per share plus 0.1703 shares of stock. The acquisition was subject to regulatory approval, though the operations of ICE and NYSE Euronext had little in common. Since ICE is largely devoted to trading commodities, as opposed to NYSE Euronext's business of trading stocks and other securities, the deal was not expected to face any resistance. The ICE planned that once the deal was closed, it would sell out the Euronext portion of the company, including securities exchanges in Amsterdam, Brussels, Lisbon and Paris.

The deal went through and Euronext became a sister division to NYSE and part of ICE. The CEO of ICE Jeffrey Sprecher continued in that position at the combined company, while the CEO of NYSE Euronext Duncan Niederauer continued to serve as president. Whereas the future of the NYSE's historic trading floor under ICE had not been announced by the time of acquisition, nevertheless, ICE closed the high profile and historic trading floors of its other earlier acquisitions such as the International Petroleum Exchange (IPE) and the New York Board of Trade in New York City.

NYSE Group and Euronext Merger

Euronext is the first integrated cross-border exchange, combining the stock exchanges of Amsterdam, Paris, Brussels and Lisbon into a single market. Issuers who meet European Union regulatory standards are qualified for listing on the regulated markets operated by Euronext. The company's exchanges list a wide variety of securities, including domestic and international equities, convertible bonds, warrants, trackers and debt securities, including corporate and government bonds. All of Euronext's markets are operated by its subsidiaries, each of which holds a national license as an exchange operator.

Before the NYSE Euronext merger of 2007, there were intense talks about big European mergers. The Deutsche Börse was holding talks with both the Euronext as well as the LSE. In 2006, Deutsche Börse AG reported that the most attractive solution for clients, shareholders and the participating financial centres is a merger with Euronext. Such a merger, it was believed, would create a unique liquidity pool under European regulation with a high level of appeal for international issuers and growth companies. European securities exchange consolidation is decisive for the advancement of the European capital market, without which a modern European economy and a functioning internal market cannot exist in the long term. The European solution among the consolidation alternatives was create the world's third largest exchange in cash trading and the number one in derivatives trading. There would be further gains in efficiency in trading, clearing and settlement.[126] Things turned out to be in favour of an American-European solution, rather than a sole European securities exchange creation.

In 2005, the expected merger between NYSE and Euronext flopped. Immediately after this flop, the NYSE merged with Archipelago Holdings in March 2006, forming NYSE Group. Then in April 2006, NYSE Group and Euronext signed a merger agreement, subject to shareholder vote and regulatory approval. Euronext shareholders gave approval to the transaction on December 19, 2006, and shareholders from the NYSE Group followed one day later. In April 2007 the Euronext shareholders tendering shares received NYSE shares and cash amounting to $11,141 million from NYSE Euronext for their assets. About 94 percent of the 112,557,259 shares were tendered in the first round. The NYSE Group and Euronext merger of April 4, 2007, signalled the creation of the world's largest and most liquid exchange group – NYSE Euronext.

The NYSE-Euronext merger was the most ambitious attempt yet at cross-border consolidation of securities exchanges. However, there are still barriers to integrating securities exchanges, ranging from distance and time zones to differences in culture and business practice. The merger offered not only access to European share trading platform but also to the Liffe derivatives market, which trades in Europe, America and Asia.[127] NYSE group merger with Euronext in April 2007 was a milestone for global financial markets, being the first to create a truly global marketplace group. This then was the world's largest and most liquid exchange group and operated six markets in five countries. The NYSE-Euronext became the world leader for listings, trading and cash equities, equity and interest rate derivatives, bonds, and distribution of market data and were, in future, to offer issuers to list in two of the world's leading currencies – the Euro and US Dollar.

---

126 Viermetz, K. (2007). Stock exchange consolidation – a tremendous opportunity for Europe, *Finanzplatz*, 5, 4-9.

127 See The Economist (2007) Market Place on the Move, 384(8546), September 15th, London.

One of the strategic objectives of the NYSE-Euronext merger was to create a win-back business from companies shying away from US markets' strict regulation. The NYSE-Euronext already has strategic alliance with the Tokyo Stock Exchange in Japan and also plans to expand operations into Asia markets. The primary savings in the NYSE-Euronext merger were to come from the streamlining of trading systems. The merger was expected to have potential for cost savings as Euronext Market Solutions, the entity that manages Euronext's technology, will supervise the integration of NYSE-Euronext's three cash trading systems and three derivatives systems into a single global cash and a single global derivatives platform. In addition, ten data centres were reduced to four – two in the USA and two in Europe – and four networks were reduced to one. Aggarwal (2006) estimated that combining the companies would result in $375 million in savings for these markets.

The April 2007 NYSE Group merger with Euronext led to the formation of NYSE Euronext – the first global equities exchange, with its headquarters in Manhattan. NYSE Euronext is a transatlantic multinational financial services corporation that operated multiple securities exchanges. The corporation was then acquired by ICE, which subsequently spun off Euronext.

Merger of NYSE Euronext and Other Exchanges

NYSE Euronext completed its acquisition of the American Stock Exchange (Amex) in October 2008 to form NYSE Amex. This transaction extended NYSE Euronext's leadership in USA option, cash equities, and exchange-traded funds (ETFs), making it then the third largest USA equity options marketplace based on number of traded contracts. Since the merger, Amex has been integrated into the company, with former Amex listings now trading directly on the NYSE, and has begun trading certain Nasdaq-listed securities. In addition, NYSE Arca was the first electronic market to offer listed ETP issuers a Lead Market Maker program, which encourages liquidity provision that contributes to the best prices and depth in the ETP marketplace. It is registered as a national securities exchange under the Exchange Act in that country.

NYSE Euronext offers a broad range of financial products and services in cash, equities, futures, options, exchange-traded products (ETPs), bonds, market data, and commercial technology. Spanning multiple asset classes and six countries, the group's acquired exchanges include the NYSE, Liffe, Euronext and NYSE Arca. With more than 8,000 listed firms – which include 90 percent of the Dow Jones Industrial Average and 80 percent of the S&P 500 – trading on NYSE Euronext's equity markets represents more than one-third of the world's cash equities volume. It also manages the leading European derivatives exchange by value of trading. NYSE Euronext is therefore part of the S&P 500 index and the only exchange operator in the S&P 100 index.

Initially, NYSE Euronext owned 60 percent interest in BlueNext with the remaining 40 percent held by CDC Climat. BlueNext operates a spot market in carbon dioxide emission allowances and credits that is the European leader in the field. It seeks to establish a leading position in trading in environment-related instruments, and has also launched a futures market with physical delivery of allowances and credits. In September 2010, NYSE Euronext announced plans to create NYSE Blue, a new global company that focuses on environmental and sustainable energy markets. NYSE Euronext contributed its ownership in BlueNext in return for a majority interest in NYSE Blue, and APX – a leading provider of regulatory infrastructure and services for environmental and sustainable energy markets – thus contributing its business in return for a minority interest in the venture. The transaction was closed in February 2011.

In addition, NYSE - Arca Europe is a Pan-European multilateral trading facility (MTF) that extends the trading scope of Euronext's regulated markets by adding blue-chip stocks from 14 European countries: Austria, Czech Republic, Denmark, Finland, France, Germany, Hungary, Ireland, Italy, Norway, Spain, Sweden, Switzerland, and the United Kingdom. Arca Europe integrates this trading facility with the other business components of the company, giving customers the flexibility in trading of an MTF while maintaining the global market reach of NYSE Euronext.

The Derivatives segment consists of NYSE Euronext's derivatives trading and clearing businesses and includes NYSE Liffe, NYSE Liffe

Clearing, NYSE Liffe US, NYSE Amex Options, NYSE Arca Option, and related derivatives market data. To begin with, NYSE Liffe comprises the derivatives market operated by Liffe Administration and Management, Euronext Amsterdam, Euronext Brussels, Euronext Lisbon, and Euronext Paris. It offers customers the advantages of one of the most technologically advanced derivatives trading platforms as well as one of the widest choices of products of any derivatives market. Through a single electronic trading platform, NYSE Liffe offers customers access to a wide range of interest-rate, equity, index, commodity and currency derivative products. This platform has been designed to handle significant order flows and transaction volumes. Orders can be matched either on a price/time or pro rata basis, configurable by contract, with transacted prices and volumes and the aggregate size of all bids and offers at each price level updated on a real-time basis. Users can continually be notified of all active orders in the central order book, making market depth easy to monitor.

Moreover, NYSE Liffe also offers its customers the Bclear and Cscreen services, which bridge the listed and OTC markets. This provides a simple and cost-effective way to register and process wholesale derivatives trades through NYSE Liffe to clearing at NYSE Liffe Clearing. Following the launch of NYSE Liffe Clearing, NYSE Liffe assumed full responsibility for clearing activities on its own London market. NYSE Liffe US, NYSE Euronext's US. futures exchange, makes available for trading full- and mini-sized gold and silver futures, options on full-sized gold and silver futures and futures on Morgan Stanley Capital International (MSCI) Indices. A significant minority equity stake in NYSE Liffe US is held by six external investors: Citadel Securities, DRW Investments, Getco, Goldman Sachs, Morgan Stanley and UBS. Under this ownership structure, NYSE Euronext remains the largest shareholder in the entity and consolidates its financial reporting. NYSE Euronext manages the day-to-day operations of NYSE Liffe US, which operates under the supervision of a separate board of directors. The NYSE Amex Options business uses a hybrid model combining both auction-based and electronic trading capabilities that is designed to provide a stable, liquid and less volatile market. This feature provides the opportunity for price and/or size improvement.

NYSE Euronext, through its wholly owned subsidiary NYSE Technologies, Inc. acquired NYFIX Inc. for $144 million in November 2009. NYSE Euronext incorporated NYFIX's trading software into the company's package of offerings to customers. Then in 2010, NYSE Euronext sold a significant equity interest in NYSE Amex Options to seven external investors: Bank of America Merrill Lynch, Barclays Capital, Citadel Securities, Citi, Goldman Sachs, TD Ameritrade, and UBS. Under the framework, NYSE Euronext remained the largest shareholder in the entity and manages the day-to-day operations of NYSE Amex Options, which operates under the supervision of a separate board of directors and CEO. The NYSE Euronext consolidated this entity for financial reporting purposes. In addition, the NYSE Arca Options, the other of NYSE Euronext's two USA options exchanges, offers immediate, cost-effective electronic order execution in nearly two thousand options issues. The NYSE Arca Options business uses a technology platform and market structure designed to enhance the speed and quality of trade execution for its customers, as well as to attract additional sources of liquidity. Its structure allows market makers to access its markets remotely and integrates floor-based participants as well.

Other successful exchange acquisitions include the Boston Options Exchange being acquired by Montreal Exchange in 2008 while the American Stock Exchange was absorbed by NYSE Euronext during the same year and the name changed to NYSE Alternext. Similarly, in 2011, CBOE Stock Exchange acquired National Stock Exchange with both the exchanges keeping their identities. In 2014, the Direct Edge merged with BATS Global Markets, with the resultant name being BATS Global Markets. There was some lull in the exchange acquisition space until in 2017 when NYSE fully acquired the National Stock Exchange, which then ceased to independently exist thus operated under the NYSE. Later in the year, BATS Global Markets was then acquired by Chicago Board Options Exchange.

NYSE Euronext – Deutsche Börse Attempted Merger

In 2011, the German exchange operator Deutsche Börse was in advanced talks to buy NYSE Euronext for $9.53 billion in a deal that would create the world's largest trading powerhouse. The shares of both companies were temporarily frozen from trading on the news due to the risk of large market price movements and clarifications of the deal. A successful deal was to see the new company becoming the world's largest securities exchange operator with a market capitalization of listed companies equal to $15 trillion.

The proposed group was to have dual headquarters, in Deutsche Boerse's newly built green tower near Frankfurt, Germany, and in New York City at 11 Wall Street. It would have led by a board with seventeen members, fifteen directors plus the Chairman and the CEO. Of the fifteen directors, nine were to be designated by Deutsche Boerse and six by NYSE Euronext. The then NYSE Euronext CEO Duncan Niederauer was to assume the same role with the newly founded company and was to lead an Executive Committee with an equal number of current Deutsche Boerse and NYSE Euronext executives.

On July 7th 2011, NYSE Euronext shareholders voted in favour of the merger, and on July 13th 2011, Deutsche Boerse shareholders also approved the deal. These decisions move the two sides closer to completing the transaction, which must still pass through forty separate regulatory approval processes to be finalized. The merger was subject to review in both the United States and with the European Union (EU) for concerns it could create a de facto monopoly.

In October 2011, the company received the EU's statement of objections, which was more than 100 pages long, and had to respond within two weeks, possibly by asking for the opportunity for an oral hearing with the regulators. The EU examination of the proposal formally began June 29th and its expanded probe had a December 13th deadline. In March, Joaquín Almunia, the EU's antitrust commissioner, expressed concern that the deal would monopolize the derivatives market due to Deutsche Boerse's vertical silo which routes all trade clearing through its own services, noting that he preferred a more open business model for markets.

On December 22nd 2011, Deutsche Boerse won USA antitrust approval to buy NYSE Euronext, on condition that a Deutsche Boerse subsidiary, the International Securities Exchange, divest its 31.5 percent interest in Direct Edge. NYSE Euronext and Deutsche Boerse AG delayed the deadline for completing their merger until March 31, 2012 so that the exchange operators could try to persuade European regulators to approve the deal.

On February 1st 2012, the European Union blocked the planned merger between NYSE Euronext and Deutsche Boerse. The European Commission – the EU's executive body – ruled against the merger noting that the combined exchange would control more than 90 percent of the trade in European derivatives. The European Commission report further stated that the merger between Deutsche Boerse and NYSE Euronext would have led to a near-monopoly in European financial derivatives worldwide, and that these markets were at the heart of the financial system and it was therefore crucial for the whole European economy that the two exchange groups remain competitive. On February 2nd 2012, the NYSE Euronext and Deutsche Börse agreed with strong opposition by the EU for the planned merger to be halted.

Deutsche Börse - London Stock Exchange Attempted Merger

The largest merger, between the Deutsche Börse and the LSE, was almost a closed deal in the beginning of this Century. On May 3rd 2000, the LSE and Deutsche Börse announced the merger that would have brought two exchanges into a joint group holding company structure – the iX International Exchanges plc. The new exchange would have been 50 percent owned by the LSE and 50 percent by Deutsche Börse. It would have consisted of all businesses on both the exchanges, including Eurex – the futures exchange, but excluding Deutsche Börse's stake in Clearstream International – its settlement arm, which Deutsche Börse would have continued to hold. The new merged exchange would have used a single trading platform, Deutsche Börse's Xetra, for all its cash markets.

At the time of the proposed merger, the Deutsche Börse was enjoying high growth. It started as one of the eight national German securities exchanges but soon became the leading and most profitable exchange in Europe. In 2000, for instance, Deutsche Börse, the company operating the Frankfurt Stock Exchange, boasted twice the profits of the London Stock Exchange. Another reason for the tremendous financial success of Deutsche Börse was its strategy to invest in and use advanced technology.

Frankfurt would have been the location for trading with stocks from the German Neuer Markt (the Frankfurt high-tech securities exchange) and its London counterpart, TechMark. Trade with these high-growth equities would have been combined in a joint company with Nasdaq, which would have been holding 50 percent of the new company's shares. In combination with Nasdaq, the new securities exchange would have accounted for 81 percent of Europe's booming high-tech growth market, putting it in an unassailable position, at least as far as Europe is concerned.

Following the approval of the merger by the board of the LSE in late May 2000, the Deutsche Börse's supervisory board voted in favour of the merger. But in order for the merger to be finalized in both the United Kingdom and Germany, it would have to be approved by 75 percent of the shareholders of both exchanges. The two shareholder meetings were planned for the 14th of September. This plan was disrupted when OM Group made a friendly bid for the LSE. This bid was however, rejected. On 11th September 2000, OM Group followed up with a £808 million hostile bid. The London Stock Exchange termed the offer inadequate and immediately reacted with safety measures postponing the shareholders' vote on the merger with Deutsche Börse and concentrating on fighting off the hostile takeover. Deutsche Börse also subsequently postponed voting. The following day, the London Stock Exchange officially announced its withdrawal from the merger until further notice. Even in absence of a hostile bid; the future of the iX International Exchanges plc was hazy due to the knot of controversial political and business interests and differences in regulatory approaches taken in Germany and the United Kingdom.

In 2017, the two exchanges again attempted to merge with each other. Let us look how these two exchanges are in terms of their subsidiaries and their products and services. Deutsche Börse AG is a diversified financial market infrastructure organisation, best known for operating the Frankfurt Stock Exchange, a regulated marketplace for trading stocks, bonds and various other financial instruments. It also operates other regulated exchanges, most notably Eurex and the European Energy Exchange (EEX), where various types of derivative products are traded. Apart from trading, its activities include the supply of post-trade infrastructure services such as clearing, settlement and custody services, as well as market data, indices and other information products.

London Stock Exchange Group is a diversified international exchange Group that sits at the heart of the world's financial community. The Group traces its history back to 1801. The Group operates a broad range of international equity, bond and derivatives markets, including London Stock Exchange; Borsa Italiana – the Italian stock exchange; MTS, Europe's leading fixed income market; and the Pan-European equities platform, Turquoise. Through its markets, the Group offers international business, and investors, unrivalled access to Europe's capital markets. London Stock Exchange Group was founded in 1698 and is based in London, the United Kingdom. The exchange group is therefore a diversified financial market infrastructure organisation, and best known for operating the London Stock Exchange. It also operates a number of other trading platforms for trading of stocks, other equity-like exchange traded products, bonds and derivatives. The London Stock Exchange is also active in the post-trading space, most notably in clearing through the London Clearing House (also referred to as LCH.Clearnet) including SwapClear, and Cassa di Compensazione e Garanzia (CC&G), the Italian clearinghouse. The exchange also offers settlement and custody services as well as indices, data, and other information products.

Deutsche Börse AG and London Stock Exchange Group submitted a proposal in 2016 to merge the two market places within Europe, as stipulated in merger control rules and procedures. The Commission has the duty to assess mergers and acquisitions involving companies with a turnover above certain thresholds and to prevent concentrations that would significantly impede effective competition in the EEA or any substantial part of it. The vast majority of notified mergers do not pose competition problems and are cleared after a routine review. From the moment a transaction is notified, the Commission generally has 25 working days to decide whether to grant approval (Phase I) or to start an in-depth investigation (Phase II).

The European Commission prohibited the proposed merger between Deutsche Börse AG and London Stock Exchange Group under the EU Merger Regulation. The Commission's investigation concluded the merger would have created a de facto monopoly in the markets for clearing fixed income instruments. The proposed merger would have combined the activities of the two largest European stock exchange operators, Deutsche Börse AG (DBAG) and London Stock Exchange Group (LSEG). They own the stock exchanges of Germany, Italy and the United Kingdom, as well as several of the largest European clearing houses.[128]

The European economy depends on well-functioning financial markets and that is not just important for banks and other financial institutions. The whole economy benefits when businesses can raise capital on competitive financial markets. The merger between Deutsche Börse and the London Stock Exchange would have significantly reduced competition by creating a monopoly in the crucial area of clearing of fixed income instruments. As the parties failed to offer the remedies required to address the European Commission's competition concerns, the Commission has decided to prohibit the merger.

Specifically, the Commission had the following concerns. First, the merger would have led to a de facto monopoly in clearing of fixed income instruments (bonds and repurchase agreements) in Europe, where the parties are the only relevant providers of these services. In particular, the merger would have combined DBAG's Frankfurt based clearing house Eurex with LSEG's clearing houses LCH.Clearnet – which comprises London based LCH.Clearnet Ltd and Paris based LCH.Clearnet SA – and Rome based Cassa di Compensazione e Garanzia.

This monopoly in clearing fixed income instruments would also have had a knock-on effect on the downstream markets for settlement, custody and collateral management. Service providers in these markets depend on transaction feeds from clearing houses. As DBAG's Clearstream competes with these service providers, the merged entity would have had the ability and the incentive to divert transaction feeds to Clearstream and foreclose the other competitors.

---

128 European Commission (2017). Mergers: Commission blocks proposed merger between Deutsche Börse and London Stock Exchange. https://ec.europa.eu/commission/presscorner/detail/es/IP_17_789.

In addition, the merger would have removed horizontal competition for the trading and clearing of single stock equity derivatives – based on stocks of Belgian, Dutch and French companies. Currently, Eurex competes with a bundled product – combining trading and clearing – offered by Euronext and LCH.Clearnet SA. After the merger, LCH.Clearnet, which has significant pricing power over the bundled product, would have less incentive to compete with Eurex. Finally, this market power could have also been potentially used to squeeze out Euronext.

The Commission raised these concerns in its decision to open an in-depth investigation and communicated them formally to the parties in a Statement of Objections issued in December 2016. The Commission also raised further preliminary competition concerns on which it eventually did not have to conclude. It is the responsibility of the parties making the application to address competition concerns either by rebutting them or by proposing adequate remedies. To be effective, such remedies have to address all of the Commission's competition concerns and be viable in the long-term.

In response, the two securities exchange groups proposed a remedy consisting of the divestment of LCH.Clearnet SA, LSEG's France-based clearing house to address the Commission's concerns. The regulator concluded that this divestment would have resolved the concerns relating to single stock equity derivatives. However, it would not have been effective to remedy the concerns stemming from the creation of the de facto monopoly in fixed income clearing. This is what emerged from the market test of the proposed remedy. Market testing is the phase of a merger investigation during which the regulator consults on proposed remedies with market participants to allow them to submit their views.

The market test revealed that LCH.Clearnet SA's fixed income clearing business was vitally dependent on trading feeds from LSEG's fixed income trading platform MTS. Without these trading feeds, the viability of this business line in the future would be severely undermined. Therefore, the Commission could not determine whether LCH.Clearnet SA would have been a viable competitor in fixed income clearing going forward. The two exchange groups parties have had the opportunity to modify the proposed commitments to address the issues identified during the market test. The divestment of MTS, a comparatively small asset compared to the parties' combined revenues and market value, would have been a clear-cut remedy to meet these concerns.

Ultimately, the parties were, however, only prepared to offer a complex set of behavioural measures but not the divestiture of MTS. They were not able to demonstrate that these measures would have been effective in practice and would have ensured that LCH.Clearnet SA would be a viable competitor in fixed income clearing going forward. The Commission therefore concluded that the proposed remedy would not have been able to prevent the emergence of a de facto monopoly on the markets related to fixed income clearing as a result of the merger, which is why it decided to block the proposed transaction. The London Stock Exchange Group continued to operate independent - despite a series of attempts by different suitors to buy it in recent years - and it looks as though it may stay that way after its unsuccessful bid for Borsa Italiana Securities Exchange.

Globally, it should be noted that the primary mechanisms for changing management or obtaining control in publicly traded firms with dispersed ownership seem to be varied. One could compare three mechanisms: proxy fights (voting only); takeover bids (buying shares only); and a hybrid of proxy fights and takeover bids in which shareholders vote on acquisition offers. It is likely to reveal how proxy fights unaccompanied by an acquisition offer suffer from substantial shortcomings that limit the use of such contests in practice. It is easier to argue that combining voting with acquisition offers is superior not only to proxy fights alone but also to takeover bids alone. When acquisition offers are in the form of cash or the acquirer's existing securities, voting shareholders can infer from the pre-vote market trading which outcome would be best in light of all the available public information. Such conditions would have implications for the ongoing debate in the world over poison pills and other directive on hostile takeovers in corporations and also in securities exchanges. The cases of mergers and acquisition undertaken in securities exchanges have features of these mechanisms.

The internationalization is evident in the tri-continental deal that has seen Nasdaq of the USA and Borse Dubai launches an agreed takeover of the Scandinavian exchange operator OMX.[129] Borse Dubai was to acquire OMX and then transfer it to Nasdaq in return for a 19.9 percent stake in a new combined company as well as Nasdaq's 28 percent stake in LSE. The Qatar exchange may trade some of its 9.98 percent of OMX to Dubai in exchange for shares of LSE to increase its 14.9 percent holding. Borse Dubai, LSE's biggest shareholder with 20.4 percent stake, also bided for Stockholm-based OMX.[130] The merger of the Chicago Mercantile Exchange and the Chicago Board of Trade created the world's largest futures exchange.

Bursa Malaysia, the Kuala Lumpur-based securities exchange, announced that it was in preliminary talks with the Chicago Mercantile Exchange, the world's biggest futures exchange, about a possible partnership that could include an equity stake. The proposal come as Bursa Malaysia was seeking to expand its business and compete with the neighbouring Singapore Exchange (SGX), whose option trading has become a main source of growth in recent years. The move followed SGX's decision during the previous month to buy out CME's stake in their joint venture, the Joint Asian Derivatives Exchange (Jade), which was set up in 2006 to trade commodity contracts such as crude palm oil and rubber futures.

The current trends suggest that the factors that have driven the demutualization and listing of securities exchanges are likely to be as relevant in the future as in the recent past. All major securities exchanges are facing increasing global competition from other exchanges or alternative trading systems. The mutual organization structure is too restrictive and frequently leads to decision gridlock as competing interests attempt to influence the strategic direction of an exchange. Most exchanges have recognized this and have already transformed themselves into traditional joint-stock corporations.

There have also been cases of demutualized securities exchanges making takeover bids for other securities exchanges. In other cases, some financial institutions have made takeover bids for, or merger proposals to demutualised

---

129 Sukumar, N. Qatar Borse Dubai Near Agreement on LSE, OMX, People Say: Bloomberg, http://www.bloomberg.com/apps/news?pid=newsarchive&sid=an.SdS.pSdQo.

130 Burton, J. (2007). Bursa Malaysia in partnership talks with CME. Financial Times, December 11th. Available online at: http://www.ft.com/cms/s/0/f9c94066-a7a1-11dc-a25a-0000779fd2ac,dwp_uuid=50b45d26-5b63

securities exchanges. In December 1998 in Australia, ASX announced a bid for the Sydney Futures Exchange (SFE). In May 1999, Computershare Limited, a firm listed on ASX, announced a rival bid for SFE. During this period, Computershare had a major business in supplying market technologies and a substantial part of the share registry services business in Australia and elsewhere. In a similarly move, the Deutsche Bourse mooted a bid for the acquisition of the LSE, an attempt that failed in 2006. As has earlier been mentioned, a more serious bid in the history of LSE was its hostile takeover bid by the Nasdaq. Following the LSE's demutualization, Nasdaq acquired 28.75 percent share through share purchase from the market and convincing the shareholders to sell to it their shares at $24.35. This effort also yielded a paltry 0.41 percent of the shares, making a total of 29.16 percent shareholding, short of the 50 percent requirement. Since 2004, several exchanges and other financial institutions had wielded at least four failed takeover bids for LSE. These include, Deutsche Boerse AG, Macquarie Bank Ltd of Australia, and the Paris-based Euronext (operator of Lisbon, Paris, Brussels and Amsterdam exchanges). Others securities exchanges planning takeover bids for the LSE include Eurex, Euroclear (owner of Cleanet, Crest), and Euronext. Following its demutualization, Euronext was acquired by the NYSE in April 2007 creating the world largest securities market, a combination worth $12billion.

As has been mentioned above, the International Securities Exchange is the fastest growing US options market. The Doutsche Boerse, having demutualized, entered into an acquisition deal with the ISE on 1st May 2007, where International Securities Exchange would be bought at $67.50 per share ($2.8billion) creating the largest transatlantic derivative market. This represented a 50 percent premium for ISE shares, reflecting the Doutsche Boerse eagerness to cinch the deal. In fact, this higher price made Nasdaq to opt out of buying its rival. During May 2007, the Dubai International Financial Centre, the owner of the Dubai Stock Exchange, was mulling over a rival bid to Nasdaq agreed $3.7billion takeover of OMX, the owner of Nordic markets.

After failing to court African securities exchanges to join a proposed pan-African listing board, the Johannesburg Stock Exchange, following its demutualization, has been seeking to undertake an all-out buyout of African exchanges.[131] Depending on how these developments are considered, they may be positive or negative consequences of demutualization.

JSE Takeover of Bond Exchange of South Africa

Excluding the above mentioned acquisitions in the Gulf region, mergers and acquisitions have been scarce in Africa and Middle East region. The JSE Ltd, following discussions with a number of shareholders of the Bond Exchange of South Africa Limited (BESA), made a conditional offer to acquire the entire ordinary share capital of BESA.[132] The purchase consideration was R90 per share, which represented a premium of 106 percent to the net asset value, excluding the BESA Guarantee Fund. The all-cash offer valued BESA at R173.22m, of which JSE offered 173.2 million Rand ($15.4 million) for the Bond Exchange of South Africa, thereby seeking to join Africa's largest stock and bond markets, Bloomberg reported.[133] This offer was more than double the BESA's net asset value. In a statement, JSE believed that integrating BESA in its operation was in line with its consolidation around the world and would improve its competitive ability in an increasingly international market for securities trading.

The JSE's offer enabled BESA shareholders to realise value for the assets of the BESA Guarantee Fund, which they did not own and would not otherwise be able to realise since the Fund is contained in a trust and is consolidated only for accounting purposes. The JSE noted that the deal was intended to create a world-class, unified multi-product securities exchange that efficiently provides sophisticated trading, clearing and settlement infrastructure to all its clients. The combined JSE and BESA team, by working with market participants and keeping an open mind, could help harness the best of what they both have to offer. The JSE was confident that together they would come up with the best solution for South Africa and

---

131 Kamau, J. (2008). JSE Now Floats Idea of Buying other Bourses in Africa. Business Daily, August 22nd pg.18.

132 JSE in bid to buy bond exchange. http://www.jse.co.za/docs/besa_deal/ MediaReleaseFINAL. pdf.

133 Africa's Stock and Bond Markets Look to Combine. http://dealbook.blogs.nytimes. com/2008/10/27/africas-stock-and-bond-markets-look-to-combine/.

the region to build liquidity, provide effective risk management to reduce counterparty risk, and lower costs for participants. JSE was of the opinion that it was hard to have a well-performing modern economy without a good financial system, and that strong capital markets are an essential part of such a financial system, allowing participants to mobilise savings, allocate capital and manage risk. It is therefore very important from a national interest perspective that there are deep and liquid markets in debt and equity products and that – as far as possible – the trading, clearing and settlement of South African financial instruments happens in South Africa in a globally competitive manner. This would enable local participants and the local economy to derive the benefits of a vibrant financial market.

According to JSE, the South African interest rate market could not continue with two exchanges and neither offering what participants really demand. The proper pricing of the interest rate spot market could also have a knock-on effect on the interest rate derivatives market: interest rate futures and options are dependent on efficient and transparent interest rate spot markets. The JSE expected the bid to be supported by a large percentage of BESA's shareholders. The JSE-BESA Group was expected to be able to grow the interest rate market while reducing the costs for users, particularly because of the ability to achieve economies of scale. The JSE has a good track record of sweating the systems for the benefit of our market participants and will apply that to this integration as well.

During that time, the JSE Group had dropped the average pricing significantly for trading in equities and derivatives products despite spending in excess of R1 billion implementing new trading, clearing and settlement technology and growing its post-tax profit by 470 percent during that same period. Over the past several years, the JSE and BESA have had numerous discussions to develop a closer relationship. These discussions had not been as fruitful as the JSE had hoped, despite what they believed to be compelling synergies between the JSE and BESA. As a result, they had not been able to make any meaningful progress towards forging the affiliation sought by market participants which in the end they hoped would convince them to trade, clear and settle South African interest rate products locally – on-exchange – rather than offshore or in the OTC market. The JSE believed that the combined expertise of BESA and the JSE will provide the market and the exchanges' respective shareholders with a powerful interest rate market.

JSE Limited, the operator of the Johannesburg Stock Exchange (JSE), in November 2020 also acquired a minority stake in UK fintech company, Globacap, for £4 million (R82.7 million).[134] The JSE acquired Globacap to progress a digital private placements platform and registry services. The deal brought together the JSE, Africa's largest stock exchange, and Globacap, a private placement and capital management platform that digitally administrates over £1 billion of private shares and debt instruments for 60 companies and over 8,000 shareholders worldwide in 35 countries. The Globacap's unique distributed ledger technology allows digital registrar services to be reflected in real-time.

The JSE planned to collaborate with Globacap to establish a private placements platform to advance and digitise capital raising for infrastructure finance and SMEs. This deal was expected to support a critical growth node across the continent in the infrastructure and SME sectors. The transaction reinforces the JSE's commitment to foster inclusive and sustainable growth by advancing access to capital markets. The JSE believes that the continent requires extensive investment into infrastructure as a vital imperative for its growth. Given that African infrastructure funding requirements are estimated to range from $130 billion to $170 billion per year, yet commitments fall short of funding requirements. JSE was to use Globacap's innovative technology and expertise to progress infrastructure finance and SME private funding. The deal would assist it to stimulate investment into those markets by narrowing the funding gap and supporting job creation and economic growth.

As part of the transaction, the acquisition reaffirmed JSE's growth strategy. The investment in Globacap was to be funded from the group's existing cash reserves and was finalised during the first quarter of 2021, having been subjected to the fulfilment of certain conditions precedent including approval by relevant local and UK regulatory authorities. This

---

134 Moyo, A. (2020). JSE Acquires R82.7m Stake in UK Fintech Firm. ITWeb News, November 5th, https://www.itweb.co.za/content/Olx4z7kn3d5v56km

acquisition moved JSE a step closer to realising its goal of the digitisation of the world's private capital markets. Therefore, the Globacap collaboration and investment was part of its ongoing strategy to sustainably grow and diversify its business. Working with a leading capital markets fintech player positions the JSE in its efforts to innovate a digital capital raise process in private placements.

On 2nd November 2020, JSE Limited, the operator of the Johannesburg Stock Exchange, Africa's largest, multi-asset class stock exchange, acquired Link Market Services South Africa (Pty) Ltd (Link SA), the second largest share registry business in South Africa (with 6 of the top 40 listed companies as clients), subject to all required approvals, for a cash amount of R224.5 million. JSE Limited acquired a 74.85 percent shareholding in Link SA with Link SA's Black Economic Empowerment (BEE) shareholder retaining the remaining 25.15 percent and the Link SA CEO remaining as CEO of the company.[135] The acquisition saw Link SA being merged into the JSE Limited structure and operated independently under a newly formed business stream, subject to all required approvals. This acquisition came after many engagements with the JSE's listed companies' which have expressed a desire to drive synergies and consolidate how they service their shareholders through a one-stop-shop.

The transaction is revenue accretive with an expected contribution of up to 6 percent of Group revenue, while exceeding the Group's return on investment hurdles. This demonstrates that even in tougher economic times there are opportunities where the JSE can make a difference to its clients by thinking creatively and working hard to deliver that difference. This also presents opportunities for both listed and unlisted companies to use these services. Through Link SA, the JSE introduced end-to-end products and services to JSE listed companies, making it easier for them to communicate and understand their shareholder base. These services include shareholder register maintenance, corporate actions, shareholder analytics,

---

135 JSE (2019). JSE agrees to acquire majority stake in share registry Link Market Services South Africa in a move to diversify business revenue. https://www.jse.co.za/news/press-releases/jse-agrees-acquire-majority-stake-share-registry-link-market-services-south

managing BEE share schemes, electronic communication and voting, and training and educating shareholders. The transaction was to enable the JSE to diversify revenue and extend the services it already offers listed companies through its Company Services team, which includes training, investor relations support and listed company annual, and interim results presentations hosting and meeting support. The exchange still seems to be searching for African exchanges for potential opportunities for acquisitions as well as mergers.

Acquisitions Strategizization by Nairobi Securities Exchange

The Nairobi Securities Exchange has been in the lookout on buy up more stakes in other exchanges across Africa with a view to eventually becoming a pan-continental exchange. The NSE, the fifth biggest by market capitalisation in Africa, already owns a 4.9 percent stake in neighbouring Tanzania's Dar es Salaam Stock Exchange, and is eyeing other bourses in countries like Nigeria and Botswana following their demutualisation. Through this, the NSE can become a Pan-African exchange in the long-term, so it is looking at how it can use this opportunity. The NSE group is keen to see the valuation of Uganda's bourse when the shares are offered to investors at a later date. To fund acquisitions, the NSE has cash reserves of up to KSh1.5 billion ($12.98 million).[136]

The NSE is also looking at buying stakes in related businesses like technology and depository services, meaning that acquisitions seem to be a key focus for it. As part of its strategy to acquire related businesses, the NSE has doubled its stake in Kenya's Central Depository and Settlement Corporation (CDSC), which offers back-office services for share trading, clearance, settlement and depository. During 2023, the NSE, which for 2021 offered investors a 17 percent dividend yield, is also holding discussions with two Kenyan technology firms to boost its securities trading infrastructure. Africa, made up of 54 nations, has just 31 securities

---

136 Miriri, D. (2022). Nairobi Securities Exchange eyes acquisitions among other African bourses. https://www.cnbcafrica.com/2022/nairobi-securities-exchange-eyes-acquisitions-among-other-african-bourses/

exchanges and 8 other alternative trading systems, meaning there will be opportunities to offer securities trading technology when the others set up their exchanges.

Evidently, the NSE is in a strong position to fend off competition from a new bond trading exchange being set up in Kenya since it offers many products, including derivatives. The NSE has been searching for a buyer to acquire its headquarter located in Westland - Nairobi in favour of leasing, arguing that property is not a space for it. Nevertheless, NSE turnover has been depressed in the past months by heightened geopolitical risk caused by the Ukraine crisis and interest rate hike in USA. Kenya also held a general election in August 2022, which also infused volatility in the market. However, the exchange has been expressing optimism that the adverse impact will ease in future as investors continue to price down the political risk.

Some selected global regional distribution of demutualization, self-listing, mergers and acquisition of securities exchanges is presented in Table 6.

Table 6: *Regional Landscape of Mergers & Acquisition of Securities Exchanges*

European- Oceania Landscape	
2000	• Consolidation/creation Euronext
2001	• Creation of Bolsas Y Mercaos Espanoles(BMX)
	• Acquisition of LIFFE by Euronext
2002	• Acquisition of Clearstream by Deutsch Group
2003	• Acquisition of Euroclear by BMX
	• Acquisition of Virt-x by Swiss Exchange
	• Merger of OM and OMX
2004	• Take-over bid of LSE by Deutsch Bourse group
2005	• Merger talks (flopped)LSE & Euronext
2006	• Merger of NYSE Group & Euronext
	• Acquisition of 25% of LSE by Nasdaq

2007	• Merger of LSE & Borsa Italiana
	• Acquisition of 28% of LSE by Dubai International Financial Exchange (DIFX)
	• Acquisition of ISE by Eurex
North American Landscape	
2005	• Acquisition of Archipelago by NYSE
	• Acquisition of Instinet by Nasdaq
2006	• Merger of NYSE Group & Euronext
	• Acquisition of 25% of LSE by Nasdaq
2007	• Merger of Nasdaq & Boston Equities exchange (BOX)
	• Merger Toronto Stock Exchange (TSE) & Bourse de Montreal
	• Acquisition of 10% in BM&F Brasil by CME
	• Acquisition of 5%in CME by BM&F
	• Acquisition of PHLX by Nasdaq
2008	• Acquisition of AMEX by NYSE Euronext
	• Acquisition of NYMEX by CME
	• Acquisition of OMX by Nasdaq
	• Acquisition of 33.34%DIFX by Nasdaq OMX
	• Acquisition of 19.9%NADAQ OMX by DIFX
Asian-Pacific Landscape	
2006	• Acquisition of 5% in Singapore Exchange by Tokyo Stock Exchange
	• Acquisition of Singapore Commodity exchange by Singapore Exchange
Africa Middle East Landscape	
2008	• Acquisition of Bond Exchange of South African by JSE Group
2010	• Planned Merger of Nairobi Securities Exchange & Uganda Securities Exchange

Future M&A Developments in Global Securities Exchanges

The international realignment and mergers and acquisitions activity are switching into high gear among securities markets, mainly in America and Europe; and this trend has the potential to spread into the Asian region, which possesses considerable capacity for economic growth. Due to this huge economic success in the Asian and Arabic region, Western securities exchanges might lose some of their importance. Growth rates of both Asian and Arabic companies as well as of private funds are extremely high and are attracted by securities exchanges. The financial exchanges of Hong Kong, Shanghai and Dubai represent interesting partners for possible alliances or mergers. Earlier, huge oil profits of the states in the Persian Gulf were invested in the foreign capital markets. Currently, Arabian investors prefer their home region because of the strict USA regulations.

Furthermore, they transfer their capital form foreign capital markets to their local one and create a concentration of funds in the Arabian region that has never been known before. In 2005 more than 510 billion euro flowed out into the Arabian securities markets, and particularly into the securities exchanges of the Gulf region.[137] The same phenomenon can be found in India and China, where funds resulting from the enormous economic prosperity are relocated and re-invested in the home economy. The ambitious Dubai International Financial Exchange (DIFX), situated in central position in the Persian Gulf, fills the gap between the existing finance places of Europe, Asia and the USA.

One of the biggest IPOs worldwide generated 10 billion dollars for the Bank of China at the Hong Kong Stock Exchange. Hundreds of other Chinese enterprises will woo for investments of the global capital. The know-how and the experience of the Western securities exchanges could be well demanded. Shanghai Stock Exchange has grown remarkably in the last few years, as have the main exchanges in India, while Brazil's Bovespa became the first quoted securities exchange in Latin America in 2007. Its IPO was so successful that it commanded a higher market value than established exchanges such as the London Stock Exchange or Nasdaq. Other centres are

---

137 See WFE (2006) Annual Report and Statistics.

now trying to get in on the mood, for example, the government of Dominican Republic is backing an ambitious attempt to build a new financial centre for Latin America, which would be set on a greenfield site close to some of the island's best beaches. With EUREX as market leader in the derivatives market, the Deutsche Bourse owned market is well positioned in this fastest growing segment of capital markets. To further develop the competitive position, a merger with the Chicago Mercantile Exchange would create a derivatives market of incomparable strength compared to the competitors like NYSE-Euronext and even Nasdaq-LSE markets.

The London Stock Exchange is continuously in the news for new attempts of takeovers or acquisition bids. Borse Dubai, the ambitious Gulf-based exchange, is now in the frame as the buyer of the 31 percent stake held by Nasdaq, the LSE's one-time hostile bidder. While it is hardly a blocking stake – it will fall to about 22 percent of the combined company once the London Stock Exchange's acquisition of Borsa Italiana is complete[138] – it is certainly a leg up should Borse Dubai decide it would like to own one of the world's great exchange brands. Borse Dubai's potential purchase of the stake looks like a key element in a deal that would head off the certainty of an expensive bidding war for OMX, the Nordic exchanges and technology group that is being courted by itself and Nasdaq. This deal would give Borse Dubai access to technology and a brand name but at a hefty price. It would be taking a stake in a company that has unambiguously demonstrated its determination and ability to see off predators. A successful bid for the full London Stock Exchange would be decidedly expensive. The prospective deal comes as competition among European exchanges is round the corner. Borse Dubai need only look at the price war among exchanges in the US from which Nasdaq is trying to escape for a vision of the future. Unless some unpredictable event interrupts the process European securities markets are likely to become fewer in number and more internationalized in their listings, trading, and membership.

---

138 LSE (2007) Borsa Italiana and London Stock Exchange Group to merge. Available online at: http://www.londonstockexchange.com/en-gb/about/Newsroom/pressreleases/2007/LSEBorsa.htm

Global securities exchange mergers and acquisition juggernauts are also snatch up fund platforms, trading venues and data analytics providers, under the increasingly vigilant gaze of European competition authorities.[139] There are notably three issues are being observed in the securities exchange landscape. First, global securities exchange giants are expanding horizontally, through acquisitions, for example Euronext's acquisition of Borsa Italiana and Tinkoff's acquisition of minority stake in Saint Petersburg Exchange, and through Joint Ventures, for example CME Group's post-trade services Joint Venture undertaking with IHS Markit. Secondly, there is the search for alternative revenue opportunities through vertical integration, and thirdly, the European leading securities exchanges are battling the tech specialists in the data analytics arena, for example Infront's acquisition of Oslo Market Solutions.

There are also notable two key drivers to these developments. One, is the global securities market institution giants are focusing on vertical integration firepower on fund platforms, for example Deutsche Börse's acquisition of 48.8 percent of Clearstream Fund Centre and Euroclear's acquisition of MFEX Group; trading platforms, for example, Johannesburg Stock Exchange's acquisition of Link Market Services South Africa; and data analytics, for example, Luxembourg Stock Exchange's acquisition of 22.8 percent of Tetrao and London Stock Exchange's acquisition of Refinitiv. Secondly, there are differing investor prerogatives loading up on liquid assets for example VTB's acquisition of 5.77 percent of Saint Petersburg Exchange and Intesa Sanpaolo's acquisition of 1.31 percent of Euronext; and offloading of non-core liquid assets, for example NPS RTS Association's disposal of 5 percent of Saint Petersburg Exchange.

So, what are the trends to watch? There is an increasing scrutiny of vertical exchange deals by UK and European competition authorities: IHS Markit's disposal of Oil Price Information Services and Coal, Metals and Mining businesses to facilitate S&P Global & IHS Markit merger;

---

139 Kotthoff, J. & Byrne, D. (2021). Financial Institutions M&A: Stock Exchanges/Trading Venues. https://www.whitecase.com/insight-our-thinking/financial-institutions-ma-stock-exchangestrading-venues

London Stock Exchange's disposal of Borsa Italiana to facilitate acquisition of Refinitiv; and London Stock Exchange and Euronext go head-to-head to attract European SPAC listings. It should be noted that a SPAC is a publicly traded shell that has a specific mandate to acquire or merge with other companies or assets. At the time of listing the company must have no operations of its own. The SPAC must be led by an experienced management team with prior M&A and/or operating experience. They usually have 24 months in which to make acquisitions or to merge with other companies/assets, as set out in the acquisition criteria, and to satisfy the basic conditions for listing. SPACs are in many ways an alternative to raising capital for acquisitions.

Therefore, the following are the future forecast for exchange mergers and acquisitions. It seems horizontal expansion is likely to remain opportunistic and under close scrutiny of European and American competition authorities. There is likely uptick in vertical diversification deals as global securities exchanges and other financial market players flex mergers and acquisition muscle to remain competitive in their effort to rejig their revenues and manage their operational costs.

Securities Exchanges, being trading venues, have publicly reported several deals aimed at achieving inorganic growth, acquisitions, joint ventures as well as some re-alignment of their market footprint.

Inorganic growth. London Securities Exchange has had its strongest start since 2006. There were 11 IPOs raising £3.24 billion in between the start of 2021 and 24 February 2021. Moreover, Amsterdam surpassed London as Europe's largest share trading centre since Brexit, with an average €9.2 billion shares a day traded on Euronext. Also, London's financial sector started to feel the full effects of Brexit on the first trading day of 2021 as nearly €6 billion of EU share dealing shifted away from the City to facilities in European capitals.

Acquisitions. Johannesburg Stock Exchange (Trading platform) undertook an acquisition of Link Market Services South Africa in June 2021; Deutsche Börse (Crypto trading and digital asset custody) acquired a majority stake in Crypto Finance in June 2021; Tinkoff Group (Securities exchange) acquired a minority stake in Saint Petersburg Exchange in June

2021; Moscow Exchange (Financial marketplace) acquired 70 percent of Inguru in May 2021; Deutsche Börse (Fund platform) acquired 48.8 percent stake Clearstream Fund Centre in May 2021; Nxchange (DLT trading platform) acquired Bondex in May 2021; Euronext (Stock exchange) acquired Borsa Italiana in April 2021; Bourse Direct (Asset management) acquired Arobas Finance in March 2021; Euroclear (Fund platform) acquired MFEX Group in March 2021; Deutsche Börse (Proxy advisory) acquired 81 percent stake in Institutional Shareholder Services in February 2021; Luxembourg Stock Exchange (Data analytics) acquired 22.8 percent stake in Tetrao in January 2021; and London Stock Exchange (Data analytics): acquired Refinitiv in January 2021.

Joint Ventures. CME Group (Trading operations) entered a post-trade services joint venture with IHS Markit in January 2021.

Re-aligning Footprint. Euronext (Asset management solutions) disposed-off Centevo in March 2021. Looking into the future, significant developments in the harmonization of regulation in markets around the world can be expected. However, with respect to the current mergers and acquisitions trend occurring in Europe and USA, there are still many hurdles to clear before the integration of these exchanges has any actual effect. An example is how to harmonize the IT systems, as well as the framework for such business areas such as trading, clearing and settlement while many differences between the structures of the markets will continue to exist. Therefore, it can be anticipated that full-fledged market integration and regulatory harmonization, and subsequently the actual effects of this integration, will occur deep into the future, rather than sooner.

Integrating Shares, Commodities and Derivatives Trading

The Markets in Financial Instruments Directive (MiFID) is a law that creates a common market for share, commodities and derivatives trading across 30 countries in Europe and entered into force in November 2007. MiFID directly touches four distinct groups of actors within the financial services industry: investment firms (which may have fairly different organisational models across countries), exchanges and quasi-exchanges (multilateral trading facilities – MTFs), and data vendors as well as specialised IT firms and solution providers, such as third party algorithm developers. It affects equity markets, commodity and derivatives markets, and to a lesser extent bond markets. Under Art. 65 of MiFID, national regulatory authorities are free to extend the strict MiFID pre- and post-trade information requirements to non-equity markets. Some already do so, such as those in Denmark, owing to the large retail investor presence in its mortgage bond market).

The MiFID was designed because it was realized that monetary union would not create a single financial market by itself and earlier studies had identified remaining barriers to the creation of such a market. This led to the launch in 1999 of the Financial Services Action Plan (FSAP) – a broad legislative and regulatory program that gave further momentum to financial integration in Europe. Combined with additional measures that were agreed in response to market developments, the FSAP built the backbone for Europe's future financial markets. As a result, financial integration in Europe has progressed significantly, most notably in the provision of wholesale financial services. The next step along the road to full integration is the implementation of the MiFID.[140]

This directive relies on several complementary levers to foster increased integration of EU securities markets. These levers include, first, competition. The new framework injects new competition among financial intermediaries at each step of a security's transaction cycle, from the provision of investment advice to the practical execution and settlement of the transaction. A major feature of MiFID is to open the execution (and settlement) of equity transactions to a variety of operators, through competing trading venues. The second lever is best execution and transparency within securities markets. To balance the risks of opaqueness and liquidity dissipation stemming from a potentially more fragmented trading infrastructure, MiFID relies on increased transparency and information requirements for the benefit of securities markets, while best execution requirements will provide more systematic investor protection.

---

140 Haas, F. (2007). The Markets in Financial Instruments Directive: Banking and Supervisory Efficiency, IMF Working Paper No. WP/07/250.

Finally, there is the lever of securities markets regulatory cooperation and supervisory convergence. Increased cooperation among securities regulators, notably thorough convergence of supervisory practices, is essential for a homogeneous implementation of the regulations envisaged within MiFID. This, in turn, is the key to ensure that more contestability and competition lead to larger and deeper securities markets rather than more but less liquid ones.

The new environment created by the new directive could trigger drastic changes in the architecture of securities markets and in the organization of financial intermediation in Europe – and which are likely to be replicated by other regulators outside Europe. Such changes could result from both the increased competition that the new directive unleashes and the technological challenges that it represents. Broader pass porting possibilities and the opening of trading venues to new actors are likely to foster competition for market shares in a large array of financial services, from trade execution to investment advice and asset management. The directive is both a business opportunity and a source of additional costs for financial intermediaries. For market intermediaries, internalizing market activity (and liquidity) is, in theory, an appealing alternative to routing orders to external trading platforms.

In the same vein, the new directive is expected to result in a significant increase in data production and data processing by financial services providers. Traditionally, securities exchanges were the predominant, almost exclusive source of market data, not least due to the concentration of trading and data reporting imposed by regulatory authorities. With this breakdown will come increased opportunities for investment firms to recapture revenue streams that were originally generated by their orders. The aggregate Pan-European market for market data is estimated at about €2.3 billion per year. This sizeable revenue pool is up for grabs by innovative firms and other financial market actors.

A group of nine London-based investment banks have set up a joint effort dubbed Project Boat, which is intended to capture back data revenue sources from trades where investment firms – and not the securities exchange – were the liquidity providers and facilitators. By opening up the architecture for trade reporting, the new directive challenge an important revenue source for demutualized securities exchanges and provide a valuable opportunity for investment firms to get in on the game. Income from the sale of trade information today accounts for about 12 percent of the revenue of the six largest securities exchanges in the EU. For some exchanges, it is much higher, reaching 32.3 percent for the LSE, although figure also includes revenues from regulatory information services. Hence, the combined effect of more internalisation by investment firms could have a direct impact on the completeness of the trade information that demutualized securities exchanges collect and sell.

Nevertheless, the new directive is a strong additional incentive for market operators to consolidate or intensify cooperation – including mergers and acquisitions. This is especially true for small and medium-sized securities markets (such as Vienna Stock Exchange strategy relative to Central and Eastern European securities markets), but is also a valid approach for larger securities markets. Connectivity is a central feature of the post-MiFID trading landscape that will be characterised by the fragmentation of liquidity pools as trading is decentralised. Connectivity necessitates the acceleration of efforts to arrive at common standards to facilitate straight-through processing in an accelerated and more competitive trading environment, as well as to ensure seamless order transmission and data retrieval, across the spectrum of business lines in a decentralised trading environment. It represents a revolution in European securities markets that is likely to lead to deep and long lasting structural changes since its impact extends far beyond mere IT and compliance alone. The unprecedented scope of harmonisation of securities markets legislation and the resulting open architecture ushered in by the new directive, especially in trade execution and reporting will cause a profound upheaval within existing securities market structures.

Trading volumes could increase as a result of greater competition between execution venues and enhanced market transparency. More competition means lower transaction costs, which should feed into higher volumes for demutualized exchanges. More transparency means more confidence in the quality of price discovery, enhancing market efficiency, which should also generate higher volumes. Securities brokers are now forced to provide best execution for their clients. This means that traders must execute a buy or sell order on any securities exchange or trading system which they feel gives the best deal for their clients. The trades, rather than being reported to a national securities exchange, can now simply be made public. That represents a substantial business opportunity, as well as a potential cost saving, for banks. With trading increasingly moving away from the established securities exchanges, MiFID makes these off-exchange markets more regulated, because more pricing information has to be disclosed.

The competition from internalization will be the biggest issue for securities exchanges. The concentration rules that make it advantageous to trade on an exchange over an alternative execution venue will now be removed. Recall, in the UK, order flow routed through the London Stock Exchange does not attract stamp duty, whereas transactions made via unregulated venues do attract these special taxes. Many securities exchanges across Europe, particularly in Central and Eastern Europe, have similar preferential arrangements. This distinction between trading venues will have to disappear. Markets like Budapest Stock Exchange (BSE) view this as a threat. BSE have four or five large companies that are heavily traded by foreign investors. The danger is that these large shares could be internalized by the investment banks. The larger financial institutions in Hungary, are mainly subsidiaries of foreign investment banks. Should these decide to internalize, deal flow will fall away and that will affect the future of the country's economy and demutualized exchanges. The domestic market participants will also stay on the securities exchange. The proposal will therefore have a direct effect on the BSE, but it could very seriously affect the domestic capital markets. The banks could close down their Hungarian operations and deal less with local players, which would also have an indirect effect on local exchange like BSE.

NYSE-Euronext, the USA and Pan-European exchange negotiated a partial re-internalization of technology linked to securities exchanges, such as trading platform systems. The exchange Group believes it has been an incredibly competitive environment since the launch of the new directive.

Technology is incredibly important, thus after the merger the exchange Group unified technology and deliver IT synergies. Therefore, the MiFID certainly brings more competition in securities markets and is substantially changing the market environment. Trading volumes can be expected to further increase as a result of greater competition between execution venues and enhanced market transparency.

Furthermore, securities exchanges like the Deutsche Börse see a chance in MiFID to extend their services portfolio. In Germany, a number of new services in the cash market and in Market Data are being prepared. The Market Data and Analytics division will offer the so called MiFID Toolbox. For Deutsche Börse customers, this means that they are exposed to a broader range of services and more information about which of these are most cost-effective for them. In the short term, the impact of the new directive is most likely to be felt by investment firms, but in the long term its implications will likely be more profound for demutualized exchanges due to their commercial and profit focus.

This can be expected because of the combination of internalisation by investment firms and increased competition to these exchanges from market actors in other business lines such as data vending, such that the traditional business model of established securities exchanges is going to be challenged as never before. Therefore, the new created will have a profound effect in the success of demutualized securities exchanges which are pursuing business as well as mergers and acquisition opportunities in European markets.

Demutualization Mergers and Acquisition Gains to Stocks Issuers

Mergers and acquisition (markets integration) and demutualization of securities exchanges are perhaps the most important developments being discussed in capital market the world over. Listed companies, also referred to as issuers, are a core stakeholder in securities exchanges, along with investors and members of securities exchanges. This is why they would be keenly interested in these developments and their implications. The concept of markets integration (M&A) of securities exchanges is intuitional – a merger of securities exchanges into a single exchange. Integration and demutualization are likely to result in a large, well-governed and dynamic securities exchange that can act as an effective economic agent.

Issuers of listed securities can expect several major advantages from exchange integration following demutualization. First, the monetary cost of listing should reduce. Of the listed firms, some are listed at more than one securities exchange and a few are listed at all the domestic exchanges. These listed firms have to pay listing fees to each securities exchange separately. With only one exchange, only one fee would have to be paid. Second, the managerial cost of time and effort spent in compliance with listing regulations should reduce. Firms which are listed at more than one securities exchange have to comply with the regulations of each exchange. For instance, each corporate announcement has to be made to each securities exchange separately. Similarly, at the time of listing, a lot of paper-work for each securities exchange has to be done independently. When there would be only one securities exchange, compliance would be simplified.

Moreover, the number and quality of financial products and services for the issuers should improve. Once the exchanges integrate then the central securities depository entity would become the subsidiaries of the integrated securities exchange. All services, from listing, trading, custody, clearance and settlement shall be provided by one securities exchange or its subsidiaries, and the exchange would have adequate economic and human resources to improve its services to issuers. For example, it could facilitate development of market for debt securities making it easier for issuers to raise capital through debt instruments. Similarly, it could fasten the pace of issuing right shares. There would also be strong incentive for a securities exchange to act as a highly efficient share-registrar through the central depository company for all listed companies.

In addition, demutualization and integration should improve price discovery and liquidity in listed securities and broaden the investor base to the advantage of issuers. Since trading would take place at only one securities exchange, rather than three exchanges, there would be a single price for a security at any one point in time. Trading volumes would increase because all the trading would happen at one exchange rather than three securities exchanges. Since securities exchanges earn most of their revenues from trading volumes, a demutualized for-profit exchange has a strong incentive to invest in having stockbrokers and trading terminals in all those parts of the country which do not have direct access to the market. Improved liquidity and price discovery and a broader investor base make it easier for new firms to raise longer term risk-capital from the capital market and reduce their reliance on conventional lenders like commercial banks. Firms would also be able to rely more on their stock prices to judge their performance.

Furthermore, securities exchanges should be better able to understand the point of view of listed firms. The demutualized exchange would be both a listed company and the front line regulator of the listed firms. It would be under constant pressure to be a role model for others. This would make it more realistic in devising and implementing regulations for other listed firms, such as the Code of Corporate Governance. Also, due to its greater economic and strategic significance, the demutualized exchanges which merged are better able to lobby with the government for the common issues facing listed firms. For instance, such securities exchanges may effectively seek concessions for the listed firms, such as lower tax rates on corporate income and dividends. There would be a strong commercial incentive for such exchanges to seek such concessions because the more the listed firms, the greater would be the listing revenue and trading fees for the exchanges.

Finally, listing on a high profile and closely watched securities exchange carries an element of prestige and help the listed firms in their overall marketing efforts. By following better governance practices, such as a high level of on-going disclosure, listed firms should be able to get better terms from lenders and other business partners than similar unlisted companies. Therefore, by demutualized securities exchanges acquiring other exchanges or merging with other securities exchanges, they stand to derive a plethora of benefits, no wonder once an exchange has demutualized they usually go on a merger and acquisition frenzy.

Share Price Performance of Demutualized Exchanges

A number of the large securities exchanges in the Europe/Oceania region have been at the forefront of demutualization. Their share prices have since soared in addition to improvement in their financial performance. In recent years Asia and America's biggest securities exchanges have followed suit, with remarkable success. Share price of the Chicago Mercantile Exchange rocketed since it went public. Since then a series of securities and derivatives exchanges, including Nasdaq, NYSE and New York Mercantile Exchange, have gone the same way. One benefit of demutualization is that it provides securities exchanges the flexibility to merge with and acquire others. Majority of the securities exchanges have therefore been changing their organizational structures due to the motives already discussed.

How are these securities exchanges performing as public organizations? Since in Europe/Oceania there have been a reasonable number of securities exchanges which have become public in nature, the European experience is used to discuss the performance of securities exchanges upon demutualization. Several European securities exchanges have recently gone public, and several other exchanges elsewhere have announced their intention to do so, including many in the USA, Asian Pacific and African Union. The following is a brief look at the ownership and performance to date of selected American, European and African exchanges that have become publicly traded firms on their own trading boards.[141]

The Deutsche Börse is in a variety of different businesses. In addition to the usual securities exchange business of *cash trading*, it also engages in derivatives trading, clearing, settlement, and the provision of information services and technology. Its cash trading platform, Xetra, is Europe's second largest cash market. It is an electronic order-driven trading system for liquid stocks that also allows for quote-driven trading and auctions for less liquid stocks. The exchange also operates and has 50 percent ownership of Eurex, the world's largest derivatives exchange. It also owns 50 percent of Clearstream, a settlement and custody business that generates substantial profits. Moreover, it also has a significant information technology division that both provides in-house technology and operates and develops

---

141 For a more detailed examination, see works by Aggarwal, (2002); WFE (2008) and Bloomberg (2008).

technology for third parties.[142] This diverse group of businesses was formed and later the exchange did an initial public offering. Its shares began trading after its demutualization and listing on the Frankfurt Stock Exchange. The shares were offered at an initial IPO price of €33.50 and the closing price on the first day of trading was €36.20. The offering was oversubscribed 23 times and this resulted in 300 additional shareholders, including banks, brokers, and regional securities exchanges.

In addition to strategic investors such as banks, brokers and regional securities exchanges who have a controlling 51 percent stake in the company other German institutions own 15 percent; USA institutions own 13 percent; UK institutions own 12 percent; other institutions own 7 percent; and retail investors own 2 percent. The five largest shareholders as of May 2002 were Deutsche Bank (10.1 percent), German regional exchanges (7.2 percent), Hypobank (4.7 percent), Commerzbank (4.6 percent) and BHF Bank (2.6 percent). The above ownership percentages, as well as the roughly 25 percent share allocation to non-German investors, reflect limits on the maximum ownership that stems from concern about the securities exchange's role as a provider of public goods. Its shares have performed well in the aftermarket both on an absolute and on a relative basis. Fifteen months after going public at a price of €33.50 in February 2001, it was trading in the €48-51 price range (May 2002). The company has also reported record earnings since going public, with the diversity of its businesses limiting its vulnerability to the slowdown in securities exchange activity.

The London Stock Exchange is the largest exchange in Europe in terms of the value of trades, the number of listed firms, and the total value of firms listed. The LSE fully self-listed with a market capitalization of one billion pounds. Institutional investors now own about 25 percent of shares outstanding, up from the original 15-20 percent; and ownership by members has fallen. Seven months later, the major shareholders included Fidelity (9.2 percent), Warburg Dillon Read (4.2 percent), Cazenove Fund Managers (4.1 percent), Credit Suisse Asset Management (2.9 percent) and

---

142 For more details, see UBS Warburg Equity Research Report on Deutsche Börse AG, August 2001.

Legal & General Investment Management (2.8 percent). The Financial Services Authority (FSA), which is the regulator of all stock trading in the UK, is also charged with listing authority for the LSE.

The LSE also provides secondary market trading for 13,000 securities, and its three major sources of revenue – broker services (exchange and membership fees), listings, and information services – are all related to cash trading. The UK equities make up 67 percent of the LSE's trading activity, while international equities account for 26 percent and AIM, the market for small growth firms, accounts for another 5 percent. The LSE's business model focuses only on stocks from which it obtains 16 percent of its revenue from listing fees, 34 percent from trading activities, and 47 percent from information services/data sales. But, as stated earlier, listing fees and data sales are likely to fall as the globalization of markets further erodes the exchanges' monopoly powers and the Internet increases investor access to information.[143] The LSE listed its stock for trading on the Main Investment Market at a price of 365 pence. nine months later, the stock was trading in the price range of 480-488 pence.

The Australian Stock Exchange was listed on October 14, 1998. The initial shares of ASX were distributed to the members of the exchange. The Act that created ASX limits ownership by any single shareholder to a maximum of 5 percent. The Exchange derives most if its revenue from four sources, first, listings providing almost 25 percent of revenue, 70 percent of which is from initial listing fees and the remaining 30 percent from subsequent listing fees. Second, equity trading, clearance, and settlement generate an additional 39 percent of the revenue. Equity trading is conducted through its Stock Exchange Automated Trading System (SEATS). Moreover, trading in options and warrants is also conducted on the exchange and contributes 16 percent of the revenue. Warrants are traded via SEATS and options are traded on its Derivatives

---

143 See HSBC and Schroder Salomon Smith Barney company report on the London Stock Exchange, August 2001 and September 2001, respectively.

Trading Facility. Lastly, another 16 percent of revenue is obtained from the sale of market data.

In addition, Otchere and Abou-Zied (2007) examined the effects of financial exchange mutual-to-stock conversion phenomenon on the performance of listed exchanges and the quality of the securities market using ASX as a case study and found that the ASX stock significantly outperformed the stock index and the control group on a market-adjusted return basis. The securities market performance was driven by strong operating performance. The profitability ratios of the ASX significantly improved in the five years following the demutualization and self-listing. The performance improvements remained significant even after controlling for growth in the Australian economy. From a market quality perspective, they reported evidence of increased trading activity by foreign investors after ASX's demutualization and self-listing. Interestingly, the bid-ask spreads of the securities market had narrowed in the post-conversion period. In particular, small-cap firms also became more liquid. These results show that securities exchange conversion from mutual to publicly traded exchange is not only value enhancing for the exchange and its shareholders, but it is also beneficial for the securities market as a whole.

Since the date of their IPOs to 29th February 2008, the shares' prices of listed securities exchanges have generally shored up with some even reaching 2030 percent. Data from WFE (2022)[144] indicates that the market capitalization of the listed exchanges are far higher than those of demutualized exchange (with the exception of Tokyo Stock Exchange), which are also higher than the market capitalization of mutual/associations and other forms of exchanges (with the exception of Shanghai Stock Exchange). Table 7 shows the shares performance of selected major listed exchanges in US dollars.

---

144 The WFE is the trade association for the operators of regulated financial exchanges with 70 members globally, and develops and promotes standards in markets, supporting reform in the regulation of OTC derivatives markets, international cooperation and coordination among regulators. WFE exchanges are home to over 57,000 listed firms.

Table 7: Shares Performance of Selected Listed Securities Exchanges

Exchange	Year listed	Share Price Change (% $)
TSX	1998	2030
SGX	2000	1167
Deutsche Borse	2001	1015
LSE	2001	464
OMX	1998	341
NASDAQ	2002	174
JSE	2006	167
NSE Kenya	2014	78
BME	2007	35
BOVESPA	2007	24
NYSE	2006	-1
BM&F	2007	-4
Source: Exchange Websites; WFE (2022); Bloomberg (2020)		

Financial Performance of Demutualized Exchanges

Since the business climate of stock exchanges is facing many challenges due to many turbulent changes, traditional stock exchanges are no longer able to keep up with these changes as they lack the required financial flexibility to do so. As a result, many have changed their ownership and governance structure by adopting the strategy of demutualization. A number of studies have focused on examining the impact of demutualization on exchange financial performance and internal governance mechanisms on an exchange's financial performance, with most of the data coming from the World Federation of Exchanges.

Exchange demutualization has also been found to lead to a significant impact on the financial performance in terms of liquidity, profitability and capital structure – mainly the debt maturity.[145] In addition, demutualization

---

145 El Azza, M. H. (2019). Evaluation of the impact of the demutualization process on stock exchange value. Cardiff Metropolitan University. Thesis. https://doi.org/10.25401/cardiffmet.12744860.v1.

of the stock exchange has a significant impact on its board composition and director's pay structure. Furthermore, the findings showed that the change in board size enhances the financial performance of a securities exchange, whereas board independence has an inverse relationship with financial performance. Thus, adopting demutualization is considered as one of the successful strategies in managing liquidity and in adjusting the capital structure through the debt maturities. As a result, demutualization supports an exchange in maintaining its financial flexibility and keeping the credit rating within the acceptable range especially in light of the uncertainty of economic environment and competitive conditions. These actions can influence critically an exchange's profitability position and in turn, improve its financial performance. On another level, demutualization sheds light on the importance of the board of directors as an effective mechanism in supporting the significant financial decisions and enhancing the securities exchange's superior performance. Overall, demutualization enhances the value of a securities exchange.

In regard to market quality of a securities exchange upon demutualization, demutualized exchanges have achieved significant improvements in market quality following their conversion from mutual to for-profit structure.[146] Demutualized exchanges have realized significant reductions in transaction costs in the post-demutualization period. The benefits are unevenly distributed, with those in developed countries realizing most of the benefits of demutualization. A further exploration of the potential sources of the reductions in spreads on demutualized exchanges showed that, consistent with the predictions of the laws of demand and supply, the increased order flow, market share, and increased listings following demutualization, contribute to the falling spreads. Interestingly, demutualized exchanges that subsequently go public after demutualization experience incremental improvements in market quality.

Changes in securities exchange ownership and governance structures has also been found to lead to better financial performance indicators,

---

146 Abukari, Kobana & Otchere, Isaac. (2020). Has stock exchange demutualization improved market quality? International evidence. Review of Quantitative Finance and Accounting. 55. 10.1007/s11156-019-00863-y.

except for fixed assets utilization in developing and emerging economies.[147] Furthermore, utilizing data on 11 out of 20 demutualized stock exchanges during the period 1996–2008, Azzam (2020) found that demutualization increases an exchange's financial performance, size, and liquidity, while lowers its debt; a securities exchange with relatively large size has relatively low profitability and high debt; and an exchange with relatively large size, low debt and high value of trade is more likely to demutualize. Therefore, securities exchange conversion from mutual to demutualized exchange is value enhancing for the exchange and its shareholders.

There has been considerable focus on the corporate governance restructuring strategies of exchanges to adapt to new market conditions following conversion into a for-profit structure. This has led to changes in the composition of the board of directors and become more international over time, and many of which have been forced to demutualize and convert to for-profit structures to compete more efficiently. Analysis of restructuring in the composition of the board on the reputation of the exchanges, has shown that securities exchanges restructured board composition and refocused them to create better value, suggesting that the conversion of an exchange to a for-profit structure brings efficiencies when accompanied by changes in the governing bodies.[148] Therefore, converting to for-profit form had a positive impact on the reputation of the exchanges. The positive impact becomes even greater when accompanied by changes in board composition, thus providing an example of successful corporate governance restructuring.

In addition, examination of the performance of mutual, demutualized, and publicly listed exchanges and found evidence of improved performance along the exchange governance continuum, with publicly traded exchanges exhibiting better operating performance than demutualized exchanges.[149]

---

147 Morsy A, Rwegasira K. (2010). Does demutualization matter to the financial performance of stock exchanges? *International Research Journal of Finance and Economics*, 40(Jun): 155–167.

148 Padilla-Angulo, L., & Ben Slimane, F. (2018). Board Restructuring and Successful Demutualization: The Stock Exchanges. *Journal of Organizational Change Management*, 31(3): 598–618.

149 Oldford & Otchere (2011). Can Commercialization Improve the Performance of Stock Exchanges Even without Corporatization? *The Financial Review*, 46(1): 67-87.

However, their robustness test, focusing on the corporatized exchanges that have gone through the three phases of the governance structure, shows that the listed exchanges do not exhibit evidence of incremental gains in efficiency and profitability beyond what they achieved at the demutualization phase. Therefore, commercialization provides sufficient freedom for exchanges to exploit monopoly rents before going public, while corporatization brings about proper valuation of the exchanges franchise.

An examination of the effects of the recent spate of financial exchange mutual-to-stock conversion phenomenon on the performance of listed exchanges and the quality of the securities market shows that the ASX stock significantly outperformed the stock index and the control group on a market-adjusted return basis. The securities market performance is driven by strong operating performance. The profitability ratios of the ASX significantly improved in the five years following the demutualization and self-listing. The performance improvements remain significant even after controlling for growth in the Australian economy. From a market quality perspective, the authors documented evidence of increased trading activity by foreign investors after exchange demutualization and self-listing. Interestingly, bid-ask spreads of the securities market had also narrowed in the post-conversion period, with small-cap firms, in particular, becoming more liquid. Available evidence therefore shows that securities exchanges conversion from mutual to publicly traded exchange is not only value enhancing for the exchange and its shareholders, but is also beneficial for the securities market as a whole.

Securities exchanges are traditionally considered as brokers club, which inconsequence tarnishes the image of these markets in mind of the people. The advancement of the technology and media explosion have broadened the wisdom of business in the field of the Pakistan market. an investigation of whether demutualization lead to better securities market performance of the Pakistan exchanges in all level of economies or for specific in Pakistan. Using data for thirteen securities exchanges obtained from WFE five years before and after the demutualization. Using Wilcoxon sign rank test to evaluate the empirical data regarding the stock market growth of the stock exchanges after the demutualization, results showed that securities exchanges are performing better in all level of economies after the demutualization in many dimension except in number of transactions in low level economies.[150]

How about the effect of demutualization on the market metrics for the listed firms themselves? After demutualization the investment rate at an exchange increase at an increasing rate as compared with the stable investment condition before demutualization.[151] There is also a positive relationship between demutualization and the number of firms listed on a securities exchange as well as the overall market capitalization.[152] If there is a proper discipline in the securities market similar to those brought about by demutualization, the number of listed securities will be traded more than before. One of the main objectives for demutualization process is to permit the securities exchange to raise more capital by selling shares and motivate the management to take effective business initiatives. Upon demutualization, the total turnover in volume at securities exchanges significantly increase. Also, it is usually expected that after demutualization, investors' trustworthiness for investment would be increased. Upon demutualization data from several demutualized exchanges reveal higher securities traded values.

Towards ensuring investors' protection and uphold transparency in the capital market, securities market regulators perform surveillance function. Most of their surveillance departments use on-line and off-line market surveillance systems to find out violation of securities related law in securities trading and also to find out whether irregularities have taken place, or any abnormalities exist in securities transactions. Upon demutualization a look at total number of irregularities found by the investigation departments under surveillance function aimed at identify whether the number of irregularities has declined after demutualization show that the number of irregularities is almost greater than after demutualization. If such

---

150 Sial, A. W., Tahir, A. Q., Zulfiqar, S., Iqbal, M. & Naqvi, S. A. B. (2014). Demutualization of Stock Exchanges and Stock Market Growth: Broader Economic Investigation of Demutualized Exchanges. *Journal of Economics, Finance&Accounting,* 1 (4): 285-294.

151 Khatun, N. (2018). Performance assessment of demutualization of Bangladesh stock market. European Journal of Business and Management, 10 (12): 174-190.

152 Ihsan, A., Nadeem, A, & Haider, M. (2019). Demutualization and Stock Market Performance: A Comparative Analysis of Karachi Stock Exchange KSE. *Business Economics.*

condition goes on, we can expect that confidence among the investors will be increased, which is one of the objectives of demutualization.

The other objective of demutualization is the opportunity to make profit by exchanges shareholders, which requires focusing on efficiency and creating more value. Upon demutualization total number of firms declaring regular dividend increased significantly in Dhaka Stock Exchange. Moreover, a look at the return on equity for demutualized securities exchanges show that they became better than before the transformation. In addition, demutualized securities exchanges have been found to exhibit higher earnings per share than they did before they underwent government structure transformation.

Furthermore, demutualization is beneficial not only for listed firms but also for its shareholders as some dimensions of liquidity such as market depth, bid-ask spread and market impact have been found to improve upon demutualization. This means that securities exchanges that are not demutualized and are facing liquidity problem, can be improved by changing its structure from mutual to demutualized.[153] There have also been significant increase in stock returns with a corresponding increase in trading volume and traded value in the post demutualization period at many demutualized exchanges in Asia.

Post-Demutualization Securities Exchange Structures

In the previous chapters it was indicated that securities exchanges could derive a myriad of advantages and benefits from demutualizing and changing their ownership and organizational and management structures. It was also noted that this could not be achieved without some drawbacks. Critics of the goals of exchange demutualization have argued that the process simply serves to substitute one private interest group for another. The broker-dealers, and later retail investors, who would be shareholders of the exchange, would likely wish the exchange to pursue profit maximization goals that may not be consistent with regulatory steps that impose burdensome listing requirements on issuers, or drive brokers

---

153 Ali, F., Wang, M., Ali, I., Ali, S. T. (2020). Does Demutualization Spur Liquidity? *SEISENSE Journal of Management,* 3(1): 15-26.

or dealers to execute their trades elsewhere.[154] Any conclusions about the success of any particular model or of exchange demutualization may only be reached by tracking the experiences of various demutualized exchanges over a longer period of time than that which has elapsed thus far. The following is a discussion of developments among various exchanges. From the update below, it can be seen that some exchanges are meeting their demutualization objectives while others are experiencing difficulties adjusting to the new pressures of public life.

The demutualization of the Stockholm Stock Exchange took place in 1992-1993 in response to legislation that effectively ended its longstanding monopoly. It sold shares to issuers and exchange members, but those shares were not freely tradable for one year. The new board of directors was considerably smaller and consisted of members elected by the shareholders. Just over five years after its demutualization, a listed company and former derivatives exchange competitor, OM Gruppen AB (OM), increased its ownership to 20 percent and proposed a merger. The merger was approved by the Swedish government because it was believed to be in the best competitive interests of both entities. However, in conjunction with the merger, the Swedish government acquired a significant interest in the combined entity. It also passed new legislation, which served to increase regulatory oversight of the combined entity. Although the demutualization of the Stockholm exchange was meant to thwart the competitive threat from OM, it actually ended up facilitating both its take-over by OM and increased government involvement in the company's regulation. Nevertheless, the beneficiaries of the take-over and, by extension, the demutualization have been the shareholders.

The initial demutualization and the subsequent merger of the two exchanges' resources and market base has strengthened its position in the market and enabled the Stockholm Stock Exchange to modernize its business operations and governance structure. Its first Act as a private company was to allow remote membership and direct execution of orders

---

154 See Cox, J. D. (2000) Premises for Reforming the Regulation of Securities Offerings: An Essay, *Law & Contemporary Problems*, 63:11.

from other cities. In 1995, a clearing link was created between OM and the Finnish derivatives exchange. In 1997, these exchanges were united by the world's first electronic trading link between independent exchanges. In 999, Sweden and Denmark launched the first cross-border joint equities trading system, Norex, designed to raise liquidity in the Baltic markets.[155]

Since the Stockholm Stock Exchange went public and listed itself on its own board it launched the first hostile take-over bid for another securities market. At the end of August 2001, OM submitted an official bid to take over the London Stock Exchange Plc. The initial bid was rejected and the bid period extended to late October and the terms of the bid were improved. The LSE shareholders also rejected that bid.

Immediately after demutualizing and listing, the Australian Stock Exchange turned its attention to a proposed take-over of the Sydney Futures Exchange, hoping perhaps to create as fruitful a union as that between the Stockholm Stock Exchange and OM. However, in pursuing the SFE, ASX experienced for the first time the competitive perils inherent in the bid process. It was caught in a bidding war and was ultimately outbid by Computershare Ltd, Australia's giant share registry and software firm. The loss was precipitated by a decision from the country's competition bureau that the merger would be anti-competition. The key issue before the Australian competition bureau was whether the exchange should receive special protection as the national capital markets institution or whether it should be treated as just another entity competing in the marketplace.

The decision was highly resisted by ASX management, who accused the competition bureau of being short-term oriented and largely unsympathetic to global market arguments.[156] Later, the Australian government expressed a desire to lift ownership limits under the Corporations Law Amendment from 5 to 15 percent. ASX has also branched into share registry work and public relations, thus competing directly with its subsidiary, Computershare

---

155 Stone, R. (1999). Swedish, Danish Bourse Link Starts Well; More Links Seen, *Dow Jones International*, 21st June.

156 Swedish Securities Dealers Association, Sweden: Country Report to the International Council of Securities Associations (May 2001); available at <http://www.icsa- intl.com/pdf sweden2001.pdf>.

Ltd. The exchange is also seeking to enter the third-party clearance and back-office support markets for brokers.[157]

Approximately a year after demutualizing, the Toronto Stock Exchange built upon its dominance of the Canadian market by announcing the planned acquisition of Vancouver's Canadian Venture Exchange (CDNX). Shareholders of both TSE and CDNX voted overwhelmingly in favour of the merger. The deal closed at the end of 2001 after the path was cleared by the OSC[158]. The CDNX is the primary exchange in Canada for junior listed companies. Once the take-over was complete, CDNX was operating as a wholly-owned subsidiary of the TSE and the two exchanges were to share a common board of directors. Under the terms of the deal, the TSE's board was expanded to 18 members from 15 with CDNX getting five of those appointments and CDNX's former chairman becoming the vice-chairman of TSE Inc.

The acquisition was part of TSE Inc.'s strategic plan to maintain and enhance its position as the best market in the world for Canadian equities and to maintain its leadership role in serving the capital-raising needs of Canadian firms.[159] The move was a successful attempt at vertical integration since just under half of the TSE's new listings had been coming from CDNX. Despite suffering through a rough first quarter of the first year that saw operating revenue drop by more than 26 percent, TSE Inc. went public in 2002 and the net income for the quarter was $13.2-million but operating revenues have been sensitive to the drop in equity trading in the last year. It remains unclear whether TSE will place limits on foreign ownership once it goes public. Given that TSE Inc. does not need additional equity capital, a secondary offering is more likely than a public treasury issue. TSE has also completed its planned technological overhaul.

In the US, both securities and commodities exchanges are required by law to have public directors. In 1975, the Exchange Act was amended and

---

157 Durie, J. (2001). Snags in the ASX Expansion Plans. *Australian Financial Review*, 2 March Issue.

158 R. Blackwell (2001) TSE, CDNX Approve Merger, The Globe and Mail (30 May),<www.globeandmail.com>.

159 Barbara Stymiest, CEO of TSE Inc. quoted in an article by G. Marr, TSE to Go Public in Next 6 to 12 Months, National Post (30 May 2001).

provided that an exchange or association must assure a fair representation of its members in the selection of its directors and administration of its affairs. It also provided that one or more directors should be representative of issuers and investors and should not be associated with a member of the exchange, broker, or dealer. The Commodities Futures Act was similarly amended in 1992 and required exchange boards to provide for a meaningful representation of a diversity of interests.

Consequently, exchanges and the NASD have for some time had large boards, which are comprised of 20-50 percent public members, and the remainder of the board are members of the securities or commodities industries. Further, various constituency groups such as specialists, wire houses, floor brokers, institutional firms and commodities producers are represented on these boards. Independent nominating committees select board members. In addition, industry committees play a large role in exchange decision-making. After exchanges demutualize, they become more like other for-profit firms where large investors may select board members and professional managers become the key decision makers. With demutualization, their boards become smaller and more focused on profitability as opposed to members' interests.

Under CME's new governance structure, the board has been reduced from 39 to 19 members and was further reduced to 10 members. Class B shareholders, representing the interests of members rather than owners; now have voting rights to elect only about 10 percent of the new board. Another governance change was at Nasdaq, where Warren Hellman of Hellman & Friedman LLC, a private equity investment firm that made a significant investment in Nasdaq, was elected to the board after demutualization. Most exchanges have conducted their demutualization as private placements, but always have plans to make public offerings when regulatory requirements and market conditions permit. The NASD later sold those shares of common stock it owned - other than shares underlying its warrants, given the market conditions and its ability to obtain a fair price. But Nasdaq could not become an independent public corporation until its registration as an exchange is approved by the SEC. Although there have been generally accepted practices, some significant differences exist. Table 8 depicts such similarities and the notable differences amongst some selected demutualized exchanges.

Table 8: Notable Similarities & Differences of Demutualized Exchanges

Securities exchange	Corporate Structure	Allocation of Equity on Demutualization	Limits on Shareholding	Management Principles	Regulatory Functions
ATHEX	– Wholly-owned subsidiary of Hellenic Exchanges Holding listed on ATHEX – Transition from a public entity – Thirty-three percent of Hellenic Exchanges Holding still under control of state	– State-owned shares are offered to financial institutions through private placement – Fifty-two percent of shares offered in 2 years	– Currently, now limitation	– Still under state control, but with broadened representation	– Regulatory functions rest with the exchanges, however, have some links with the state regulatory agencies
ASX	– The exchange is a listed company	– Shares distributed equally among firms and individual members	– Initial limit of 5 percent has been increased to 15 percent after 2 years – Any amount more than this requires special permission	– No decrease in the number of directors, there is a broadened representation	– Regulatory functions done by a wholly-owned subsidiary of review (ASX SR), backed by an independent review by ASIC

SGX	– Is a listed holding company created from the merger of Stock Exchange of Singapore & Singapore International Monetary Exchanges – The exchange is a fully-owned subsidiary	– Shares were distributed to the members of merged entities (SES, SIMEX) based on amount invested – Ownership then expanded through private placement and IPO	– Initial limit of 5 percent has been increased to 10 percent subject to prior limit on the total shares owned by brokerage houses of 75 percent	– No decrease in the number of directors, but there is a broadened representation	– Regulatory functions rest with the holding Co. while trading & clearance are done by separate subsidiaries – Monetary Authority of Singapore empowered to exercise supervisory powers over the exchange
SSE	– Is a wholly-owned subsidiary of OM Gruppen, which is also listed on SSE	– Share capital split equally among members and then distributed according to the fees paid to the exchange over the past 5 years	– Swedish Finansinspectinen (SFI) assess anyone who proposes to acquire more than 10 percent of shares	– Has much more smaller board but with also representatives from investors	– Supervision is by SFI and strengthened after merger with OM

Key: ATHX- Athens Stock Exchange; ASX- Australian Stock Exchange; SGX- Singapore Exchange; SSE- Stockholm Stock Exchange.

Source: Author's literature compilation; Exchanges Annual Reports; Exchanges' websites.

Structural Similarities & Differences in Demutualized Exchanges

It has been noted that since the early 1990s, securities exchanges around the world have been undergoing major organizational and operational changes, with the most visible trends being demutualization and integration. In some cases, the demutualized exchanges have taken the further step of becoming publicly listed companies by issuing shares on their own trading boards. There are some structural similarities and differences among selected demutualized securities exchanges.

From organization science, especially organizational design, organization structure tends to follow organizational strategy. These dramatic changes in the organizational form of securities exchanges reflect major changes in their business environment – notably, the rise of global competition and technological advances – and in the competitive strategies designed to respond to such changes. Until recently, the main sources of revenue for securities exchanges have been transaction fees, listing fees, membership fees, and sales of information services such as market data.

But, as competition among securities exchanges intensifies and more corporations have the option of listing on overseas exchanges, many exchanges are being forced to reduce their listing fees. In fact, it is not even clear that the exchanges themselves will continue to certify firms for listing. As discussed in more detail below, that function may increasingly be left to other entities. Membership fees are also likely to fall in a demutualized exchange environment, as broker-dealers find it advantageous to trade on multiple exchanges rather than committing themselves exclusively to one. At the same time, technological innovations have sharply reduced the cost of providing data on quotes and trades, thereby diminishing the importance of this source of revenue. What is likely to produce revenue, however, is trading commissions, and the key to an exchange's success in generating commissions is likely to be its ability to generate trading volume.

As the industry continues to consolidate to achieve scale economies, the eventual winners in the process will be securities exchanges that attract order flow and so provide liquidity to investors. It is not too difficult for new entrants to set up a trading system and even outsource some required regulatory functions. However, investors will be reluctant to move their order flow to a new trading system until that system can attract sufficient liquidity. If most investors wait for this liquidity to be generated before changing, it will be difficult for new entrants to oust the incumbents.[160] For the dominant exchanges, then, the major source of revenue will be transactions and related services. Most securities exchanges can also be expected to expand their offering of products and services. For example, the businesses of some securities exchanges like the Deutsche Börse now include derivatives trading, clearance and settlement, and information technology and services. Also, Nasdaq has introduced the exchange traded fund, that has been extremely popular and achieved high trading volume. One way to accomplish such product and revenue expansion is through strategic alliances like joint-ventures.

There are a number of alliances which have been formed between securities exchanges. Particularly for the exchanges in emerging markets, such alliances have been seen as a means of ensuring survival. For many of the local exchanges, the recently acquired ability of their own blue-chip companies to list on the NYSE or LSE resulted in sharp declines in their trading volumes and listings. In response to this competitive threat, the securities exchanges formed alliances designed to coordinate trading technology, membership, listing requirements, and order execution – all with the ultimate aim of building revenue and reducing operational costs. Securities regulators from different countries have also signed a number of memoranda of understanding to achieve the standardization of regulatory requirements. Part of the attraction of such alliances is that they enable securities exchanges to maintain their individual identities, something that would not have been possible with an outright acquisition or merger.

However, in most cases, the proposed linkages and benefits have failed to materialize either because of regulatory hurdles or because all the parties involved were not able to achieve proportional benefits. And because of the disappointment with such alliances, there is once again a trend toward

---

160 See Lee, R. (2002). The Future of Securities Exchanges. *Brookings-Wharton Papers on Financial Services*, January 10-11.

outright mergers and acquisitions of securities exchanges. At the same time, the smaller exchanges now find themselves in a very difficult position – they cannot survive independently and there is little if any demand to acquire them. In fact, there are stiff competitions these exchanges face from trading venues such as alternative trading systems.

Implications for Regulatory Framework

The conversion of securities exchanges to for-profit entities raises several questions about the regulation of securities exchanges and financial markets. What role should governments play in regulating private securities exchanges? What role should private securities exchanges play in regulating exchange activities and members? And what happens in a country with only one major securities exchange that suddenly goes bankrupt? In many developed and several developing countries, securities exchanges were state-owned because they were viewed as serving a public interest. Securities exchanges play an important role in both the financial sector and the functioning of the overall domestic and regional economy.

The possibility that for-profit securities exchanges may fail and go out of business can create serious problems if listed firms suddenly find it difficult to raise capital and investors face reduced liquidity for their holdings. Of course, to the extent that there are competing exchanges, the effect of a failure by one would be limited by the ability and willingness of other exchanges to buy the financially troubled exchange. But even so, regulators may need to closely monitor the financial condition of demutualized securities exchanges. For example, in Australia a reserve fund was created to provide a capital cushion. In Canada, TSE provides an early-warning reporting system as it is required to maintain certain financial ratios and to notify regulators when not in compliance. Securities exchanges are regulated entities in the sense that they must apply to market regulators for a license to operate and must comply with certain regulatory guidelines including those setting up in their own procedures and rules.

However, in most developed countries, market regulators also have the authority to delegate certain regulatory functions to securities exchange. In many countries, securities exchanges need to register with the designated market regulator and are responsible for regulating the activities of their members, assuring compliance by members and by issuers whose firms are listed on a securities exchange with the rules laid out in the regulations. Thus market regulation and self-regulation are supposed to protect investors and serve the public interest by ensuring fair and orderly markets. As a result, most securities exchanges in developed countries have historically operated as SROs. A major concern among market regulators is that the attempts to maximize profits and shareholder value by demutualized securities exchanges will come at the expense of reduced self-regulation and supervision.[161] The self-regulating functions of securities exchanges typically consist of trading, setting rules for trading, conducting surveillance, and enforcing market manipulation rules, overseeing the trading system to prevent abuses; and membership, through the establishment of rules to govern the conduct of members and monitoring compliance with and enforcement of rules. These functions must continue to be carried out by securities exchanges that demutualize as they will no longer act as member associations.

A number of regulatory models have been proposed and/or adopted, and three of them are distinct. First, a demutualized exchange continues to perform all of its regulatory functions, even after becoming a for-profit firm. Although conflicts of interest arise in both non-profit and for-profit exchanges, concerns have been raised about whether a demutualized exchange will take enforcement actions and impose penalties on those who are major providers of revenue. The NYSE, for example, had argued that the regulatory function is an integral part of the exchange's reputation; and it had earlier backed away from demutualization because of the market regulator's insistence that it first set up an independent regulatory body.

Exchange reputation and branding is even more important in a demutualized environment to protect the commercial viability of the securities exchange. The OM Group of Sweden had adopted this model. The exchange had made a case that privately operated and owned market

---

161　For details see, Aggarwal, R. (2001). Integrating Emerging Market Countries into the Global Financial System: Regulatory Infrastructure Covering Financial Markets. *The Brookings-Wharton Papers on Financial Services*, January.

places do not stand in any opposition to high regulatory and supervisory standards required by the market and the authorities. It is not just a question of morality. To me it is a question of being a good businessman as a privately owned exchange can take full responsibility in building and enforcing a good regulatory framework.[162] Such a framework is critical to a securities exchange's commercial success.

Moreover, for-profit securities exchanges can establish a separate entity to conduct regulatory functions, thereby avoiding some of the conflict-of-interest issues. Nasdaq has taken this approach. In April 2000, the Nasd started to demutualize and created two subsidiaries: NASD Regulation Inc. (Nasdr), which was the regulatory arm, and the Nasdaq Stock Market, the commercial trading arm. This set-up reduces the problem of conflict of interest. The Chinese walls between Nasdr and Nasdaq have been strengthened as Nasdaq moves ahead with its plans for a public offering. Then in January 2002 Nasd sold its remaining 27 percent ownership to Nasdaq, thereby completing the spin-off. NASD is moving in the direction such that other exchanges will outsource their regulatory activities to Nasd.

Third, an exchange can also outsource its regulatory functions to a completely independent third party. This approach may help avoid conflicts of interest. However, there must be some way to ensure that the third-party regulator is accountable and will perform its functions effectively to avoid harm to the reputation and brand name of the exchange. In the USA futures market, the National Futures Association performs this function for several securities exchanges. This third party can be a registered futures association, or an entity registered with and regulated by the Commodity Futures Trading Commission, to ensure direct governmental oversight of the party carrying out the regulatory function. Therefore, both for-profit and non-profit securities exchanges can be inadequately regulated, particularly if they have market power. With the rise of competition, for-profit securities exchanges are likely to have even stronger incentives to self-regulate. But one thing is clear, competition and globalization will continue to make the regulatory question even more challenging as cross-border mergers and

---

162 See for example, Speech given at 26th Annual Conference, IOSCO, Stockholm, June 2001.

alliances between securities exchanges take place during the consolidation phase.

Implications for Disclosure Requirement

Demutualization has changed the management and ownership structures of securities exchanges. They will now be required to conduct their affairs just like other public firms do theirs. Particularly, the public and listed securities exchanges will have to remain accountable to their shareholders, and all the recently crafted issue such as of tightening the internal control aspects of the firm and the corporate governance status of securities exchanges will become high on the agenda.

To see how these issues have become relevant in demutualized public securities exchanges is an excerpt, below, from LSE depicting the governance issues, which are likely to crop up should a securities exchange decide to demutualize. It reveals some of the information appearing in the LSE financial report to shareholders as at 31st March 2022.[163] "...the Financial Reporting Council has adopted a revised Combined Code for reporting. The Board is satisfied that it has complied with all the provisions... the Board believes that these exceptions are justified given the wide experience and calibre of the two non-executive directors concerned. Under the provisions of the new Code, the Board is required both to determine the independence of non-executive directors and to ensure a balance of independent non-executive directors. The Company will be seeking to recruit new directors to enable it to meet the Combined Code requirements..."

Board of directors. The 2022 LSE Board for example, was comprised of nine non-executive directors, including the Chairman and Deputy Chairman and two executive directors and nine non-executive directors. Of the non-executive directors, five were considered to have been fully independent during the year within the meaning of the Combined Code. The senior non-executive director, who was not regarded as being independent, was only one. The Board had six scheduled meetings a year and meets more frequently as required.

---

163 LSE (2022) Corporate Governance: LSE annual report 2022, for the year ended 31 March 2021.

The roles of Chairman and Chief Executive are distinct and separate with a clear division of responsibilities. There are directors serving on the Board's committees. The Remuneration Committee comprises four non-executive directors including a chairman. One member of the Committee is not regarded as being independent and, in this respect, the Company does not comply fully with the Combined Code. The Committee has written terms of reference and meets at least twice a year to review and present recommendations to the Board regarding remuneration and the conditions of service of the Chairman, Chief Executive and executive directors, including the grant of entitlements under the exchange company's share schemes.

The Audit Committee comprises five other non-executive directors including a chairman. It has written terms of reference and meets at least twice a year, normally with the external auditors present, to consider the audit plan and the interim and annual results, as well as any matters raised by the auditors. It also reviews the adequacy and effectiveness of the key systems of internal control and monitors the efficiency and independence of the internal audit function. The Committee reviews the exchange company's financial statements and makes recommendations regarding their approval by the Board as a whole. In order to ensure an appropriate balance between cost-effectiveness, objectivity and independence, the Audit Committee also reviews the nature of all the services provided by the external auditors each year. Factors taken into consideration include: the cost, appropriate use of the auditors' existing business knowledge and their procedures for ensuring compliance with professional and regulatory requirements.

The exchange company normally expects to retain the external auditors to provide audit-related services, including work in relation to shareholders' circulars and transaction related work, and certain tax and similar services. The external auditors have provided no general consulting or internal audit services during the year. The Nomination Committee comprises five non-executive directors including the Chairman. The Committee meets as necessary to make recommendations to the Board on all new Board appointments.

Internal Control. In its financial reports, the exchange Board usually confirms that procedures have been in place throughout the year and up to the date of that report which comply fully with the published guidance Internal Control Guidance for Directors on the Combined Code. The exchange company's systems of internal control over business, operational, financial and compliance risks are designed to assist in meet its business objectives by appropriately managing, rather than eliminating, the risks to those objectives. The controls can only provide reasonable, not absolute, assurance against material misstatement or loss. The Board has ultimate responsibility for the systems of internal control and, through the Audit Committee, review the effectiveness of the systems. The Board is committed to their continual enhancement. The principal features of the exchange company's control framework are described below.

Delegation of Authority. Matters reserved for Board approval only are clearly defined. Executive directors have the general responsibility for making and implementing operational decisions and for overseeing the Company's business. All directors have access to the advice and services of the Company Secretary. In addition, all directors are able, if necessary to obtain independent professional advice at the exchange company's expense.

Planning and Reporting. The Board approves strategic decisions and the budget for the forthcoming year and receives a report on key business matters from the Chief Executive at each meeting. Monthly reports to the management contain key performance indicators and compare actual financial performance with the annual budget or forecast. Management action is taken where variances arise and revised forecasts are prepared on a regular basis.

Audit Committee. The exchange company's internal audit department reports to the Audit Committee on the effectiveness of key risk management and internal control procedures and appropriate action is taken where necessary. The Audit Committee also receives reports from the exchange company's external auditors, who are appointed from time to time during the AGM of shareholders.

Risk Management. Effective risk management is the responsibility of all line managers. Each business area updates and evaluates its documented key risks and controls as necessary. Periodic reports confirming the effectiveness of all significant control policies and procedures are produced by management and reviewed by the most senior executive in each business area. The exchange company's internal audit department reviews these reports and independently summarises any significant matters arising for the Audit Committee.

Detailed procedures. The procedures and controls for key business areas – including the exchange company's finance function are set out in detailed departmental manuals. These are reviewed and kept up-to-date to meet changing business needs of the securities exchange.

Relations with Shareholders. The exchange company conducts regular dialogue with institutional investors, holding meetings throughout the year in the jurisdiction they operate in and on overseas visits. Communication with shareholders also takes place by way of annual and interim reports, quarterly trading updates and through the presentation of preliminary and interim results, which are made accessible to all investors by webcasts available on the Investor Relations section of exchange website. The AGM provides the opportunity for shareholders to question the Board and meet informally after the event. The procedures for the AGM must be in line with the applicable market regulations and the event is normally attended by all directors and the exchange company's external auditors.

As have been noted earlier, it is a requirement that the management should make disclosures divulging to the shareholders of a firm relevant issues shown above, and such disclosures should accompany the financial reports of demutualized publicly listed securities exchanges.

Why are Some Securities Exchanges Resisting Demutualization?

Having discussed the pressures on securities exchanges to demutualize worldwide due to increasing competitive pressures, and the resulting changes in these markets, why haven't many larger securities exchanges restructured through demutualization? Although many securities exchanges in different jurisdictions are moving first to demutualize, other old exchanges have been resisting this global trend. Although demutualization began in 1993, large and old exchanges, which should have shown the way, took too long to demutualize. The NYSE is the biggest securities exchange in terms of trading volume but resisted pressures to demutualize until 2006 when its owners yielded to the demutualization pressure.

The NYSE was therefore forced to demutualize due to major changes in its business environment, notably due to increased competition and technological advances, so that it could adapt to new market conditions. The exchange improved its financial performance after demutualization and is now regarded as an example of successful corporate governance restructuring by exchanges. It is worth asking why it took it 15 years, since the first exchange demutualized, in order to restructure its governance system. One possibility is that these exchanges have, unlike other exchanges, not faced significant competition.

Let us venture to traces the reason why securities exchanges may delay or resist demutualization by using the example of the NYSE. This exchange may have taken this long to demutualize because it may not have had significant competition. The NYSE had over the decades benefited from a favourable regulatory environment. There are three main reasons for limited competition in listed stocks. There was the delayed posting and cancellation of limit orders on the exchange. Consequently, limit order traders face tremendous 'adverse selection' risk. The largest trading cost faced by limit order traders is 'adverse selection' – the fact that the probability that your order will be executed is greater if the market is about to move against you. Limit order traders mitigate this cost by monitoring the market carefully and cancelling their orders when they detect evidence of an impending adverse move. When they cannot predict short-term market direction well or when they are unable to cancel quickly, they adjust by pricing less aggressively. This impedes limit order use and results in higher quoted spreads – and less liquidity.

Also, there is a favorable regulatory procedure of the trade-through rule – a regulation that forces brokers to allow the securities exchange time to find the best price. This allows the specialist to *jump ahead* of limit orders by filling market orders at an 'improved' price, and limit orders are unable to compete on a level playing field with the specialists. Lastly, the intermarket trading systems in many markets are notoriously slow which discourages its use. As a result, regional exchanges and alternative trading systems that link via a regional exchange, like ArcaEx were unable to compete with NYSE as genuine alternative pools of liquidity.

If the securities exchanges have benefited from these regulations, the benefits may be observable in the form of monopoly rents to specialists. Becker (2003) conducted an analysis of the profitability of the NYSE specialist and found that compared to Nasdaq dealers and other benchmarks (including firms in the financial services industry) the NYSE specialist makes higher profits. For instance, Van der Moolen and LaBranche, two market makers on NYSE earned 2.4 and 1.3 cents revenue per share traded in 2001, respectively, compared to 0.3 cents made by Knight Trading (a Nasdaq dealer).

Despite the evidence on monopoly rents, other studies indicate that the spreads on the exchange were lower relative to alternative trading venues such as Nasdaq. Comparing the costs on NYSE and Nasdaq over time, Kothare & Laux (1995) studied the spreads on these exchanges over time and reported that spreads on NYSE had significantly fallen. This implies that over time the NYSE brought in policy changes, which had kept its spreads low, and helped it to maintain its dominant position. Apart from Nasdaq whose wide-spreads provided Instinet with an opportunity to compete with it, the relatively low spreads on NYSE discouraged potential competition.

A classic case of such a policy change was the NYSE's response to broker-dealers such as Madoff Securities who threatened to siphon off block trades from the exchange's trading floor. A consequence of this pressure, the exchange started the upstairs market where large trades could be negotiated anonymously and price impact minimized. Another one is the response to competition from Nasdaq in which NYSE during the same period partially adopted electronic networks through the introduction of SuperDot – for designated order turnaround – an electronic order-routing system that links exchange member firms to specialists' posts on the trading floor. SuperDot sends orders up to 99,999 shares directly to the specialist's computerized order book, without passing through the hands of a floor broker.

There was also the NYSE's response to customer demands for automatic execution, and competition from the ECNs. In 2000, it launched NYSE

Direct+, an automatic execution system for small orders up to 1,099 shares, which executed every 30 seconds per user, when the limit price was equal to or better than the published bid or offer. Also, in 2002, the exchange attempted to attract institutional order flow through the introduction of Institutional XPress and Open Book. Institutional XPress provided institutional traders with systematic delivery of information, anonymity for routing orders and improved execution capability.

On the other hand, Open Book allowed the upstairs traders to view the top five best bids and offers on the specialist's limit-order book, with a 10-second delay. Lastly, exchange in response to complaints of *penny-jumping* from upstairs traders in 2003, launched a pilot of Liquidity Quote – a real-time quote that showed the depth of market beyond the best bid or offer. It was a compilation of orders on the limit-order book, the trading-crowd interest and the specialist as principal.

These cases above show that whenever the NYSE faced potential competition, it has been able to bring in policy changes as required. But this raises another interesting question – why was exchange able to anticipate potential competition and respond effectively, when other exchanges were not able to do so? Usually the members, in some typical member-owned securities exchanges, pay fees to become a member of the exchange, and do not really buy a seat per se.

In contrast, the NYSE's governance structure was quite different. Unlike LSE, members of the NYSE bought and sold seats. If the exchange was to dissolve, seat-holders would receive equal net proceeds from the liquidated assets. Thus, seats were analogous to equity in the exchange and the seat-holders were the residual claimants. The dynamic behaviour of monthly NYSE seat prices of the exchange showed that unexpected changes in the prices of exchange-listed stocks or in the volume of shares traded on the exchange were important new information about the value of seats and this information was quickly incorporated into the seat prices. The seat values were therefore linked to the profitability of the brokerage business. Thus, if competition was eroding the members' revenues, it would be reflected in the exchange seat prices. If the seat-holders wished to keep seat prices high, they would be willing to take steps to respond to competition.

Moreover, LSE had a one-member, one-vote governance structure while the NYSE had a one-seat, one-vote governance structure. Thus, NYSE members could own more than one seat, and could thus cumulate their votes. Prior to demutualization, there were seven specialist firms on NYSE who together owned one-third of the seats and thus one-third of the votes. These members appear to already have a mechanism in place for members to vote according to their stake in the exchange. Thus, the residual claimants to the exchange could respond whenever there was a threat of potential competition.

This example therefore suggests that some large securities exchanges have been able to survive without demutualizing because of two complementary reasons: they have managed to suppress competition by capturing the market regulator, and there are unique features in their governance structure which have let them respond effectively to competition without demutualization. Another important consideration which is difficult to measure, but may influence the impact of competition on a securities exchange, is that the network externalities an exchange enjoys makes it especially difficult for other trading venues to compete effectively with it. Due to industry consolidation, over time the number of specialist firms in NYSE significantly reduced from thirty-eight specialist firms in 1992 to 12 firms in 2001.

Later, Securities and Exchange Commission in USA scrutiny brought in regulatory changes, which introduced significant competition, and NYSE could not have been able to survive without demutualization. In spite of the policy changes that the NYSE initiated to date, it still retains the floor-based specialist system where trades take much longer to execute as compared to electronic exchanges. Large institutional investors continue to trade on NYSE because the losses due to trading delays are offset by the large pools of liquidity available on the floor. With competition from electronic exchanges intensifying, these losses will soon increase to the extent that some large traders may decide to defect to electronic exchanges – the ECNs. Thus exchange would have faced the threat of technological obsolescence and would have to move to an electronic execution system to survive. To counter this, made a proposal to the SEC in USA to be granted permission to allow its biggest customers to use an existing electronic system, which was previously reserved for small orders. An electronic execution system made the role of the specialist – in its earlier form – redundant. Probably, this led to changes in the membership and NYSE eventually demutualized in 2006 with a new ownership and governance structure.

As we shall see in chapter eight, there are other reasons which have made securities exchange in other jurisdiction such as Africa to resist demutualization. Although some of these reasons may be unique to securities exchanges in developing markets, others may also be applicable to other emerging and developed exchanges depending on the ownership of those exchanges as well as the development level of the economies in question.

Market Risk in Demutualized Self-listed Exchanges

An important question to ask is whether there is some market risk in demutualised self-listed exchanges? The ownership and governance structures of securities exchanges around the world have changed dramatically in the last decade or so. The major theme has been the abandonment of the traditional mutual structure, where a securities exchange is owned by trade-executing brokers, in favour of a corporate form of ownership, where stocks of a securities exchange may be owned by non-broker third-parties. As already been discussed, these structural changes have opened up opportunities for the merger of exchanges and related settlement systems, and the formation of joint ventures and alliances with other exchanges and settlement systems, both nationally and internationally. And concomitantly, the changes in ownership and governance have raised regulatory issues relating to the ability of a for-profit exchange – self-listed securities exchanges which are often monopolistic – to properly exercise its responsibilities regarding trading, settlement and the surveillance of market behaviour including, in an increasing number of instances, its own.

The debatable issue here is whether self-regulation is inconsistent with demutualization and often, though not always, self-listing, that has most dominated discussion of the global changes in ownership and governance.

Certainly, it has been high on the agenda for securities regulators. While the demutualization and subsequent self-listing of the Australian Stock Exchange was not associated with a complete rewrite of market provisions, the amended legislation did include: provisions that no person (or group of associated persons) should own more than five (now fifteen) percent of its share capital; a fuller articulation of the obligations of securities exchanges, especially for market monitoring and supervision; requirements for reports detailing compliance with supervisory obligations and powers to enforce compliance; and other powers directed to the Australian Securities and Investment Commission as listing authority and market supervisor.

As both a market operator and commercial entity, ASX works closely with oversight bodies to ensure the appropriate supervision of its own market and the management of any conflicts of interest that may arise with its for-profit activities. This successful balance underpins the integrity of the market.[164] Similarly, in the Singapore Exchange, the five business divisions are kept separate from the regulatory division. In addition to this, there are two additional safeguards are in place. One is the Monetary Authority of Singapore, the securities market regulator, which supervises the exchange's compliance with its listing requirements. The other is a conflict's committee, set up to consider all possible conflicts of interest and to notify the markets regulator of all identified conflicts.[165]

Generally, the balance of opinion of both market regulators and exchanges worldwide is that exchange demutualization (whether not-for-profit or for-profit), with and without self-listing, is no less consistent with the development and enforcement of appropriate listing and disclosure standards, surveillance and discipline, financial and operational compliance, and fair and equitable treatment of customers and client, than mutualisation. However, an additional concern that has received rather less attention is whether the act of demutualization and self-listing has facilitated risky business activities that may be of concern to securities market regulators, which simply did not arise when the exchanges were mutual.

---

164 Australian Stock Exchange (2022) <http://www.asx.com/>
165 Singapore Stock Exchange (2021) <http://info.sgx/com/>

For instance, the IOSCO Technical Committee had even expressed concern that the profit-seeking actions of a demutualised securities exchange may provide further encouragement to enter businesses other than those directly ancillary to its traditional trade execution functions.[166] This, it suggests, entails new financial risks for securities exchanges that may merit regulatory intervention, such as the imposition of firewalls to protect the resources necessary to run the exchange's core activities. Thus the self-listed exchange's role as a market regulator and its role as a commercialised entity enable them to pursue business initiatives in many directions thereby opening up the scope for conflicts, and the potential for new forms of risk through global links, including clearing and settlement arrangements.

Demutualization and self-listing patently appear to have also played a major role in freeing-up the ability of securities exchanges to engage in many commercial activities – part of their stated purpose after all. For example, a few months after demutualization, the ASE announced a merger proposal (unsuccessfully) with the Sydney Futures Exchange, and within a year entered a strategic alliance with Nasdaq, formed a joint venture with Perpetual Trustees, created an operational trading link with both North America and Singapore, launched a futures market, and by 2003 had entered MOUs with the Philippines, Thailand, Singapore, Tokyo, Hong Kong, Shanghai and Shenzhen exchanges.

The increased pace of expansion in less-core non-domestic commercial activities, is found in many other demutualised exchanges, like Deutsche Börse, LSE, Singapore Stock Exchange, and Nasdaq. And yet other differences have arisen in business conduct. For instance, various WFE cost and revenue surveys of its member exchanges have concluded that demutualised exchanges generated about twice as much service income from (less-traditional) market data dissemination as did mutuals, and much less from (more-traditional) transaction fees. Likewise, while all demutualised and self-listed exchanges in this survey identified themselves as being for-profit, more than one-third of member exchanges and less

---

166 IOSCO (2001) Issues Paper on Exchange Demutualization, June: pg.14.

than one-half of mutual securities exchanges did not identify profits as a business goal.

Clearly, the financial risk of securities exchanges may have increased substantially relative to their traditional domestic market with the process of demutualization. This is especially likely to be the case for self-listed exchanges, where ownership is usually more dispersed – albeit with limitations on maximum holdings – than demutualised-only entities whose ownership is sometimes concentrated in the hands of prior mutual holders, domestic financial market risk in demutualised and self-listed securities exchanges intermediaries, and even governments.

It is worth ascertaining the changes in risk in selected demutualised and self-listed securities exchanges and examine if this risk has increased substantially for exchanges post-demutualization and self-listing and the freeing-up of commercial behaviour. To this front, empirical research[167] has examined market risk in four demutualised and self-listed securities exchanges: the ASX, the Deutsche Börse, the LSE and the Singapore Stock Exchange. Using the daily company and MSCI index returns to provide the respective asset and market portfolio data, and a bivariate MA-GARCH model to estimate time-varying betas for each exchange after self-listing, Worthington and Hellens (2005)'s results are striking. While the results indicate significant beta volatility, the unit roots tests show that despite significant variability in each exchange's beta over time, they are covariance stationary and mean reverting.

Such findings suggest that despite concerns that demutualised and self-listed securities exchanges entail new market risks that merit regulatory intervention, the betas of the self-listed demutualized exchanges have not changed significantly since listing. This has obvious and well-known for implications the capital asset pricing model, efficient markets hypothesis, event studies, and more importantly, the forecasting of securities exchange returns. However, market risk does vary considerable across these exchanges,

---

167 Worthington, A. & Higgs, H. (2005) Market risk in demutualised self-listed stock exchanges: An international analysis of selected time-varying betas. School of Accounting and Finance, University of Wollongong.

with mean time-varying betas of 0.56 for the Deutsche Börse, 0.66 for the LSE, 0.78 for the Singapore Stock Exchange, and 0.95 for the ASX. While none of the exchanges had been listed for more than seven years, there is still ample evidence that the betas for these exchanges are stationary and have neither trended up nor down since listing. This suggests that despite ample evidence of operational and financial change since demutualization, and concerns that risky business decisions could impact upon the ability of demutualized securities exchanges to perform their traditional monitoring and supervisory roles, there has been no significant change in financial risk.

There are still much unknown concerning demutualised and self-listed securities exchanges and their impacts. Empirical research, for example, could follow the theoretical models of Hart and Moore, and Pirrong and attempt to account for the ongoing demutualization movement. While the former has been criticised for over-emphasising the role of member heterogeneity and the apparent trade-off between exchange costs and profits, as against the role of internationalisation and corporatisation of membership and market competition, and the latter because he fails to take account of the choice of demutualised exchanges to take an additional step of widening their ownership by self-listing, these scholars still provide a convenient starting point. Another line of work could examine the relative performance, as variously defined, of demutualised securities exchanges, in reference to both their own mutual form and current demutualized form. Similarly, they could examine differences, if any, between the roughly equal number of demutualised but not listed exchanges and listed exchanges. Finally, there is scope for work to merely assay the current situation regarding ownership and governance structures in securities exchanges. Such surveys may enrich the decisions by securities exchanges, like those in Asia and Africa and Middle East, which are contemplating demutualization, self-listing and consolidation via mergers and acquisitions and other forms of strategic alliances.

Changes in Exchanges Investment Behaviors

The securities exchange industry has been subject to unprecedented dynamics in recent decades, particularly in Europe, Middle East and USA.

Overall, competitive pressure has increased on many securities exchanges due to a range of significant changes of the industry environment. Besides globalization tendencies that led to less home-biased investors and issuers and consequently stronger competition between national securities exchanges for order-flow and listings, the deregulation of financial markets resulted in lower barriers to entry, making the incumbents' home markets more contestable. A major catalyst for increased competitive pressure is also advances in communication and information technology, creating new forms to conduct business in securities exchanges globally.

Remote membership, electronic order book trading, alternative trading systems, and the internalization of order flow by financial intermediaries all became viable threats to the core business of securities exchanges, the traditional floor trading activity. Furthermore, the trading members of securities exchanges have become increasingly heterogeneous in nature. On the one hand, these members differ in the activity they perform at their securities exchange. As an example one should think of stockbrokers, dealers or broker-dealers, each with diverging preferences on securities exchange-related issues such as the imposed fee structure or the investments undertaken. On the other hand, exchange members also vary in size and the scope of activities outside their exchanges. Some commercial banks, for example, are engaged in activities such as over-the-counter trading, derivatives trading and post-trading services. To the extent that securities exchanges were also active in these fields, they became competitors of the exchanges.

Increased competition and divergence in the interests of the trading members led to a decline in the prosperity of securities exchanges. Some of them found themselves in an environment where their viability was at stake. In many cases, this resulted in a restructuring of the governance system of securities exchanges. As a consequence, their organizational form converted from the traditional mutual structure towards a regular outsider-owned, for-profit corporation. Take as an example the NYSE, whose seat price, a proxy for the profitability of possessing a licence to trade on the Big Board, declined sharply in the last years because of ever-growing pressure from competing trading venues like ECNs and its members' resistance to implement a modern trading platform. In 2006, NYSE demutualized, migrated towards electronic trading and even floated its shares on its own market.

Meanwhile, new business opportunities emerged, partly due to the same technological advances that threatened the exchanges' core business. Securities exchanges could, for example, embrace the new computerized technologies to modernize their trading and information dissemination systems. This promise lower transaction costs and potentially higher rents for their members. Furthermore, related business activities that offered both growth opportunities and new sources of income induce exchanges to diversify into these fields. Vertical integration of post-trading services, for example, is easier to accomplish with the availability of modern IT-systems and promise efficiency gains due to straight-through-processing possibilities. The strong growth in the derivatives market induces many securities exchanges to horizontally integrate this business field by offering a derivatives trading platform.

Hence, securities market seems to experience both a trend towards demutualization and diversification into related business activities. The number of exchanges that are organized as mutuals, or are state-controlled, have decreased substantially by over fifty percent in the last decade. During the same period, the number of demutualized exchanges increased the almost the same percentage. The main difference between demutualized and self-listed exchanges is that the latter not only underwent a demutualization process, but also sought a public listing.

The number of exchanges that added post-trading services to their business portfolio have risen by about forty percent, while the number of entities that operate a derivative-trading platform marked up by about twenty-five percent. Despite the strongest relative increase, providers of software solutions remained rather scarce, with the number of securities exchanges offering this service increasing by one-hundred-thirty percent.

Could there be a link between these two trends? One could argue that, since demutualized exchanges are profit-oriented entities, they are more likely to invest into related business segments to increase their revenues and possibly profits. One can compare both the average degree of diversification and the development in operating revenues of securities exchanges that underwent governance restructuring with entities that remained organized as mutuals. It seems that the change in governance, especially for securities exchanges that have self-listed, have a profound effect on both dimensions.

The average excess degree of diversification seems to increase after demutualizing and going public. Securities exchanges that have experienced such an 'event' have already been more diversified on average than mutual exchanges prior to the event. Self-listed securities exchanges have outpaced their mutual counterparts on average after performing IPOs. Demutualized securities exchanges do not however experience significant excess rise in their core-function revenues. The lion's share of the increase in revenues may stem from these new related activities. Although one could propose that securities exchanges may have also earned more from the traditional cash market operation, a look at data from WFE lends only limited support to this notion. There has been an exceptional rise in revenues from cash trading-related activities by some smaller securities exchanges like Oslo Exchange, whose trading-related revenues increased by more 78 percent, Wiener Borse by 350 percent in the last decade. Nevertheless, majority of the securities exchanges do not have a significant rise in their cash-trading revenues.

The mutual securities exchanges are exposed to the possibility of runs, as a member's exit exerts a negative externality on the remaining members. In most circumstances, the outsider-owned securities exchange can exploit this fragility, thereby undermining the ability of the mutual securities exchange to invest, despite the existence of a countervailing second-sourcing effect, which supports the investment propensity of a mutual. Second-sourcing connotes a situation where the mutual securities exchange invests into the project, even though it knows that its members will migrate to the competing for-profit securities exchange. This is as a result of the fact that the mutual can improve the price conditions of the transfer for its members by investing into the project.

There are important practical implications, as market participants are concerned about certain investments undertaken by securities exchanges, such as the vertical integration of post-trading services, which are profitable for the securities exchange, but may be detrimental to its users. In Europe, outsider-owned Deutsche Borse, which acquired post-trading services provider Clearstream, is therefore under particular scrutiny by both users and market regulators due to fears of anti-competitive behaviour. The emerging trend point to the fact that outsider-owned securities exchanges are less constrained in their investment behaviour, which could lead to overall welfare losses, if the negative externalities borne by the users are larger than the gains for the exchange and its owners.

Are there options of an incumbent mutual exchange to survive in a competitive environment? There can exist viability of a mutual securities exchange, which competes against an outsider-owned securities exchange. When experiencing fierce competition from a for-profit trading platform, a mutual securities exchange can only survive if it converts to a similar governance regime. This may further explain the rationale for the recent wave of demutualization amongst securities exchanges that were exposed to increased competitive pressure, as has already been discussed. Therefore, once a securities exchange demutualizes within a jurisdiction, it is predictably that other competitors within the same market will move to demutualize whether to derive the same benefits which come about by demutualization, or just due to the herding mentality.

Chapter Summary

Due to global competition, consolidation, advances in technology and increasing operational costs, among other factors, securities exchanges worldwide have been re-examining their business models and becoming more entrepreneurial. A majority have responded by demutualizing, thus bringing a change in their ownership and corporate governance structure. Through converting member-owned, non-profit securities exchange into profit-driven investor-owned corporations, demutualization could give such exchanges access to capital that can be used both for investment in new technology and for participation in the ongoing consolidation of the industry. In the process of providing the exchanges with capital, demutualization can also strengthen the corporate governance of securities exchanges. There are some differences and similarities of demutualization in different jurisdictions. There are also important lessons being learnt from demutualization worldwide in relation to management and ownership structures and exchange financial performance, and market regulation important for securities exchanges in developing continents of Africa and Asia.

The final part of this chapter examined the reasons why some securities exchanges resist or delay the process of demutualize. It was noted that such exchanges have not faced significant competition due to both regulatory advantages and certain unique features in its governance structure, which has helped them, remain member-owned. Evidence also exists suggesting that despite concerns that demutualised and self-listed exchanges entail new market risks that merit regulatory intervention, the risk of these exchange have not changed significantly after demutualizing and even self-listing.

Chapter Eight

DEMUTUALIZATION OF SECURITIES EXCHANGES IN AFRICA

Introduction

Despite the plethora of analyses examining the governance of securities exchanges, those devoted to African securities markets are scanty. Nonetheless, securities exchanges form the basic structure of African development financing source. However, their future role lies in their growth and development, which calls for the need to restructure their ownership and management structures. This chapter first, explores the prospects and possible benefits that African exchanges stand to derive from demutualization.[168] Secondly, it discusses in details possible challenges that stand on the way for Africa in its attempt to demutualize it securities exchanges. Finally, it describes the African demutualization cases and draws some experiences and lesson for other securities exchanges in Africa and other developing economies.

Past research highlights numerous advantages of exchange demutualization and analyzed the share performance and valuation of listed exchanges and found a positive link between the fraction of equity sold to outside investors and securities exchange performance.[169] There also seems to exist a positive impact of demutualization on cost efficiency of European and American exchanges. African securities exchanges may also stand to derive these benefits should they resolve to demutualize.

---

168 This chapter is based on some material in Onyuma, S. O. (2006) Demutualization of Stock Exchanges in Africa: Prospects and Problems. *OSSREA Bulletin,* 3(3) (October): 25-35.

169 See, for example, works by Pirrong (2000); Gompers et al. (2001); Mendiola & O'Hara (2003; Serifoy (2005); Aggarwl (2006).

Demutualization may be the key solution to many of the problems bedeviling African mutual exchanges. Based on the extensive discussions in earlier chapters, demutualization can improve the competitiveness of African exchanges. The main motives of, and expected benefit from demutualization include tapping new sources of capital, through self-listing needed to modernize exchange-trading systems. Such capital cannot be obtained through mutualized status. In fact, stockbrokers and governments cannot enable a commercial entity to raise such capital from shareholders, as do corporations. Second, demutualization can enable African securities exchanges to pursue business opportunities unconstrained by vested interest issues since it allows for diversification of the exchanges' shareholder base, thus improving their corporate governance systems. This enables the separation of ownership rights from trading rights.

In fact, boards of directors of African exchanges would be made up of shareholders and other investors without state representation. Although state appointments may be conducive to mitigate entrenched vested interests in the short-run, they can prove counter-productive leading to unhealthy interference by the state in the long run. It can also enable African exchanges to increase investor participation better than they currently do.

Moreover, demutualization can allow African exchanges to achieve better operational cost controls, and increase flexibility, efficiency and competitiveness through reviewing their commercial strategy. Such demutualized exchanges elsewhere have achieved consolidation in their domestic markets by merging the derivatives and cash segments or including trading, clearing and settlement services under one roof to create economies of scale and scope. Usually, demutualization is accompanied by the development of cross border exchange linkages and international alliances among various exchanges. Several demutualized exchanges in the America, Europe, Canada, and Asia Pacific have trading links and dual listing agreements with each other. Thus, this form of governance structure transformation can speed up the on-going process of integrating African securities markets.

The demutualization of African securities exchanges would also strengthen their governance and ensure their financial sustainability since they will be in a position to raise capital through rights issue or even bond issuance. Through demutualization African securities exchanges stand to benefit through enhancement of corporate governance within the exchange for sustainable protection of all their stakeholders, as well as access to the efficiently priced source of funds to finance the exchange's growth and capital markets development in their respective countries, including capital investments in trading technologies as well as introduction of new products and services.

Moreover, demutualization is responding to the increased competitiveness within the African regional financial centres in relation to finance and investment choices and allocations. In the process, the few securities exchanges in Africa which have demutualized have evolved towards new corporate, legal and business models to strengthen governance and face competition. Consequently, across the African continent securities exchanges are now re-thinking their business strategy and models in order to find ways of how best to survive.

In addition, demutualization would allow African exchanges to sell their equity stake to a mix of shareholders; decision-making would be based on the new ownership structure, not on the rights of intermediation or state representation, which ensures an effective oversight of the board of directors. Using new capital raised, exchanges would have the incentive and the resources to invest in the competitiveness of their information systems. They would be capable of introducing new products, recruit high-calibre staff, compete on an expensive technology level, leverage the value of the exchange as a brand name, and bring African exchanges to international standards.

Furthermore, the new structure would ensure that the management of African exchanges are fully qualified and motivated to act in the best interests of the shareholders and conduct the business in a prudent manner, which enhances orderly and fair-trading in African capital markets. Before delving into details of demutualization of securities exchanges in Africa, let us look at the development issues of these exchanges and identify which of them could act as catalyst or constraints to efforts to demutualize African securities exchanges.

Securities Markets Landscape in Africa

The African Stock Exchange Association was established in 1993 with the NSE as the founding member followed by the Stock Exchange of Mauritius, USE and Dar-es-Salam Stock Exchange (DSE). The ASEA's membership is composed of securities exchanges and market infrastructures within the African continent as well as entities affiliated with the growth and development of the African capital market. The members are able to interact among themselves in a bid to exchange information and share experiences and best practices. The total membership count stands at 32 members made up of 27 full members serving 37 African countries. There are about 1100 listed firms boasting $2.1 Trillion market capitalization.

Financial systems in many African countries remain underdeveloped, which results in low investment rates and high credit constraints for corporations. The African financial sector is dominated by commercial banks, with very few investment banks. Other than Egypt, African countries have only one securities exchange. A part from the African Development Bank and the Development Bank of South Africa, development banks and other specialised banks in many African economies are very limited in their capacity to raise adequate external finance to fill the financing needs of firms. Consequently, financial constraints have been identified as the most severe obstacle to doing business in Africa and a major hindrance to business start-ups and innovation by firms.[170] This has led to very low investment rates in Africa (24%) compared to other emerging global economies, such as China (40%), East Asia and Pacific (32%) and South Asia (28%).

The Covid 19 Pandemic overturned most of the progress that had been achieved on the continent in the last decade. This also includes developments in the capital market space which conversely was yet to be fully demystified. However, like other regional players, Africa must not relent. As at the beginning of 2020, the top 5 securities exchanges in terms of market capitalization include Egyptian Stock Exchange ($41.3b), Botswana

---

170 Ayyagari, M., Demirgüç-Kunt, A., & Maksimovic, V. (2011). Firm innovation in emerging markets: The role of finance, governance, and competition. *Journal of Financial and Quantitative Analysis,* 46(6), 1545-1580.

Stock Exchange ($36.3b), Rwanda Stock Exchange ($3.6b), Malawi Stock Exchange ($2.3), and Cape Verde Stock Exchange ($75.2m). These are very subdued market performance when compared to performance just before the pandemic. The 24th Annual ASEA Conference was held on 24th – 25th November 2021 and hosted virtually by Bourse de Casablanca.[171] This was followed with the 25th meeting in which the Bourse Regionale des Valeurs Mobilieres (BRVM), the regional securities exchange of the West African Economic and Monetary Union, hosted the Annual General Meeting and Annual Conference of the ASEA in Abidjan, Côte d'Ivoire from December 7th - 9th, 2022, on the theme 'African Capital Markets: Game Changers for long term development'.

These conferences featured industry experts and thought leaders across the globe who addressed topical subjects such as capital markets development, African economic integration, disruptive technology and impact investing among others. The event attracted distinguished participants, most of whom are key stakeholders in the development of the African capital markets as well as entities that have continued to champion the growth of financial services and system in the region.

Securities markets, nonetheless, play a critical role in complementing commercial bank financing in the African continent. For example, more than US$640 billion have been raised through bonds by African states and private firms in Africa since 1992. Moreover, the number of securities exchanges in Africa has grown from five in 1989 to twenty-nine in 2023, with securities markets growing continuously in the number of shares listed and the traded volume. Between 1992 to 2023, the capitalisation of African securities markets grew tenfold from $115 billion to more than $1,139 billion.

Despite these improvements in securities markets, African capital markets remain underdeveloped. Based on data from PwC 2022, the top four stock exchanges in Africa (in terms of nominal market capitalisation)

---

171 ASEA (2021) Press Release: 24th Annual ASEA Conference – November 24-25, 2021 Hosted virtually by Bourse de Casablanca. Tuesday, October 26th, https://african-exchanges.org/download/24th-annual-asea-conference/

are in South Africa, Morocco, Egypt and Nigeria. The market capitalisation of each of these is greater than $30 billion. Where data is available, the capitalisation of most of the securities exchanges in Africa is less than $6 billion. Also, excluding South Africa featuring a market capitalization ratio of 235 percent (market capitalization of the GDP), the highest securities market capitalisation in Africa was in Mauritius of 69 percent of GDP in 2019. That for Stock Exchange of Mauritius was way below the average market capitalisation in the East Asia and Pacific region of 83 percent and in high income countries of 119 percent, during the same period.[172]

The underdevelopment of securities markets is caused by many factors, including the small size of the domestic economies, volatile macroeconomic and business environment, as well as quality of institutions and financial infrastructures, among other. The share and bonds listing and issuance requirements in most African securities exchanges are binding constraints in relation to the structure and capacity of the domestic firm. The complex, tedious and lengthy administrative procedures for listing, the high transaction costs, the lack of training and knowledge about capital markets, as well as the lack of transparency in some of these marketplaces are some key constraining factors for the development of many African securities markets.

The size of the securities exchanges in African countries, with size measured by the ratio of securities market capitalisation to GDP low, according to 2023 data from World Development Indicators, is small. A look at the largest securities exchanges in Africa in terms of market capitalisation as share of GDP show that South Africa has the largest securities exchange, among other countries including high-income economies. The second largest securities exchange in Africa is Mauritius, which is close in size to those of the South Asian economies, but smaller than those of high-income and East Asia and Pacific countries. The size of the third largest African securities exchange – Casablanca Stock Exchange – lies between the securities exchanges of South Asian countries and the countries of Latin

---

172 Soumaré, I. (2020). Innovations in equity and stock market financing. Background Paper for Economic Report on Africa 2020, UNECA.

America and the Caribbean. The other three – Nigerian Stock Exchange (NGX), Tunisia Stock Exchange (TSE) and Egyptian Exchange (EGX) - are the smallest among the selected group of countries.

Considering the 2020 trading data from WFE, the top four securities exchanges in Africa show dismal market capitalization figures as compared to other emerging markets. Except for the JSE from South Africa, all the other major exchanges in Africa are less capitalised in absolute terms and as a percentage of GDP than the other four frontier markets of Asia considered. The JSE, the top securities exchange in Africa, is less capitalised than the Korea Exchange and the National Stock Exchange of India in nominal value. However, when normalising nominal values by economy size, JSE becomes the most well capitalised (235%), followed by Malaysia (112%), Korea (87%), India (76%), Morocco (52%), Indonesia (47%), Egypt (17%) and Nigeria (8%). The market capitalisation-to-GDP ratio of South Africa is greater than the average value of the high-income countries (118.9%), greater even than the ratio of the United States of America (148.5%). This may be due to the number of listed firms (365) and the variety of instruments offered by this market, not typical of other African securities exchanges.

Given the trend in the above two market metrics, except the JSE, African securities exchanges are under-developed compared to securities exchanges in other regions globally. One main constraint of securities exchanges development in Africa is the limited diversity of instruments available for trading and the very small number of listed securities. Most of the securities exchanges are in their early developmental stages, although some of them have been around for quite some time. Except for South Africa, where derivatives securities are currently traded, the available financial instruments are only equity shares and bonds in all the other markets. More generally, securities markets in Africa attract very few investors and are not so liquid.

The main problems encountered by African securities exchanges in their development are the lengthy administrative procedures for listing, the binding listing conditions deemed not accessible to all companies, the high transaction costs, the lack of training and knowledge about securities markets, the lack of transparency in some securities exchanges, as well as the lack of privately managed local pension funds with the capacity and incentives to evaluate different kinds of securities. In some other markets, macroeconomic and other market conditions that are not conducive to listing and investing are a major impediment.

Comparing the transaction costs of some of Africa's most advance securities exchanges to transaction costs applied in developed markets around the world shows that fees are relatively expensive in Africa. For example, there is an upper limit for fees applied to firms for admission and further issuance of securities on the LSE. Meanwhile, in exchanges like the *Bourse Régionale des Valeurs Mobilières* (BRVM) and the Stock Exchange of Mauritius, the transaction fee is a percentage of the transaction value – except for government securities in Mauritius. In Mauritius, for example, the fee for a transaction not exceeding 3 million Mauritian rupees is 1.25 percent, decreasing to 0.9 percent for transactions above 10 million rupees, but there is no upper limit for fees. So, a transaction of 100 million rupees (approximately £2.15 million) costs 0.9 million rupees (£19,330). The maximum cost for such a transaction on the LSE is £11,250.[173]

Technology can contribute to lowering transaction costs in many of these markets. Many securities exchanges across the Africa continent and around the world have modernised their trading system by moving away from the manual trading system of clearing and settlement they had in the past. Most of them have changed to automated trading systems. For example, the Botswana Stock Exchange introduced the automated trading system in 2012 to increase transparency and efficiency in the trading of securities. Its trading was previously conducted manually, with brokers meeting daily at the Exchange House to execute trades for their clients. Ghana also introduced an automated trading system, and opens for continuous trading every working day from ten to three o'clock Greenwich Mean Time. The Bank of Ghana's Central Securities Depositary handled the settlement of trades on a T+3 (business days) basis. The trading system

---

173 Soumaré, I., Kanga, G., Tyson, J. & Raga, S. (2021). Capital market development in sub-Saharan Africa: Progress, challenges and innovations. Working Paper No. 2, A joint FSD Africa–ODI research programme for financial sector development in Africa. London: ODI.

was manual. The East African exchange NSE, DSE, RSE and USE have all changed their clearing and settlement procedure. The NGX adopted the Nasdaq X-Stream trading platform in 2013 – a technology which moved the dealers away from slower automated technology and sped up trading. As of March 2023, all derivative products listed on the JSE Derivatives Market are tradable using the Trading Technologies platform.

Considering the indicators for bond markets in Africa and Asia in 2023, as reported by WFE, in both continents, bonds listed on the domestic exchanges have been mainly issued by domestic issuers, especially the public sector shows that corporate bonds markets dominate in terms of number of issuances only in Tunisia, South Africa and Botswana. For the rest of the countries the market is dominated by public bonds issuances. However, the outstanding amount is dominated by government bonds in all the countries where data is available.

The other central feature is that most of the government bonds have short-term maturities compared to corporate bonds. In fact, about 85 percent of corporate bonds listed on the African domestic markets that have not yet matured have an average maturity of 11 years, while 81 percent of government bonds have an average maturity of 8 years. The majority of government papers are T-bills with a maturity of less than a year. The T-bills are usually used for liquidity management, particularly in the conduct of monetary policy. Only 12 out of 42 countries issued very long-term (more than 20 years) bonds listed on the domestic market: Angola, Botswana, Egypt, Ghana, Kenya, Mauritius, Morocco, Namibia, Nigeria, South Africa, Tanzania, Tunisia. This can be explained by the pool of investors, their risk-taking behaviour which is also related to macroeconomic fundamentals, country risk and the limited depth of local markets. The lack of a benchmark yield curve that can provide pricing signals to potential corporate issuers impedes development of corporate bond markets.

Securities exchanges, African government and quasi-government bonds perform better than other indices around the word, including the S&P 500. The returns of African government and quasi-government bonds were less volatile compared to other indices even between March 2020 and December 2021, a period when most world stock indices dropped sharply due to the Covid-19 pandemic, which resulted in lockdown of economies and stoppage of trading in securities exchanges.

Most local securities markets in Africa are clearly very small in size. Due to this, regional integration could be a route to deepening African securities markets, with countries coordinating to pool their strengths. As such consolidation and securities market development advances, there may be opportunities for existing smaller domestic exchanges within a region to specialise in different industry sectors or types of share issues as a way of improving efficiency.

Regional securities market integration is basically a market or institutionally driven process of broadening and deepening the securities markets interrelationships within a region. It is expected to create larger capital markets and expand the spectrum of opportunities for financial intermediation, which makes it more cost-effective to improve financial infrastructure and diversify financial services offerings. Efficiency effects also arise from the increase in the number of market participants promoting diversification and healthy competition, and thus, eventually results in lower prices for services. It can also increase capacity to withstand financial crisis even though greater regionalism may mean greater contagion effects in the future, as was seen in USA during the global financial crisis of 2007/2008.

There are several ongoing initiatives to create regional securities exchanges in Africa. One of the most accomplished is the regional securities exchange of the West African Economic and Monetary Union (WAEMU) region - the BRVM, shared by eight countries in the region. A similar initiative was undertaken to consolidate the regional securities exchanges of the Central African Economic and Monetary Community (CAEMC) by merging the Bourse des *Valeurs Mobilières de l'Afrique Centrale* (BVMAC) with the Douala Stock Exchange in 2019 – a move expected to assist create economies of scale and scope to increase the size, depth and liquidity of the region's securities market.

The West African Capital Markets Integration Council (WACMIC) has also been initiated to allow the integration of securities markets in the Economic Community of West African States (ECOWAS). The main objective of the Council is to establish a harmonised regulatory environment for the issuance and trading of financial securities across the region. The Council is striving to create cross-border securities markets, where a passport mechanism exists with a single listing system: the passport allows a registered broker in a given jurisdiction to trade on other securities exchanges; while the single listing allows a firm to be listed on a single securities exchange with the stock available for transactions by all brokers in the defined area. The passport system would start on a regional basis within the existing regional economic communities.

The ECOWAS is a leading example on this phenomenon, where the WACMIC was inaugurated in January 2013 as the governing body for the integration of capital markets in ECOWAS. Its key objective is to establish a harmonised regulatory environment for the issuance and trading of financial securities across the region, as well as to develop a common platform for cross-border listing and trading of such securities within the region. The WACMIC is made up of the Director Generals of the region's securities regulatory authorities and CEOs of the WAEMU securities exchanges, Ghana, Nigeria, Sierra Leone and Cape Verde. The WACMIC is also tasked with designing the policy framework and managing the implementation of the process that will facilitate the creation of an integrated capital market in West Africa.

Specifically, it supervises the securities market integration programs; set up standards and validate all works done by the technical committees; coordinates relevant stakeholders such as ECOWAS, the West African Monetary Institute and WAEMU; monitors and assess the state of preparedness of the member states in the integration process; sources funds and other resources for the implementation of capital market integration; and monitors standards and compliance after integration. From these functions, WACMIC is to lead to the integration of financial markets in three major phases aimed at integration through sponsored access trading (brokerage firms), having a common passport for qualified West African brokers in ECOWAS, and establishment of a common trading platform in the region.

These initiatives to integrate securities markets are also ongoing in the East African Community (EAC), where concrete progress has been made, including achievement of relative success in attracting cross-listings on at least a few of the domestic securities exchanges and cross-border investment by the EAC's institutional investors, despite the lack of a common currency. The EAC partner states have since created the EAC Financial Sector Development Regional Project (FSDRP) structured into six components: Financial inclusion and strengthening market participants, Harmonization of financial laws and regulations, Mutual recognition of supervisory agencies, Integration of financial market infrastructure, Development of the regional bond market, and Capacity building.

On 23rd February 2018, the EAC Heads of State directed the EAC Council of Ministers to expedite the establishment of the East African Monetary Institute (EAMI) according to the roadmap of the East African Monetary Union (EAMU), and on 1st February, 2019, the EAC Heads of State assented to the Bill for the Establishment of the Institute.[174] Then on 26th February 2021, the EAC Council of Ministers designated 1st July 2021 as the date for the coming into being of the EAMI – the precursor to the East African Central Bank (EACB).

The operationalization of the EAMI effectively sets the EAC on a journey towards the single currency by 2024 as envisaged in the EAMU Protocol. The Sectoral Council of Finance and Economic Affairs was to develop an institutional structure for the EAMI by 30th September 2021, with the Secretariat initiating the process of identifying the Institute's host Partner State. The EAMI is therefore a transitional mechanism to the EACB that will issue the single currency that is expected to be in place by 2024. Three of the securities markets – DSE, Rwanda Stock Exchange (RSE) and Uganda Securities Exchange (USE)– have since connected their trading systems and linked with the EAC Capital Markets Infrastructure platform, although the NSE – the largest securities exchange in the region – had initially bolted out of this project, but later joined in 2023.

---

174 EAC (2021). EAC pronounces 1st July, 2021 as date for coming into effect of East African Monetary Institute, 26 February, https://www.eac.int/press-releases/145-financial-sector/1941-eac-pronounces-1st-july,-2021-as-date-for-coming-into-effect-of-east-african-monetary-institute.

Regarding bonds, a regional bond market development agency known as Agence UMOA-Titres was created in 2013 by the Central Bank of the WAEMU countries to help member states use their domestic securities markets to raise the resources they need to fund their economic development policies at reasonable costs. This is a market dedicated to public bonds and Treasury bills, shared by the eight countries of WAEMU with a common currency. Moreover, another attempt to deepen African securities markets is represented by the African Continental Free Trade Area signed in March 2018 by 44 African Heads of States to establish a single continental market for goods and services, with free movement of capital and business travellers.

There are also plans to integrate all the regional as well as domestic securities exchanges in Africa, with the journey having started with the African Exchanges Linkage Project (AELP) aiming at coming up with a Pan-African Securities Exchange. To this end, the African Securities Exchange Association and African Development Bank (AfDB) launched the AELP- an E-Platform linking seven African capital markets with $1.5 trillion market capitalization. On 18th November 2022, the AELP went live on integrating the African capital markets by facilitating cross-border trading and free movement of investments in the continent through the AELP Link platform.[175] The go-live happened when the platform was officially switched on. The interconnectivity platform enables the trading of exchange-listed securities across 7 participating securities exchanges.

This go-live of the AELP Link was a great milestone towards achieving ASEA's mission to engage African capital market ecosystems in order to foster capital mobilization, promote sustainability, and enhance financial inclusion for the benefit of Africa's economic development. Trading infrastructure harmonization through the Link is expected to ease existing trading processes and potentially reduce the cost of trading across African capital markets. The participating exchanges and the respective brokers therefore became front-runners in this great Pan-African securities exchange integration initiative.

---

175 ASEA-ADB (2022) African Exchanges Linkage Project (AELP) Goes Live on Cross-border Trading. *African Securities Exchange Association/African Development Bank*

The AELP, a flagship project of the ASEA and AfDB is aimed at facilitating cross-border trading among seven participating Exchanges and select broker firms. The AELP Phase 1 was funded by a grant from the Korea-Africa Economic Cooperation (KOAFEC) Trust Fund managed by the African Development Bank. The seven Exchanges participating in Phase 1 of the AELP are: Bourse Regionale des Valeurs Mobilieres (BRVM), Bourse de Casablanca, The Egyptian Exchange, Johannesburg Securities Exchange, Nairobi Securities Exchange, Nigerian Exchange Limited, and Stock Exchange of Mauritius.

Earlier in July 2021, ASEA signed a contract with DirectFN Ltd for the design and implementation of the AELP Link trading system in the seven markets. The Link which is hosted on the Oracle Cloud Infrastructure (OCI) has been designed to integrate with securities exchange and broker trading systems, and is available in English, French and Arabic. It aggregates live market data from the participating exchanges and enables stockbrokers to access information and see the market depth and liquidity of the foreign market of interest. Stockbrokers and securities dealers are critical stakeholders in the Linkage process. Through the coordination of the exchanges and the African stockbrokers and securities dealers association (ASSDA), each exchange will connect 5 stockbrokers or securities dealers to the AELP Link.

In the first phase of the project 33 stockbrokers have connected as at the time of go-live. The selection of participating stockbrokers and securities dealers was based on agreed criteria, and expression of interest by approved licensed dealing members from each of the participating Exchanges. The development was a historic moment for Africa, to finally actualize the linking of stock exchanges across Africa after many unsuccessful attempts over the last 2 decades. The AELP test environment has been operational since July 2022 enabling the stockbrokers and securities dealers to familiarize themselves with the platform and execute mock trades. This culminated in the completion of the User Acceptance Testing on 7th November paving the way for the technical go-live in November 2022.

The participating stockbrokers have already embarked on signing counterparty broker agreements between different securities markets. The sponsoring stockbrokers enable access to their domestic markets to the sponsored stockbrokers from other markets and vice versa. The sponsoring stockbrokers will clear and settle trades in the host market using their local currency in compliance with the host market's rules and practices. The regulatory bodies in all the participating markets are already apprised on the progress. A ceremonial launch of Phase 1 and demonstration of live cross-border trades was held alongside the 2022 ASEA Annual General Meeting & Annual Conference on 7th December 2022 in Abidjan, Cote d'Ivoire. Future phases of the project may include automated cross-border payment systems, participation of additional ASEA member Exchanges and their respective brokers and additional brokers from the current participating Exchanges after the pilot phase. Botswana Stock Exchange and Ghana Stock Exchange kicked off Phase 2 of the AELP with technical connectivity to the Link expected to commence in 2023.

In order to prepare for the commencement, the African Securities Exchanges Association in partnership with the Zimbabwe Stock Exchange hosted the 11th Building African Financial Markets (BAFM) Seminar on April 12th-14th, 2023 in Zimbabwe.[176] The BAFM Seminar is a Pan-African capacity building initiative by ASEA. The seminar seeks to build the capacity of financial market players on the continent empowering them to effectively address existing and emerging risks and opportunities facing African financial markets. The seminar placed special focus on capital market policy and regulations, market integration and cross border capital flows, liquidity, product development, trading technology as well as climate financing opportunities. Themed Managing Risk in Turbulent Times, the seminar featured industry experts and leaders across the continent as well as other key stakeholders in the development of African financial markets. It is usually a unique opportunity to enhance the knowledge and capacity of African markets players enabling the continent build on continued growth of African markets. The seminar provided extensive coverage and offered latest insights on key issues facing financial

---

176 ASEA (2023). 11th Building African Financial Markets Workshop. African Securities Exchanges Association. April 12th -14th, 2023 at Elephant Hills Resort, Victoria Falls, Zimbabwe.

markets on the continent enabling players to stay ahead of the changing landscape of African markets.

Based on the above discussion, on the growth of Africa's securities markets and whether the continent has the right foundations in place to support intra-African securities trade, Africa seems not to have built the foundations that it needs. There are pockets of excellence, but African securities exchanges do not seem do enough together. There is the need to bring these markets closer and build links between their market infrastructures. Africa's securities markets focus on putting in place procedures that suit the international markets when they should focus on attracting African investment. They need to focus on what they can do for Africa within Africa. There is more than enough capital available from investors on the continent. There is no need to completely rely only on investment from the rest of the world. There is the need to improve connectivity between markets and make them accessible to other African investors.

However, the challenge of increasing intra-African investment may not just be about linking infrastructure. Connecting infrastructure is crucial, but African markets are getting investment from Europe and American investors, so clearly there is already some access to African markets. Is it also a problem of lack of information or insufficient marketing? Maybe there is concern about a lack of diversification by other African investors. Standards and good governance are also critical. Investors are looking for good governance and stability. Over the years, market regulators have stepped in, which has increased investor confidence to some extent, however, within Africa there are still challenges in terms of market regulation. Securities markets need to work with market regulators to come to a consensus as to what form of regulation is actually needed given the emerging competition, integration and demutualization trends.

This will increase investor confidence even further.

In order for African securities markets to experience sustainable growth, another issue is also fundamental: supply. Currently the number of listed financial products on most African exchanges is severely restricted and this prevents local investors from gaining exposure to African growth and international investors from increasing their exposure to African securities markets. Policy makers and securities exchanges need to provide incentives that encourage firms to raise money through the capital markets instead of relying on bank lending to fund their growth. There is fundamental a lack of listings which are critical if markets are to grow and develop greater liquidity. There is a need for privatisation in Africa, especially in the utilities market as too much still sits with governments. This calls for a framework to bring about private sector involvement. Money seems to be there for investment, but it is waiting to be employed.

It is important to underscore the value of African securities markets but asked whether they could be stronger together. Despite slumps and obstacles in these markets, international investors are hungry for new markets and opportunities. These investors know that there are few remaining investment frontiers. African countries with robust securities markets need to be positioned as attractive investment hubs for Europe, Asia, America and Middle East. Africa inherently has very strong growth potential and therefore, African securities exchanges can play an important role in enabling this growth.

Currently, Africa holds many success stories, including the creation of international financial hubs. Africa's emerging financial hubs are posting marked improvements on a global index, signalling an opening up of regional economies – and jostling for status. Cities across Africa are rising into the ranks of most preferred global financial hubs, significantly raising their capacity to attract investment and drive economic growth across the continent. Johannesburg, Mauritius, Nairobi, Kigali, Lagos and Casablanca have emerged as serious financial hubs. There is also Ghana's decision to consolidate two central securities depository systems into one – demonstrating the right approach and reduced risk. In addition, there is the creation of Strate in South Africa – another important success story of integration with other markets. The consolidation of two securities exchanges (Cairo, Alexandria) in to the Egyptian Exchange has also brought market expansion. All of these success stories can be adopted by other markets.

Africa, therefore, does not have the luxury of wasting time and money to redefine models or standards. Too many successful examples already exist, and which can be reused and re-implemented. The key takeaway from all these issues is that collaboration is king. Africa's securities markets will be stronger together, so connecting infrastructure, working with regulators, addressing exchange governance challenges, and clear communication between all parties are critical. In order to create investor confidence, transparency is critical and this can be achieved through securities exchange demutualization.

Nevertheless, nothing is lost. It is well documented that Africa has one of the lowest financial inclusion rates in the world, but this situation is changing thanks to developments in the mobile money services pioneered by Kenya. The financing of the economies is essentially bank-based, with underdeveloped securities markets across the continent except in South Africa. These markets are composed mainly of securities exchanges and bond markets, even if other capital markets such as private equity markets and crowdfunding platforms are gaining ground. While stocks traded on securities exchanges are issued mainly by big firms, for bonds, governments are the main issuers. Corporate bonds constitute a tiny part of the securities markets in most African countries. Despite this under-development, there is still huge potential for market expansion given both the financial development gap and the huge infrastructure development gap in Africa.

African securities markets can increase their investor base by tapping into the huge financial resources sitting in deposit accounts of African pension funds and sovereign wealth funds. African pension funds hold about $700 billion, and the assets of sovereign wealth funds in sub-Saharan Africa are estimated at $16.4 billion.[177] If these funds were channelled into the continent's local securities markets, they would improve the liquidity of many African exchanges and bonds markets. However, this would require appropriate market mechanisms (sound regulatory framework, transparent management structures and safe business environment), which do not fully exist currently, with some markets having made significant progress and others much less so. In many cases, not only are the investment vehicles offered domestically too risky from the perspective of institutional investors, but funds are prevented from investing abroad. One successful use of

---

177 Soumaré, I. (2020). Innovations in equity and stock market financing. Background Paper for Economic Report on Africa 2020, UNECA.

pension and other public funds for economic development is the case of the Province of Quebec in Canada, where the *Caisse de Dépôt et Placement du Québec* pools public funds in a fund management vehicle for investment in financial markets and in the economy. Similar successful examples are the *Caisse des Dépôts et Consignations* in France and the *Caisse de Dépôt et de Gestion* in Morocco. These pooled funds managers are some of the largest institutional investors in their domestic securities markets and around the world. To enable pension funds and other indigenous institutional investors to contribute significantly to the growth of their domestic economies, management institutions in Africa need to be set up with specific objectives and must have sound regulatory frameworks and business environments.

Parastatals, also known as state-owned enterprises, are among the big economic players in many African countries. In South Africa, 5735 large companies have been formally registered, but less than 400 of them are listed. The privatisation of some of these parastatals through transparent initial public offerings and listing them on local exchanges will increase the number of listed firms and offer investors more choices to diversify their portfolio. Allowing citizens to hold shares and bonds in these large firms will not only increase the number of market participants, but also increase the number of traded stocks available. The listing of these parastatals could increase not only their ability to mobilise additional financial resources for innovative projects, but also improve their corporate governance and performance. Such initiatives require continuous improvement of the business environment, with sound and reliable regulatory frameworks, financial literacy and management structures, all of which do not yet fully exist in many African countries. Based on some of the development challenges securities exchange in Africa face, the next section documents how some of these issues and standing on the way for demutualization of African exchanges.

Impediments to Demutualization of African Securities Exchanges

Academic analysis point to the fact that, along with the above benefits, some problems may confront demutualization process. There are many obstacles on the way of Africa in demutualizing its exchanges. These obstacles stem from its economic, political, and other non-economic factors like the nature of its rudimentary capital markets, and its ability to deal with problems inherent in demutualization.

Cost of Demutualization. The costs associated with an exchange self-listing are huge. Deutsche Borse and Euronext, respectively paid 36.8 million and 46 million euros for their quotation. Although the proceeds received from an IPO naturally more than recouped these costs, the IPO-costs amounted to 3.7 percent of the new proceeds in Deutsche Borse's case and 12.7 percent for Euronext. Besides these one-off costs, there are also additional running costs such as stricter disclosure requirements and need to convene AGMs. A strategic implication is that African exchanges may become more easily to be taken over by other foreign giant exchanges with higher investment capital endowment.

Partial Market Liberalization. Capital markets in Africa are not yet sufficiently liberalized to enable a for-profit securities exchange to explore an expanded opportunity set. For example, markets such as Ghana still have capital account restrictions that limit the ability of a securities exchange to implement cross-border strategies such as cross-listing. Other markets, including Kenya, have stringent and expensive listing requirements, while other still have capital gain tax.

Exchange Financial Sustainability. Of the 30 securities exchanges in Africa, only about 7 are likely to be financially viable. These are those exchanges with a combined market capitalization of at least \$2 billion and at least 40 listings.[178] Securities exchanges in Egypt, Kenya, Mauritius, Morocco, Nigeria, South Africa and Zimbabwe may have such critical mass.

Conflict-of-Interests. Ownership in demutualized exchange becomes problematic, as there are the difficulties in the choice of the financial institutions to become shareholders and marrying powers wielded by former member-owners and other new shareholders. The power wrangles in most African countries, may trickle into securities exchanges, thus

---

178 see Mensah, S. (2005). Demutualizing African Stock Exchanges: Challenges and Opportunities. Paper Presented at the 9th Annual Conference of the African Stock Exchanges Association, Cairo, Egypt, 10-12 September.

increasing the possible effect of conflict-of-interests between old owners and new shareholders, and an exchange and its market regulator.

Political Bottlenecks. Where they still provide financial support to exchanges, African governments may not be in urgency to demutualize their securities exchanges. As long as African exchanges are in their current mutualized form and seen as national symbols, governments will continue to provide financial support, with the usual under-funding and intermittent disbursements. They may only act when put under pressure by donors. After all, some donors have preference for supporting securities exchanges, for instance, the IFC provided seed money for the Ghana Stock Exchange and the BRVM, while SIDA has long supported Tanzania, Uganda and Zambia securities exchanges.

Thin-Illiquid Markets. For a long time, Africa had only eighteen securities exchanges. Mozambique and Cameroon have just established their exchanges, bringing the total number of securities exchanges to twenty. African exchanges are small, illiquid and poorly regulated, with most markets classified as frontier-markets, and not emerging-markets. The Economist magazine that publishes weekly economic data on emerging markets only classifies South Africa and Egypt. Exchange market capitalization to GDP is as low as 3 percent in Swaziland, compared to about 71 percent in other emerging markets like Malaysia, or 262 percent in UK and 131 percent US.

Low Turnover. African securities markets lag in terms of market turnover. According to the 2004 Standard & Poor Global Markets Fact Book, liquidity as measured by market turnover in African securities exchanges is low. Markets such as Ghana have turnover ratios as low as 4 percent, Kenya (7.4%) and BRVM (1.6%). Even South Africa and Egypt, the largest and most liquid markets in Africa have turnover of 44.8 percent and 13.7 percent respectively, and Nigeria 11 percent. Other like Namibia even shows zero turnover. This contrasts with turnover ratios in developed markets of US (123%), UK (101%) and in other emerging markets such as India (138.5%). The number of listed firms is very low for most countries. Egypt and South Africa are outliers with listings of 967 and 426 respectively. Countries like Tanzania and Uganda have as few as 8 listed firms although there are countries such as Nigeria, Zimbabwe and Kenya and Morocco with over 50 listings. This may create supply constraints and worsen liquidity, a critical success factor for demutualized exchanges.

Dominance by Foreign Firms. African securities exchanges are dominated by foreign firm listings of local subsidiaries of multinationals like StanChart Bank, Barclays Bank, Unilever and Guinness. While the parent company may be cross-listed in a number of developed markets, the subsidiary listing is domesticated, with no incentive for the listed local subsidiaries to migrate.

Poor Macroeconomic & Regulation. Some factors impeding performance of African states may also influence their exchange demutualization. In fact, many African states still have high budget deficits, high inflation, volatile and fast depreciating exchange and interest rates. Policy inconsistency and macroeconomic instability undermine investor and issuer confidence, thus dampening business flow to securities exchanges. Most African capital markets also lack robust regulatory frameworks since fifteen out of twenty-nine markets have a formal oversight agency. There are rules for members and listings for every securities exchange, shortage of experienced supervisors and the absence of a strong culture of compliance with rules. Such poor regulatory enforcement may increase the problem of conflict-of-interest common with demutualization.

A demutualized exchange focuses on profit and wealth maximization of its shareholders. Therefore, it has less incentive to take enforcement actions against its customers or users, who are a source of income. Given their rudimentary nature, most African exchanges would have the problem of balancing regulation by themselves and by their market regulators. Self-regulatory functions of a demutualized securities exchange pose a challenge both for the exchanges themselves and the capital markets regulators.

Market Infrastructure. Given their sizes, African securities exchanges lack the resources needed to acquire key infrastructure for market operations. Roughly ten African exchanges do not have central depository systems. Although this is a positive driver for demutualization, it is constrained by the limited profitability prospects of most African exchanges.

Poorly Trained Finance Staff. In more developed countries, a large part of the training in capital markets is done on-the-job. Working in modern capital markets requires fundamentally different skills than working in rudimentary markets. Training in management of financial institutions is still thin in many African countries. With demutualization, securities exchange management who previously operated in a cooperative mode, might find it difficult to assimilate commercial mind-set or develop the necessary capacity to execute sound business strategies, common with demutualization.

Thin Stocks Investor Base. African securities markets are characterized by a small investor-base as most people have low incomes with little to save and invest. There is also a small institutional investor-base with most markets having as few as five securities markets service firms. This limited investor-base may influence the financial viability of demutualized exchanges.

Wrong Reasons for Setting up Exchanges. With the exception of older exchanges like South Africa, Kenya, Egypt, Zimbabwe and Nigeria, most African exchanges have been set up as state initiatives, and benefit from state subsidies to cover operating costs. In fact, the reasons why African states promote exchanges are both technocratic and political. The technocratic reasons are the standard economic reasons normally advanced by technocrats to justify formal capital markets like a source of long-term finance, improved capital allocation and savings mobilization.

Other complex non-economic factors, which underpin government objectives for promoting securities exchanges, are inconsistent with the market reasons for demutualization. Most exchanges emerged as symbols of international legitimacy of a country. Other came to being due to geographical advantage; for example, BRVM is a regional exchange for the 8 West African countries belonging to WAEMU, while BVMAC is a regional exchange for 6 Central African countries under CEMAC bloc. Prior to BRVM, there was only one exchange within the zone, in Code d'Ivoire. Lastly, there is the FMDQ Holding Plc (FMDQ Group) – the first vertically integrated financial market infrastructure group, strategically positioning to provide seamless trading, clearing, settlement, risk management and depository services for financial market transactions, as well as data and information services, across the debt capital, foreign exchange, derivatives and equities markets, through its wholly owned subsidiaries – FMDQ

Securities Exchange, FMDQ Clear, FMDQ Depository, and FMDQ Private Markets.

Securities exchanges are sometimes seen as symbols of democratising state corporations and tools for indigenisation of economy. The implication is that demutualization in Africa may not be driven by market-based reasons.

Securities Exchange Demutualization Experiences in Africa

The demutualization fever has not yet fully caught up with securities exchanges in Africa as compared to other emerging markets. Not many exchanges in Africa have gone an extra mile to fully convert themselves from mutual to public outfits through self-listing. Only 7 exchanges, among them Johannesburg Securities Exchange (2005), Nairobi Securities Exchange (2011), Dar es Salaam Stock Exchange (2015), Zimbabwe Stock Exchange (2015), Botswana Stock Exchange (2018) have so far restructured their governance system with some even self-listed their shares on their own trading boards.

A handful, especially exchanges that were established in recent times, such as Stock Exchange of Mauritius, BRVM, Rwanda Stock Exchange, Trop-X (Seychelles) and Lesotho Stock Exchange were registered from the onset as companies limited by shares and have never had to experience the transition from a mutual to a demutualized securities exchange. Perhaps, with this background, it is worth exploring demutualization and self-listing perspectives with respect to African exchange landscape especially that the two are the only next and ultimate steps in the evolution of African securities exchanges. These perspectives are to do with maintaining a balance between serving the regulatory functions, financial sustainability and pursuing the corporate objectives without jeopardy to stakeholders. A few others are working on their demutualization strategies as discussed below. This global trend is likely to continue across the continent and will bring more transparency and inclusiveness in the way stock exchanges are managed.

It should be noted that more often than not, demutualization is just an interim step for many securities exchanges in their evolution process. Post-demutualization, securities exchanges can evolve further by listing on their own platform – a process called self-listing. Globally, a number of securities exchanges progressed to self-list after they demutualized as a way of further enhancing their governance and competitiveness given that a listing expands the shareholder base and enables access to deeper pools of capital. Early examples of global major securities exchanges that underwent a self-listing are the Stockholm Stock Exchange AB in Sweden, Australian Stock Exchange, Hong Kong Stock Exchange and Singapore Stock Exchange. As time progressed Deutsche Bourse, London Stock Exchange, Euronext and NASDAQ followed suit, among others.

The same trend has been experienced in Africa, where for example, the Johannesburg Stock Exchange was the first securities exchange in Africa to self-list in 2006, a year after its demutualization. The Nairobi Securities Exchange self-listed in 2014, three years following its demutualization. The most recent self-listing in Africa was by the Dar es Salaam Stock Exchange in 2016, a year after its demutualization. Notwithstanding, few of the demutualized exchanges in Africa, such as Zimbabwe Stock Exchange, Stock Exchange of Mauritius, and Bourse de Casablanca remain unlisted. Botswana Stock Exchange Ltd as a newly demutualized securities exchange is also unlisted, thus yet to fully complete the whole hog of making the exchange to be widely held by the public.

A self-listing is a privatization of a securities exchange. Experience and empirical evidence elsewhere shows that privatization brings about a broader mix of shareholders ranging from institutional investors, retail investors, listed companies, technology companies, the public at large, and in some cases foreign investors. Often, as is common practise in most government-driven privatization efforts, foreign institutions might become owners of newly privatized entities to a certain extent.

In the context of African demutualized exchanges, demutualization has ushered the exchanges into an era of corporatization. This is particularly necessary as a securities exchange itself is mandated to regulate corporatized institutions, being listed firms. Corporatization brings about significant expectations from the shareholders of these exchanges. One such is the expectation that the exchange, once listed, should maximise profits and value for its shareholders.

The listing of a securities exchange strongly accentuates the business orientation of the exchange. As with any listed company, the exchange can be expected to be more value oriented, more efficient, more innovative and growth oriented and, as a result, highly motivated by short-term profit maximisation. This is because where the open ownership attracts outside investors, they will expect a return on their investment that is commensurate with the return they could earn on their investment alternatives. However, this probably will not be the case if the owners are insiders (members, issuers) with other interests in the exchange than outsiders.

The three demutualization cases profiled below can be regarded as evidence of these exchanges venturing in to unchartered waters of success, which has only been witnessed in foreign markets. As has been noted earlier, being a torturous and complex journey, majority of African securities exchanges are still putting a wait and see attitude before venturing in it.

Demutualization of Johannesburg Securities Exchange

The discussion about the need for African exchanges to remove their veils and prospects with demutualization cannot be complete without profiling the African securities exchange pacesetter, the JSE.[179] Of the bonds markets, only the Bond Exchange of South Africa had demutualized in 2007. There are a few other African securities exchanges, which are limited by shares and in theory demutualized. However, there is a significant overlap between licensed stockbrokers and shareholders. They are, therefore, yet to be copiously restructured through demutualization process.

Founded in in 1887 during the first South African gold rush, the Johannesburg Stock Exchange (JSE) is one of the world's 20 largest securities exchanges by market capitalisation and the largest exchange in Africa. Following the first legislation covering financial markets in 1947, the JSE joined the World Federation of Exchanges in 1963 and upgraded

---

179　The discussion here is based on material in Onyuma, S. O. & Shem, O. A. (2007) Reorganizing Corporate Governance Structures in African Stock Exchanges. *African Journal of Business & Economics*, 2(1):60-85.

to an electronic trading system in the early 1990s. The JSE acquired the South African Futures Exchange (SAFEX) in 2001.

The Road to Restructuring. The JSE, currently known as JSE Securities Exchange Ltd has operated through years of almost continual change. It began in May 1994 with the publication of a research report into the structure of the JSE, and the subsequent changes have affected every aspect of the structure, operation and ownership of this Securities exchange. The big bang started with the introduction of corporate membership and the abolition of the requirement that only South African citizens could be stockbrokers in the country. This paved the way for the large international corporate brokers to establish businesses in South Africa, and saw the HSBC, JP Morgan, Merrill Lynch and Salomon Smith Barney become members of, and began trading on the JSE. The next dramatic change was the closure of the open outcry floor in 1996 and the introduction of a computerised order-driven, centralised, automated trading system, known as JSE Equities Trading, then the launch of the Stock Exchange News Service (SENS) in 1997, and perhaps the most dramatic and noticeable change for investors was the introduction in 1999 of electronic clearing and settlement, the Share Transactions Totally Electronic (STRATE) that swept away the old paper-based share certificate settlement system.

The Demutualization Process. As at April 2005, demutualization of securities exchanges had been completed globally in only 5 jurisdictions out of a total of 76 emerging market jurisdictions. By this time, the demutualization fever had not caught up with Africa as compared to other emerging markets. During the meeting of May 26th 2005, the individual and corporate members of the JSE, who owned the exchange by virtue of holding trading rights, approved the demutualization of the exchange. On June 27th 2005, the South African Financial Services Board approved the proposal to demutualize the JSE.

On announcing the privatisation, Russell Loubser, the then CEO of the JSE, noted that demutualization was an exciting milestone in the JSE's history. It offered the exchange additional capital-raising opportunities and would allow it to implement more easily, a broad-based black economic empowerment strategy. It laid also the foundation for the self-listing of the JSE and put it at par with its international competitors.[180] The change therefore, ushered in a new era in July 2005.

After 118 years as a mutual securities exchange, JSE joined the world's most prominent international exchanges in operating as a fully-fledged publicly-owned corporate when the exchange became a public limited company. Therefore, on July 1st 2005, JSE began operating as a public unlisted securities exchange, going by the name JSE Limited. In the past, the ownership of the exchange was inextricably linked with the right to be its member. Under the new demutualised dispensation, any person is free to purchase shares and become part owners of the JSE Ltd, and ownership of shares is no longer a requirement for membership of the exchange.

To give effect to the demutualization, all existing rights holders received 1,000 new JSE Ltd shares in exchange for each right held. As a result of a statutory requirement, no single shareholder could own more than 15 percent of the shares in issue. In order to create a market for the shares, the JSE Ltd first created an OTC trade using its own trading system with Strate as the settlement agent. This was necessary to enable the future listing of JSE Ltd own shares as other international securities exchanges have already done. Initially, JSE Ltd had 8.3 million shares each trading on the OTC market at between R220-250. To meet its own listing requirements that a listed firm needed more than 25 million shares in issue, the JSE Ltd split its shares before its IPO issue ten to one, implying a post-split listing price in the range of R22-25. This was necessary to enable the future self-listing of its own shares. Following the amendments to the Income Tax Act that resulted in the securities exchange losing its tax-exempt status, the exchange decided to self-list.

Listing of JSE Limited Shares. The JSE Ltd had been giving listing consideration a thought for some time, but the final push came in the form of amendments to the Income Tax Act that resulted in the exchange losing its tax-exempt status. This did not seem a particularly compelling reason to many, given the fact that most other mutual and limited companies and institutions have been paying tax for decades. On June 5th 2006, JSE Ltd self-listed on its own trading board by offering for sale, 84.27

---

180 JSE (2005) Demutualization of the JSE. Web Announcement, www.jse.co.za.

million shares, which based on their OTC trading prices, were valued at R2.1b ($310.7m). The self-listing was expected to increase the exchange's liquidity and open additional avenues for raising capital.

The cynics were watching out for the "snouts-in-the-trough syndrome" as directors, executive management and staff were showered with excessive share options or allocations. Fortunately, the JSE Ltd has a good track record of remuneration disclosure, and in view of the fact that its size and profitability as a listed firm were far more modest that many of its company listings then. Given this, the chairman of the South Africa Shareholders' Association noted that the long and the short of the JSE demutualization was that it would have little impact upon anyone, and it was very much business as usual.[181] The exchange currently operates a financial derivative market, an interest rate product market, and an agricultural products derivatives market, in addition to the vibrant equity and bonds markets.

Post-Demutualized Structure & Value. The JSE demutualized structure envisages a board and executive management that remained same. JSE Ltd has 17 directors as before, of which, four are females and the rest, males. The board has a CEO and a Chairman. It has an executive committee made up of 15 members, six of whom are females, the rest, are males. The operations of the exchange and its contractual relations were not affected, and no capital raising was undertaken. During 2005, the board meet 6 times probably deliberation on the demutualization agenda.

At listing time, the market capitalization of the listed companies was R3.5trilion ($517.5b). According the WFE, this JSE market capitalization was double the market value of Norwegian securities market, and half the size of the Swiss exchange. Upon demutualization, the number of transactions increased from 3.9 million (2004) to 5 million (2005). There was an increase in market capitalization from R2.5billion (2004) to R3.5 billion (2005).[182] Turnover also increased from R.1000, 000 million (2004) to R1600, 000 million as at 31st December 2005. During this period, JSE

---

181 Sylvester, D. (2006) Johannesburg Demutualization: Business as Usual? *Personal Finance Online Magazine* Saturday, March 11th.

182 World Federation of Exchanges (2000, 2001) Annual Reports and Statistics. Paris: WFE.

was ranked 17 worldwide by the WFE. In terms of liquidity, it was ranked 33 worldwide as opposed to 38 in 2004. Within emerging securities markets, it was positions four.

Post-demutualization period has seen the JSE Ltd acquire the Bond Exchange of South Africa (BESA) in 2009. On 25th February 2021, the JSE announced its results for the financial year ending December 31st 2020. Earnings before interest increased by 19 percent while net profit after tax grew by 12 percent to R778 million (2019: R695 million). This represents a strong performance given the effect which Covid 19 Pandemic may have inflicted in the JSE's business, and whose revenue for the period under review was spread across capital markets (listing, equities, currency derivatives, bond and interest rate, commodity derivatives) – 45 percent, post-trade services – 39 percent, information services – 16 percent.

The demutualization and self-listing of the JSE was a milestone in Africa securities exchange landscape since even up to early 2011, only JSE had fully demutualized in Africa. Other African exchanges could only lean from the JSE demutualization case.

Demutualization of Nairobi Stock Exchange

The process of demutualizing the NSE was winding and tedious. The formula for splitting ownership interest between government and stockbrokers was the most contentious issue in the long-drawn demutualisation debate. Both the CMA and NSE had incurred millions of shillings in consultation fees paid to consultants to advice on how the securities exchange assets would be shared, but a consensus had throughout remained elusive.

The first Demutualisation Study Report prepared by KPMG (2007), commissioned by CMA, suggested that the government should own, at least, a quarter of the securities exchange, drawing fierce opposition from the then board chairman of the NSE, Jimnah Mbaru, who said "the government had never given NSE even a cent." The brokers therefore, rejected an earlier proposal by consulting firm KPMG that the government gets a quarter of the NSE ownership stake. Stockbrokers had all along argued that the government did not deserve to get any direct stake in the demutualised securities exchange.

The Kenya Government, on 23rd December 2008 placed a Request for Expression of Interest following the General Procurement Notice for the project that appeared in the United Nations Development Business No. 674 of March 16th 2006 and was updated in United Nations Development Business No.707 of July 31st 2007. Having received a credit from the International Development Association and a Grant from the UK DFID towards the cost of the Financial and Legal Sector Technical Assistance Programme (FLSTAP), it intended to use part of the proceeds in procuring consultancy services for Demutualization of the NSE. It was intended to support the development of a policy and legal framework to demutualize the exchange.

The consultant was to do the following four tasks. First, review the reports prepared by NSE and CMA on proposed modalities for demutualizing the NSE taking note of the difference in the recommendations with regard to the desirable legal framework for demutualization, value determination, value allocation, governance structures, and post demutualization listing process; and conduct one-on-one discussions with relevant stakeholders and make independent recommendations that reflects local consensus as well as international best practice on demutualizing the NSE including determination of the value of the NSE; value determination/share allocation, taking into consideration contributions of various stakeholders, conflict resolution mechanisms between different interested groups.

Secondly, the consultant was to recommend a suitable demutualization model taking into consideration the overall objective for regional integration of the East African capital markets and the study conducted by IFC/ ESMID on the EAC capital markets regionalization model; and appropriate legal framework for demutualization. In addition, they were to propose a roadmap to guide implementation of the demutualization process taking into consideration input from key stakeholders; and finally, they were to present the draft report to stakeholders' forum/workshop for views and comments.

A second recommendation by a 2008 Ernst & Young Demutualisation Study report, commissioned by the NSE, however noted that the then value of the NSE was attributable to existing members as NSE had not received any direct government funding. The study proposed that NSE's assets were to be shared in an 80:5:5:10 ratio between stockbrokers, NSE staff, previous directors and the Investors Compensation Fund. According to this report, the NSE assets were to be shared amongst brokers in the proportion of the value of business transacted since 1997. This report argued that this was the only time during which transaction records of the NSE were available.

But the government had on the other hand argued that it had facilitated development of the securities market over the years by setting up a regulatory body and privatising state corporations through the exchange thereby increasing the number of listed firms. In fact, it was the government which had always came into the scene to maintain investor confidence whenever a stockbroker collapsed or shown signs of financial distress. After all, the investor compensation fund, from which investors whom have lost their investments through inappropriate trading by stockbrokers, is management by a government agency.

Of significance, a Demutualization Steering Committee (DSC) was formed to steer the demutualization process of the NSE. The DSC had membership from various relevant sectors, comprising: Capital Markets Authority Chief Executive Mrs. Stella Kilonzo (Chairperson); Chief Executive of the NSE Mr. Peter Mwangi (Vice Chair); representations from the Ministry of Finance, the Attorney General's office, Central Bank of Kenya, an Investment Expert Mr. Davinder Sikand, and Mr. George Oraro, the Legal Expert and consultant.

Reforming the Regulatory Framework. Before demutualization could be undertaken, certain ownership and management, operational and regulatory frameworks had to be instituted. A study was conducted by KPMG (2007) to assess the industry's perception on demutualizing the NSE. Ernest and Young also made recommendations to the Exchange on demutualization. There was the acquisition of financial advisors and financial institutions to perform the valuation of the NSE. A demutualization steering committee was then formed to see through the process, in addition to the drafting of the market regulatory Act. The NSE had to conduct a meeting of its members to approve the intended project before seeking the approval from CMA to perform demutualization. The NSE made an application seeking approval from CMA on March 26th 2008 to demutualize and self-list. This application was however, preceded by an NSE board decision to demutualize and appoint Ernest & Young Company to undertake a study on the process and also develop an implementation plan and a roadmap for securities exchanges integration or merger.

The Draft of the Memorandum of Association, and the Articles of Association of the NSE were first redrafted and approved by the AGM of the exchange. A Draft Demutualization Act was then drafted by the Legal Consultant and the Demutualization Steering Committee, and forwarded CMA for approval. The approved Act was then forwarded by the Capital Markets Authority to the National Treasury (Ministry of Finance). Through the Ministry, a Cabinet Memorandum was prepared for the Cabinet and upon Cabinet approval, the Treasury then forwarded the draft Act to the Cabinet for approval. Thereafter, the Treasury submitted the draft Act to the Attorney General's Office. The Demutualization Bill was then presented to Parliament for consideration.

Lobbying for Stakeholders' Support. On 20 November 2009, the DSC for the NSE demutualization process invited Capital Markets Stakeholders to a workshop on demutualization of the NSE in Nairobi. On Tuesday 24th November 2009, the Steering Committee successfully hosted a stakeholders' workshop at the Sarova-Stanley Hotel in Nairobi under the sponsorship of FLSTAP, a World Bank programme under the Ministry of Finance, with the event attracting 150 participants.

The objective of the workshop was to sensitize key stakeholders in the Capital markets on the process and implications of demutualising the exchange and build consensus on the benefits of demutualization, key among them being the restoration of investor confidence in the securities markets. Furthermore, the workshop intended to create a forum for the stakeholders to exchange views on the details of the demutualization project which aimed at reforming the ownership and improve the governance structures of the NSE to make it more attractive to investors and issuers.

The workshop, whose attendance was only by invitation, was officially opened by the then Deputy Prime Minister and Minister for Finance Hon. Uhuru Kenyatta. The forum was addressed by, among other resource persons, the demutualization project consultant Mr. John Carson from Canada, representing the FLSTAP. Invitees who attended include members of Kenya Association of Stockbrokers and Investment Banks (KASIB), Association of Fund Managers, Association of Collective Investment Schemes, representatives of the Government regulatory institutions, listed companies, other financial regulators, legal and financial experts, members of the Board of the CMA, the NSE and the Central Depository and Settlement Corporation (CDSC), and capital markets representatives from the East African Community region, and media.

According to Micah Cheserem, the Chairman of the CMA, demutualization was one of the many initiatives being implemented to restore investor confidence and facilitate the capital markets to effectively perform their role of mobilizing long-term financial resources to support realization of the Kenya Vision 2030 developmental aspirations. The DSC planned to demutualize the NSE by 31st December 2009, after which, the NSE was to undertake internal reforms that would lead to self-listing within a period of 1 to 3 years. At the time of demutualization and during the transition period prior to self-listing of the NSE shares, the shareholding of NSE would be amongst stockbrokers and investment banks who were members of the exchange, and the Investor Compensation Fund and the government.

Upon demutualization, stockbrokers were to have 2-3 seats in an 11-member Board of Directors. Majority of the Board seats were subsequently to be taken up by independent directors with knowledge of the capital markets and who were able to oversee the business of the NSE to maximize shareholder returns. After the transition period the shareholding by members of the NSE were further divest in the demutualized exchange.

As at the 20th November Workshop, the following were the remaining steps of the NSE demutualization process: the draft legal instruments to be presented to Cabinet through the Treasury for approval; publication of the Demutualization Bill by the Attorney General; sensitization of Members of Parliament upon publishing of the Demutualization Bill; debate of the Bill and enactment of the Demutualization Act by Parliament; formal application by NSE for demutualization upon enactment of the Demutualization Act; and the CMA approval to demutualize the NSE.

Approval of Demutualization. On Thursday 4th March 2010, the Members of the NSE held an Extra-Ordinary General Meeting (EGM), which came at a crucial juncture in the history of the exchange as the demutualisation process neared completion. The members of the exchange took cognizance of the remarkable growth of the market since its inception and also noted that with such growth change must follow. The Exchange needed to continually adapt itself to the changing realities of the economy and the market. The decisions made by the members reflected the negotiated position arrived at after extensive consultations and lobbying. The members were also guided on the process and the legal effect of demutualisation by the Chairman of the Legal Sub-Committee of the DSC Mr. George Oraro, a Legal Consultant and Renowned Nairobi Lawyer.

The members unanimously approved: the demutualization of the NSE subject to the coming into force of the relevant provisions of law that provide the legal framework to achieve demutualization; the authorized share capital of the shareholders of the new proposed post demutualised NSE to be Ksh.1 billion; the shareholding in the proposed post demutualised company was be: the current Members – 80 percent; Investor Compensation Fund (ICF)– 10 percent; the Government of Kenya – 10 percent; the proposed post demutualization Memorandum and Articles of Association of the NSE; and authorisation of the Board of Directors of the exchange to deal with any other matters, including statutory requirements, necessary to facilitate the demutualization of the NSE.

The Members again reiterated their commitment towards fostering a vibrant capital market. The resolutions passed were to enable the NSE to effectively play its role in sustainably developing the Kenyan economy. Demutualisation was expected to transform the exchange and position it to realize its vast potential and attain its vision of being a leading securities exchange in Africa, with a global reach.

The NSE thus moved closer to public ownership after the stockbrokers, who controlled it, agreed on an ownership structure that will enable them to sell shares to investors in the planned initial public offering. The long awaited removal of the exchange from the hands of the 20 brokers was to see the government gain a 20 percent shareholding in the exchange leaving the stockbrokers with a collective 80 percent stake. A stakeholders' meeting held in Nairobi therefore agreed to allow the Treasury to get a 10 percent stake in the exchange and an additional 10 percent to be held by the ICF – another State-owned agency that is managed by the market regulator – the Capital Markets Authority.

Under the new ownership structure that was to pave the way for sale of shares to the public, stockbrokers were to get 80 percent of the Sh.850 million exchange and divide it equally among themselves in readiness for the planned IPO. This means that each broker or investment bank was to get an estimated 4 percent of the market but was to remain with much smaller stakes after the public share sale. Each stockbroker was expected to have ceded at least half of their stake in the next two years, according to the regulations meant to take the market public. The new ownership structure was largely in line with the structure that the CMA had tabled before the exchange members as a pre-condition to the planned transfer of the exchange's ownership into the hands of the investing public through demutualisation.

The NSE, which was then ranked as the fifth biggest securities market in Africa by total value of listed shares, had existed as a mutual company owned by stockbrokers since its formation in 1954. But this ownership structure had emerged as a major drawback for the smooth operation of the exchange as the stockbrokers had found it hard to punish rogue counterparts resulting in the collapse of four stockbrokers in as many years.

Reforming Ownership Structure. The Nairobi Stock Exchange had been grappling with the ownership structure for nearly ten years with some of the big stockbrokers insisting that the market-share should be used as the basis of share allocation. However, the smaller players argued that credibility was the value that was being shared and could only be divided equally among all the exchange members. In the 4th March 2010 meeting, the stockbrokers sought to downplay past differences with the State, with NSE Chairman Mr Eddy Njoroge declaring that the decisions made during the March 4th 2010 Workshop by the members reflected the negotiated position arrived at after extensive consultations. Demutualisation was expected to curtail stockbroker's influence on the day-to-day running of the exchange and convert it into a public limited company with an independent board to oversee the exchange's role as a self-regulating organisation. It was one of the ways of continually adapting itself to the changing realities of the economy and the global capital market.

The proposal settled on left out former directors of the NSE and employees who had jointly been proposed for a 10 percent stake in a proposal commissioned by the exchange. The agreed ownership structure was to see the government hold majority stake in the exchange to become the single largest shareholder after the stockbrokers agreed that Treasury will be the sole custodian of the shares that were be allocated to the stockbrokers who were then under statutory management. These include Francis Thuo and Partners, Nyaga Stock Brokers, Discount Securities and Ngenye Kariuki, placed under statutory management because of facing financial distress thus being unable to meet their market obligations. These brokerage firms therefore got a reprieve after all stockbrokers agreed to have them take their proportion of ownership, but their financial benefit were to be transferred to the creditors if they got liquidated.

All the 20 members of the Exchange received equal number of shares, suggesting that a breakthrough had been reached in what was previously also a hotly contentious issue. It was agreed that the ownership separation process was to commence as soon as the demutualization Bill which was still before Parliament was passed into law. The Bill was later passed and gazetted on June 18th 2013. On June 24th 2014, the NSE received a formal approval from the CMA to operate as a demutualized entity and also to self-list its shares on its own trading board.

Upon demutualisation, the NSE changed its name to Nairobi Securities Exchange Limited and an approved share capital of Ksh.1 billion. It was expected that the exchange would gain value over time before its IPO. Thus, the transitional period after demutualisation was to allow time for the exchange to realize its value before selling its shares to the public. The authorized shares of the NSE Ltd were then consolidated into 212.5 million shares of Ksh.4 each totalling to Ksh. 850 million. The exchange then proceeded with its self-listed on 9th September 2014 on its Main Investment Market Segment. Therefore, on September 9th 2014, the NSE listed 194,625,000 shares at a stock price of Ksh. 9.50 per share. This was after a successful IPO which attracted over 17,000 local and foreign investors, where it raised Ksh.4.8 billion in new capital recording an overwhelming subscription rate of 763.9 percent.

Of the twenty stockbrokers who held a combined 59 per cent controlling stake in 2014 when the NSE issued its IPO, eleven have either exited the securities market or substantially reduced their shareholding in the NSE Ltd. Despite Stockbrokers holding a 26.7 percent stake in the NSE Ltd in 2017, foreign investors were controlling over 40.8 percent of the exchange as at the second quarter of 2018, from 36 per cent in 2017.

The NSE Ltd continues to deliver substantial shareholder value in the midst of the volatile macro- economic environment in 2015. Shareholders of the exchange received a payout of Ksh. 0.49 per ordinary share for the year 2015, an increase of 29 percent from the dividend paid in 2014. For the first time since its listing, the exchange made a bonus issue of one new ordinary share for every three fully paid up ordinary shares. This accentuates the company's long-term growth strategy. Overall, the NSE Ltd realized a marginal decrease of Ksh.13.6 million (1.7%) in total income of Ksh.808.3 million compared to 821.9 million the previous year. Profit after tax stood at Ksh.305.6 million, a 4.5 percent decrease in net earnings of Ksh.320 million recorded in 2014. Equity turnover dropped by 3 percent to Ksh.419 billion from Ksh.431 billion and fixed income market performance declined by 39.7 percent from Ksh.1.012 billion in 2014 to Ksh.610 million in 2015.

This financial performance in 2015 was impacted by the introduction of the capital gains tax that had a negative effect on trading activity. In addition, the rise in interest rates and volatility of the currency also impeded market performance. In spite of the decline in profit, the exchange was confident of better performance in the coming years in light of the new products the exchange was to be bringing to market. The NSE company was to continue to deepen shareholder value as evidenced in the increase in dividend payout for 2015. The exchange was working towards a future improvement in performance through its growth strategy initiatives such as the launch of new products which include derivatives trading, exchange traded funds ETFs, while aggressively seeking new listings in its existing product lines. The exchange has also upgraded its automated trading system to support its new product and service offerings.

Other developments at the NSE include the 2015 launch of day trading aimed at increasing market liquidity and volatility, exchange traded funds in 2017, the 2019 introduction of the NSE derivatives market (NEXT) to facilitate trading of securities market equity index futures and single stock futures in the Kenyan market, as well as the 2020 launch of the re-modulated Automated Traded System to support the trading of new equity and quasi-equity instruments in a robust platform with dynamic surveillance capabilities.

The NSE, the fifth biggest by market capitalisation in Africa, already owns a 4.9 percent stake in neighbouring DSE, and is eyeing acquisition in other exchanges like NGX and BSE following their demutualisation as a way of becoming a Pan-African exchange. Lastly, the exchange also became the fourth stock exchange in Africa to join the United Nations Sustainable Stock Exchanges which works towards enhancing corporate transparency among financial markets. It has also participated on the development of regulations for the introduction of securities lending and borrowing in an effort to enhance liquidity in the securities market.

Demutualization of Botswana Stock Exchange

The modern day Botswana Stock Exchange Limited (BSEL) traces its origins to the Botswana Share Market (BSM) that was established in 1989. Back then there was only one stockbroker (Stockbrokers Botswana) and it created the market by matching orders from the public on the shares of the then five listed firms. The buoyancy of Botswana's economy led to more firms and more stockbrokers coming to the market and ultimately creation of the BSE in 1994 through an Act of Parliament.

Following the establishment of the BSE as a securities exchange resulted in the BSE opening for trading in 1995. The securities exchange was owned by its member-stockbrokers through ownership of Proprietary Rights as well as the Government of Botswana. Proprietary Rights were defined in the BSE Act as a share in the assets of the exchange acquired for the purposes of registering as a member of the exchange in order to trade on the exchange.

Historically, government has provided majority of the financing targeted at developing the BSE infrastructure and undertaking market development initiatives, and jointly, government and stockbrokers have played a vital role of developing various facets of the BSE and the market as a whole. This includes establishing a favourable regulatory environment, driving marketing efforts and investor awareness, among others. This ownership of a securities exchange by a government is a common practice globally in many developing markets.

The Demutualization Process. The commencement of demutualizing the exchange came on 1st December 2015, when the BSE (Transition) Act of 2015 came into operation to initiate the process of conversion of the BSE from a mutual exchange to a public company limited by shares under the Companies Act. The BSE Transition Act was primarily aimed at governing this process by outlining the details of conduct of the BSE whilst it is undergoing conversion, following conversion, and defining the powers of the relevant stakeholders overseeing the transition of the BSE during this period, being the Minister in the Ministry of Finance and Economic Development. Although BSE was regarded as a mutual entity, it was by and large a parastatal, thus belonging to the Government of Botswana.

The Main Committee of the BSE, comprising of representatives of stockbrokers and Government representatives, whose responsibility was to oversee the affairs of the BSE played a strategic role in the commencement of the demutualization. As the BSE would become a company, the BSE Act would become repealed effective the date of conversion and in its place would be the Companies Act, which then required the promulgation of the Constitution of the BSEL as a governing document of the exchange with respect to governance issues.

Valuation of the Botswana Stock Exchange. Some of the heated issues that delay demutualization include the allocation of shareholding in the new company by way of converting the Proprietary Rights (ownership of the brokers) and the capital injection by Government into shares on the company. By and large, the BSE has operated with just four members for a long time, each having a certain number of Proprietary Rights amounting to various amounts. Government has financially supported the Exchange for many years by way of a subvention, majority of which has gone towards the development of the BSE's technology infrastructure and initiatives around market development. For purposes of demutualisation these investments by both stock brokers and the Government had to be converted into shares in the BSEL. Based on global best practise, the Main Committee of the BSE appointed an independent consultant in 2017 to determine the value of the exchange and attribute shareholding of the BSE between the brokers and Government, and among the brokers as individual shareholders, and make a report with the recommendations.

Allocation of the BSE Limited' Shareholding. Given that the Transition Act stipulates that the shareholding of the Company shall be open to Government, securities brokers, employees of the Exchange and members of the public, consultant's share allocation recommendations were to be line with the same, thus the provision formed the basis for apportioning the share capital of the BSE. However, an independent valuation by an independent consultant – appointed through an open international tender which was impressively contested for – was to provide the appropriate, independent and objective basis for such allocation and subsequent determination by the Minister of Finance and Economic Development. The process of determining the share capital, value of the exchange and the attribution of shareholding in the BSE was completed in November 2017, by a consultant.[183] This was an impressively shorter period of time from the commencement of the Transition Act, which was just under 24 months.

In line with the provisions of the Transition Act, the Minister had the power to determine the shareholding of the BSEL, therefore, the independent valuation and share attribution report merely provided guidance, anchored on fundamentals, independence and objectivity, to this crucial decision. Perhaps, owing to the meticulousness of the report,

---

183 Benza, B. (2017). Botswana Stock Exchange to self-list after demutualization. https://www. african-markets.com/en/stock-markets/bse/botswana-stock-exchange-to-self-list-after-demutualization

the Minister approved the shareholding of the Exchange as presented in the report, paving a way for each of the four brokers to then take note of their individual shareholding on the basis of the number of Proprietary Rights held by each. The ministerial approval signalled the commencement of the conversion of the securities exchange by way of registration of the company by Companies and Intellectual Property Authority.

On 2 August 2018, the Companies and Intellectual Property Authority completed the registration of the securities exchange as a public company limited by shares accordance with the Companies Act. This is therefore the day of the full demutualization of the exchange to a company called Botswana Stock Exchange Limited (BSEL). In line with Section 12 of the Transition Act, the BSE Act was the repealed to be in tandem with the conversion.

Transition from Parastatal to Exchange Company. The complete conversion of the of the exchange to a company called BSEL through demutualization represented a historic milestone for Botswana and the capital market as a whole. This has been a fairly shorter process, and one that was characterized by diplomacy and a concerted mission by the management of the exchange, the members of the exchange and Government of Botswana to modernize the domestic securities market. The conversion happened at the time that the exchange was one-year shy of its 30 years of existence. This evolution elevated the position of the BSE in the African continent, as just a few of the then 28 members of the ASEA servicing 32 countries in Africa, have demutualized whilst just 4 have proceeded to self-list. The full demutualization of the securities exchange to a company called BSE Limited represented a historic milestone for Botswana and the capital market as a whole.

Arguably, the milestone was worth undertaking looking at the various facets of the organisation itself and the need to promote the competitiveness of the securities exchange in the face of global competition and its internationalization strategy. The BSE was converted to a Government Parastatal through an Act of Parliament in 1994, having operated as an informal share market. In the earlier years, the BSE was mainly funded by Brokers through the purchase of Proprietary Rights from time to time. In subsequent years, Government started funding the exchange through a subvention primarily financing the capital projects of the exchange and its market development activities. This investment gradually translated into improved performance of the market which positively impacted the performance of the organisation. In 2012, the exchange moved from negative profitability position to one characterised by generation of significant profits annually.

Balancing Public Interests and Profit Motives. Traditionally, securities exchanges are viewed as institutions for public good and being a government parastatal, the exchange was seen as a national strategic asset that operates for the broader and more inclusive benefits of all the citizens. This perception was expressed in the various activities that the exchange was undertaking, those which being undertaken to promote the reach of the exchange, the inclusion of all in the securities market and without due priority to lament on the cost or expect a return on investment.

As a public good, a securities exchange exists to provide three basic functions to the public. These include: Allocation, where they are a platform on which scarce capital is allocated to worthy investments; Valuation – in which they assist in the price discovery of the listed securities and this is achieved by ensuring transparency and nurturing liquidity in the securities market; and Control in which they are also tasked with ascertaining that shareholders have meaningful control of their firms by protecting and upholding the rights of the minority shareholders.

These three functions ought to be equally pursued by securities exchanges, because if there is inefficiency in one function there will be market disequilibrium. There would be an instance where there is poor disclosure by issuers – caused by laxity in regulation by the securities exchange – leads to inaccurate market pricing, which in turn leads to inefficient allocation of capital in the market. Such has the risk of distorting rewards in the market and further threaten the stability of the market.

Therefore, a transition from a parastatal to a fully demutualized securities exchange operating as a company or a corporate poses one fundamental challenge in that the exchange has to reconcile being responsible for providing a public good with maximizing profit for its shareholders. The primary sources of income for securities exchanges are listings and annual sustaining fees as well as trading fees. On one hand, if the exchange is to impose the burden of responsibilities and obligations on its issuers in favour of protecting the investors, it may crowd out the issuers and therefore lose out on the listings and annual sustaining fees, and thereby fail to maximize shareholder return. On the other hand, there is a possibility that a securities exchange might relax its regulation so as to attract and keep issuers for their fees, much to the detriment of the investors.

As such, it is important that demutualization efforts are preceded by bolstering and adequately capitalizing the supervision of the securities market. A was explained earlier, most markets have set up standalone public agencies, regulatory authorities and securities exchange commissions that regulate the capital markets. In the case of Botswana, the Non-Bank Financial Institutions Regulatory Authority, being the regulator of BSE Limited, with the Market Act is well equipped to accommodate this regulatory conundrum of ensuring adequate supervision of a securities exchange pursuing for-profit objectives whilst balancing the protection of investors and ensuring adequate compliance by the listed firms.

As a way of improving the financial sufficiency of securities exchanges and cushion the heavy reliance on listing fees, annual sustaining fees and trading fees, some securities exchanges have sought to increase revenues by expanding their product offerings to include post-trade services as well as information and data services. This has helped to diversify exchange revenue from the main sources, and BSEL also has in the pipeline a number of new revenue sources it plans to create.

Post Demutualization BSE Ltd. The corporatisation of the BSE by way of demutualization has been well thought out in the manner in which the securities exchange has gradually been behaving like a corporate entity. So far, the exchange has successfully balanced the public interests and profit motive. The BSEL has over the years been embarking on initiatives to diversify its revenue streams, whilst putting in place robust programs to equally rationalise expenditure. The exchange has signed several data vending agreements with international data vendors. Besides promoting the visibility of the exchange and enhancing the reach of market statistics, these have generated new revenue for the exchange. This brings in an immense potential for an exchange which owns the Central Securities Depository in the country, which also functions as a data repository with respect to listed and unlisted instruments and can offer a broad range of cash generating services at its maximum capacity. The pre and post-trade data services represent a growing income avenue for the exchange.

Notably, there has been modernization also in the manner in which the exchange has undertaken its market development initiatives. Before demutualization, the exchange used to undertake public roadshows across various places primarily in various public arenas and these would be characterized by entertainment to pull the crowd. This was a necessary mode of execution given the low levels of awareness at the time, the myths and misconceptions about the securities market and the low retail investor participation in the securities market. As the financial literary improved over the years, along with retail participation from as low as 3 percent to 15 percent, the exchange has remodelled this approach to be represented by highly targeted Open Days, still open for free to the public and also introduced targeted annual listings and investment conference to cultivate the supply side of the market. As an institution moving towards corporatization, the remodelling of these highlighted activities was inevitable as, as a corporate, the focus will be on striking an optimal balance between attaining shareholder expectations without compromising the broader reach and inclusion of everyone in the securities market, more so that the government remains the majority shareholder in the demutualized exchange – but this stake will need to be reduced because worldwide, governments are not known to be good investors.

These aspirations of becoming a competitive corporate and a world-class securities exchange are enshrined in the Strategic Plan 2017-2021, whose design had foresight to the demutualization of the exchange. The strategies are highly cost and revenue conscious, there is greater indication of product and services diversification, a shift towards optimising the technology infrastructure, commitment towards building a conducive regulatory environment, human capital uplifting and traction towards previously unchartered territories such as the derivatives market. The BSE Limited, however, will refine its strategic plan to capture post-demutualization initiatives.

BSE Limited and the Self-Regulatory Issues. Demutualization and self-listing of a securities exchange presents a number of conundrums and one such is to do with maintaining an optimal balance between serving its regulatory functions and pursuing its corporate objective without jeopardy to its stakeholders. A common and widely observed practise is to delegate a demutualized securities exchange a Self-Regulatory Organization status. Earlier, it was noted that an SRO is an organization whose object is to regulate the operations of its members or of the users of its services and include the organizations that may be recognised as such. Under this status, the exchange maintains its primary regulatory functions of developing listing requirements, enforcing compliance by listed firms with the listing requirements, facilitating listings and trading and conducting market surveillance. These may be financially demanding functions in the context of an increasingly competitive environment. However, not doing these functions can be detrimental to the reputation of an exchange and the definition of the securities market as a whole, whereas doing them may be unfavourable to the value maximisation objective of the exchange.

So why does an exchange strive to maintain an optimal balance? It had been explained earlier that there are several approaches which have been explored and adopted to deal with this. For example, when the Stockholm Stock Exchange demutualized it created an independent Disciplinary Committee to handle compliance of the exchange with its own listing requirements. Prior to this, the function had been handled by the Board of the exchange. The securities exchange law was later amended to require that all authorised exchanges organise such committees. When the JSE demutualized and self-listed its shares listing requirements were amended to include the establishment of the SRO Oversight Committee which was a Board Sub-Committee responsible for overseeing the issuer regulation and market regulation functions of JSE Limited. Subsequently, compliance of JSE Limited with its own listings requirements was seconded to the financial market regulator, the Financial Services Board. These two examples represent some of the strategies used to work around promoting the independence and objectiveness of the exchange with respect to its regulatory function and the compliance of the exchange to its own listing requirements in order to ensure that the exchange discharges its functions in a manner that is transparent and equitable to all.

These efforts have been made as a means of regulating the SRO. In the case of Botswana, the Non-Bank Financial Institutions Regulatory Authority regulates the exchange and the regulatory Act provides that an institution such as BSE Limited can be declared a SRO. However, if declared, the status will not absolve the exchange of its supervision by market regulatory Authority, which will therefore continue with its role of approving any rules, including the amendment of listings requirements. In fact, Sec. 36 of the regulatory Act outlines this relationship and due process by SRO in detail.

Recent developments are that the Authority is undertaking this assessment regarding BSEL being declared a SRO and will submit a recommendation to the Minister of Finance who will make this declaration. The declaration of SRO status will evolve and possibly expand when BSE Limited progresses to the next phase of its development which is a self-listing at a future point in time. International best practice suggests that once BSEL is self-listed, it will continue to regulate firms and securities listed, the listings and trading platform, and the market regulatory Authority will regulate BSE Limited with the same set of listing requirements that BSE Limited uses to regulate companies listed on its platform. This way, the demutualized exchange will be subjected to the same regulations used to oversight the other listed firms.

The BSEL is currently in the sixth year of its five-year strategy in which it, amongst others, aims to grow the ratio of the BSEL's market capitalisation to gross domestic product from 34 percent to 40 percent by 2021 as well as increase the number of domestic companies listed from 24 to 30 by 2021. In the 2016 financial year, the BSE realised revenues of P31.7 million and posted a profit of P8.4 million.

Demutualization of Zimbabwe Stock Exchange

Zimbabwe has three securities exchanges: Zimbabwe Stock Exchange (ZSE), Victoria Falls Stock Exchange (VFEX), Financial Securities Exchange (Private) Limited (FINSEC). Of these, the Zimbabwe Stock Exchange planned to demutualize by seeking to transform itself into a company limited by shares and at the same time update its member rules and listing requirements to synchronize them with the Securities Act (Chapter 24:25) and Statutory Instrument 100 of 2010. The ZSE, one of the oldest exchanges on the continent, was before the demutualisation exercise, controlled by stockbrokers through a mutual society.

The Securities Exchange Commission (SEC) in September 2013 was seeking to procure the services of a legal advisor who was to work in close co-operation with appointed financial advisors, the ZSE and other stakeholders as appropriate, to provide legal advice generally regarding the transformation process, prepare the founding documents to corporatize the ZSE, review and align member rules to current legislation and the transformation objective, and review the proprietary rights of current members of the ZSE and their entitlement, if any, to shareholding in the new corporatized ZSE.

Reforming the Market Regulation. The explicit objectives of the consultancy included:[184] legal advice on the best transformation process; incorporation of the ZSE as a corporate body limited by shares; legal advice on the completeness of the Membership register and the proprietary rights entitlement; legal advice on the equity entitlement of proprietary rights in the ZSE as currently constituted and in the corporatized ZSE; and review and alignment of member rules to current legislation and in sync with the transformation objective. Any legal analysis or advice was to focus on the legal risk, liabilities and compliance as at 31 July 2013 - the effective date.

Acting on behalf of the ZSE the consultant was required to assist and advise Corporate Excellence and Imara Corporate Finance Zimbabwe (the Advisors) on the following three issues:[185] first, the current contractual obligations was to include an investigation into and comment on all outstanding material disputes, including but not limited to pending lawsuits, unpaid or disputed claims of any nature and unresolved labour settlements; confirmation of the status of any lease, marketing, service,

---

184 See, The Tender Notice: Zimbabwe Stock Exchange – Demutualisation Terms of Reference For Legal Advice. September 4th 2013.

185 See, http://wwww.zimbabwe-stock-exchange.com/profiles/investor/ResLibraryView.asp?

employment, or supply agreements that may be in existence with various agents and/or customers, in particular whether any of these agreements may become void or expire as a consequence of demutualization; and assistance with regard to the transfer, innovation re-execution, as the case may be, in respect of said agreements in favour of the demutualized entity.

Second, in terms of the regulatory environment, the consultants were to summarize the regulatory environment within which the ZSE operated and the level of regulatory risk inherent in the ZSE's operations; provide an overview of the reporting responsibilities of the ZSE Compliance function. Including local regulators, international regulators overseeing the financial markets/ activities in which the ZSE is active, such as securities dealers, and commodity trading. Third, in terms of corporate governance issues, the assignment was to focus conceptually on separation of ownership and membership. The Advisor was required to assist and advice on the following; scrutiny of the existing general legislation and provisions in the existing legislation and the current Member Rules, and making recommendations as to whether provisions of Member Rules should be added or deleted, including proposed amendments; re-drafting founding documents to deal solely with company matters.

The ZSE Constitution needed to be replaced with Memorandum and Articles of Association, and regulation of rights and obligations between shareholders and between shareholders and the company need to be defined. The advisors also required specific advice on converting from a mutual society to a company with share capital, including conversion of rights to shares and removal of linkages between membership and ownership; and the advice on converting the current ZSE board to a corporate board compliant with best practice from a governance perspective. They were expected also to be available during the assignment to advise the ZSE, the financial advisors and other stakeholders on an ad-hoc basis to ensure a successful transformation process by the end of the 1st week of October 2013 – the closing date.

The Legal Advisor was to work directly with the Financial Advisors and the ZSE or other agents the ZSE may appoint as appropriate. In seeking to attain the objectives stated, they were to carry out the work as specified under the scope of work and any additional work they deem necessary to meet the objectives, and ensure that knowledge of the process and methodology of the work were, whenever possible, transferred to suitable representatives of the ZSE. The Legal Advisors were to provide a detailed plan of work, including milestones and reviews required by the Financial Advisors and the ZSE for progress monitoring to ensure conclusion by the closing date. The key deliverables were expected to include: litigation statement; cessation by current body and assumption of existing contracts by new body; transformation structure/route legal advice; ZSE body corporate founding documents and incorporation; and updated/revised member rules. The Commission expected applications to be sent by electronic mail before close of business of 6th September 2013.[186]

Delays to Demutualization. Despite the above efforts, the demutualization of the ZSE was already facing a fresh hurdle with six non-participating members said to be demanding substantial shares in the new entity. The ZSE was in the process of transforming itself into a company limited by shares and at the same time updating its member rules and listing requirements to synchronize them with the Securities Act. Under a recommendation, Government was to own 54 percent shareholding in the new company while the remaining stake was to be distributed among stockbrokers.

While the distribution formula was being worked on, it emerged that some non-practicing stockbrokers had demanded a substantial stake on strength they purchase proprietary rights. Furthermore, the non-practicing stockbrokers contended that they had been paying quarterly fees to the exchange and therefore had a claim to the assets of the exchange. But what had riled other stockbrokers was the amount of shares the non-members were demanding despite not contributing to the brokerage fees, market sources. These non-paying members included Trudy Chashel and Mike van Bleck.[187] At some point, the ZSE wanted to deregister them but that failed after the High Court ruled against the Exchange and they seemed to

---

186 To: legaladvice@zse.co.zw

187 See, the Herald (2013) ZSE Demutualization Faces Fresh Hurdle. http://www.herald.co.zw/
zse-demutualisation-faces-fresh-hurdle/, December 3rd.

be riding on that. They had kept on paying fees and on that strength, they needed to be allocated some shares.

In 2012, the stockbrokers also had a misunderstanding with the Government over the ownership of the Exchange, arguing that since they pay proprietary rights then they were entitled to be owners of the exchange. However, it can be argued that merely purchasing the proprietary rights does not translate to ownership but gives the brokers the right to use the Exchange and make a profit out of it. The ZSE operations executive Martin Matanda reported that while the demutualization process was progressing, he was not aware of how the shares would be allocated among brokers. However, the SEC of Zimbabwe chief executive Alban Chirume reported that the demutualization would proceed despite emerging controversies. Earlier in 2013, Chirume said the demutualization of the Exchange would be completed by end of 2013 but the new entity would not immediately self-list. The self-listing would not be looked at immediately but would be considered in the medium to long term.

Conversion into a Limited Company. In pursuance of the demutualisation process, a new company known as the Zimbabwe Stock Exchange Limited was registered under the Companies Act (Chapter 24:03) on December 31 2014. The functions and operations of the new company remained the same as that of a securities exchange regulated under the earlier Securities and Exchange Act (Chapter 24:25). The Companies Act (Chapter 24:03) was to continue providing the governance framework, capital structure and financial reporting requirements and obligations.

Allocation of Share Ownership. Under the processes of demutualisation, the ZSE was corporatized first where it changed its name although the Government was to be 100 percent shareholder. Soon after the corporatisation, there was a capital raising, which was to bring in various Government-related institutions for the majority stake (in this case the 54 percent) while the stockbrokers, the public and/or a strategic partner were to take up the rest. Once demutualisation was complete the exchange was to democratize and create a second-tier exchange or more exchanges.

The Exchange also changed its name to Zimbabwe Stock Exchange Ltd. Stockbrokers and the government were in the interim to own 68 percent and 32 percent, respectively. This equity stakes would later be halved to 34 percent and 16 percent, respectively to attract new investors. The remaining 50 percent equity stake was to be shared among private financial institutions and individuals.

Post-Demutualization Performance. By July 2016, the ZSE had effectively completed its demutualisation exercise after it held its first meeting as a private company in July 2016. However, it reported a US$1.1 million loss for the full year to December 2015 compared to a profit of US$300,000 in prior comparative period owing to weak trades. The weakening of share prices across the board resulted in a significant drop in market capitalisation of 29 percent from US$4.327 billion recorded on December 31 2014 to US$3.073 billion recorded on 31st December 2015. According to minutes of the ZSE Ltd annual general meeting (AGM) held in July 2016, the ZSE fears a gloomy outlook.[188] The decline in market turnover had a significant impact on the profitability which declined from a surplus of US$0.338 million in 2014 to a deficit of US$1.101 million incurred during the financial year ending December 31 2015.

The board took a decision to fair value the investment in Chengetedzai Depository Company (Private) Limited and this resulted in an impairment charge of US$0.381 million to the profit or loss. Expenditure related to the implementation of the ATS, property development and the once-off costs had a further negative impact on the performance of the Exchange. The ZSE Ltd anticipates that the operating environment will remain challenging and this calls for innovative business processes and solutions. At the macro-economic level, the foreign debt arrears clearance strategy being spearheaded by the Ministry of Finance and Economic Development was anticipated to unlock fresh funding and encourage foreign direct investment.

As at 2016, the Exchange was planned to seek partnerships with major data vendors such as Bloomberg and Thompson Reuters to ensure that its market data is easily accessible to investors worldwide. The ZSE Ltd

---

188 Mpofu, B. (2016). Zimbabwe Stock Exchange Demutualisation Exercise Done. Zimbabwe Independent, July 11th. Zimbabwe.

is mindful of the high market charges that make it less competitive than other regional exchanges. ZSE will continue to lobby the government in order to have the charges reduced or associated taxes removed altogether in order to stimulate trading.

Planning for Self-listing. The ZSE has been over the years planning to perform an IPO on itself but lacked regulation to facilitate self-listing. In April 2023, the Securities and Exchange Commission of Zimbabwe developed Securities Exchange (Self-Listing) Rules for Exchanges to guide exchanges wishing to self-list following demutualization. The Act gives the Commission powers to list and supervise the listed exchange. The implication is that in the near future, the Exchange has no intension to remain as unlisted company.

Enhancing Demutualization of African Securities Exchanges

Experience from countries where demutualization has taken place show that many issues arise during and after demutualization. Evidence from Europe, Oceania, America, and Asian Pacific reveal that certain preconditions are important for successful demutualization of securities exchanges. Let us look at these issues.

Self-Listing. In order to achieve the full benefits of ownership and management restructuring, demutualization is not simply turning into a for-profit entity owned by members. A truly demutualised securities exchange would be better placed if it were able to unlock its hidden value for all stakeholders in order to maximize its potential market capitalization and shareholder value. Being self-listed is likely to improve the value of an exchange to operate more efficiently. More often than not, demutualization is just an interim step for many exchanges in their evolution. Post-demutualization, the exchange can evolve further by listing on its own platform, and this is referred to as self-listing. Globally, a number of securities exchanges progressed to self-list after they demutualized as a way of further enhancing their governance and competitiveness given that a listing expands the shareholder base and enables access to deeper pools of capital.

Early examples of securities exchanges that underwent a self-listing are the Stockholm Stock Exchange AB in Sweden, Australian Stock Exchange, Hong Kong Stock Exchange and Singapore Stock Exchange. As time progressed Deutsche Bourse, LSE, Euronext and Nasdaq followed suit. The same phenomenon has been experienced in Africa. For example, the JSE was the first stock exchange in Africa to self-list in 2006 following its demutualization in 2005. The NSE self-listed in 2014 in the same year that it demutualized. The most recent self-listing in Africa was by the Dar es Salaam Stock Exchange in 2016, a year after its demutualization in 2015. Notwithstanding, few of the demutualized exchanges in Africa, such as Zimbabwe Stock Exchange, Stock Exchange of Mauritius, and Bourse de Casablanca, Botswana Exchange remain unlisted. Therefore, African exchanges should include self-listing in their demutualization plans.

Improving Profitability. The justification for demutualizing African securities exchanges in terms of the mobilization of resources for investment and the unlocking of securities exchange value depends on the assumption that these exchanges will be profitable in future. Excluding Johannesburg, Egypt, Nigeria, Kenya, and Mauritius, African securities markets operate below breakeven due to their small sizes. Since most of them rely on states and donors to financially support their functions, demutualization is unlikely to result in more resources.

Financial Sustainability. Successful demutualization of a securities exchange implies that there must exist a market justification based on a critical mass of trading activity that supports financial viability. Demutualization calls for exchange's ability to raise more capital and make investment that bring home more revenues, other than from traditional sources like membership subscription fees, listing fees, trading charges, clearing and settlement fees, and fees from sale of listed company news and quote data. African securities exchanges operate at a deficit and have enjoyed financial support from government and donors. As stand-alone entities, some may become insolvent. African securities exchanges must develop profitable operation driven by well-developed economies, market size and business strategies. They must also possess the ability to introduce new financial products to increase liquidity and turnover since for-profit demutualized structure does not guarantee profitable existence. Securities market regulators must be able to closely monitor the financial condition of demutualized exchanges. In Australia a reserve fund was created to provide a capital cushion, while in Canada provides an early warning system whereby a demutualized securities exchange is required to maintain certain financial rations and to notify market regulators whenever they seem not to in compliance. African exchanges may consider these options if they are to become financially sustainable.

Mechanism for Dealing with Conflicts-of-Interests. Demutualization raises many questions about the regulation of securities exchanges. Traditionally, exchanges are self-regulating, in which they set trading rules, conduct surveillance and enforcing the rules; market manipulation, oversee the trading system to avoid abuses; establish rules governing the conduct of their members; and monitor compliance with the rules. Attempts to maximize profits could undermine self-regulation.

Demutualized African exchanges can establish a separate entity to conduct regulatory functions, thereby avoiding conflict-of-interest issues like has been seen in other countries. Nasdaq has created two subsidiaries, Nasd Regulation Inc – regulatory arm, and the Nasdaq Securities Market – commercial trading arm). They can also outsource their regulation to a third party. This approach may help avoid the perception of conflict of interest. However, the third party regulator must be accountable and perform its functions effectively. Most conflicts in demutualization already exist with the mutual exchanges like the temptation to hurry through a lot of listings is high even for mutual securities exchanges.

Demutualization may aggravate this due to stronger profit motive, unless the listing approval is taken away from the securities exchange. In Africa where regulatory systems are fragile, an effective relationship between the for-profit securities exchange and the market regulator must be forged, and investor confidence maintained. African securities market regulators must be a significant player in the exchange demutualization process. There is also a need to establish a dispute resolution system to resolve conflicts of interest among securities exchange members, and between the exchanges and securities markets regulator.

Risk Management & Investor Protection. Development of sophisticated risk management tools for the capital market is critical. The more securities exchanges improve their risk management techniques, the more investors are protected and transparency increased. Areas worth considering may include capital adequacy ratios, margin trading rules, short-selling regulations, etcetera. African securities exchanges must have the capability to provide investor protection by improving good corporate governance and disclosure mechanisms of listed firms.

Further Market Liberalization. Capital gain taxes discourage securities investments. Capital accounts are also not conducive for the creation of a for-profit securities exchange as they could inhibit exchanges' abilities to implement business strategies like cross-border dealings. Africa must sufficiently liberalize its capital market where for-profit exchanges can survive with new business strategies.

Commitment from all Stakeholders. The most important task to demutualized exchanges is remaining financially viable. The road to demutualization is a complex one that requires total commitment from former broker-owners, managers and the state. The process of demutualization seems to have been uneven between developed, emerging, and developing securities markets. In developing and emerging markets, the decision-making process is largely policy-led while in developed markets it is market-led. Because the impact of market forces may not be at the same level as a developed market, securities exchange restructuring issues are considered from the perspective of national policy.

Strong support by the state is needed to resolve thorny issues like how to allocate ownership of an exchange that was limited by guarantee prior to demutualization, and the relationship between the market regulator and a demutualized securities exchange. The post-demutualization also calls for continued state support and the support from other stakeholders. Valuation of shares held in a securities exchange is complex and challenging and a critical issue demutualization since before demutualization, broker-owners may own seats, which have to be converted into monetarized shares. Accommodating all stakeholders will be crucial or else, demutualization efforts in Africa would collapse.

Chapter Summary

There seems to be no a one-size-fits-all demutualization model. There are several exchange governance models, based on local business practices and cultural patterns. Larger and financially sustainable securities exchanges in Africa should be the ones to think of demutualization. Once a demutualization decision is made, African exchanges must desist from rushing. They should move cautiously through preparation, detailed process, and post-demutualization, while viewing it as a long-term objective for growth, development and sustainability. The factors that have fuelled demutualization in developed and the larger emerging markets are largely absent from Africa. In addition, the key preconditions such as a sufficiently liberalized market and critical mass of exchange trading and related services do not exist in most African securities markets. However, there are few African securities exchanges that may have the readiness for demutualization, especially the larger securities exchanges with market capitalization and listings that are adequate to sustain profitable operations upon demutualization and whose markets are currently sufficiently liberalized.

Therefore, for mutual African securities exchanges, potential conflict of interest could pose huge problems, since current regulatory structures are still undergoing restructuring to meet international standards. In many African countries, the establishment of formal securities exchanges preceded the creation of formal independent securities regulators. However, it could also be argued that perhaps being a private venture, demutualized exchanges could speed up the formation of strong regulatory systems in Africa. The policy of demutualization should not be of immediate concern to most African exchanges. The reason is that most African exchanges have barely existed for three decades, and are grappling with teething issues of poor infrastructure and illiquidity. Demutualization would, therefore, be more relevant in the medium to long-term when the teething issues have been properly managed. Indeed, demutualization should be the step after African markets have consolidated gains on improving liquidity problems and strengthening cooperation through market integration.

African securities exchanges must however avoid pressure from the World Bank and other donors to demutualize. They should seize control of the demutualization agenda and only move when the objective and conditions are favourable to them. Demutualization does not have to be an all-or-nothing model. Securities exchanges that do not have the necessary preconditions for demutualization at this time should consider demutualization as a long-run objective. In the transition period, which may be long for many exchanges in Africa, some of the benefits of demutualization can be partially captured by re-engineering of Africa's mutual exchanges through corporate governance, increasing representation of non-members; continuous improvement in trading and post-trade technology to remain competitive and avoid possible migration of liquidity as firms mature on their exchanges. Continuous market liberalization will enhance the prospects of the demutualized securities exchange.

Finally, improving corporate governance is not just a box ticking exercise, thus African exchanges need a wealth of experience and practical guidance in order to conceive and implement successful demutualization. Training on capital markets development and modern day investment strategies are a critical as balancing majority and minority shareholders' interests. Exit routes and dispute settlement mechanisms are needed to deal with conflicts-of-interest that may arise during demutualization. The Egyptian Exchanges' experience shows how an emerging market can integrate successfully corporate governance principles to improve its capitalization and liquidity. The journey has been started by JSE, NSE, DSE, NGX, USE, BSE and ZSE, therefore, other African exchanges should learn from their experiences as a demutualized exchange and solder on. Admittedly these African demutualization cases pose a challenge for advocacy for a regional exchange for SADC, WAEMU, CEMAC and EAC. This is because a regional exchange in these jurisdictions in the near future is expected to be demutualized given the current stance of the above demutualized African exchanges.

Chapter Nine

MUTUAL SECURITIES EXCHANGE STRUCTURE AND EFFICIENCY OF ATTRACTING LISTING

Introduction

In this chapter, a deliberate departure from the existing literature on demutualization is made by considering the possibility that the non-profit form actually created important efficiencies that could be lost upon demutualization. The nonprofit member firm is therefore viewed as a more efficient form of exchange organization than the newly emerging for-profit securities exchanges. Later, the chapter speculates on why an entity would choose to demutualize when doing so would be inefficient. To analyze the nonprofit exchange structure as the solution to an information problem, this chapter applies the theory that views a nonprofit as a consumer-owned entity.

In particular, the discussion describes a general model of nonprofits in which the highest demanding consumers of a non-rival good organize themselves to produce that good together. In the case of a securities exchange, the non-rival good is the liquidity, which is viewed as the ability to act in the market as a price-taker and which provides enormous benefits to issuing firms and investors. The high demanders are financial intermediaries. Therefore, the focus is on investment banks for the purposes of understanding the inherent lemons problem. As intermediaries between large investors and firms seeking to issue securities, these investment banks have special access to information from issuing firms. Demutualization was also expected to enable securities exchanges to grow through attraction of more firms to gain listing. But, majority of these for-profit exchanges, especially in emerging markets like in Africa, seem to be struggling in this effort.

Complexity of Demutualization Process

The move to demutualize has been less straightforward than the literature suggests. If demutualization were in fact more efficient, why does it take so long to implement? The possibility of alternative trading systems based on computerized networks first emerged in the 1960s. The argument that the private club-like form of securities exchanges was archaic was vetted in the 1930s. Yet, the first exchange to demutualize was in 1993. As early as 2004, for example, the Nairobi Stock Exchange had expressed its desire to shift to for-profit form and its board had already begun the process. In September 11th 2006, the NSE again announced, during the launch of its automated trading system, that it would demutualize and even self-list in three years. Then in November 2007, the NSE signed a memorandum of understanding of dual listing of stocks between the Uganda Securities Exchange (USE) and itself. This marked the beginning of the first major step towards its merger with USE and transformation from a nonprofit membership organization to a standard for-profit corporation. This process was only completed in 2014 after many false starts and severe arm-twisting of stockbrokers by the Kenya government.

Demutualization was needed to assure the continued competitiveness and position of the NSE as the world's pre-eminent equity market. The decision to change its organizational form caped a decade-long trend among securities exchanges around the world. Yet the NSE delayed the change, probably due to the apparent internal tensions. It took several years and a change in leadership of the exchange to accomplish demutualization. Significant shifts in NSE governance structure have been rare and stability has been the norm. The two most notable constitutional moments for the NSE, prior to its transition, occurred in 1991 when it was registered as a company guaranteed by shares. It then slightly opened up its board to outside directors representing the investing public, listed companies and institutional investors.

The entrenched interests of insular securities exchange members may have delayed the inevitable. In fact, when the move to demutualize was finally made in the wake of the change in management, the media's view was that the NSE leadership had blocked the reforms in order to protect those entrenched interests. But the leadership also raised many of the same arguments as those found in the scholarly literature. If the presumed leading defender of insular member interests at the securities exchange was in favor of for-profit status yet was unable to carry out such a reform, an alternative explanation for the failure to complete the transition much earlier than 2014 is required. The nonprofit form benefited members, as well as the issuing firms and investors they served, and thus preserving that structure was rational. One can only speculate as to the reasons for the delay. The NSE Chairman, Jimnah Mbaru's push for a change was met with internal tension, a tension that may have reflected debate over the relative value of retaining the hostage system versus the potential for short term gains by selling out one's membership.

The arguments in favour of demutualization offered typically contend that a for-profit firm is better able to make new investments, especially in technology, and that for-profits are more responsive to heightened competition from other securities exchanges. It is also argued that, by placing the assets of a securities exchange in a corporation whose shares itself are traded, the competitive pressures of the capital markets will drive the new entity to more efficient behavior than that of the *clubby*, insular - and outdated - nonprofit. Much of discussions therefore focuses on various perceived weaknesses of the non-profit mutual securities exchange. For instance, decision-making at a nonprofit securities exchange is problematic because nonprofit decisions require consensus,[189] respond to a median voter, which shifts as membership diversifies,[190] or produce an increasingly insular, *clubby* membership.[191] In the past, most mutual securities exchanges have been marred by confusion in operations and management. They have been run as members' clubs where the operations and control are at the behest of their members who are also the broker-dealers. The exchanges envisage

---

189 Aggarwal, R. (2002) Demutualization and Corporate Governance of Stock Exchanges," *Journal of Applied Corporate Finance.* 15(1):105-113.

190 Macey, J. R. & O'Hara, M. (2005) From Markets to Venues: Securities Regulation in an Evolving World. *Stanford Law Review,* 58:563-599.

191 Bradley, C. (2001) Demutualization of Financial Exchanges: Business as Usual? *Northwestern Journal of International Law & Business,* 21.

an old-boys network among the stockbrokers, a feature that encourages collusion and inhibits competition.

These exchange members, who are also stockbrokers also underwrite new issues and provide lead advisory services during IPOs, mergers and acquisitions, and debt issuance. This has perpetuated the dominance of securities exchanges by these broker-dealers at the expense of other stakeholders. Since the retail investors are not represented on board of securities exchanges, this gives the broker-dealers to dictate terms, generating skewed decisions and causing financial loses to such investors. Where broker-dealers have been found to have violated the market regulations, such as inappropriate dealing in client's shares and money, it is the same broker-dealers who are sort to determine whether there was violation of the law and to act as arbitrator between the aggrieved investors and the broker in question. The brokers have become so powerful, as in the case of Kenya, that they completely influence the appointments at the Capital Markets Authority, the entity that regulates the capital markets, including the securities exchange.

Therefore, demutualization should bring about better, faster decisions as the for-profit responds to the market for corporate control, by investing in new trading and depository technologies. The timing of demutualization is largely seen as being brought about by new competition from ECN's – the alternative trading systems, but also by an increase in trading volume internationally, the integration of securities markets globally.[192] These alternative electronic trading platforms allow securities buyers and sellers to match orders directly without routing the order to a broker-dealer or specialist. An alternative trading system is simply a network of broker-dealers without a trading floor or specialists. Arguments for these systems include the likelihood of faster execution, greater transparency and better pricing. However, several caveats have been made, as the merits of the nonprofit form are acknowledged for being more responsive to regulation.[193]

---

192 Karmel, R. (2000). Demutualization: Implications for the Regulation and Governance of Securities Exchanges. Paper presented at the 25 IOSCO Annual Conference.

193 Cox, J. (2000). The Future Content of the U.S. Securities Laws: Premises for Reforming the Regulation of Securities Offerings. *Law & Contemporary Problems*, 63: 11-34.

Certain rules, including high listing standards and a difficult delisting process, helped firms that list on securities exchange to signal their quality and commitment. Nonetheless, few discussions consider the possibility that the mutual exchanges in their nonprofit form could be efficient organization. Yet, despite recent changes in their surrounding mutual environments these exchanges maintained that form for centuries, undergoing only moderate structural change in response to periodic crises. Right up to their debut as publicly traded for-profit, the earlier mutualized exchanges, like the LSE, NYSE, Nasdaq, remained the largest and most prestigious exchanges globally.

The main rationale behind many securities exchanges' IPOs seems not primarily driven by efficiency-enhancing objectives. An IPO is more likely to be used as a solution vehicle for the diverging interests between few large international financial intermediaries and many small local stockbrokers. The exchange's old member-owners possibly viewed a public listing as a catalyst to both maximizing the value of their venue and creating an exit option for those members that are unwilling to bear the costs of an operations restructuring. The fact that most of these IPOs occurred during the bull market until 2006, when relatively high sales prices were feasible, further strengthens this argument. Therefore, in anticipation of a substantial appreciation of the value of their voting rights, many small brokers give up their reluctance to demutualize and their hitherto relatively large share of the control structure in favour of cashing out these rights on the securities market. Securities exchanges with a relatively homogeneous member structure are able to respond to a changing environment without significantly altering their governance structure. Whereas, securities exchanges with a highly heterogeneous composition cannot overcome their conflicts other than providing side payments through an IPO to resolve deadlocks on important decisions concerning the exchange's future strategy, anticipated to engineer growth and development.

Demutualization and the Lemon Problem Issue

Could it be that the stability of mutual securities exchanges forms a rational response to the lemons problem? The lemons problem has been identified as the existence of asymmetric information between buyers and sellers in a market that would allow bad items to drive out good items over time.[194] At a securities exchange, the potential for a lemons problem exists because of its corporate forms and the difficulty in extracting truthful information about firms whose shares trade on the exchange and then persuading investors of that truthfulness. But, how does a non-profit securities exchange, organized by stockbrokers and investment banks to produce liquidity, overcome its lemons problem? There are two mechanisms that these financial intermediaries might employ. First, during the listing process, stockbrokers and investment banks assess prospective securities issuers and screen out bad firms. A second mechanism, observed in venture capital deals,[195] is the taking of *hostages* to motivate truthful disclosure of information by insiders at issuing firms. Insiders always know more about their firms than outside stockbrokers and investment banks irrespective of how sophisticated the due diligence process. Information quality is always a potential problem, since insiders may wish to misrepresent the financial condition of their firms. Cases of inside managers taking advantage of outside investors are enormous as was discussed in Chapter 2 on corporate governance.

As underwriters, stockbrokers and investment banks allocate shares of an IPO to the insiders of other listed firms. These IPO allocations typically come with an expectation that the shares be held for some period of time - a lock-up period, market bubble behavior notwithstanding.[196] This lock-up served a dual purpose, stabilizing the stock price of a new issue and creating mutual vulnerabilities to bad information among insiders of issuing firms. That is, if the management of an issuing firm were to lie about their firm to the investing public, insiders at other listed firms who own shares in their firm would also suffer. Although this may not be a strong deterrent, and does not perhaps rise to the level of hostage taking like in venture

---

194 Akerlof, G. (1970) The Market for Lemons Quality Uncertainty and the Market Mechanism, *Quarterly Journal of Economics* 9, 629-650.

195 Kuan, J. W. (2005). The Use of Hostages in Venture Capital Syndicates. Working Paper, Institute of Economics and Policy Research, Stanford University.

196 See Kuan, J. W. & Diamond, S. F. (2006) Ringing the Bell on the NYSE: Might a Non-profit Stock Exchange Have Been Efficient? Working Paper, The Berkeley Electronic Press.

capital financing, there are indications that scrutiny by exchange's peers matters. For instance, during decades of securities exchanges' operation as a nonprofit, first as a membership association and later as a formal nonprofit corporation, their members carefully decided which firms would list on the securities exchange and then extracted hostages in order to motivate firms to disclose information truthfully.[197] With the demutualization of securities exchanges, the era of the stockbroker/investment banker-owner relationship seems to disappear.

But, could there be a significant difference between the period of investment banking dominance of a securities exchange and the pre-investment banker dominant period? Over the years, the securities exchange itself served as gatekeeper for new firm listings during that earlier period. Since the creation of securities exchanges, listing standards are designed assuring investors that they had accurate information regarding the capital structure of firms. It can be argued that a form of hostage taking has prevailed during at least the broker-dealer dominant period. The rise to prominence of the investment banks' role in listing securities in many markets rather than reforming the disclosure requirements was key to the establishment of a credible modern disclosure regime at securities exchanges like NYSE.[198] In fact, modern hostage system emerged only after trial and error. Securities exchanges had to weather quite volatile periods in their early years as non-repeat players behaved opportunistically.

In its reality, what does a for-profit exchange signify? As broker-dealers relinquish ownership of the securities exchange, they also give up control and their formal role as gatekeepers. The for-profit exchange will then assume the role of gatekeeper. But if the business models of existing for-profit securities exchanges are any guide, a for-profit exchange, which profits directly from trading volume, is unlikely to be as elective as investment bankers, who

---

197 Kuan, J. W. & Diamond, S. F. (2006). Ringing the Bell on the NYSE: Might a nonprofit stock exchange have been efficient? Working paper No. 1451, The Berkeley Electronic Press, bepress Legal Series.

198 Mahoney, P. G. (1997). The Allocation of Government Authority: The Exchange as Regulator, *Virginia Law Review*, 83.

profit only indirectly from trading profits.[199] But selection is only part of a securities exchanges' success. Unless a for-profit securities exchange can also facilitate hostage taking, through IPO allocations, firms' incentive to disclose information will never be as good as under nonprofit ownership of a securities exchange. Without hostages motivating securities issuers to disclose information, the quality and reliability of firm information they provide will deteriorate and a lemons problem could potentially re-emerge. A closer look at the existing literature, show there is little evidence that the agency and other problems that cause opportunistic behavior by firms' senior insiders has diminished as securities exchanges demutualize.

Admittedly, instead, there have been cases of outbreak of manipulation of stock prices in many mutual as well as demutualized securities exchanges, as has been recently witnessed at Nairobi Securities Exchange concerning KenolKobil share trading following talks of a takeover by Rubis. In July 2019, Andre DeSimone – the CEO of Kestrel Capital (stockbrokers) was fined Ksh.2.5 m ($24,356) by the market regulator for sharing price sensitive information with two traders, and was later banned from holding a senior role in a listed firm or a brokerage for a period of year. The Nairobi-based Kestrel acted as the transaction adviser for KenolKobil in that deal. The CMA investigation established that DeSimone disclosed price sensitive material relating to the impending takeover of KenolKobil by Rubis to two stockbroking agents Aly Khan Satchu and Kunal Bid. The CMA banned Satchu from holding a key post with a listed company or a brokerage for a period of three years and forced to give up Ksh.4.69 million in commissions from the suspect trades, while Bid was give up Ksh.23.41 million in gains from the trading accounts he managed. Kestrel voluntarily gave up Ksh.9.86 million in commissions on the trades executed through the two agents, without accepting or denying liability, thus ending the investigation against the brokerage firm.

The announcement of plans for demutualization, and future self-listing at mutual securities exchanges could be greeted by a mixture of applause and

---

199 Karmel, R. S. (2002). Turning Seats into Shares: Causes and Implications of Demutualization of Stock and Futures Exchanges, *Hastings Law Journal* 53, 367.

concerns. Announcing the arrival of a publicly traded for-profit securities exchange, the negative reaction could come mostly from the exchange's own floor traders. For them, the implications of demutualization are clear: an end to their way of life as floor trading is gradually replaced by automated on-line order matching. Executives at the exchange would also be replaced, one after another, by those executives from the merging exchange. The plans to merge with other exchanges before or after demutualization, is part and parcel of what appear to be a gradual degradation of the exchange quality. For instance, as the Eastern African premier securities exchange, the NSE has had imitators around the EAC. Yet it has maintained a position of leadership, with the highest valuations, the largest market capitalization, and the biggest trading volumes, even without the largest number of issuers. Currently, the valuation of the Nairobi Securities Exchange is about Ksh.2.47trillion – more than the Uganda, Tanzania, Eritrea and Rwanda exchanges combined. This is a comparison which may just be made with what NYSE is in the world. For example, the market value of firms traded on NYSE's floor before demutualization was $24,000 billion – more than the Tokyo, London, Nasdaq, Euronext and Deutsche Boers exchanges combined.[200]

Incumbency alone, however, cannot explain this superior performance, as entrants have tried and failed over time to displace the larger exchanges like NYSE, LSE or Nasdaq. There have been hostile takeovers attempts on these exchanges by others, with no success. One explanation for their sterling performance is their higher level of integrity – their successful resolution of the lemons problem. One way they may have solved the lemons problem is through the use of a hostage exchange system embedded within the non-profit form. For various reasons, including the difficulty of observing the system itself, this solution is difficult to imitate. Could be also that over time those who recognize the advantage of a hostage based system have moved into other settings, particularly the private equity world where, as the venture capital environment is concerned, there is an established

---

200 Hughes, J. & Authers, J. (2006). Taking the Floor: How a Screen Role Will Challenge New York's market debutant, *Financial Times*, Mar. 7: 13.

hostage exchange process. That leaves the public trading securities markets exposed to the potential downside of a slide into a hostage-free world of commoditized trading. And, automated trading has been responsible here.

Under the non-profit model, securities exchange with investment banking subsidiaries have an incentive to be selective about which firms traded on the securities exchange. Therefore, solving the lemons problem led to greater investor confidence and hence liquidity, which in turn meant more and higher underwriting fees. Increased activity by small individual retail investors would profit broker-dealers directly rather than investment banks which deal only with issuing firms and large institutional investors. So limiting the firms that trade on the securities exchange to only those who meet certain listing criteria and whose most important managers post hostages benefits investment bank through higher fees from listed firms. Such bankers thus profit only indirectly from greater liquidity. A for-profit securities exchange, like the JSE, NSE or NGX profit directly from liquidity, charging investors for each buy or sell transaction. They thus benefit only indirectly from investor confidence that results from solving the lemons problem, so maintaining the quality of firms and the quality of information is of interest only indirectly. Given these incentives, there could be a reduced incentive for the for-profit demutualized securities exchange to maintain informational integrity. In turn, this is likely to lead to an increase in the growth rate of firms allowed to list and hence an overall decline in investor confidence.

However, a question arises from these predictions. If the mutual form of governance is that good, why would a securities exchange choose to demutualize? One possibility is that a form of market segregation is now occurring in securities markets. Technological change is both driven by, and combined with, the rise of institutional investors who value speed of order execution over best price. Thus, with the growth of internet-based computing power, a market for trading as a commodity has arisen. That has created a new form of competition for the traditional securities exchanges from the alternative trading systems, first Nasdaq and then Archipelago, Instinet and others. Rather than beat them, competitors like the NYSE has decided to join them in order to reduce the potential losses, as has been explained earlier. Meanwhile, private equity and other forms of off-exchange trading of financial instruments seem to offer much higher rewards to individuals who might have gone into traditional investment banking several years ago. In the off-exchange world it is once again possible to recreate stable hostage systems.

This is particularly the case in markets that are controlled by certain key players with a first mover advantage: those who build the club get to set the rules. This approach is important in understanding the origins of the highly successful venture capital environment. What remains now is to apply the approach to the emerging frontiers of finance, especially in the emerging securities markets of Africa and Asia, South America. It is however evident that demutualization is in general efficiency enhancing but may cause conflict in terms of regulatory powers of market regulators and the exchanges themselves. Operational and financial performance is enhanced as converting to a securities exchange from a mutual structure offers the possibility of raising capital to ameliorate perceived financial constraints and the ability to provide high-powered incentives to managers and employees.

That being the case, have mutual securities exchanges outgrown their original purpose and become vestiges? The recent wave of demutualization will undoubtedly force the remaining mutual securities exchanges to reassess their value to members. Also, the economic theory on conversion, discussed earlier in Chapter 3, highlights two structural weaknesses of mutual structure: governance and access to capital, among others. If mutual securities exchanges are to survive in an increasingly global, deregulated, competitive and capital-intensive business environment, they will need to address these major organization structure constraints. The demutualization benefits may not materialize, in any case, the benefits may conflict with each other. In fact, the costs as well as benefits of demutualization need to be critically considered. Finally, the benefits may be obtainable in mutual securities exchange structure. Mutual securities exchanges therefore are not condemned to disappear as long as they are well capitalized and managed while adopting effective corporate governance rules to safeguard member control.

Chapter Summary

A host of securities exchanges in developed markets have completed their demutualization processes by converting from non-profit to for-profit organization forms. A few have done so in developing economies such as from Africa. The change from non-profit to for-profit has mostly been viewed as a long-overdue response to new, on-line competition from the emerging alternative trading systems such as the electronic communications networks. It can be seen that demutualization is productive for African securities exchanges in their overall trajectories. It shows that democratic governance structure is more progressive than the mutual governance structure for the securities exchanges.

The implication is that demutualization is a concept which leads the securities exchanges from autocratic culture toward the democratic culture. When culture of securities exchange is based on the autocratic governance structure where the board of the directors consists of only as few as 3 directors, the decision made by the board will be based on the mutual consensus which leads toward the interest of stockbrokers. In consequences it discourages listed firms from decision making authority. In this type of scenario market forces disturb badly and inside trader make the abnormal profit and derail the ethics of the market and code of governance. When the securities exchanges go for initial public offering and convert to for profit organization, governance structure totally change. After that, the board of the directors comprised of minimum five directors and decision of the market and regulation about the control on the market are made through special resolution. If the decisions of the board are based on the majority voting and consensus of all stakeholders as well as shareholders, then the securities exchanges provide the suitable and good governance atmosphere in which no one will not involve in window dressing for the competing of its competitors, inside trading for the abnormal and illegal way of gaining profit and also market abusing for the artificial desired ups and downs in the market. Consequently, the good governance and focusing on all stakeholders the decisions of the African securities exchanges will lead towards the growth and stability for the normal working and profit gaining.

Nevertheless, there has been little assessment of the strengths or efficiencies of the non-profit form of securities exchange. This chapter presented some discussions on the possibility that a securities exchange choice of organization form is an efficient solution to a classic *lemons problem*, in which misinformation from bad securities issuing firms – firms whose shares trade on the exchange – could drive out good issuing firms from the market.

The chapter applied a robust theory of non-profits in which the highest demanding consumers of a non-rival good organize the production of that good. In this case, stockbrokers, investment bankers and other financial intermediaries organize to produce liquidity. The resulting non-profit is the former mutual securities exchange, which was able to align issuing firms' incentives to disclose with those of investors. Stockbroker-owners and investment banker-owners of the mutual securities exchange acted as gatekeepers to the exchange, screening issuing firms through an extensive *due diligence* process, providing capital through underwriting, and connecting issuing firm insiders to one another, again through initial public offering allocations. For decades, this system maintained an equilibrium in which issuing firms, large and small investors, and securities exchange members could participate with relative ease, transparency and fairness in the exchange.

The shift to a for-profit securities exchanges, no doubt, have a significant, and potentially deleterious, impact on this equilibrium as it breaks up the age-old components of the non-profit structures. Mutual securities exchanges therefore are not likely to vanish as long as they are well capitalized and managed while adopting effective corporate governance rules to safeguard member control. In fact, they are likely to exist side by side of their demutualized counterparts. Remember, demutualization has been a new issue in securities markets globally. As in the case of many other securities exchanges all around the world, steps have been taken to turn the traditional mutual securities exchanges into demutualized ones. However, most of securities exchanges around the world use a two-step demutualization process initially they change the organizational structure and then go for public listing. Some exchanges do move very fast to adopt both the changes at a time. However, their management should be careful about any future conflict of interests. It would not be easy to handle the pressure and new challenges initially. Such exchanges would not be also easy to implement new policies overnight. So, securities exchanges should apply new rules and regulations carefully.

Hopefully the demutualization will be a blessing for the securities exchanges in African countries as it will ensure efficient corporate governance and attract foreign investments through the exchanges. Many multinational institutions in African countries must follow many regulatory frameworks as per guidelines of their parent companies. Demutualization is one step towards ensuring a level playing field for those companies and let the local companies adhere to it. The more accurate the structure of the securities exchanges is, the more interested will be the investors to divert their savings to capital markets. Demutualization will also create new jobs in investment banks, brokerage houses, credit rating agencies and fund management firms. With the passage of time general investors will start getting benefit of demutualization. The most challenging step will be to teach the general investors about the effect of demutualization. But as the time goes by, general investors, listed firms as well as the government will benefit from demutualization securities exchanges.

Chapter Ten

STRATEGIC DIRECTIONS FOR RESTRUCTURING GOVERNANCE STRUCTURES OF AFRICAN SECURITIES EXCHANGES

Introduction

Securities market integration has encouraged a process of disintermediation and demutualization. With the emergence of new structures, there may be no need for formal floors of securities exchanges or financial market intermediaries and participants, as they do not add value (to match the cost) to trading of securities. Exchanges with low market capitalization and weak trading volumes have had to particularly re-examine their operations and organizational structures with the view to increasing their competitive offering and price mix to minimize further diversion of trading volumes. The powerful trends of internationalisation, migration of order flow, and change to corporate structures are putting pressure on securities exchanges around the world. For some exchanges, already more than half of trading and listing has migrated offshore. Migration may make it difficult for countries to sustain a full-fledged local securities exchange. As trading volumes further decrease, financing the fixed overhead of maintaining market oversight, clearing and settlement systems, and generating enough business for local investment banks, accounting firms, and other support services will become even harder, especially for smaller emerging markets. The trend towards increased migration will thus make it more difficult for small securities exchanges to survive.

In order to survive in this environment, securities exchanges need to diversify and move towards commercially oriented business practices with greater focus on improving efficiency, accessibility and ease of use of their systems. These issues call for a re-examination of their organizational and legal structures. Since securities exchanges have higher overhead costs compared to ECNs caused by, among other things, the cost of building and facilities, they need to strive harder to achieve profitability and economies of scale, while offering competitive services and fees compatible to those being provided by the ECNs. These considerations have driven securities exchanges to consider alliances, consolidation and demutualization. By merging two securities exchanges and adopting for-profit structures, the securities exchange can multiply the volume at the same overhead cost, provided cost cutting synergy is fully explored. It can thus offer to the investors and brokers more listed securities for trading on the same platform. Probably by 2035, there will be fewer than five major securities exchanges; and, perhaps two or three of these will be entirely electronic markets, which have not yet been established, and all will be operated as for-profit demutualized securities exchanges.

These dramatic changes in the organizational form of securities exchanges reflect major changes in their business environment - notably, the rise of global competition, consolidation and technological advances, and in the competitive strategies designed to respond to such changes. In the new competitive environment, the promise of demutualization is that, along with the capital necessary for investments in technology, the shareholders of the newly demutualized exchanges will provide a new corporate governance structure that is far more effective in managing conflicts among market participants. In the long run, for-profit securities exchanges run by entrepreneurs and disciplined by profit-seeking investors should produce better-financed organizations with a greater ability to respond quickly to preserve the value of their franchises. Global competition, consolidation and advances in technology, among other factors, are causing securities exchanges around the world to examine their business models and become more entrepreneurial.

Restructuring Exchange Corporate Governance Structures. Corporate governance usually improves with demutualization for a number of reasons. The board of directors becomes more diversified. As a mutual, the board will often largely reflect social single group of exchange owners. The social culture probably plays a role, and their perspective is that of a broker, although their interests are not always uniform. The idea of shareholder value introduces new disciplines to exchange management. Hopefully, the culture shifts to a service culture. This is partly dependent on the ability of the management to act as agents of change and of staff to embrace change.

A more diversified board represents a greater diversity of business views. The priority of the board shifts from brokers' interest to shareholder value. This changes the organization in many ways and, significantly, introduces customer focus. There is a widening of the groups recognized as customers. Staff can be rewarded in line with improved efficiencies. It is usual for a mutual exchange not to distribute profits and use any reserves to even out good and bad years. The levelling effect also applies to staff salaries, so staff may expect regular pay increases and promotions regardless of the company's performance. Profit distribution changes that and allows better rewards in good times and for productivity gains. Market discipline will apply, particularly if the entity lists. Because the exchange company is paying a return on capital it can be measured against other investments doing the same.

There is now a widespread recognition that securities exchanges are handling commodity business of buying and selling securities. As such, they are increasingly opting to operate as a firm that seeks business for profit and gears its business strategy to respond to different competitive forces from the automated proprietary systems including ATS and ECNs, and other international operators. The survival of securities exchanges is contingent on their ability to generate trading volumes and offer efficient and cost effective execution services. These factors have required a re-examination globally of the role of securities exchanges and their business relations, model and governance structure.

A number of securities exchanges are transforming from members' associations into for-profit corporations, and, in some cases this has involved consolidation and merger with other exchanges and/or with clearing, settlement and depository institutions. The approaches and modalities for the restructuring of securities exchanges have in part differed from case to case depending on prevailing conditions and the degree of success of exchange transformation and alliances whose trends and structure have varied across the globe and region.

Strategic Realignment by African Securities Exchange

Optimizing Expected Benefits from Demutualization. Demutualization has, generally been, observed to offer a wide range of advantages. It allows securities exchanges to abolish the members'/traders' monopoly over intermediation and be responsive to the needs of its issuers and investors by allowing them direct and cost effective access to the exchange. The for-profit motive of securities exchanges allows it to generate the desired levels of investments, while offering appropriate returns to the owners. Provided the incentive structure of demutualized exchange is developed effectively, demutualization lends itself to improved governance. This can be achieved through a shift in the ownership of the exchange from member-brokers and dealers to a wider group of investors with adequate safeguards to prevent excessive concentration of ownership and power, the appointment of a professional board and management, and appropriate investments in automated trading to offer competitive services. The for-profit securities exchanges have further been observed to adopt strategies and incentives to enhance competitiveness through cost effective measures and broadening and diversification of the revenue base. The corporate culture of demutualized securities exchanges has been observed to lend themselves better to deploying profits into investments for the modernization of exchanges and improving the SRO functions and performance.

Specifically, demutualization allows securities exchanges to raise capital to develop their businesses. Such needed capital may not be obtained through a mutualized status, unless securities exchanges privatise. In fact, stockbrokers and government cannot offer a business-oriented entity to raise such capital from shareholders, as a business corporate. Demutualization also allows for the diversification of the exchanges' shareholder base and so modifies and improves their corporate governance structures. Also, demutualization enables the separation of ownership rights from trading rights, thus many demutualized securities exchanges have opened the access of their trading platforms to other participants, which increases their trading turnover. This can enable securities exchanges to increase investor participation. Moreover, demutualization may also allow securities exchanges to review their commercial strategy. Many securities exchanges have achieved consolidation in their domestic markets by merging the derivatives and cash segments or including trading, clearing and settlement services under one roof, in order to create economies of scale.

The forces of globalization and integration dictate that securities exchanges have to reorganize themselves to become viable entities of international standards. Stiff competition amongst exchanges and between exchanges and ATS calls for mechanisms to minimize costs and generate more revenues in order to shield themselves from such competition. Demutualization is usually accompanied by the development of cross-border exchange linkages and international alliances among various exchanges. The board of directors of exchanges is made up of shareholders or investors with no government representation. A recent World Bank Study noted that while in the short-run government appointments, may be conducive to mitigate entrenched vested interests, in the long-run, they can prove counter-productive leading to unhealthy government interference.

Furthermore, demutualization allows exchanges to sell their equity stake to a mix of shareholders, decision making will be based on this new ownership structure – not on the rights of intermediation or government representation – which ensures an effective oversight of a governing board. It can also provide securities exchanges with the necessary capital to introduce new products, recruit calibre staff, compete on the always expensive technology level, as well as leverage the value of the exchange as a brand name. The new structure ensures that the management of a securities exchange is fully qualified and motivated enough not only to act in the best interests of the shareholders, but also to conduct the business in a prudent manner so as not to disrupt the orderly and fair trading in capital market. To remain competitive, the privatised exchanges must follow international best practices in rules, ethics and procedures.

Optimizing Market Competition and Demutualization. Advances in telecommunications introduced competition to traditional securities exchanges, which forced them to change their governance structure from member-owned mutual monopolies to demutualized entities. The members were interested in maximizing their individual profits, and as competition intensified, the dominant exchange needed a residual claimant who would maximize securities exchange value as against the member's profits. Thus, many exchanges demutualized. This analysis contained in this book has provided evidence of competition being the major motivation for demutualization.

Throughout the book it has been shown that introducing a residual claimant in the governance structure of securities exchanges is definitely beneficial for a securities exchange. Demutualization can also help a securities exchange to increase its order flow. The impact of this governance change for investors is not as unequivocal. The impact differs depending on whether a securities exchange is facing competitive pressures. In the case of securities exchanges, which faced competition and demutualized in response to competition like the LSE, introducing a residual claimant has been beneficial to investors as trading costs have continued to decline post-demutualization. On the other hand, those securities exchanges, which demutualized in a non-competitive environment and where the government may have had a hand in restructuring like Borsa Italiana investors appear to be worse off. As Botswana Stock Exchange navigates through post-demutualization era, its investors could also undergo such loses. Demutualization has helped the dominant exchange become even further entrenched and trading costs to increase. These experiences indicate that competition contributes to differing effects of demutualization, and highlight the importance of competition in securities markets.

It was showed that competition reduced trading volumes and reduced bid-ask spreads on exchanges, which forced the members to demutualize their exchange. Post-demutualization, the introduction of the residual claimant helped such exchanges to increase trading volumes, but competitive pressures kept trading costs low on these exchanges. Considering the impact of pure demutualization – where an exchange did not face competition but was privatized by the government – it was noted that there is possibility of increasing exchange volumes pre-demutualization; and an accelerated increase in trading volumes post-demutualization. Exchanges like Borsa Italiana gained 98 percent market share (from 71 percent pre-demutualization) in ten months after demutualization. Strikingly, bid-ask spreads also increased post-demutualization – a reflection of limited competition.

Demutualization is therefore beneficial to a securities exchange as it helps it regain trading volumes, while the effect of demutualization for investors depends on the competitive environment. If investors have to gain from exchange demutualization in terms of lower trading costs, the exchange has to operate in a competitive environment. Demutualization in a non-competitive set-up entrenches the exchange even further and increases trading costs. This argument validates the theoretical arguments that in a competitive environment, outside ownership is a more efficient governance structure, while in a non-competitive setting, the cooperative governance structure is more efficient.

Managing Potential Challenges in Restructuring Securities Exchanges. There are concerns that demutualized exchanges may have an inherent degree of conflict of interest, given that stricter enforcement of market regulations can be costly and may result in loss of business. The loss of investor confidence because of weak regulation may itself lead a securities exchange to lose its competitive edge. In some instances, some securities exchanges have opted to segregate the market and regulatory roles within their organizational set-up or have established a separate subsidiary corporate entity to handle SRO functions or outsourced this function to an independent entity. Independent of these arrangements, the structure of a securities exchange can only make a difference if the outfit is well governed and managed efficiently and fairly, while ensuring high standard market surveillance and trade practices monitoring, and effective checks and balances on securities market participants.

A demutualized securities exchange aims to maximize profits and dividends for its shareholders, and is argued to have less incentive to take enforcement actions against its customers or system users, who are a source of income. There is also the problem of balancing regulation by exchanges and by their regulators. Self-regulatory functions of a demutualized exchange possess a challenge both for securities exchanges themselves and for the securities markets regulators. This calls for a harmonious relationship with the regulator. Ownership in a demutualized securities exchange may also become problematic. There are difficulties in the choice of the financial institutions to become shareholders and marrying powers wielded by former member-owners and new shareholders. The most important task for demutualized exchanges is remaining financially viable. Substantial capital is required, which is not available at most exchanges and may not be provided by the government, due to other priorities. It is very difficult to achieve securities exchange's goals, unless the required capital is available, which is not possible, unless the securities exchanges are privatised.

The new governance structure enables securities exchanges to operate as a business oriented entities and raise capital from shareholders, as a business corporation. The road to demutualization is a complex one that requires total commitment from former exchange owners, market regulator and more important, from the government, and this was exhibited in the case of demutualizing the Nairobi Securities Exchange Limited. The post demutualization period also calls for continued government support and the support from other stakeholders. The serious challenge of demutualization is found in the attempt to value the shares of the securities exchange. This has been a critical issue for those exchanges that have been demutualizing, since before demutualization, owners may own seats, which have to be converted into shares with monetary value. However, there have been counterarguments that a demutualized securities exchange cannot afford to risk its reputation, customers and market integrity given their implication on business and revenue streams. Such securities exchanges will implement a governance structure to lessen the conflicts of interest. Some demutualized securities exchanges have been seen to separate their commercial activities from the regulatory functions. The market regulators take over all the powers and functions of exchanges regarding their self-listing. There is also the imposition of a ceiling on the ownership of any one entity in a demutualized exchange, the most common being five percent.

Seizing the Future of Demutualized Securities Exchanges. Having analysed different aspect of the industry of securities exchanges, applying different theories and displaying various drivers of the industry, such as demutualization, mergers and acquisition, and other forms of strategic alliances, and new regulations, it is equally important to discuss some future aspects that might result from this new trend in securities market. It had earlier been asserted that the forces of globalization lead to less home-biased investors as well as issuers of stocks. Similarly, competition has, over the decades, increased between domestic securities exchanges for order-flow and listings. Also, deregulation measures for financial markets have resulted in lower market entry barriers. Moreover, advances in technology through computerization and ICT have opened new ways for doing business for securities exchanges. Internalisation of order flow by financial intermediaries makes them compete with securities exchanges.

A look at the potential sources of the reductions in spreads on demutualized securities exchanges indicate that, consistent with the predictions of the laws of demand and supply, the increased order flow, market share, and increased listings following demutualization, contribute to the falling spreads. Interestingly, evidence also suggest that demutualized securities exchanges that subsequently self-list by going public after demutualization experience incremental improvements in market quality.[201] In addition, the conversion of exchanges from member-owned not-for-profit to for-profit companies improves stock liquidity, with positive relation achieved through the market development level and the exchange strategy channels. In fact, this positive relation is stronger for securities exchanges with higher operating performance and revenue diversification. Moreover, the competitive effects of demutualization exhibit asymmetric patterns on exchange market share. Furthermore, domestic order flow and the level of market development enhance the positive impact of exchange demutualization on the securities exchange market share.

These factors, together with consolidation, among other factors, are causing securities exchanges around the world to examine their

---

201 Abukari, K. & Otchere, I. (2020). Has stock exchange demutualization improved market quality? International evidence, Review of Quantitative Finance and Accounting, 55(9): DOI: 10.1007/s11156-019-00863-y.

business models and become more entrepreneurial. Many exchanges have responded by demutualizing, which is bringing about major shifts in ownership and corporate management structure. By converting member-owned, non-profit organizations into profit-driven investor-owned corporations, securities exchanges are able to access the much-needed capital for making investments in new technology and for participation in the ongoing market consolidations. Securities exchanges are expanding the products and services that they provide, such as data processing, the distribution of information, the provision of custody and registry services, and the operation of clearing and settlement systems. The profit-seeking actions of a demutualized exchange may provide further motivations to enter businesses other than those directly ancillary to its traditional trade execution functions. The potential for increased conflicts of interest may produce, particularly those arising where a securities exchange is seeking to provide services or products, which compete with those offered by users of the exchange's other services, has been mentioned above.

The network externality theory suggests that, ceteris paribus, firms want to be listed where other firms are listed – the direct-network effect – and especially where many intermediaries trade – the cross-network effect – as more liquidity is on the market. Securities market intermediaries want to be present at exchanges where more firms and intermediaries are present as they are more attractive to their final customers-investors and for themselves – their own portfolios and all the risk-management services. Larger securities exchanges with more liquidity are therefore the consequence which would lead to further consolidation in the industry with a few but large financial exchanges surviving this process.

Firms are more likely to cross-list in countries with better investor protection, and more efficient courts and bureaucracy, but not with more stringent accounting standards. The main customers of securities exchanges are the sell side of investment banks and issuers. They are both putting more pressure on securities exchanges, leading to more competition, as there are more and more alternatives in terms of execution venues and deep major financial centres to raise capital. Intense competition from substitute services comes from alternative trading platforms like Project Turquoise, which is created by seven large investment banks, which in Europe will trade under MiFID in competition with established European securities exchanges.

With the increased consolidation of the securities markets to achieve scale economies, the eventual winners in the process will be the securities exchanges that attract order flow and so provide liquidity to investors. Companies will cross-list on a foreign securities exchange alone if most of the group of investors who have a comparative advantage in evaluating their firm trade in the foreign securities exchange rather than in the domestic exchange, and the foreign securities exchange has the same or greater transparency than the domestic exchange. Firms will dual-list when they have a significant base of low-cost information producers in their own country, but would like to enlarge that base by listing in the foreign securities exchange, or take advantage of the higher transparency of the foreign exchange. They can also do both. This has important implications for African governments and their securities exchange given the current talks of creation of a Pan-African securities market.

About 70 percent of the world's total securities market capitalization is now on publicly listed exchanges. Securities exchanges that have demutualized but not listed their shares account for an additional 19 percent. The dominance of listed exchanges is widespread across the Americas and Europe. In Asia there are yet only 26 percent demutualized and listed exchanges, but the total proportion of demutualized securities exchanges account for 81 percent. Nevertheless, the success of the demutualization process is too early to evaluate. There are several issues that will need to be followed closely. The main one is how best to regulate privately owned securities exchanges. Given the potential conflicts of interest between the shareholders of securities exchanges and their consumers, it will be interesting to see how these conflicts are resolved. Again, of the exchange which have demutualized in Africa, over 50 percent have chosen to remain unlisted.

While the wave of demutualization and public listing of securities exchanges seems to have run its course, it may well be followed by an era of consolidation of exchanges both geographically and across products.

Advances in technology allow adding more trades to an electronic trading system at close to zero cost which is seen as the main driving force behind the consolidation wave in the securities exchange industry. The current trends suggest that the factors that have driven the demutualization and listing of exchanges are likely to be as relevant in the future as in the recent past. All major securities exchanges are facing increasing global competition from other exchanges or alternative trading systems. Unless some unpredictable event interrupts the process African securities markets are likely to become fewer in number and more internationalized in their listings, trading, and membership and only the most efficient exchanges should survive, trading stocks from all the other African countries and offering the most innovative and competitive financial instruments, especially derivatives. This situation is likely to be mirrored also in European countries.

Asian and Arabian securities exchanges are gaining importance and represent interesting partners for possible alliances or mergers. Arabian investors prefer to invest their oil profits in financial exchanges in their home region because of the strict US regulations. They prefer to transfer their capital form foreign capital markets to their local one and create a concentration of funds in the Arabian region that has never been known before. The same phenomenon can be found in India, China, and of late Africa, where funds resulting from the enormous economic prosperity are relocated and re-invested in the home economy. It can be predicted that the full-fledged market integration, regulatory harmonization and subsequently the actual effects of this integration, will occur a little bit further in the future, thereby restructuring the securities markets more.

New legislations will challenge an important revenue source for exchanges and provide a valuable opportunity for investment firms to get in on the game. They will further intensify competition among exchanges and again trigger the consolidation process. Furthermore, they will encourage traditional exchanges to lower fees and increase the speed of transactions to become more attractive. Business opportunities for further internalisation of share trading as well as for information services will arise, and could be taken advantage of by more efficient securities exchanges or alternative trading loops.

Securities exchanges were, in the past, viewed as the hardest and longest-lasting part of financial trade. Whether this might now be changing and whether securities exchanges will be necessary at all is a subject of further discussions elsewhere, and beyond the scope this book. Remember, it had been noted that technology makes it relatively easy to set up new exchanges, but few will be needed. It is possible that one single exchange might emerge in each region, but this is unlikely and especially undesirable. The risk of bankruptcy and dependence on such single monopoly exchange would be too high. It will be interesting to see where these possible three or five competing global networks of securities exchanges would locate themselves, that is if at all they will have a physical location.

Whether securities exchanges can be transformed into perfect ordinary public firms is another interesting question. Securities exchanges are much more than market places for trading securities and commodities. They are quasi-public bodies that function as SROs and are treated as national champions and symbols elsewhere. If an exchange becomes an ordinary public firm it becomes subject not only to the advantages of public ownership, but also to the perils and burdens of such a business's unaccustomed mode of operation. Publicly owned securities exchanges have to make a full disclosure of their financial condition and business operations than they have done before and they must become subject to the pressures of investors to realize shareholder value. They also have to learn to deal with security and market analysts.

Securities exchanges might become overly focused on stock prices and begin to follow short term instead of long-term strategies. They could become the targets of a hostile takeover initiative or a bidder in a losing acquisition effort. Five years after the demutualization of the Stockholm Stock Exchange, a listed firm and former derivatives exchange competitor, OM Gruppen AB (OM), increased its ownership to 20 percent and proposed a merger. The Swedish Government approved the merger because it was believed to be in the best competitive interests of both entities. However, in conjunction with the merger, the government acquired a significant interest in the combined entity. It also passed new legislation, which served to increase regulatory oversight of the combined entity.

Although the demutualization of the Stockholm exchange was meant to thwart the competitive threat from OM, it actually ended up facilitating both its take-over by OM and increased government involvement in the company's regulation. This has already happened in the OM Gruppen and Nasdaq bids for the LSE. A market breaks and the fall of the stock price of a securities exchange could accelerate investor loss of confidence in the market generally. Many exchanges, for example those from Africa and other nascent economies, have a smaller capitalization than some of their members and listed firms, but they have a mystique that places their trading activities on the new screens every day. As public firms struggle for profits and market share, exchanges could lose that mystique. However, that may be the price of survival in the securities markets of the future. Although there have been generally accepted practices, some significant differences exist, as have been discussed in the earlier chapters.

Demutualized securities exchanges actually have fewer endemic conflicts of interest with investors and issuers than mutualized exchanges, thus lessening the need for strict regulatory interventions to mitigate the effects of such conflicts. This is because demutualized exchanges are not wholly owned by broker-dealers, which have a clear incentive to design the trading architecture to maximize their own trading profits. This incentive structure has the effect of lowering investor returns and raising capital costs to listed firms. Securities markets regulators are highly dependent on public directors to mitigate the inherent conflicts of interest between the broker-owned exchange and the trading public, but it is dangerously naïve to believe that such directors can be independent of the members' interest when they are nominated by an exchange nominating committee and then elected by the membership. If, on the other hand, a securities exchange is organized as a normal public company with a diversified shareholder base, or at least primarily owned by entities independent of brokerage firms, the board is much less likely to pursue the interests of brokers at the expense of investors and listed firms.

Securities exchange regulators therefore face many challenges in the current environment which may be intensified when a securities exchange, operating in a competitive marketplace, decides to restructure its operations as a for-profit entity. Some of the issues discussed in this book have been considered by regulators facing demutualization in their jurisdictions. The responses taken vary, reflecting the regulators' assessment of the particular circumstances in their jurisdiction. Whereas the new business lines for securities exchanges may reduce financial risks by diversifying the exchange's sources of income, they also bring new risks. It is worth considering whether the ability of the exchange to engage in commercial activities should be unfettered, or whether it should be subject to some limitations, such as segregation of core and non-core businesses, firewalls to protect the resources necessary to run the exchange's core activities, a restriction to products and services that are ancillary to its core business or a requirement for prior regulatory approval.

Consequently, securities market regulators must accept that some regulatory responsibilities simply cannot be privatised. Whoever owns a securities exchange is primarily interested in the financial gains such ownership affords, as with any other private business. A mutualized exchange is no exception. Although insider trading is one drawback of mutually-owned exchanges, there are many, much narrower, areas where governments routinely implement securities market regulations and then inappropriately leave private vested interests to implement and enforce them. A significant by-product of the current wave of exchange ownership and governance reforms may well bring much greater clarity in the formulation and allocation of regulatory responsibilities in the securities trading industry. If that is the case, securities exchange demutualization will make a significant contribution both to the efficiency and integrity of global securities markets.

Future Serious and Critical Questions in Demutualization. Future demutualization may raise other issues that will require different approaches and strategies to deal with, and which African securities exchanges need to seriously consider. For instance, how far will technology reach in the securities markets? Would technological threats wipe out the traditional exchanges? The sharp gains in share prices, and all the deal activity, are due in large part to advancing technology. Trading can be conducted much faster now, and at much cheaper costs for securities exchanges. That helped prompt the realization that securities exchanges, most of which had previously been run as mutual associations, can be very profitable. Much of the recent activity reflects a one-off adjustment to a world where exchanges exist to make a profit. But those technological advances could threaten the long-term future of securities exchanges. They make it much easier for new forces to enter, avoiding traditional exchanges altogether.

Secondly, could securities exchanges, in future, go under? The success of the demutualization process is too early to evaluate. There are several issues that will need to be followed closely. One of the major open questions is how best to regulate privately owned exchanges. Given the potential conflicts of interest between the shareholders of exchanges and their consumers, it will be interesting to see how these conflicts are resolved. So far the financial performance of listed exchanges has been quite strong. However, if there will be periods in the future when for-profit exchanges face major financial difficulties, will they be allowed to go bankrupt just like any other listed company? If this happens, would the securities exchange still maintain its integrity and rationale to exist? How would the capital or the financial markets deal with such phenomenon? How about the stocks of the firms listed therein and the investors who holding the listed firms' securities and the exchange-own stocks, as these will not have a market for trading?

Moreover, could reduce competition due to consolidation – mergers, acquisitions and hostile takeovers – lead to creation of regional monopolies? As all the biggest names in the global securities markets arena have sought to spread from their traditional territory, both geographically, and by moving into new asset classes, one can just speculate a future bogged with more securities exchange consolidation. Through reduction in competition, leading clients of the securities exchanges worry that this wave of consolidation could lead to higher profit margins for exchanges – and higher prices for clients. The consolidation, whether domestically or regionally, indeed amounts to creation of monopolies. This could lead to increase in IPO costs, market surveillance costs, prices for securities exchange information and data, and other services.

In addition, the production cycle of a securities exchange is divided into three parts: listing, trading, and clearance and settlement. These three different stages of the production cycle lead to the formation of different goods that the exchange can sell: listing services, trading services, clearance and settlement services, and price-information services. In fact, inefficiencies in each part of the cycle fall upon the whole community (negative externality), not only on the entities that actually trade. Low quality information tends to form wrong prices that contribute to a bad allocation of resources; inadequate clearing and settlement procedures can threaten the stability of the whole financial system. Therefore, could the resultant poor quality thereafter threaten the whole financial system? The threat for the whole system could become bigger, with more concentration of securities exchanges.

Given the current heat for consolidation, will the smaller developing securities exchanges keep pace with the emerging Asian, Arabic and African exchanges? The JSE, EGX and NGX are emerging in Africa and other exchanges like Qatar and Dubai in Arabia, and Hong Kong, shanghai and Tokyo in Asia, becoming more important and powerful in the international exchange scene. It will be interesting to see where alliances and mergers will be implemented. In Europe, the Euronext has already been acquired by the NYSE and LSE is continuously in the spotlight of takeover bids and the Deutsche Börse keeps its strong position in the derivatives market. For other small exchanges with less international importance competition is already intensified by the new EU directive MiFID. Also we saw how American exchanges like Nasdaq and NYSE are consolidating locally and with other exchanges in Europe, Asia and Arabia. The influence of Asian and Arabic exchanges will certainly grow in recent years while at the same time geographic locations of the securities markets might lose importance as the advances in technology grow. It might be possible that in future, only three major exchanges might survive the consolidation process with one being an American-European-Gulf region, American-European-Asia region, and an African-Gulf region. Alternatively, there could emerge large continental securities markets of Americas, European, Asian-Pacific and Middle East and African ones.

Finally, will the emerging of a raft of regulations, being responses to consolidation and demutualization, trigger the extinction of securities exchanges? The traditional business model of established securities exchanges is going to be challenged as never before by the new legislations in some jurisdictions. For instance, the new law – MiFID – in Europe will challenge an important revenue source for exchanges and provide a valuable opportunity for investment firms to get in on the game. It will also intensify competition among exchanges and again trigger the consolidation process. It will further encourage traditional exchanges to lower fees and increase the speed of transactions to become more attractive. If other forms of off-exchange trading are able to handle the effects of such new legislations faster and more effective, it will be interesting to see whether traditional securities exchanges will be necessary at all as trading platforms or will they be rendered irrelevant.

The inexorable trend towards securities exchanges operated as for-profit public companies with non-member ownership is a direct product of the automation of trading systems. Much deeper changes in the industrial structure of the securities trading business are on the horizon. As the traditional role of stockbrokers as conduit between investor and exchange is increasingly rendered obsolete by electronic communications technology, the trading function will become increasingly disintermediated. Cross-border exchange and CSD consolidation will be driven by the competitive need to exploit massive economies of scale and network effects in trading, and regulatory arbitrage will increasingly determine the legal domicile of the resulting entities. Whereas regulators are becoming increasingly comfortable with the notion that securities exchange ownership and governance reforms can be conducive to greater capital market efficiency, there remains deep scepticism about the ability of these new commercial exchange entities to carry out self-regulatory responsibilities.

Nevertheless, these concerns are misplaced on at least three major counts. Much of what is currently classified by government regulators as a self-regulatory obligation of a securities exchange is actually wholly consistent with profit-maximizing behaviour, and does not, therefore, need to be imposed upon securities exchanges in order to ensure protection of public interest. One example that can be fronted is the formal listing of securities. The problem is not merely that such obligations are redundant, but that they can function as a barrier to entry for potential competitor trading systems. Article 1.13 of the EU's Investment Services Directive, for example, appears to indicate that an exchange is only entitled to a single passport to provide services outside its home market if it meets the requirements of the Listing Particulars Directive. This would mean that securities exchanges which trade stocks listed elsewhere may be denied the right to compete in certain EU national markets. It is my considered opinion that there is no public interest being served by obliging exchanges to implement redundant listing services.

Preconditions for Restructuring Securities Exchanges. The decision to demutualize must take several points into account. To this end, African securities exchanges contemplating demutualization need to be cognizant of these conditions if they are to succeed in their demutualization journey and benefit from it. The local market must be sufficiently developed, with issuers using financing instruments in the market and the country on a large scale. There should exist a diversified and growing investor base comprising individuals, institutions, foreign investors, as well as, a well-structured regulatory basis, with highly rated market regulators and supervisors providing the market with the credibility required to implement this important change in the structure of exchanges. Similarly, there is the need for a sufficiently liberalized financial market since demutualization involves the privatisation of the organizational structure.

Moreover, there is also the need for market justification based on a critical mass of trading activity that supports financial viability. Similarly, the support of the ruling government, financial and capital markets regulatory agencies in managing the demutualization process is critical. Securities exchanges should be comfortable with becoming a self-regulatory organization that sets its own rules and regulations to react faster to market participants. The ability of an exchange to introduce new financial products to increase its liquidity and turnover is also as crucial as the capability to provide investor protection by improving corporate governance and disclosure of listed firms.

Furthermore, a securities exchange should be able to establish a dispute resolution system to resolve conflicts among its members. In addition, it must be capable of developing sophisticated risk management tools for the whole capital markets. This includes capital adequacy ratios, margin trading rules, short-selling regulations, and circuit breakers. The more a securities exchange improves its risk management techniques, the more investors are protected and transparency increases. There is also the need for the willingness to become a more efficient securities exchange by providing better quality services tailored to the needs of issuers and broker-members, which in turn would increase the revenues of the exchanges.

Larger and financially sustainable securities exchanges in both developed and developing countries should be the ones to think of demutualization. Once a decision has been made, securities exchanges should move cautiously through the preparation, the process, and the post demutualization period. Demutualization should be viewed as a long-term objective for growth, development and sustainability. Some benefits of demutualization can be captured by re-engineering mutual securities exchanges, through corporate governance, increasing representation of non-members, continuous improvement in trading and post-trade technology to stay competitive, and pursuing on-going market liberalization. Therefore, securities exchange from developing countries such as those from Africa should avoid donor pressure to demutualize, and seizing control of the demutualization agenda. The technicalities and merits of demutualization will evolve as further experience is gained. However, the creation of commercial, for-profit trading exchanges with appropriate incentive structures is of high priority in developing Africa and Asian countries where the entrenched vested interests have undermined the opportunities for financial diversification and penalized investors.

Some securities exchanges from Africa have responded by demutualizing, which brings about major shifts in ownership and corporate governance structure. By converting member-owned, non-profit organizations into profit-driven investor-owned corporations, demutualization gives securities exchanges access to capital that can be used both for investment in new technology and for participation in the ongoing consolidation of the industry. In the process of providing securities exchanges with capital, demutualization should strengthen the corporate governance of the exchanges in the African continent. Again, it is too soon to tell whether demutualization will live up to its promise in Africa and other developing continents. After all, demutualization might not be the answer for all exchanges in all countries. But the evidence so far available from America, Asia-Pacific, and Europe-Oceania, in the form of the stock-price performance and profitability of securities exchanges that have been operating as publicly-traded companies for at least few years, is encouraging.

There is no universal right regulatory path to follow. However, given the importance of a securities exchange in the financial and economic system of a country and the additional complexities posed where a securities exchange becomes a for-profit entity actively competing for business, these issues will continue to demand regulatory attention both from capital market development experts and from regulators. In the meantime, more rigorous discussions supported with quantitative findings are needed, in the form of the stock-price performance, profitability and liquidity of demutualised securities exchanges from America, Asian Pacific, Europe, and Africa that have been operating as publicly-traded companies for at least ten years, for comparison with such performance before they demutualized.

Without good doses of the above ingredients and without a solid business model proposal, a securities exchange may fail to be an attractive company in the eyes of investors. In this case, stockbrokers would also fail to recover their investments in the securities exchange at fair prices. However, if the right conditions for developing the market are present, demutualization and self-listing can be successful and the result will be a strong and competitive exchange that – even without the control of the brokers – can provide infrastructure efficiently for all participants in the market: its shareholders, the brokers, listed companies, investors and society as a whole, thus supporting the country's economic growth and development. The ground has already been set for African securities exchanges to justify their existence and make themselves relevant.

African Securities Exchanges Moving Forward

Securities exchange industry globally is in a state of turbulence. Securities exchanges are constantly developing new revenue sources and financial products, try to expand their market share through ferocious competition and pursue integration with other exchange and financial institutions. A prerequisite for this development is their transformation into market-oriented for-profit ownership and management structure entities that are dominated by outside investors through a process called demutualization.

Demutualization is therefore the transformation of a securities exchange governance structure from a mutual association of stockbrokers operating as not-for profit entity into a for-profit company accountable to its shareholders. It has become a widespread phenomenon – one with increasing appeal in developed markets. It challenges the traditional approach to regulation of securities exchanges and raises issues regarding their role in capital markets regulation.

We have seen that in restructuring the exchange ownership structure, broker-members' seats are monetized and financial values assigned per seat. Members can then keep or sell their shares. Ownership restrictions are placed on individuals and groups to prevent potential takeovers by other exchanges. The legal and organizational change normally leads to a securities exchange becoming a typical for-profit company.

Securities exchange demutualization has gained popularity due to competition among exchanges, need for increased capital, good corporate governance in exchanges and the urge to open up ownership of exchanges to public investors. It is expected to reduce governance problems in mutualized exchanges by opening up trading rights, admitting new trading partners, and broadening ownership to allow the public to invest in securities exchanges. The absence of these in mutual exchanges tends to breed poor governance structures. In a mutualized exchange, traders and brokers enjoy monopoly power through exclusive rights and access to trading systems, resulting in a protection of vested interests for traders. In a demutualized exchange there is a vote per share and once incentives for equity stakes to non-members exists there is separation of powers.

Demutualization in Africa can therefore induces better corporate governance systems as decision making is based on ownership structure and not on trade's intermediation. In addition, undue governmental influence in mutual exchanges in Africa is likely to be absent in demutualized exchanges since appointment of government officials become unnecessary due to the fact that a demutualized exchange is a private company.

Indeed, improving the ownership and management structures of African securities exchanges through demutualization can increase access to services of the exchange and removes excessive investment costs for fund managers. Stockbrokers usually package non-trade related fees for research, computer systems and IPO access into institutional traditional commissions often known as soft or bundled commissions and pass them on to clients. With demutualization, therefore fund managers can directly access such information without the use of stockbrokers. Also, demutualization can also instil efficiency and better structures in securities exchanges thus resulting in commercial gains for the exchanges.

The major challenges with demutualization are the inherent conflict of interest and regulatory challenges, given that securities exchanges tend to shy away from taking enforcement actions against their own customers who are the major source of revenue. Furthermore, there is commercialization of services such as trading data and information that traditionally is offered freely. Listing standards and oversight can also be compromised by the exchange concerned. These conflicts can however be solved through self-listing via an initial public offering.

For markets in developing countries like those in Africa, potential conflict of interest could pose huge problems, since current regulatory structures are still undergoing restructuring to meet international standards. In African, for example, the establishment of securities exchanges preceded the creation of formal independent securities regulators. Perhaps being a private outfit, demutualized exchanges could speed up the formation of strong regulatory systems in African capital markets. We have noted that in spite of its popularity as a strategy for catalysing securities exchange development in emerging economies, the pace of demutualization in Africa has been excruciatingly very slow. Consequently, African securities exchanges have therefore remained underdeveloped compared to their peers in other emerging markets.

This book has provided answers as to how African securities exchanges facing the challenge of integration and better technical and institutional development can address the problem of underdevelopment through demutualization. It has explained how demutualization can enable greater and swifter securities market development in Africa. It has also espoused the role that government regulators should play in demutualization of exchanges in African countries. In addition, it has proposed the right self-regulatory model applicable to African exchanges, and how to effective manage conflicts of interest and other barriers to separation of ownership from management and trading rights. Moreover, the book provided the type of investments needed to enhance the effectiveness of African's capital market. Lastly, it discussed how securities exchange demutualization can facilitate Africa's destiny to become leading capital markets globally.

Moving forward, the demutualization of Africa securities exchange should not be hurried since most these exchanges have barely existed for a decade, and are grappling with teething issues of poor trading infrastructure and illiquidity. For demutualization in Africa to become more relevant these teething problems have to be properly addressed with exchanges consolidating gains on improving liquidity problems and strengthening market integration through mergers, acquisition and other forms of strategic alliances. African securities markets must therefore improve their trading infrastructure and strengthen cooperation and other forms of strategic alliances. These exchanges need to examine the demutualization of other major African securities exchanges in South Africa, Kenya, Botswana, Zimbabwe and Nigeria to learn from their experiences and avoid the pitfalls.

The demutualization poses a challenge for advocacy for developing regional securities markets in Africa. The construction of a regional securities market in any part of Africa in the near future would be expected to be demutualized given the current status of JSE given its link and cooperation agreements with many African securities markets. The demutualization also poses a further challenge for advocacy for developing an integrated Pan-African securities market in Africa, one which whose integration infrastructure was launched in 2023 through the Exchanges Linkage Project – an E-Platform linking seven African capital markets with $1.5 trillion market capitalization. This project aims at integrating the African capital markets by facilitating cross-border trading and free movement of investments in the continent through the AELP Link platform. The AELP Link interconnectivity platform enables the trading of exchange-listed securities across 7 participating securities exchanges. Therefore, to become successful, the touted Pan-African securities exchange will have to be linking demutualized exchanges and even the Pan-African Exchange itself will have to itself be demutualized.

FURTHER READING

Abukari, K. & Otchere, I. (2020). Has stock exchange demutualization improved market quality? International evidence. *Review of Quantitative Finance & Accounting*, 55: 901–934.

Aggarwal, R. (2002). Demutualization and corporate governance of stock exchanges. *Journal of Applied Corporate Finance*, 15(1):105–113.

Aggarwal, R. (2006). Demutualization and public offerings of financial exchange, *Journal of Applied Corporate Finance*, 18(3): 96-106.

Akhtar, S. (2002). Demutualization of Asian stock exchanges-critical issues and challenges. In S. Akhtar (ed.) Demutualization of Stock Exchanges: Problems, Solutions and Case Studies. *Asian Development Bank*, Manila, 3–32.

Akpesey, P. (2008) Publicly owned stock exchanges - Prospects and challenges: http://www.modernghana.com/news/169336/1/publicly-owned-stock-exchanges-prospects-and-chall.html

Amihud, Y. & Mendelson, H. (1986). Asset pricing and the bid-ask spread. *Journal of Financial Economics*, 17:223–249.

Andersen, A. (2003). Competition between European Stock Exchanges. Helsinki School of Economics Working Paper.

Angel, J. J. (1998). Consolidation in the global equity market: An historical perspective', Working Paper, Georgetown University.

Armstrong, M. (2006) Competition in Two-Sided Markets, *Rand Journal of Economics*, 37(3): 668-691.

Arnold T., Hersch, P., Mulherin, J. H. & Netter, J. (1999). Merging markets. *Journal of Finance*, 54:1083–1107.

Ayogu, M. D., (2001). Corporate governance in Africa: The record and policies for good corporate governance. *African Development Review*, 13(2): 308-330.

Azzam, I. (2020). Stock exchange demutualization and performance. *Global Finance Journal*, 21(2): 211-222.

Baikie, T. (2002). Toronto Stock Exchange-from Toronto Stock Exchange to TSE Inc.: Toronto's experience with demutualization. In S. Akhtar, ed. Demutualization of stock exchanges: problems, solutions and case studies. *Asian Development Bank*, Manila, 283–298.

Berle, A. A. & Means, G. C. (1932). The modern corporation and private property, Harcourt, Brace and World, New York.

Bessembinder, H. & Kaufman, H. M. (1998. Trading costs and volatility for technology stocks. *Financial Analysis Journal*, 48:64–71.

Bessembinder, H. & Kaufman, H. M. (1997). A cross-exchange comparison of execution costs and information flow for NYSE-listed stocks. *Journal of Financial Economics*, 46: 293-319,

Black, D. (1948). On the rationale of group decision-making. *The Journal of Political Economy*, 56(1), 23–34.

Blume, M. E., Siegel, J. J. & Rottenberg, D. (1993). Revolution on Wall Street: The rise and fall of the NYSE, Norton, W. W. &, Company, Inc., New York.

Boehmer, E., Saar, G. & Yu, L. (2005) Lifting the veil: an analysis of pre-trade transparency at the NYSE. *Journal Finance*, 60:783–815

Bradley, C. (2001). Demutualization of financial exchanges: business as usual? *Northwestern Journal of International Law & Business*, 21(3).

Brailsford, T. J., Frino, A., Hodgson, A. & West, A. (1999). Stock market automation and the transmission of information between spot and futures markets. *Journal of Multinational Financial Management*, 9(3–4), 247–264.

Buchanan, J. M. (1965). An Economic theory of clubs. *Economica*, 32(1): 1–14.

Buti, S., Rindi, B. & Werner, I. M. (2017) Dark pool trading strategies, market quality and welfare. *Journal of Financial Economics*, 124:244–265.

CACG (2000). Guidelines on principles for corporate governance in Commonwealth. Commonwealth Association for Corporate Government Bulletin, London.

Cadbury, A. (1992). Report of the committee on the financial aspects of corporate governance: the code of best practice (Cadbury Code), December.

Cameron, Alan (2002). Demystifying demutualization. http//www.sec.or.th/nbfi_2002.

Carson, J. W. (2003). Implications of demutualization for the self-regulatory and public interest roles of securities exchanges. Mimeo.

Chaddad, F. R. (2003). Waves of demutualization: an analysis of the economic literature. Working Paper, Washington State University.

Chaddad, F. R. & Cook, M. L. (2004) The economics of organization structure changes: a US perspective on demutualization. *Annals of Public and Cooperative Economics*,75(4): 575–594.

Charoenwong, C., Ding, D., & Thong, T. Y. (2016). Decimalization, IPO aftermath, and liquidity. *Review of Quantitative Financial Analysis*, 47:1303–1344.

Chemmanur, T. J. & Fulghieri, P. (2006). Competition and cooperation among exchanges: a theory of cross-listing and endogenous listing standards, *Journal of Financial Economics* 82 (2006) 455-489.

Chesini, G. (2001). Changes in the ownership structure of stock exchanges: from demutualization to self-listing. 10th International Conference on Banking and Finance, University of Rome, 5-7th December.

Chung, K. H, & Chuwonganant, C (2009). Transparency and market quality: evidence from SuperMontage. *Journal of Financial Intermediation*, 18:93–111.

Chung, K. H, Elder J, Kim J-C (2010). Corporate governance and Liquidity. *Journal Quantitative Financial Analysis*, 45:265–291.

Claessens, S., Klingebiel, D. & Schmukler, S. L. (2002). Explaining the migration of stocks from exchanges in emerging economies to international centers. World Bank Working paper no. 2816. Washington, D.C.

Claessens, S., Klingebiel, d. & Schmukler, S. L. (2002). the future of stock exchanges in emerging economies: evolution and prospects. Financial Institutions Center Working Paper No. 02-03. Pennsylvania: Wharton School.

CMA (2009). Stakeholders workshop on demutualization of the NSE. Press Release. http://www.nse.co.ke/newsite/pdf/Year 2009/General/

Cochran, P and Wartick, S. (1988). Corporate governance: A review of the literature, Financial Executives Research Foundation, Morristown, New Jersey.

Coffee, Jr. & John, C. (2002). Racing towards the top? the impact of cross-listings and stock market competition on international corporate governance, *Columbia Law Review*, 102(7): 1757-1831.

Cohen, N. (2007). Danger may be looming yet again for the LSE. Financial Times, September 20th. http://www.ft.com/cms.

Comerton-Forde, C., Malinova, K. & Park, A. (2018). Regulating dark trading: order flow segmentation and market quality. Journal of Financial Economics, 130:347–366.

Cybo-Ottone, A., Di Noia, C. & Murgia, M. (2000). Recent development in the structure of securities markets. Brookings-Wharton Working Papers.

Demsetz H (1968). The cost of transacting. *Quantitative Journal of Economics,* 82:33–53.

Denis, D. K. & McConnell, J. J. (2003). International corporate governance. ECGI - Finance Working Paper No. 05/2003. ECGI Finance Working Paper No.05, ECGI.

Dewenter KL, Han X, Koski JL (2017). Who wins when exchanges compete? evidence from competition after Euro conversion. *Review of Finance,* 27:1–35.

Dewenter, K. & Chang-soo, K. & Ungki, L. & Novaes, W. (2007). Race to the top among stock exchanges: theory and evidence, Financial Times Report – World Financial Centers & Exchanges.

Di Noia, C. (1998). Competition and integration among stock exchanges in Europe: Network effects, implicit mergers and remote access, Wharton Financial Institutions Center, http://fic.wharton.upenn.edu/fic/papers/98/9803.pdf.

Di Noia, C. (1999). The stock-exchange industry: network effects, implicit mergers and corporate governance. Commissione Nazionale Per Le Societa E La Borsa.

Di Noia, C. (2001). Competition and integration among stock exchanges in Europe: network effects, implicit mergers and remote access, *European Financial Management,* 7(1), 39-52.

Diether, K. B, Lee, K. H. & Werner, I. M. (2009). It's SHO time! Short-sale price tests and market quality. *Journal of Finance,* 64:37–73.

Dimsdale, N. & Prevezer, M., (1998). Capital markets and corporate governance. In H. J. Blommestein (ed) The new financial landscape: 257-261, Clarendon Press.

Domowitz I, & Steil, B. (2001). Automation, trading costs, and the structure of the securities trading industry. In: Davis, E. & Steil, B (Eds) Institutional Investors. MIT Press, London: 347–397.

Donnan, F. (2002) Self-regulation and the demutualization of the Australian Stock Exchange, *Australian Journal of Corporate Law,* vol.10.

Du, B. (2019). Relative option liquidity and price efficiency. *Review of Quantitative Finance Accounting,* 52:1119–1135.

ECB (2007). The stock markets´ changing structure and its consolidation: Implications for the efficiency of the financial system and monetary policy, *ECB Monthly Bulletin,* 11/2007: 61-74.

Economides, N. (1996). Economics of networks. *International Journal of Industrial Organization,* Vol. 14, 673-699.

Economist (2007). Big headache or big bang? – EU securities regulation. *The Economist*, Oct. 27th, Issue No. JF980238.

El-Azza, M. H. (2020). Evaluation of the impact of the demutualization process on stock exchange value. *Unpublished Thesis (Cardiff Metropolitan University)*.

Elliott, J. (2002). Demutualization of securities exchanges: A regulatory perspective. Working Paper 02/119, International Monetary Fund.

Erickson, T. J. (2000). Futures exchange demutualization, commodity futures trading commission, Preliminary Study.

Foley S, & Putniņš, T. J. (2016). Should we be afraid of the dark? dark trading and market quality. *Journal of Financial Economics*, 122:456–481.

Frame, W. S. & White, L. J. (2004). Empirical studies of financial innovation: Lots of talk, little action? *Journal of Economic Literature*, 42(1), 116–144.

Franks, J. R., Mayer, C. & Rossi, S. (2005). Ownership: Evolution and regulation. ECGI - Finance Working Paper No. 09, ECGI.

Gresse, C (2017). Effects of lit and dark market fragmentation on liquidity. *Journal of Financial Markets*, 35:1–20.

Hansmann, H. (1996). The Ownership of enterprise, Harvard University Press, Cambridge.

Hart, O. & Moore, J. (1996). The Governance of exchanges: members' cooperatives versus outside ownership. *Oxford Review of Economic Policy*, 12(4), 53–69.

Hasan, I. & Schmiedel, H. (2003). Do networks in the stock exchange industry pay off? European evidence. Discussion Paper 2-2003, Bank of Finland.

Hasan. I., Malkamäki M. & Schmiedel, H. (2003). Technology, automation, and productivity of stock exchanges: International Evidence. *Journal of Banking & Finance*, 27(9):1743–1773.

Hazarika, S. (2005) Governance change in stock exchanges. Working Paper, City University of New York, January.

Hendershott T. & Moulton, P. C. (2011). Automation, speed, and stock market quality: the NYSE's hybrid. *Journal Financial Markets*, 14(4):568–604.

HolmstrÄom, B. (1999). Futures of cooperatives: a corporate perspective, *Finnish Journal of Business Economics*, 48(4), 404-417.

Huang, R. & Stoll, H. (1996). Dealer versus auction markets: A paired comparison of execution costs on Nasdaq and NYSE, *Journal of Financial Economics*, 41, 313-357.

Husband, M. (1999). Egypt leading the way: institution building and stability in the financial system. Euromoney Publications.

ICG (1992). Standards of self-regulation of the securities markets. International Capital Markets Group.

IOSCO (1998) Objectives and principles of securities regulation, September, IOSC.

IOSCO (2002). Issues Paper on Exchange Demutualization. Report of the Technical Committee of IOSC, June.

IOSCO (2005). Exchange demutualization in emerging markets. emerging markets Committee of the International Organization of Securities Commission, April: IOSCO.

Jensen M, & Meckling W. (1976). Theory of the firm: managerial behaviour, agency costs and ownership structure. *Journal of Financial Economics*, 4:305–360.

Jensen, M. C. & Meckling, W. H. (1976). Theory of the firm: Managerial behaviour, agency costs, and ownership structure. *Journal of Financial Economics*, 3(3), 305–360.

Karmel, R. (2000). Demutualization – Implications for the regulation and governance of securities exchanges. Paper presented at the 25th IOSCO Annual Conference.

Karmel, R. S. (2002). Turning seats into shares: Causes and implications of demutualization of stock and futures exchanges. *Hastings Law Journal*, 53(2), 367–430.

Kasch, H. & Theissen, E. (2007). Competition between exchanges: Euronext versus Xetra. EFMA 2003 Helsinki Meetings, SSRN: https://ssrn.com/abstract=407781

Kaserer, C. & Schiereck, D. (2007). The Costs of going and being public – Frankfurt and London Compared, *Finanzplatz*, l(2):14-15.

Keim, D. B. & Madhavan, A. (1998). The information contained in stock exchange seat prices. Working Papers 07-98, Wharton School Rodney L. White Center for Financial Research.

Kloess, S., Exner, E. & Silli, N. (2006). Stormy waters ahead: Stock exchanges are heading towards a turbulent future. Accenture.

Koendgen, J. (1998). Ownership and corporate governance of stock exchanges. *Journal of Institutional and Theoretical Economics*, 154(1), 224–251.

KPMG (2007). NSE Demutualization study report. Submitted to the NSE by Financial Advisory Services. Nairobi: KPMG East Africa, June 15th Presentation.

Krishnamurti, C., Sequeira, J. M. & Fangjian, F. (2003). Stock exchange governance and market quality. *Journal of Banking and Finance*, 27(9), 1859-1878.

Kuan, J. W. & Diamond, S. F. (2006). Ringing the bell on the NYSE: Might a nonprofit stock exchange have been efficient? Working paper No. 1451, The Berkeley Electronic Press, bepress Legal Series.

Lannoo, K. & Levin, M. (2004). Securities market regulation in the EU, CEPS Research Report in Finance and Banking, No. 33, May 2004.

Lazaroff, L. (2006). NYSE Trading on Future Stock Sale, Merger for Future, Chicago Tribune, Feb. 26.

Lee R (2002). The Future of Securities Exchanges. Brook Whart Papers in Financial Services, 14:1–26.

Lee, R. (2003). Consolidation and Demutualization. Paper Presented at the 5th Round on Capital Market Reform in Asia. Tokyo, Japan.

Lendle, D. (2007). The Effects of the Mifid on Derivative Trading. *Finanzplatz*, 2: 20-21.

Licht, A. N. (2007). Stock Market Integration in Europe, Harvard Law School, Program on International Financial Systems.

Liu B., Tan, M. & Cam, M. (2019). Reinvestigate the bid-ask bounce effect and pricing of idiosyncratic volatility: The Case of the Australian market. *Review of Pacific Basin Financial Markets Policy*, 22:1–23.

Macey, J. R. & O'Hara, M. (2005). From markets to venues: securities regulation in an evolving world. *Stanford Law Review*, 58(2): 563-599.

Mahoney, Pau,l G. (1997). The Allocation of Government authority: the exchange as regulator. *Virginia Law Review*, 83(7): 1453-1500.

Malinova, K. & Park, A. (2015). Subsidizing liquidity: the impact of make/take fees on market quality. *Journal of Finance*, 70:509–536.

Marek, M. T. & Haris, P. (2008). Stock exchange M&A, FDI & demutualization: Industrial Organization Changes to the Better or to the Worse? Paper presented at the 8th Global Conference on Business and Economics, Florence, Italy October 18-19.

Mendiola, A. and O'Hara, M. (2004). Taking stock in stock markets: The changing governance of exchanges. Working Paper, Cornell University.

Mensah, S. & Moss, T. (eds.) (2004). African emerging markets: Contemporary Issues 2. Accra, Ghana: African Capital Markets Forum.

Mensah, S. (2005). Demutualizing African stock exchanges: Challenges & Opportunities. Paper presented at the 9th Annual ASEA Conference. Cairo, 10-12 September.

Mügge, D. (2006). Reordering the marketplace: Competition politics in European finance, *Journal of Common Market Studies,* 44(5): 991-1022

Nielsson, U. (2009). Stock exchange merger and liquidity: The Case of Euronext. *Journal of Financial Markets,* 12:229–267.

NSE (2010). Members of the NSE approve demutualization at extra-ordinary Meeting: Press Release. http://www.nse.co.ke/newsite/pdf/Year2010/General/

OECD (2003). Demutualization and corporate governance of stock exchanges. *Financial Market Trends,* No.85, 89-117.

OECD (2014). Privatisation and demutualisation of MENA stock exchanges: To be or not to be? OECD Directorate for Financial and Enterprise Affairs.

Oldford, E. & Otchere, I. (2011). Can commercialization improve the performance of stock exchanges even without corporatization? *The Financial Review,* 46(1): 67-87.

Onyuma, S. O. (2020). Securities markets development in Africa: Mobile financial services, efficient remittance flows & diaspora investment securities. Chennai, India: Notion Press.

Onyuma, S. O. (2017). Analysis of financial deepening determinants influencing securities market development in Kenya. Unpublished Doctoral Thesis (Laikipia University, Kenya).

Onyuma, S. O. (2015). Paradigm shift in stock exchanges: automation, competition, governance, integration and regulation of stock markets. Senegal: CODESRIA.

Onyuma, S. O. (2011). Developing the management and ownership structures of African stock exchanges. *African Management Development Review,* 10 (1): 35-66.

Onyuma, S. O. (2012). Capital markets development in emerging economies: Institutions, macroeconomic & microstructure reforms determining stock markets development in Kenya. Saarbrucken, Germany.

Onyuma, S. O. & Shem, O. A. (2007). Reorganizing corporate governance structures in African stock exchanges. *African Journal of Business & Economics,* 2(1):60-85.

Onyuma, S. O. (2006a). Regional integration of stock exchanges in Africa. *African Review of Money, Banking & Finance*: 99-124.

Onyuma, S. O. (2006b). Demutualization of stock exchanges in Africa: Prospects and problems. *OSSREA Bulletin,* 3(3):36-46.

Otchere, I. (2006). Stock Exchange self-listing and value effects. *Journal of Corporate Finance*, 12:926 - 953.

Otchere, I. & Abou-Zied, K. (2008). Stock exchange demutualization, self-listing and performance: The case of the Australian Stock Exchange. *Journal of Banking & Finance*, 32(4): 512-525.

Padilla-Angulo, L., & Ben Slimane, F. (2018). Board restructuring and successful demutualization: the stock exchanges. *Journal of Organizational Change Management*, 31(3): 598–618.

Pagano, Marco. & Randl, O. & Röell, A & Zechner, J. (2001). What makes stock exchanges succeed? evidence from cross-listing decisions. European Economic Review 45: 770-782.

Pati, A. P (2005). Prospective governance problems in demutualized stock exchanges of india: issues and prescriptions. Dept. of Commerce, NEHU, Shillong.

Pirrong, C. (1999). The Organization of financial exchange markets: theory and evidence. *Journal of Financial Markets*, 2: 329-357.

Pirrong, C. (2000). A Theory of financial exchange organization. *Journal of Law & Economics*, XLIII, October.

Pirrong, C. (2000). Technological change, for-profit exchanges, and self-regulation in financial markets. Working Paper, Washington University, pp.1-39.

Preece R. (2012). Dark pools internalization and equity market quality. CFA Institute Paper, 1–76.

Prentice, R. A. (2006). Regulatory competition in the securities law: a dream (that should be) deferred. McCombs Research Paper Series No. IROM-01-06, *Ohio State Law Journal*, 66(6): 1155-1230.

PSCGT (2002). Principles of corporate governance and its status in Kenya. The private sector initiative for corporate governance. Paper read at PSCGT Workshop, 30th Jan-1st Feb. Kenya School of Monetary Studies, Nairobi.

Rajan, R. G. & Zingales, L. (2000). The governance of the new enterprise, corporate governance, theoretical and empirical perspectives, Xavier Vives (ed.), Cambridge University Press.

Rajan, R. G. & Zingales, L. (2001). The influence of the financial revolution on the nature of firms, Working paper, University of Chicago.

Rajan, R. G. & Zingales, L. (2003). The great reversals: the politics of financial development in the twentieth century, *Journal of Financial Economics*, 69(1), 5–50.

Reiffen D. & Robe, M. (2011). Demutualization and customer protection at self-regulatory financial exchanges. *Journal of Futures Markets*, 31:126–164.

Sahid, S. A. (2004). Demutualization of stock exchanges: what could be done by CASE? paper for workshop on North African emerging capital markets. Cairo, 31st March.

Sandier, T. & Tschirhart, J. T. (1980). The economic theory of clubs: an evaluative survey. *Journal of Economic Literature*, 18(4):1481–1521.

Schmiedel, H. (2003). Technological development and concentration of stock exchanges in Europe. In I. Hasan & W. Hunter, eds, *Research in Banking and Finance*, 3, Elsevier, Amsterdam.

Schwert, G. W. (1977). Stock exchange seats as capital assets. *Journal of Financial Economics*, 4(1): 51–78.

Segal, J. (2001). Market demutualization and privatisation: The Australian experience. In public documents of the 27th Annual Conference of the International Organisation of Securities Commissions, 23-29 June, Stockholm, Sweden.

Segal, J. (2002). Market demutualization and cross-border alliances: The Australian experience. remarks at the fourth round capital market reform in Asia held in Tokyo, Japan.

Serifsoy, B. & Tyrell, M. (2006). Investment behaviour of stock exchanges and the rationale for demutualization - theory and empirical evidence - http://www.finance.uni-frankfurt.de/master/brown/155.pdf.

Serifsoy, B. (2005). The impact of demutualization and outsider ownership of stock exchange performance – empirical evidence, Goethe University Frankfurt Finance Department.

Serifsoy, B. (2007). Stock exchange business models and their operative performance, *Journal of Banking & Finance*, 31:2978-3012.

Serisfoy B (2008) Demutualization, outsider ownership, and stock exchange performance: Empirical evidence. *Economics & Governance* 9:305–339.

Shahid, S. A. (2005). Corporate governance issues and stock exchanges: The Egyptian Example, CASE.

Sial, A. W., Tahir, A. Q., Zulfigar, S. T., Iqbal, M. & Naqvi, S. A. A. (2014). Demutualization of stock exchanges and stock market growth: broader economic investigation of demutualized exchanges. *Journal of Economics, Finance& Accounting*, 1(4): 285-294.

Steil, B. (2002). Changes in the ownership and governance of securities exchanges: Causes and consequences. In R. E. Litan & R. Herring (eds.) Brookings-Wharton papers on financial services. Brookings Institution Press, New York, pp. 61–91.

Tahir, A. Q. & Sial, A. W. (2013). Does demutualization enhance financial performance of stock exchanges in developing and emerging economies? *Strategic Change*, 22: 461–469.

Treptow, F. (2006) The Economics of demutualization: an empirical analysis of the securities exchange industry. Doctoral Dissertation, Universität München. Sofort lieferbar

Verousis, T., Perotti, P. & Sermpinis, G. (2018). One size fits all? High frequency trading, tick size changes and the implications for exchanges: market quality and market structure considerations. *Review of Quantitative Finance and Accounting*, 50:353–392.

World Federation of Exchanges (2013). Annual research & statistics-1999-2013 https://www.world-exchanges.org

Worthington, A. & Higgs, H. (2005). Market risk in demutualised self-listed stock exchanges: an international analysis of selected time-varying betas. School of Accounting and Finance, University of Wollongong.

Zhu, H. (2014). Do Dark Pools Harm Price Discovery? *Review of Financial Studies*, 27(3):747–789.